ALL · IN · ONE

PMI-ACP®
Agile Certified
Practitioner

EXAM GUIDE

Joseph Phillips

Mc
Graw
Hill
Education

New York   Chicago   San Francisco
Athens   London   Madrid   Mexico City
Milan   New Delhi   Singapore   Sydney   Toronto

Cataloging-in-Publication Data is on file with the Library of Congress

McGraw-Hill Education books are available at special quantity discounts to use as premiums and sales promotions, or for use in corporate training programs. To contact a representative, please visit the Contact Us pages at www.mhprofessional.com.

PMI-ACP® Agile Certified Practitioner All-in-One Exam Guide

1 2 3 4 5 6 7 8 9 LCR 21 20 19 18

ISBN: Book p/n 978-1-260-11594-9 and CD p/n 978-1-260-11595-6
of set 978-1-260-11596-3

MHID: Book p/n 1-260-11594-1 and CD p/n 1-260-11595-X
of set 1-260-11596-8

Sponsoring Editor Wendy Rinaldi	**Technical Editor** James L. Haner	**Production Supervisor** Lynn M. Messina
Editorial Supervisor Janet Walden	**Copy Editor** William McManus	**Composition** MPS Limited
Project Manager Poonam Bisht, MPS Limited	**Proofreader** Richard Camp	**Illustration** MPS Limited
Acquisitions Coordinator Claire Yee	**Indexer** Karin Arrigoni	**Art Director, Cover** Jeff Weeks

For the love of my life, Natalie…thank you for the encouragement, laughs, friendship, and time to write.

ABOUT THE AUTHOR

Joseph Phillips, PMP, PMI-ACP, ITIL, Project+, CTT+, is the Director of Education for Instructing.com, LLC. He has managed and consulted on projects for industries including technical, pharmaceutical, manufacturing, and architectural, among others. Joseph has served as a project management consultant for organizations creating project offices, maturity models, and best-practice standardization.

As a leader in adult education, Joseph has taught organizations how to successfully implement project management methodologies, adaptive project management, information technology project management, risk management, and other courses. He has taught at Columbia College, University of Chicago, Ball State University, and for corporate clients like IU Health, as well as the State of Indiana and Berkeley National Laboratories. A Certified Technical Trainer, Joseph has taught more than 50,000 professionals and has contributed as an author or editor to more than 35 books on technology, careers, and project management.

Joseph is a member of the Project Management Institute and is active in local project management chapters. He has spoken on project management, project management certifications, and project methodologies at numerous trade shows, PMI chapter meetings, and employee conferences in the United States and in Europe. When not writing, teaching, or consulting, Joseph can be found behind a camera or on the working end of a fly rod. You can contact him through https://instructing.com.

About the Technical Editor

James L. Haner, PMP, PgMP, PMI-ACP, PMI-RMP, PMI-SP, is the head of Ultimate Business Resources Consulting, specializing in "Building Better Businesses." James' management and leadership roles have included establishing a corporate Web presence, creating a successful organization-wide employee development plan, and developing the IT infrastructure for a start-up company.

James brings more than three decades of dynamic experience as a distinguished college professor, award-winning author of books, articles, and blogs, and successful management and leadership consultant to each learning experience.

He is a member of the Project Management Institute (PMI) and the American Society for Training & Development (ASTD). James has won the Dale Carnegie Course "Highest Achievement Award." He earned the Vietnam Service Medal while serving in the U.S. Air Force.

CONTENTS AT A GLANCE

CONTENTS

ACKNOWLEDGMENTS

Books, like projects, are never done alone.

Thank you to Wendy Rinaldi for all of your help, great conversations, and guidance on this book and others. Thank you, Claire Yee, for your management and organization of this book—you are fantastic. Thank you to Janet Walden for your keen eye, attention to detail, and for all your hours and help. Bill McManus, thank you for helping me be a better writer. Thank you to Production Supervisor Lynn Messina for her work on this book. Thanks also to the production teams at McGraw-Hill Professional and MPS Limited for your hard work in making this book a success.

I would also like to thank the hundreds of folks who have attended my project management classes over the past years. Your questions, conversations, and recommendations have helped me write a better book. A big thank you to my friends Greg and Mary Huebner, Jonathan Acosta, Brett and Julie Barnett, Don "Just Publish It Already" Kuhnle, Greg Kirkland, my Sarasota pals, Monica Morgan, and all my clients. Thank you also to my friends and in-laws Bernie and Alice Morgan. Finally, thanks to my parents, Don and Virginia Phillips, and my brothers, Steve, Mark, Sam, and Ben.

INTRODUCTION

This book is all about preparing you to pass the PMI Agile Certified Practitioner examination. While this book will help you become a better agile project management, it's not a guide on how to implement agile. My goal is simply that you pass the PMI-ACP exam on your first crack. You don't want to spend hours and hours poring over information that you won't be tested on, so I've only included information on what the exam covers. No fluff. No filler. This whole book is arranged based on the seven PMI-ACP exam domains:

- Domain I: Agile Principles and Mindset
- Domain II: Value-Driven Delivery
- Domain III: Stakeholder Engagement
- Domain IV: Team Performance
- Domain V: Adaptive Planning
- Domain VI: Problem Detection and Resolution
- Domain VII: Continuous Improvement (Product, Process, and People)

Some exam domains are a little heftier than others, but for the most part the exam is distributed evenly among the seven exam domains. As you move through this book we'll cover these domains in detail and in order through seven chapters. I'll focus only on the processes, tasks, and agile information that you'll likely see on your exam.

All About the PMI-ACP Certification

The PMI-ACP exam will challenge your understanding of agile project management practices. This means you'll need to be familiar with all the different flavors of agile: Scrum, Kanban, eXtreme Programming (XP), Lean, and a few other adaptive life cycle approaches. I'll cover all of those in this book. I think it's fair to say, however, that the Scrum project management approach is the most widely accepted agile practice and you'll see plenty of Scrum tasks and philosophies on your exam.

Because there are several different types of agile project management practices, it does create a challenge to create an exam, master all the different approaches, and certainly to write a book that addresses all the nuances of each project management approach. Fortunately for you and me, PMI tells us exactly what the exam will focus on. I've used PMI's exam content outline as the basis to write this book—and to ensure that it delves just enough into each of the agile practices you'll encounter.

Exploring the Role Delineation Study

The Project Management Institute (PMI) commissions a Role Delineation Study (RDS) for each of its examinations. The RDS for the PMI-ACP exam, completed in 2014, focuses on the day-to-day work that an agile project manager should be able to complete as part of their role in any agile organization. The study identifies the most common agile knowledge, skills, and tasks that you, as an agile project manager, should be able to readily identify and correctly answer questions about.

The PMI-ACP RDS helped PMI to develop and update the content of the exam. Basically, based on the agile information PMI collected in the RDS, it created the exam domains, created the exam test questions, and determined an appropriate passing score (which it keeps a secret) for the PMI-ACP exam. The PMI-ACP exam domains and tasks are based on the RDS—and I've based this book on the exam outline from PMI. In other words, there's a direct link between what I'm providing here and what you'll be tested on.

Qualifying for the PMI-ACP Exam

Not everyone qualifies for the PMI-ACP exam. Applicants must have a high school diploma or better, for starters. Then, you need to validate that you have 2,000 hours of experience working on project teams within the last five years; if you're a PMP or PgMP in good standing, you don't have to document these 2,000 hours. You also need to establish that you have 1,500 hours of experience using agile methodologies within the last three years (this is in addition to the 2,000 hours of general project management experience). Finally, you need to verify that you have 21 contact hours of agile project management education—such as by completing my PMI-ACP Exam Prep class on Instructing.com.

Applying for the PMI-ACP Exam

To start the application process, visit www.pmi.org; you'll have 90 days to complete the application once you start the process. If you don't complete the application within 90 days, you have to start the application over. To be clear, you don't have to complete the application in one sitting—you can save your work and return to the application later; just don't take too long or you'll have to start over.

Like all PMI exam applications, a random audit of your PMI-ACP application is possible. Audits require a copy of your diploma or transcripts for your formal education. You'll use PMI's experience verification form as part of the audit process to gain signatures from your supervisors that can vouch for your documented experience. If you're audited, PMI will provide directions on how the supervisor is to sign the form. You'll also provide a copy of your agile project management education certificate or transcripts proving that you've completed the 21 contact hours of agile training.

Paying for the PMI-ACP Exam

Of course, there are exam fees for this test. You'll submit payment as part of submitting your application. Once you've submitted the payment, you'll find out if your application is being audited or not. That's right, you pay, then you find out if you'll have to complete the audit process—PMI doesn't tell you about the random audit so audit gamblers don't run away without completing the process.

The exam fee is \$435/€365 if you are a PMI member. If you are not a PMI member, the fee is \$495/€415. As of this writing, it costs \$129 to join PMI, plus an additional \$10 processing fee, so basically \$439 to join PMI. You should also factor in the cost of joining your local PMI chapter—fees vary, but most chapters cost around \$30 per year. So, all in, you're looking at \$600 to join PMI and take the test.

While our focus is on passing the test the first time, there is a reexamination fee should you not pass the exam on your first attempt. The retake fee is \$335/€280 if you're a PMI member, or \$395/€330 if you abstain from PMI membership. You can take the exam up to three times in one year before having to start the process over.

If you need or want to reschedule your exam, you must do so outside of 30 days of your scheduled exam date. Within 30 days it'll cost you \$70 to move the exam. Within two days of your scheduled exam date, you'll forfeit the exam fee. If you have an emergency, you can contact PMI and ask them to accommodate the emergency and they'll decide if the emergency is valid or not. Be forewarned: a work emergency is not a PMI emergency. You have one year to complete the exam once your application is approved—you can't reschedule the exam beyond your one year eligibility period.

So what happens if you don't take the exam within a year after your application has been approved? You lose the exam fee. If you don't show up for the exam without rescheduling, you'll also lose the exam fee. My advice is to schedule the exam within a few weeks of getting your application approved. You don't want to stretch this process out for a year. Study, schedule, pass the exam, and get back to your life.

Passing the PMI-ACP Exam

This is a pass-fail exam and PMI does not reveal the passing score. The scoring model for the test is based on four categories: Needs Improvement, Below Target, Target, and Above Target. At the end of your exam you'll see where you land on this scale. Of course, you need to be on Target or Above Target to pass the test. I know, that's not much information to go on when it comes to preparing or quantifying an exam score, but that's all that PMI tells us. In my classes, and now in this book, my advice is to aim for 80 percent for your practice exams and quizzes. In my experience, people who consistently score at an 80 percent mark or better clear the PMI-ACP exam.

Preparing a Study Strategy

People ask me all the time for a study strategy. The truth is, there is no silver bullet for passing the exam. There is no secret code or shortcut to getting to your goal of PMI-ACP. You have to dig in, do the work, and clear the exam. However, I do have some general guidelines on studying to pass the exam:

- **Flashcards**   More than anything else, make and study flashcards every single day. Get a stack of index cards and on each one put a term on one side and the definition on the other. Every day buzz through all of the terms at least once. If you know the terms you'll be able to better answer the questions. Do not purchase flashcards! Making the flashcards is part of the learning experience. Yes, it's time consuming and painful, but so is taking the exam twice. The glossary in this book is an ideal place to start your flashcard creation.

- **Focus on the most important exam domains**   Adjust your study strategy to spend more time on the valuable domains than the lesser domains:
  - II. Value-Driven Delivery, 20 percent
  - III. Stakeholder Engagement, 17 percent
  - I. Agile Principles and Mindset, 16 percent
  - IV. Team Performance, 16 percent
  - V. Adaptive Planning, 12 percent
  - VI. Problem Detection and Resolution, 10 percent
  - VII. Continuous Improvement (Product, Process, People), 9 percent

- **Create a place to learn**   When I study to pass a test, I have a test learning headquarters. It's quiet, with no distractions, and it's only for exam studying. You should do the same. When you're studying, give yourself a couple of hours to focus on the exam content—much like when you're taking the actual exam. Use this study time to seriously immerse yourself in the content and prepare to pass.

- **Quizzes in this book**   Throughout this book you'll find end-of-chapter quizzes that'll test your comprehension of what's been covered in that chapter. Take these quizzes over and over until you can answer the questions perfectly every time. If you miss a question, do the research to understand why you missed the question. Repetition is the mother of learning.

What to Expect on Testing Day

The PMI-ACP exam is a computer-based test hosted at Prometric Test Centers. Once your application has been accepted, PMI will provide you with directions on how to schedule your test at a Prometric Test Center. PMI will send an e-mail with a testing code, a URL for scheduling the exam, and specific directions on how to complete the exam registration process.

On your testing day you should arrive at the Prometric Test Center about 30 minutes before your exam start time. The receptionist will check you in and confirm that your valid, government-issued ID matches the PMI application. Be smart and use the exact same name on your application and training certificate as appears on your government-issued ID. Note that your government-issued ID must have a photograph, or else you'll need a secondary ID with your name and photo. Social Security cards and library cards are not accepted.

After the Prometric receptionist checks you in, you'll be assigned a locker for your belongings. You cannot take anything into the testing room with you. All phones, purses, wallets, and items you've brought with you must go into the locker until the exam is over. You cannot access the locker for snacks or drinks, so ask if you can leave those somewhere handy if you need them during the three-hour exam.

The testing administrator will have you turn out your pockets and roll up your shirt sleeves. Next, they'll wave a magnetic wand over you to confirm you're not trying to smuggle anything into the test center. You cannot take anything into the center other than the clothes you're wearing—and those must stay on for the duration of the exam. You can't shed sweaters or jackets (and certainly not your pants) during the test, so dress comfortably.

You'll be seated at a computer workstation and given either six sheets of paper and two pencils or a small whiteboard and a dry erase marker. You don't get to choose which; the testing center decides. The proctor will log you into the software and get you started. You'll have a 15-minute tutorial, if you choose to complete it, on how to use the exam software. You are not allowed to write anything down during this tutorial. Once the tutorial is done, your exam timer begins and you can now jot down any notes and start answering test questions. The exam software will allow you to move backward and forward in the questions, mark questions for review, highlight key words, and even strike out answers you don't want to choose. You cannot pause the timer, but you can take a break.

Most testing centers will also provide ear plugs or headphones if you want complete silence. Talking or disturbing other test takers is not tolerated, so behave. You can't eat or drink in the testing room. You can't cheat, of course. You can't tamper with the computer. Basically, you must be on your best, professional behavior or you're booted from the testing center and you'll fail the exam. If you do take a break, you'll have to turn out your pockets and have the magnetic-wand treatment again before you go back into the testing room, so be prepared.

After you've answered all the test questions, you'll have an opportunity to review any questions that you've marked for review. After you're done reviewing, the testing software will make you confirm that you're done to end the test. Before you actually get to see your score, you'll have to complete an irritating, but necessary, survey of the testing experience. And then, after that survey, your pass/fail results will be displayed. You'll exit the testing room and the testing administrator will give you a stamped and signed score report. Get your stuff out of the locker and go celebrate!

Reviewing the PMI-ACP Exam Contents

Your exam, and this book, is based largely on PMI's *PMBOK Guide, Sixth Edition* and *Agile Practice Guide* (which is included with the *PMBOK Guide*). Throughout the *PMBOK Guide* you'll see that with each knowledge area, PMI has added small sections that address agile-specific content. The *Agile Practice Guide* has six chapters just on agile:

- An Introduction to Agile
- Life Cycle Selection
- Implementing Agile: Creating an Agile Environment
- Implementing Agile: Delivering in an Agile Environment
- Organizational Considerations for Project Agility
- A Call to Action

It's a short book—just over 100 pages total. As you might be guessing, everything you want to know about the PMI-ACP exam isn't included in that *PMBOK Guide* addition. Like the *PMBOK Guide*, the *Agile Practice Guide* addresses topics at a high level with assumptions that you already know, or can find, more information about the topics. Throughout this book I've addressed the contents for your PMI-ACP exam in detail. I'm focusing on the PMI-ACP exam domains, tasks, and objectives to help you clear the exam without having to scour the Web for additional info from the *PMBOK Guide* and the *Agile Practice Guide*.

Reviewing the PMI-ACP Exam Domain Blueprint

Your PMI-ACP exam has seven domains that you'll be tested on. Starting with Chapter 1 in this book, we'll be diving right into each domain and exploring the topic in detail. Your PMI-ACP exam domains, exam percentage, and expected questions are listed here:

PMI-ACP Exam Domain	Exam Percentage	Expected Number of Questions
I. Agile Principles and Mindset	16%	19
II. Value-Driven Delivery	20%	24
III. Stakeholder Engagement	17%	20
IV. Team Performance	16%	19
V. Adaptive Planning	12%	14
VI. Problem Detection and Resolution	10%	12
VII. Continuous Improvement (Product, Process, People)	9%	11

If you sum up the number of expected questions, you'll see that the total is 119. This is because the percentages provided by PMI don't quite equate to the total of 120 questions. Bear in mind, there are 20 seeded test questions that don't count in your score, so you might have slightly more questions in one exam domain than what's actually expected. These seeded questions may become part of the PMI-ACP exam pool in the future depending on how the PMI-ACP candidates answer these questions. You won't know if you're answering a live question or a seeded question, so answer all the questions with the same intensity.

Studying the PMI-ACP Exam Handbook

PMI provides to you, for free, the *PMI-ACP Handbook* through its website, www.pmi .org. I highly recommend you download and read this short book as you prepare to pass the PMI-ACP exam. This is the source for all things related to the exam: costs, application requirements, exam content, and policies. What I've provided herein is based on the current *PMI-ACP Handbook*, but PMI can change anything about the exam at its discretion. Do yourself a favor and hop out to PMI's website, visit the Certifications area, click the Prepare for the Exam link on the right, and download the *PMI-ACP Handbook* to confirm PMI hasn't made any updates that'll affect your study strategy.

The *Handbook* is short, an easy read, and defines several things about the PMI-ACP exam in the following sections:

- Overview of the PMI-ACP Certification
- How to Complete the Online Application
- PMI-ACP Application & Payment
- PMI Audit Process
- PMI-ACP Exam Information
- Exam Policies & Procedures
- Certification Complaints Process
- Certification Policies and & Procedures
- Continuing Certification Requirements (CCR) Program

Now that this foundation of the PMI-ACP exam is out of the way, let's hop into the specifics for preparing to pass your PMI-ACP exam.

Agile Principles and the PMI-ACP Mindset

In this chapter, you will

- Define the nine exam tasks of agile principles
- Explore the agile values for projects
- Define leadership qualities for organizational agility
- Learn the Agile Manifesto
- Compare agile project management approaches
- Review the qualities of agile project leadership

This is a book on how to pass, not just take, the PMI-ACP exam. In each chapter I'll dive into the exam specifics you'll need to know to clear that specific exam domain. This chapter is all about the agile principles and embracing the agile mindset. The PMI-ACP exam is more than just recalling facts about agile, and it'll test your ability to review a scenario-based question and then choose the best course of action—often based on the agile mindset.

You will need a strong foundation of agile principles—and if you've worked on agile projects, you likely have an understanding of how agile projects operate. I don't believe that the PMI-ACP exam is overwhelmingly difficult, but it can be tricky. Agile projects are tricky too—you must follow a framework, allow flexibility for the project team, and serve as a leader. On the PMI-ACP exam, you'll likely face questions for which more than one answer is acceptable, but to be scored correctly, you'll have to choose the best answer—not just an acceptable answer. I know, it's tricky.

 For a more detailed explanation, watch the *Passing Your PMI-ACP Exam* video now.

The first exam domain, on agile principles and the agile mindset, is worth 16 percent of your exam; that's about 19 questions. While it's not the largest exam domain, it's an important one. Fortunately, the topics in this exam domain and chapter are pretty easy to grasp, and I suspect you already know much of this information. If you're nervous about your chances of passing the PMI-ACP exam, this chapter will help you build a strong foundation on agile and bolster your confidence.

 EXAM COACH Throughout the book I'll drop in these little coaching tips and tricks. These serve as a quick reality check, to encourage you, and to remind you that while there's lots of information to learn, know, and recall, you can do this. Thousands of others have passed the exam, and you can do it too. Be confident, do the work, and you'll get it done. Like an agile project, we're breaking down all this exam preparation into manageable chunks.

Introducing the Agile Principles and Mindset Tasks

This first exam domain is about understanding and applying the agile principles and mindset within your project team and within your organization. To have the agile mindset means that you're not a silo, but that you're leading others within your organization to also embrace the agile approach. If you're the only person in your organization that has the agile mindset, you're going to feel frustrated as not everyone is going along with the principles of agile. Your role is to be an agile evangelist and convert others to agile and all its glory.

To have the agile mindset, you first must understand agile, then embrace agile, and then help others learn and embrace agile, too. The agile mindset embraces the values of the Agile Manifesto (which I'll discuss later in the chapter), solid principles of agile project management, and effective practices and leadership in agile projects. The agile mindset also requires having a good attitude, learning to fail and learning from failure, and helping others understand what they need to know to deliver in the project.

Reviewing the Nine Tasks for Exam Domain I

You'll need to know the following nine tasks, all centered on the agile principles and mindset, for this first exam domain:

- Advocate for agile principles by modeling those principles and discussing agile values in order to develop a shared mindset across the team as well as between the customer and the team.

- Help ensure that everyone has a common understanding of the values and principles of agile and a common knowledge around the agile practices and terminology being used in order to work effectively.

- Support change at the system or organization level by educating the organization and influencing processes, behaviors, and people in order to make the organization more effective and efficient.

- Practice visualization by maintaining highly visible information radiators showing real progress and real team performance in order to enhance transparency and trust.

- Contribute to a safe and trustful team environment by allowing everyone to experiment and make mistakes so that each can learn and continuously improve the way he or she works.

- Enhance creativity by experimenting with new techniques and process ideas in order to discover more efficient and effective ways of working.

- Encourage team members to share knowledge by collaborating and working together in order to lower risks around knowledge silos and to reduce bottlenecks.

- Encourage emergent leadership within the team by establishing a safe and respectful environment in which new approaches can be tried in order to make improvements and foster self-organization and empowerment.

- Practice servant leadership by supporting and encouraging others in their endeavors so that they can perform at their highest level and continue to improve.

Applying the Nine Agile Principles

On your exam, you'll be faced with scenarios about these nine principles. For example, a typical exam question could be something like this:

John is the project manager for his organization and he's leading an agile project. Some of the stakeholders are confused about the actual progress of the project and how agile is working. Of the following choices, which is the best method for John to convey actual project progress, create trust with the stakeholders, and keep everyone informed about the project progress?

A. Host a weekly status meeting with the project stakeholders

B. Create a project website and share status reports

C. Create an information radiator that includes a project burndown chart

D. Create a wall of status reports for each iteration within the project

While all the choices could work, you must choose the best answer, which is C, to create an information radiator. While we've not yet discussed the concept of an information radiator, that's a key term directly from the fourth task and it refers to a method that helps to communicate project status and is highly visible for everyone to see actual project performance. You must always choose the best answer, even if some of the other choices are good ideas, too. And don't worry, I'll be covering the terms in the preceding answer choices in this chapter.

Your experience as an agile project manager might differ from the principles I'm sharing with you here—and that's okay. I'm sharing the mainstream approaches that you'll be tested on. The PMI-ACP exam tests your knowledge of the most common agile methodologies and concepts, not the very specific applications and process tailoring you may have created and embraced in your organization.

Defining Agile Values for Projects

If there's one word to sum up agile projects, it'd be *value*. Value is what you and your organization care most about: it's the value of the work you do, why your organization exists, and the value you have for the people and their talents in the project and in the organization. Value is so important in agile projects, there's an entire exam domain just on creating value. Value touches all areas of an agile project—and all exam domains for your test. In this first exam domain, we need to discuss the value of doing and being agile.

The whole goal of project management is to get things done, and that's the first definition of value—reaching "done" in a project. The project manager, the project team (sometimes just called the development team), the customer, and all other stakeholders need a common vision of what the definition of done is. You, the agile project manager, and the customers need to agree on what done looks like. Once everyone knows what constitutes done, you can work toward that vision. Of course, in agile, the requirements that equate to done can be evolving or changing throughout the project life cycle, but everyone needs a general idea of what done means.

Once you have that shared vision of the project's product, you can utilize the adopted agile approaches to continue to work to achieve that value. As changes enter the project, the changes are prioritized based on their value in relation to other components of the project. Agile, at its core, welcomes and expects changes throughout its life cycle, but the framework of agile has principles established to prioritize changes that affect the expected value of what the development team is working toward.

Project management is about getting things done. Agile projects have that same goal, but the management of the project is different than predictive projects. Agile projects, and the processes therein, have some special considerations you'll need to know for your career and for the PMI-ACP exam.

Managing Knowledge-Work Projects

Agile projects are most commonly associated with knowledge-work projects. Knowledge-work projects are driven by creativity and brain power more than projects like construction or moving a call center. This isn't to say that industrial-work projects are less valuable than knowledge-work projects; they're just different. Industrial-work projects, like construction, require up-front planning, exact designs, and specifications that are well known at the launch of a project. These types of projects follow a predictive life cycle where everything is predicted at the start of the project.

Progress in an industrial-work project is easy to see because you can view the results of the construction, for example, as it's happening. Progress in a knowledge-work project is tougher to see because lines of code don't mean much to a customer. This is the reason why one of our exam tasks in this domain is to maintain a highly visible information radiator—a wall on which to openly and easily share project information—which is vital to being open and transparent and showing honest progress.

Project management in industrial-work projects is also different than in knowledge-work projects. Industrial-work projects have a defined sequence, rely on exact answers and plans, measure performance based on results, and establish the project manager as the center of command and control over the project team. Agile project managers have a servant leadership role, meaning they help the project team by removing impediments, shielding the team from interruptions, and encouraging the team to be autonomous and self-directed.

Knowledge-work projects are more ambiguous and expect change, and the actual work is invisible because the work is taking place in your brain rather than at a construction site. Agile is best-suited for knowledge-work projects, like software development. Agile expects change and provides a framework to manage changes that will happen in its life cycle. Knowledge-work projects have less structure and more innovation, more creativity, than industrial-work projects.

 EXAM COACH Knowledge-work projects have higher uncertainty than industrial-work projects because change is likely, they can be complex, and there is risk in their probability of success. Agile project management addresses change, complexity, and risk.

Comparing Empirical Processes and Defined Processes

If you and I were going to put together a store-bought packaged bookshelf, we'd unpack the bookshelf, dig through the instructions, and follow the defined plan. That's a simple analogy to defined processes. *Defined processes*, as the name implies, are processes for project work that have been defined for us. In construction, manufacturing, or any other industrial work, there are processes for the work and tasks that follow a defined and generally accepted approach to getting the work done. In a predictive project, where everything is planned upfront, the project manager and team are creating and using defined processes because they know exactly what the project is intended to create.

Empirical processes, by contrast, are based on observation, trial-and-error, and the experience of the person doing the work. Empirical processes are what you use when you put together a puzzle—or perform knowledge work. Agile projects rely on the knowledge worker to be creative and innovative, and to figure out the work to reach the desired results. You could bring ten developers together and have each of them create a simple "Hello, World" application based on the same set of requirements and you'd likely have ten different approaches to reach the same result in the application. Each developer would use their experience, observations, and creativity to build the app to get the "Hello, World" result. That's an example of empirical processes.

By embracing the values of agile, you're encouraging your dev team to utilize empirical processes to create value. Of course, in an agile project you'd want the ten developers to work together to create a common plan to create the value of the deliverable, rather than ten individuals working on their plans separately. We want teams to be collaborative and to have a common, agreed-upon approach to solutions.

Embracing the Agile Mindset

A term you'll see throughout the *Agile Practice Guide*, on websites, and in other books is the *agile mindset*. The agile mindset is a way of thinking about and doing agile projects. Having the agile mindset is to exemplify the values and principles of agile in how you work, how you lead a project, and how you share your passion for agile with others. To fully embrace the agile mindset means that you first must follow a formal agile approach.

You must know the rules, the processes, and the formalities of agile as a solid base to embracing the agile mindset. Once you completely understand the agile methodology that you and your organization will follow, then you can begin tailoring the process to suit your environment and projects. If a project manager begins changing the established agile approach without really understanding how the approach works, then risk can be introduced to the project, frustration and confusion can plague the project team, and stakeholders may lose engagement and support of the project. So, basically, know what you're doing before trying to change what you're doing.

The second step to fully embracing the agile mindset is to utilize agile to reach organization and customer goals, not just to "do agile." You might break a product into increments for several product releases, or help the customer find the most valuable requirements, or trim requirements from scope to meet time and costs constraints. To fully embrace the agile mindset, you'll use agile to create value, not just follow a nifty project management formula.

Reviewing the Declaration of Interdependence

The core people who established the guiding principles of agile project management released a document in 2005 called the "Declaration of Interdependence" to serve as a value system for agile project managers. The idea behind this document is that all participants in an agile project are interdependent on one another: the project manager, development team, customers, and other stakeholders all contribute to the same goal of creating value for the organization. Here's the content of this straightforward document for the agile community (see www.pmdoi.org):

We are a community of project leaders that are highly successful at delivering results. To achieve these results:

- We **increase return on investment** by making continuous flow of value our focus.

- We **deliver reliable results** by engaging customers in frequent interactions and shared ownership.

- We **expect uncertainty** and manage for it through iterations, anticipation, and adaptation.

- We **unleash creativity and innovation** by recognizing that individuals are the ultimate source of value, and creating an environment where they can make a difference.
- We **boost performance** through group accountability for results and shared responsibility for team effectiveness.
- We **improve effectiveness and reliability** through situationally specific strategies, processes and practices.[1]

While you likely won't have direct questions about this document on your PMI-ACP exam, you should know that this document clearly defines the concept of the agile mindset. These are some guiding principles you'll want to know for answering questions on the exam.

Being Agile and Doing Agile

As you might expect, there's a real difference between doing agile and being agile. You can accomplish *doing agile* by taking a seminar, following some preset rules and guidelines, and following a formula of sorts for an agile approach. Doing agile encompasses the mechanics of agile project management. *Being agile*, however, includes not only the mechanics of agile but also the agile mindset of engaging your project team, working collaboratively with stakeholders, providing open and honest communication, allowing leadership from anyone in the project, embracing change, and being excited about the project.

Being agile is more than just understanding the rules and principles of an agile approach. Being agile is understanding the depth of process application that's needed, how to tailor the approach, and how and why to bend the rules, and keeping the team and stakeholders engaged and focused on creating value. Being agile is the actualization of the agile mindset. While the PMI-ACP exam can't precisely test you on whether you're just doing agile or really being agile, having the agile mindset will greatly help you both pass the exam and find success as a PMI-ACP.

Inverting the Triple Constraints

If you're like most agile project managers, you already have a good grasp on the traditional, predictive approach to project management. In traditional project management, we often refer to the "iron triangle" (or "triple constraint") where we wrestle with the project to maintain the balance of schedule, costs, and scope. Scope in predictive projects that follow the iron triangle is the factor of project management that is fixed, and we generally try not to change scope—unless we'll accommodate the change in the other two factors of schedule and cost. In other words, for the project to be successful, scope is fixed, but the schedule and costs may vary.

---

[1] ©2005 David Anderson, Sanjiv Augustine, Christopher Avery, Alistair Cockburn, Mike Cohn, Doug DeCarlo, Donna Fitzgerald, Jim Highsmith, Ole Jepsen, Lowell Lindstrom, Todd Little, Kent McDonald, Pollyanna Pixton, Preston Smith, and Robert Wysocki.

Figure 1-1 Agile inverts the common triple constraint of traditional (predictive) project management.

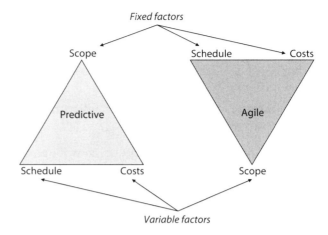

In an agile project we flip this equation and fix schedule and costs and allow scope to change as much as the customer likes, as shown in Figure 1-1. With this inverted triple constraint, we know how much the stakeholder can spend, based on the cost of the knowledge-work labor in the project, and we know the duration of the project, based on iterations of work or a realistic deadline that we must meet. Now the requirements of the project scope can grow or shrink to meet how much time and how much money we must spend. This introduces the prioritized product backlog, which I'll talk more about in adaptive planning, but for now, just know it's the prioritized product backlog that make up the project scope in an agile project.

Leading Organization Agility

If you're the only person in your organization who embraces agile, you'll feel anxious and frustrated as you work with others who don't embrace it. You may have the agile mindset, and that'll help you to some extent, but your team, stakeholders, and the rest of the organization won't be in the same mindset when it comes to getting things done. If your project team comes onboard and begins to embrace agile, that'll help the team get things done, but the rest of the organization will still be outside the agile mindset and how agile works. Finally, if the whole organization learns how agile works, then the whole organization can prosper, and the organization can move deeper into organizational change, continuous improvement, and some of the loftier goals of agile.

While your PMI-ACP exam won't focus too much on how you convert project teams and organizations to agile, it's part of the agile mindset: to teach others how agile works, why it creates value, and how it helps us all become more effective in our roles and responsibilities.

Thinking About Agile

As you prepare to pass the PMI-ACP exam, you'll be thinking a lot about agile. In your study efforts, look for opportunities to apply agile techniques both in your plan to pass the PMI-ACP exam and in your projects. Seeing how agile can create value, streamline project management, and empower others to innovate and be creative is crucial for exam (and agile) success. While you may be the sole individual in your organization to embrace the agile mindset, great things can come from converting individuals, then teams, and, hopefully, the entire organization to the agile mindset.

Doing Agile Project Management

While I just discussed the need to be agile, not just do agile, you have to start somewhere. Agile project management is really a generic term to describe all the different flavors of agile: Scrum, XP, Lean, Kanban, and Crystal, to name a few. Whatever approach you use out there in the real world, you must first understand the rules, sometimes called *ceremonies*, of agile and how it all works. The PMI-ACP exam will first test you on doing agile—on understanding the rules and framework of agile—by testing your knowledge of these different agile flavors. You don't have to be an expert in every agile approach, but you need to know enough to understand the framework, recognize the terms, and follow the generally accepted practices. Then, when you've fully mastered the agile approach, you can begin tailoring the approach to work best in your environment—that's being agile.

Encouraging Others to Embrace Agile

To be an agile project manager, you need to understand the principles of agile and then evolve into being agile. That's what'll happen with your project team and with the organization. We all have to start somewhere—so the basic rules are a great place to start. By showing others, not just telling, how effective agile is, they'll want the approach in their life too. This is true for the project team and for others in the organization. You'll encourage others to try agile, and that means you'll be doing some teaching of how agile works, its goals, and how to best apply it. You'll likely see a question or two on this concept on the PMI-ACP exam, as it's part of being agile.

When we think about organizational agility, we must think from the organization's perspective. Many of the people in an organization are going to be resistant to changing to agile practices, let alone being agile. People don't like change, of course, so you'll need to think of things from their perspective, think of what concerns them, what they expect from a project. To encourage others to embrace agile means you'll need open and honest communication—no secrets in agile project management. You'll also need to constantly think about the values of the organization: what constitutes value for your customers, and how can you create that value quickly, effectively, and with quality?

Reviewing the Agile Manifesto

If you've been around agile for more than a few minutes, you've likely heard of the Agile Manifesto. Technically, this document is called the Manifesto for Agile Software Development, but Agile Manifesto is the name you'll encounter most often. In 2001, a bunch of software developers and software project managers met up to discuss the nuances of software project management and to try to establish some general guidelines for managing software development projects. From that meeting the Agile Manifesto was created, and it has grown in popularity over the past decade and a half.

EXAM COACH You don't have to know about the origins of the Agile Manifesto or the names of the 17 people who signed the original document. I'm just providing some light history of the document here for reference.

The Agile Manifesto is a broad document that establishes the values of agile project management and provides some good advice for leading agile projects. The four values you want to know are

- Individuals and interactions over processes and tools
- Working software over comprehensive documentation
- Customer collaboration over contract negotiation
- Responding to change over following a plan

Let's take a closer look at each of these values.

Valuing Individuals and Interactions over Processes and Tools

The first value of agile project management is that we value individuals and interactions over processes and tools. Projects are performed by people, not by equipment, software, or tools and techniques. People get things done, people create the business value for the organization. In agile projects, we focus on collaboration, synergy, and creating a sense of community within our projects. We want people to feel safe, empowered, and trusted to do the right thing. We don't focus on doing processes just because we were instructed to do them. We take the time to think, to see the obvious, and to get things done.

Processes and tools are great for helping us to get things done, but sometimes organizations and project managers get bogged down in the bureaucracy of managing a project and fail to get out of the way and let the team do its work. That's the goal in agile: if a process or tool doesn't add value to the project, we likely don't need it. Our focus is on collaboration, teamwork, and working together to get things done.

Valuing Working Software over Comprehensive Documentation

One of my pet peeves is documentation: reports, meeting minutes, manuals, and other items documenting why or how the team accomplished something. In my experience, these documents are standard tasks for management rather than tasks with meaning and value. Sure, some documentation is good, but if no one is reading what's been written, who cares?

In agile, we are pragmatic and focus on creating working software, not comprehensive documentation. If the team is having to spend time documenting decisions and work processes rather than staying "in the flow" of creative problem solving and getting things done, it's a big waste. No one is going to spend time reading lengthy reports, manuals, and documentation. Value is in working software. Value is in results. Agile focuses on the priorities of the customer, not documentation that is glanced over and then tossed in the recycle bin. We do need some documentation, but the documentation should be barely sufficient, completed at the last responsible moment, and sometimes, just because. "Just because" means that sometimes, like in the case of regulations or strict policies, we have to document things.

Valuing Customer Collaboration over Contract Negotiation

Consider the customer–vendor relationship in traditional project management, where proposed changes to the product the vendor is creating for the customer often involve some negotiation and haggling. Now consider how agile expects change, how agile priorities can shift based on the customer needs and realizations of value, and how the project scope in an agile project varies at the start of the project. Rather than negotiating with the customer regarding each change to the project, in agile, the customer and the project manager and team all work together to create the best solution for the customer.

Valuing customer collaboration over contract negotiation doesn't mean there isn't a contract between the customer and the vendor, but that the terms of the contract are defined, with flexibility in mind, and then we focus on collaborating through the agile framework. We don't have to haggle over a shift in priorities, but instead we'll focus on what's creating value, accepting some tradeoffs, and working through the project collaboratively, rather than bemoaning and dreading every meeting with the customer. Collaboration is a key theme in agile project management.

Responding to Change over Following a Plan

The Agile Manifesto is about software development projects, not industrial-work projects like construction projects. Construction projects rely on a predictive life cycle, where design specs, blueprints, engineer drawings, architects, and the customer are all in agreement about what the project is intended to create before the project team begins executing. In a predictive life cycle, the project manager and project team are often averse to change because of the time and monies that have been invested in planning.

Of course, in agile projects, we expect and even welcome change. Change is not a big deal like it is in a predictive life cycle. Changes to the project scope can, and do, occur often, but agile also considers changes in the technology the development team is working with. Technology can change daily. The customer expectations can change. The marketplace can shift. If the project manager and team are married to a plan, then they ignore the opportunity to deliver value, or at least are resistant to the change. Agile welcomes change, and our planning is at a high level initially, and then specific to our current iteration. I'll talk more about iterations and iteration planning when we get into adaptive planning in Chapter 5—something to look forward to.

Embracing the 12 Principles of Agile

In addition to the four values of the Agile Manifesto, there is a supporting document that defines the 12 principles of agile project management. Know these for your exam. As you prepare to pass the PMI-ACP exam, embrace these 12 principles of agile project management. While the PMI-ACP exam likely won't ask specific questions about these 12 principles, knowing these will help you recognize the best answer on your test.

Create Value Through Continuous Delivery Value is in working software, not documentation, meetings, or great ideas. The highest priority of an agile project team is to satisfy the customer by delivering value. Above all other choices on the PMI-ACP exam, look for opportunities to deliver value to the customer through continuous delivery of working software as soon as possible in the project.

Working with Changing Requirements Agile welcomes change at any point in the project, even at the end of the project. The goal is to create value for the customer, so if a change will add value, bring it on. This principle is "Welcome changing requirements, even late in development. Agile processes harness change for the customer's competitive advantage."

Delivering Working Software Frequently Agile isn't a surprise party: create value quickly for the customer through timeboxed iterations. This principle is "Deliver working software frequently, from a couple of weeks to a couple of months, with a preference to the shorter timescale."

Working with Business People Often in predictive projects there can be an "us against them" mentality, but not in agile. Agile projects collaborate with business people. This principle is "Business people and developers must work together daily throughout the project."

Creating Results This principle is straightforward: "Build projects around motivated individuals. Give them the environment and support they need, and trust them to get the job done." As in the Agile Manifesto, results are created by people, not by equipment, tools, or processes. Agile empowers the project team rather than the project manager to be in a command-and-control position.

Communicating Face-to-Face Face-to-face communication is one of the best ways to communicate and to share information. That's the thrust of this principle: "The most efficient and effective method of conveying information to and within a development team is face-to-face conversation."

Building Working Software   Variance analysis, earned value management, and performance measurement are all great, but the real measure of progress is working software. This principle is "Working software is the primary measure of progress."

Providing Manageable Environments   It's no secret that overworking the project team creates tension, defects, and frustration. Agile projects promote sustainable development by establishing a workable pace in a manageable environment. This principle is "Agile processes promote sustainable development. The sponsors, developers, and users should be able to maintain a constant pace indefinitely."

Paying Attention to Details   The devil is in the details, and agile is no exception. By paying attention to details, being committed to excellence, and practicing good design, the development team is creating value for the customer. This principle is "Continuous attention to technical excellence and good design enhances agility."

Keeping Things Simple   Simple doesn't mean easy, but it's focused on the prioritized requirements, approachable, and creates reliable solutions through stable architecture, good code, and valuable software. Agile projects don't need to create more than what's needed. This principle is "Simplicity—the art of maximizing the amount of work not done—is essential."

Relying on Self-Led Teams   Agile teams are self-led and self-organizing, and they work collaboratively on the software solutions. The project manager gets out of the way and lets the team do the work as it sees fit. This principle is "The best architectures, requirements, and designs emerge from self-organizing teams."

Adjusting the Project Practices   One of the beautiful things about agile is that there is opportunity to pause and reflect on what's working, or not working, and then to adjust. Rather than continue to suffer, as in some predictive projects, agile teams have an opportunity to communicate honestly and make corrective actions in the work to improve the project. This principle is "At regular intervals, the team reflects on how to become more effective, then tunes and adjusts its behavior accordingly."

Comparing Agile Project Approaches

There are lots of different approaches to doing agile and no single way is the best way. For your PMI-ACP exam, you'll need to know a bit about each of these common agile approaches, but you won't have to know everything about every single approach—just the good stuff. In this section I address the seven most common agile approaches that you'll likely see on your exam. I cover them to a depth that's reflective of what's popular in the industry. I'm not going into every facet of every approach, but will provide detail where detail is warranted.

The two most common agile approaches in the software development industry, and on the PMI-ACP exam, are Scrum and XP. You'll likely see questions about these two approaches the most on your exam, but you'll also likely see questions about the other approaches at a high level. I seriously doubt you'll get many questions about the nuances of any of these approaches. The PMI-ACP exam is about being agile, not specifically about Scrum, XP, Kanban, or even Crystal.

Reviewing the Basics of Scrum

As of today, Scrum is arguably the most popular agile project management approach. Scrum uses timeboxed iterations, called *sprints*, to create prioritized requirements for the customer. Sprints last from two to four weeks. Scrum is based on three core principles of agile software project management: transparency, inspection, and adaptation. Know these three principles and how to apply them in a Scrum project.

- **Transparency** Transparency begins with a clear understanding among all stakeholders of what the definition of "done" is. Transparency communicates with a common language, evidence of accomplishments in each iteration, and an understanding of what everyone on the project is doing.
- **Inspection** Scrum utilizes intermittent inspections of the work to ensure quality. The inspection of the work catches defects before they're released into production (called *escaped defects*) and gives the team opportunity to fix the glitches before the defects cause the work to become unacceptable.
- **Adaptation** Scrum is agile, meaning it's flexible, adaptive, and allows tailoring of the processes being used in the project. If a process within a project isn't adding value, you don't just live with the broken process, you adjust the broken process. It's silly to continue to run a project on and on when there's something that's not working.

Exploring the Five Scrum Values

There are five Scrum values that all project team members, including the project manager, strive to adhere to:

- **Commitment** Commit to achieving the goal of each sprint.
- **Focus** Focus on completing the goals of the sprint and the goals of the team.
- **Openness** Be open and transparent about the challenges of the project work.
- **Respect** Respect each other as capable, independent people.
- **Courage** Do the right thing and work through tough problems.

Leading a Scrum Project

There are just seven steps in a Scrum project—that's it! I'll talk more about each of these steps later in the book, but for now, here are the seven steps to the Scrum framework:

1. The product owner creates a prioritized list of everything the project might deliver. This list is the product backlog.

2. The team and product owner meet in sprint planning and the team decides how much work it can take on in the next sprint. The team pulls requirements from the prioritized product backlog that it can achieve in the sprint. This chunk of work becomes the sprint backlog.

3. The team decides who'll do what and creates the items in the sprint backlog for the current sprint. The team will meet each day for a 15-minute meeting, called the Daily Scrum, to share progress updates.

4. The project manager, called the ScrumMaster, helps keep the team working toward the sprint goal.

5. A sprint review happens at the end of each sprint to demonstrate for the product owner what the team has accomplished.

6. After the sprint review the team participates in a sprint retrospective to discuss what did or did not work in the last sprint. This gives the ScrumMaster and the team an opportunity to adjust the processes and work for the next sprint.

7. The whole process repeats itself by the project team selecting the next chunk of prioritized requirements from the backlog and getting to work in the next sprint.

Sounds easy, right? Well, the Scrum approach is easy to understand, but implementing it in an organization can be tricky—especially the first time. Like most things, with practice it does get easier and easier, and as people begin to see value in the results, more and more people in the organization will want to adapt the Scrum approach.

Identifying the Scrum Roles and Responsibilities

There are three distinct roles in the Scrum environment and they all work together throughout the project. First up is the product owner. The product owner has one job: manage the product backlog. As previously mentioned, the product backlog is the long list of prioritized project requirements. The product owner arranges these items from most valuable to least valuable. The ordering and content of the product backlog can change for each sprint, but what's in the backlog and the ordering of the items is transparent to the whole team. The management of the product backlog is called *grooming* or *refining*.

Next up is the development team, sometimes just called the dev team. The development team is responsible for sizing the requirements of the product backlog and getting work done in each sprint. The development team is self-organizing and self-led, and its members are called *generalizing specialists* because they can often do more than one function on the team. An ideal Scrum team has no less than five people and no more than eleven people. Some people argue that seven people on a Scrum team is perfect.

Finally, there's the ScrumMaster. This is analogous to the project manager role, but a ScrumMaster is less focused on command and control and more focused on being a servant leader. The ScrumMaster ensures that everyone understands the rules of Scrum, removes impediments for the team, facilities Scrum meetings, helps the product owner groom the backlog, and communicates the vision of the project to everyone that's involved.

Reviewing the Scrum Ceremonies

Scrum ceremonies sounds so formal, but it's the terminology for the meetings and events within the Scrum practice. Scrum ceremonies are straightforward, but there are some guidelines for each of the events:

- **Backlog refinement meeting** This event is where the product owner, the ScrumMaster, and the development team work together to discuss the backlog items and prioritize the items.

- **Sprint planning meeting** The team determines how much work they can take on from the prioritized backlog for the next sprint. This determination is based on estimates of the items in the product backlog and past sprints. The selected items from the product backlog become the sprint backlog and the goal of the sprint.

- **Daily Scrum** This is a 15-minute meeting, sometimes called a standup meeting because everyone stands for the duration. The Daily Scrum happens every day at the same time, in the same place. This meeting is for the development team and the ScrumMaster only. In the meeting each person addresses the entire team by answering three specific questions:
  - What have I accomplished since the last Daily Scrum?
  - What will I accomplish before the next Daily Scrum?
  - Are there any impediments blocking my work?

- **Scrum of Scrums** In a big Scrum project there might be multiple teams working together. Rather than having a huge Daily Scrum, the teams meet separately and then a representative from each team meets in a Scrum of Scrums to report on each team's progress. The team representatives answer the same three questions, but for the team rather than as individuals. In addition, a fourth question is often addressed: Will our team be putting something in another team's way?

- **Scrum of Scrums Scrum** Yes, this is getting silly, but you should know it. If there are many teams, you can create another layer of Scrum meetings with representatives from the Scrum of Scrums. This isn't very common, but it's just the type of question scenario that you could see on your exam.

- **Sprint review** At the end of each sprint, the development team demonstrates for the product owner, the ScrumMaster, and other key stakeholders the work they've accomplished in the past sprint. This review is an opportunity for the development team, not the ScrumMaster, to show the results of what they've created. It's also an opportunity for the product owner to offer feedback on whether the work has reached the done stage, and, if it hasn't, describe what's missing and elaborate on corrections or modifications for the increment of work created.

- **Sprint retrospective** After the sprint review, and before the next sprint planning meeting, the development team meets to discuss three items: people, product, and process. The team discusses what's worked well with each item in the project, what needs improvement, and the feedback from the product owner from the sprint review meeting. Note that *people* means the project team and the ScrumMaster; this isn't a gossip session, but an opportunity to give an assessment and offer suggestions for improvement, done with respect for one another.

 EXAM COACH This is a quick primer on Scrum. Throughout the book I'll reference Scrum as needed. The important thing to remember here is that the PMI-ACP exam doesn't test you specifically on Scrum, or other agile methodologies, but on how to perform agile. You'll only need to know the fundamentals of Scrum and these agile approaches. Don't get bogged down in trying to learn all that you can about each of these agile approaches.

Reviewing XP

XP is short for eXtreme Programming, an agile approach that is focused, of course, on software development. XP also uses iterations of development, but these iterations last for two weeks in a typical project. The requirements are called *user stories* and the development team sizes up the user stories to see how much work they can accomplish in the next iteration. At the beginning of the project, and as needed through the project, the XP team will host a release planning meeting. The purpose of the release planning meeting is to create the high-level estimate for the project work and define when the product will be released, either through increments or as one final deliverable.

Spike is an XP term that you should know. There's an architectural spike, which is an iteration to set up the environment, ensure the design is not overly complicated, and examine the plan's feasibility to accomplish the project goals. A risk spike aims to mitigate or eliminate risks that have been identified in the project and threaten project success.

Reviewing Five XP Values

In an XP project, the development team utilizes pair programming. As the name suggests, *pair programming* means that programmers work together in pairs; one person codes and the other person checks the code. When thinking through these values, keep in mind the concept of pair programming. XP has the following five core values, which aren't much different than the values you've already seen in the Agile Manifesto:

- **Simplicity** Find the simplest thing that could possibly work. Keeping things simple means removing complexity and waste in the development.

- **Communication** Transparent, face-to-face communication is best for a project team.

- **Feedback** Fail fast and fail early to get feedback on what's not working before getting too invested in the project approach.

- **Courage**   All the code is visible to everyone all the time on an XP project. It takes courage to put your work out there for others to review, inspect, and edit.

- **Respect**   The team respects each other, and respects others' culture, values, and how they work to get results. The success, or failure, of the project is everyone's responsibility.

Introducing the XP Roles and Responsibilities

There are four roles that you'll work with in an XP project. Know these four roles for your PMI-ACP exam:

- **Coach**   The project manager as a coach is more of a mentor, a facilitator, and she coaches the people on the project team, helps get things done, and serves as the hub of communications for the project stakeholders.

- **Customer**   This is the person that represents the business, and the role is similar to that of the product owner in a Scrum project. The customer helps prioritize requirements and is onsite with the development team.

- **Programmers**   These are the development team members for the project. These members are also known as developers or coders.

- **Testers**   These are the people that test the code before the code is released into production. The tester role can be fulfilled by a programmer.

Learning the 13 XP Core Practices

There are 13 XP core practices that wrap around different layers of a circle, as depicted in Figure 1-2. While I do think it's important to know these core practices, you don't need to memorize them for your PMI-ACP exam. Be more familiar with the mindset and intent of these practices and how to apply them—that'll help you more. Let's take a quick look at these 13 core practices now:

Figure 1-2   The 13 XP core practices are situated on different layers of a circle.

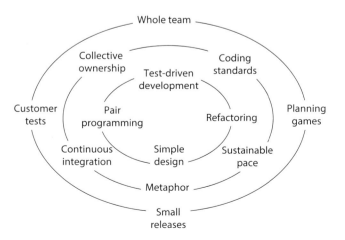

- **Whole team**   The whole team acts as a collaborating unit where team members can serve more than one role and are ideally colocated. The individuals in the team are sometimes called generalizing specialists.

- **Planning games**   The team plans for iterations and incremental releases. Iterations are the two-week segments of work, and releases happen within six months.

- **Small releases**   With two-week iterations, the development team can create, test, and release the code in quick, small releases for fast feedback and corrections as needed.

- **Customer tests**   The code is tested from the customer perspective to confirm that the code meets the expectations of the customer before releasing the code to production.

- **Collective code ownership**   Any pair of programmers on the development team can edit anyone's code.

- **Code standards**   All programmers on the development team follow defined and communicated standards for developing the code.

- **Sustainable pace**   As in Scrum, the team works at a sustainable pace to get the iteration done.

- **Metaphor**   A metaphor for the project is used to explain the goal and function in plain, understandable language for all stakeholders.

- **Continuous integration**   By integrating code frequently throughout the iteration, issues are discovered quickly and are easier to fix than when integrating code right before testing.

- **Test-driven development**   An acceptance test is written before the code is written so the developers know what it takes to pass the acceptance test and can program accordingly.

- **Refactoring**   Refactoring involves cleaning up the code to remove waste, redundancy, dependent connections, and shortcuts. This "mess" that developers are cleaning up is called *technical debt*. Technical debt can pile up and become trickier and heavier to clean up the longer the mess is ignored.

- **Simple design**   Do the simplest thing that can work. Keep it simple.

- **Pair programming**   Developers work in pairs; one person codes while the other checks the code. The pair switches roles periodically.

Like Scrum, I'll mention XP as needed throughout the book, but you won't have real in-depth questions about the nuances of XP on your exam. Be familiar enough with these principles and intent to answer agile questions about the approach.

Working with Kanban

Kanban (pronounced "con bon") is a Japanese word that means signboard. The Kanban approach started at Toyota as a way to help visualize the flow of work through a system.

Figure 1-3 Kanban boards visualize the flow of the work in a project.

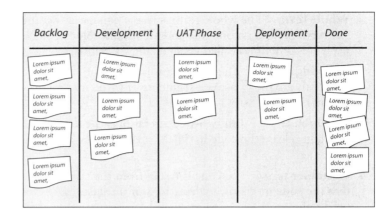

Figure 1-3 is an example of a simple Kanban that shows the work that's in queue (the Backlog column), the work that's in progress (the middle three columns), and the items that have been completed (Done column). The work that's in progress is called the WIP and that's what the team is working on right now. The signboard is often a big white board and items are pulled from the leftmost column and moved progressively to the right columns either by erasing and rewriting the items in each column or by using sticky notes. This use of low-tech, high-touch tools to help manage and visualize the project workflow is an agile concept.

Kanban is a pull system, pulling work from the queue into the WIP and workflow. When a team member completes an item, it triggers the next item to be brought into the system. When there are additional steps, such as testing, the item pulled into the next task column can also trigger other team members to address or pull that item in their queue of work. Kanban doesn't use iterations like Scrum and XP, but just continues to pull to-do items into the WIP and through the established workflow. The items in queue can be prioritized, but Kanban is about getting things done, rather than creating increments.

Reviewing the Five Kanban Principles

Kanban has five principles you should know:

- **Visualize**   The big principle of Kanban is the most obvious: you visualize the workflow that you and the team have created. Your workflow can have as many steps (columns) as needed from the queue to completion.

- **Limit the WIP**   Don't pull too many items into WIP in an attempt to increase productivity. Switching between work items creates waste, bottlenecks, and defects. By limiting the WIP, your team members focus on completing one item at a time before bringing new work into the workflow.

- **Manage the workflow**   By visualizing the work and controlling the WIP, you and the development team can better control defects, easily track work items, and better manage changes.

- **Clearly define the process and policies**   When everyone understands the policies and how agile processes work, any changes to processes are made based on value, rather than subjective reasoning.

- **Collaborate**   The team works together to get the work done, but also works as a team to consider any changes to the processes or workflow.

The most important thing about Kanban is limiting the WIP. By limiting the WIP, the development team is more effective and can complete the work faster. Little's Law, identified by John Little, states "the average number of items in a queuing system equals the average rate at which items arrive multiplied by the average time that an item spends in the system." In other words, the more items that are in the WIP queue, the longer it will take the team to complete the items in queue. It's like standing in line at the grocery store: the longer the line you're in, the longer it takes the cashier to process all the orders ahead of you. If your team can minimize waste and increase speed, then the duration of the queue will diminish. Too many items in WIP equates to too much motion—and motion is waste.

Introducing Lean Product Development

Lean Product Development, commonly called Lean, began in Toyota manufacturing as a refinement of Henry Ford's manufacturing approach, but it's been adapted to agile and other environments. Like other agile approaches, Lean visualizes what needs to be done, creates requirements based on the customer's definition of value, and includes opportunity for learning and process improvement throughout the project.

There are seven principles within Lean that you should recognize for your exam:

- **Eliminate waste**   Waste is anything that is a detriment to the customer-identified value. Waste includes partially done work, the addition of unnecessary features, rework in test and fix cycles, and waiting too long to test after creating the code.

- **Quality is built in**   As a project manager, you likely know that quality is planned into a project, not inspected in. That's the same principle here: you build quality into the project by keeping things simple in the code, refactoring often, and utilizing continuous integration.

- **Create knowledge**   Architecture validation happens as the code is created, offer early and frequent releases for customer feedback, have daily builds, perform continuous integration, and use modular architecture to add features and changing requirements in future builds. Through learning we create more knowledge.

- **Defer commitments**   By not making irreversible decisions until the last responsible moment, you're creating opportunities for better design, features, and flexibility in the software. You don't want to lock in design solutions until it's necessary to do so.

- **Deliver fast**   Fast delivery creates value, keeps customers from changing their minds about the established and agreed-upon product requirements, allows the development team to be self-led and self-organizing to get the work done, and reduces defects because of higher quality demands.

- **Respect people**   Development teams are given goals and the empowerment to achieve those goals, leaders are more entrepreneurial than traditional project managers, and the development team is made up of technical experts that can deliver on requirements. We treat people as professional colleagues, not as underlings to do our bidding.

- **Optimize the whole**   We consider the whole project: the people, processes, alignment with organizational goals, and how everything must contribute to the value of the product.

In addition to these seven principles of Lean, there are also the following seven areas of waste we aim to remove from the project. These are often called Poppendieck's Seven Wastes of Software Development, as they were identified by Lean experts Tom and Mary Poppendieck.

- **Partially done work**   Value is in working software, not partially done work. The development team should work on and complete one item at a time.

- **Extra features**   Adding bells and whistles that the customer hasn't requested is not a value-add. This is scope creep and robs the project of time and energy that should be spent on the identified requirements.

- **Relearning**   When information goes missing, due to poor knowledge management, and teams members have to relearn the information, that's wasted time and energy in the project.

- **Handoffs**   When information is passed from one person to another and another, rather than through a centralized communication system, the message and information can change and that contributes to waste.

- **Delays**   Waiting time is wasted time. When team members are waiting for information or outputs from stakeholders, this is waste.

- **Task switching**   Hopping from task to task is wasteful, sucks time, and creates partially done work. Instead, the development team should focus on completing one task at a time.

- **Defects**   Defects cause rework, create frustration, and can cause stakeholders and the project team to lose support of the project. Defects that make it through the testing process and are released into production are called escaped defects.

Working with DSDM

The Dynamic Systems Development Method (DSDM) is one of the predecessors of today's agile project management and relied on a business case to show value and a feasibility study to determine if the development team could create the architecture and requirements the customer identified. While you likely won't see many questions about DSDM on the PMI-ACP exam, you should recognize these eight principles:

- Business need is the primary goal.
- Deliver working software on time.

- Collaborate with the development team and the business people.
- Quality cannot be comprised.
- Build incrementally based on firm foundations.
- Develop iteratively.
- Provide clear and consistent communications.
- Demonstrate control.

The project manager and the development team work together to ensure that all eight of these principles are implemented in the project. You cannot shortcut any of the eight principles without affecting the quality of the project management process and the quality of the deliverable presented to the project customer.

Utilizing Feature-Driven Development

Feature-Driven Development (FDD) is an iterative approach to software development that bases its progress on the client's values of features the software will provide. Like other agile approaches, FDD utilizes a backlog of features that are prioritized based on customer values then created through iterations of project work. Figure 1-4 shows the FDD process.

There are five stages to the FDD process:

- **Develop an overall model** This stage establishes a high-level description of the project scope. The scope is broken down into domain models and passed through a peer review to reach consensus on the models that will be part of the project's overall model to be created.

- **Build the features list** The domain models are decomposed into subject areas. The subject areas are broken into business activities and features. Features are written as <action><result><object>, such as "Calculate the total price for a purchase" or "Validate a user login." Features are small enough that they won't take longer than two weeks to create.

- **Plan by feature** A features list is compiled, and a development plan is created. The development plan assigns ownership of features to developers.

- **Design by feature** The chief programmer chunks out the set of features that can be created in the two-week iteration by the class of programmers. The chief

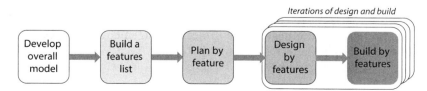

Figure 1-4   Feature-Driven Development has five stages in its development process.

programmer also creates a sequence diagram for the selected features and updates the overall model. Design by feature repeats for each iteration of the project work.

- **Build by feature**   The development team develops the code, then the features pass through unit testing, and finally code inspection ensures that each feature is of quality and ready to be added to the build. Build by feature also repeats for each iteration of the project work.

Throughout the process, the project manager utilizes configuration management to document and track changes to the code. The team participates in regular builds to ensure the features they're creating work with the existing build. The compiled code is demonstrated for the client on a regular basis (often every two weeks). The project manager also tracks the completion of milestones and overall progress.

Working with Crystal

The last agile approach you need to be familiar with is Crystal. Crystal isn't a singular approach to agile project management, but a family of methodologies created by Alistair Cockburn. Crystal uses eight different schemes of agile project management based on several factors, such as the complexity of the project, the number of project team members, and the criticality of the project. Sometimes, these approaches are described as project criticality and the weight of the processes used in the project. The higher the priority of the project, the more weight and ceremony is needed to control the project.

Crystal utilizes methodology, techniques, and policies to manage the project. In addition, Crystal focuses on people, interaction, community, development team skills, talents, and communication as its core principles. From lightest criticality to most serious project criticality, here are the eight levels of Crystal:

- Crystal Clear—small, easy projects
- Crystal Yellow
- Crystal Orange
- Crystal Orange Web
- Crystal Red
- Crystal Maroon
- Crystal Diamond
- Crystal Sapphire—top priority projects

The bigger the project, the more complex it is, and the more people involved, the more formal the project and the heavier the project management processes will become.

EXAM COACH   Crystal isn't something that you'll need to know a great deal about for your exam. Just know that the colors of the Crystal approach represent different priority levels. I suspect you may see one or two questions on this approach.

Leading an Agile Project

Leading an agile project is different than leading a predictive project. Predictive projects plan everything, for the most part, up front. Agile projects follow a methodology of not being too invested in planning and instead focusing on handling chunks of work throughout the life cycle. An agile project manager can go by lots of different names: ScrumMaster, coach, team leader, or even facilitator. The responsibility of the agile project manager will vary based on the methodology selected and the organization, but as a rule, the agile project manager follows more of a servant leadership role and ensures that the team has the resources, knowledge, and tools to complete their project work. Sometimes the agile project manager is known to "carry the food and water for the project team." This doesn't mean you're literally carrying jugs of water and snacks for the team, but that you're getting the team the stuff they need so the team can continue to be productive.

Within agile there are four types of life cycles you'll be leading as a project manager, and you should recognize these characteristics for your exam:

- **Agile**   Working with dynamic requirements for the development team to deliver working software frequently through small releases
- **Incremental**   Working with dynamic requirements for the development team to quickly deliver working software through increments of product releases
- **Iterative**   Working with dynamic requirements for the development team to create a single delivery of the software solution at the end of the project
- **Predictive**   Working with fixed requirements for the project team to create a single delivery of the product, manage costs, and manage the project schedule

While the agile, incremental, and iterative life cycles have overlapping characteristics, there are some difference in the delivery of the product the project is creating. Of course, predictive is the traditional approach to project management that you'll often see in industrial-work projects.

Comparing Management and Leadership in Agile Projects

There's an obvious difference between management and leadership. Management is about getting things done and leadership is about getting the project team to want to do what needs to be done. Leadership is about aligning, motivating, and inspiring the project team. Management is about command and control of the project tasks and directing people to get stuff done. Sure, there are some cute idioms about management and leadership, but the truth is that you need to know both approaches to complete a project successfully. Agile projects, and your PMI-ACP exam, will lean toward the attributes of leadership over management.

Make no mistake: all agile projects need management to ensure that the ceremonies, framework, and processes are being followed. Call that management facilitation, or mentoring, or coaching—it's all management to get things done. You, the agile project manager, must have some control over the project without getting in the way of the project team, creating unnecessary bureaucracy, or creating layers of approval that can delay delivering value quickly for the customers. Servant leaders focus on the purpose of the project, the people working on the project, and then the processes needed to complete the project.

Serving as a Leader

The project manager doesn't always have to be the leader in an agile project. Agile supports the idea of emergent leadership, where anyone can become the leader based on what's happening in the project. You will be seen, at least initially, as the project leader. You'll need to embrace these seven attributes of servant leadership:

- **Promoting self-awareness** Servant leaders use emotional intelligence to understand and control their emotions and to understand the emotions of others. This also includes how the servant leader behaves, responds, and takes time to think before speaking or acting.

- **Listening** Servant leaders listen to the project team and the stakeholders. This means listening to the whole message, body language, and nonverbal clues to really understand the message's meaning. By understanding the message, you can better serve the needs of the project.

- **Serving the project team** Servant leaders protect the project team from interruptions, remove any impediments the team reports or the project manager identifies, often communicate the project vision to everyone, and provide what the team needs to do their work.

- **Helping people grow** Servant leaders provide opportunities for people to learn from the project work and from one another. Often, when people are challenged and interested in what they're doing, they're happier, create better results, and are willing to take on tasks. Servant leaders promote collaboration and peer learning.

- **Coaching versus controlling** Servant leaders coach and mentor rather than command and control. The project manager may have to enforce certain rules and policies of the organization but should do so in a way that explains the policies so the team understands why they need to follow the policies.

- **Promoting safety, respect, and trust** Servant leaders ensure a safe environment for the team to experiment, to be creative and innovative without a fear of repercussions should they fail in their innovations. The team members need to show each other respect and need to trust one another. Trust also means the team must learn to trust the process, the approach, and be willing to collaborate with one another to create value.

- **Promoting the energy and intelligence of others**   Servant leaders promote and encourage the team to be creative, to try new things, and to collaborate on ideas. The project team should be self-organizing to determine what's the best use of their time without the project manager being in control of every decision. The team members should be encouraged to practice emergent leadership where anyone can become a leader for the project team.

Visualizing Transparency

Transparency is a concept you'll see promoted in every agile approach. Transparency means that we're honest about both good news and bad news, and that we don't hide information about progress or setbacks in the project. To visualize transparency means that the project manager and the development team are open about their work's progress, the actual code of the work, and how well they're meeting the iteration's goals and objectives. For example, in Scrum, the team commits to taking on a chunk of the product backlog and then throughout the sprint communicates daily about what's been accomplished and any issues they've experienced in their progress.

Visualization is another key agile concept. Through signboards, charts, and dashboards, we openly communicate our progress. As previously mentioned, an information radiator is an agile concept of a wall of signs, charts, or even electronic displays that "radiates" information about the project work. An information radiator may be referred to informally as "a big, visible chart" or the stuffier "informative workspace." The information radiator visualizes that the team has nothing to hide from stakeholders, the project manager, and each other. Everything, good or bad, is out there for everyone to see.

Creating a Safe and Trustful Environment

I've seen, and perhaps you've seen it too, a manager encourage the team to experiment and try new methods of getting work done only to later criticize the team when their innovations didn't work out. That's just awful. In agile, project managers embrace innovation, empower the team to try new things, to be creative—all without the fear of repercussions. Because agile, for the most part, uses short bursts of work, if something isn't working out, the failure is considered fast, thereby avoiding a long, drawn-out failure by sticking to a plan that is doomed. It's better to experiment, fail early, learn from the mistake, and move on.

Fast failure is good for several reasons:

- The team now knows something that didn't work.
- New success is based on failed innovations.
- Failure is a learning opportunity for the whole project team.
- Failure without repercussion promotes trust and continued innovation.

The project team should be empowered to try new approaches, make decisions, learn from what didn't work, adjust their approaches, and try again. Too much studying, planning, and analysis can slow things down versus simply experimenting to see what'll happen. This isn't to say that the development team doesn't think before acting, but rather they don't overthink a problem that they could test and then move forward based on the results. An agile project manager wants the team to experiment and discover new ways of doing things to find innovations.

Encourage Emergent Leadership

Emergent leadership means that leaders emerge from the project team at different times of the project. Different team members will lead various initiatives of the project work based on what's happening within the project. When a new leader emerges, ideally a power struggle will not ensue over who's leading and all team members will acknowledge that others have talents to offer and should be followed when those talents are needed. This isn't a formal voting process to identify the new leader; rather, leaders are self-selected in an effort to help the team, not themselves.

Emergent leadership doesn't mean that the agile project manager ceases to offer leadership as new leaders emerge from the project team. The project manager has four distinct leadership roles:

- **Directing** When the team first comes together, called the *forming stage*, the project manager needs to direct the team, as they'll likely have low competence about the project's values and goals, but a high commitment to getting things done.

- **Coaching** When the teams shifts into storming, where there's a power struggle and conflict among the team, the project manager offers directions and supportive behavior to help the team move forward in the process of team development.

- **Supporting** As the team settles into their project roles, called the *norming phase* of team development, the project manager scales back directing but continues supportive behavior.

- **Delegating** When the team is working collaboratively and the project is moving forward, the team is in the *performing stage* of team development. During the performing stage, the project manager offers minimal directing and low supportive behavior. This means the project manager gets out of the way and allows emergent leaders to lead.

Chapter Summary

You're done with Chapter 1. Congrats!

In this chapter, we talked about the agile principles and the agile mindset you'll need to master for the PMI-ACP exam. Remember that the agile domain of Agile Principles and Mindset has nine tasks that center on the values of agile projects. Agile projects are creative, knowledge-work projects that deal with invisible work and complex requirements to create value for the project customers. This complex work requires the use of trial and error, observation, and innovation through empirical processes rather than the use of defined processes as in industrial work.

You also reviewed the Agile Declaration of Interdependence, which outlines the values and principles of an agile project team. This document has just six items that create a framework of goals and behaviors for agile project managers and the project team. Based on this document, you also reviewed the difference of being agile and doing agile. Of course, your goal is to be agile, to embrace the agile mindset, and create a safe environment for your team to create value for the project customer. You'll also work to educate others in your organization about agile and why it's something the whole organization should embrace rather than just one individual or just one project team.

In this chapter you also took a quick look at the Agile Manifesto and its four values for the project. This is the document that defines how agile projects value people and interactions over processes and tools, working software over comprehensive documentation, customer collaboration over contract negotiation, and responding to change over following a plan. You also explored the 12 principles of agile that support the goals of the Agile Manifesto.

Next, you walked through the various agile project management approaches. This discussion included an in-depth look at Scrum and XP, two approaches you'll likely see on the PMI-ACP exam. Other, less popular approaches you might encounter on the PMI-ACP exam include Kanban, Lean Product Development (Lean), Dynamic Systems Development Method (DSDM), Feature-Driven Development (FDD), and Crystal. Finally, we wrapped things up with a frank talk about agile project leaders and the concept of emergent leadership.

Keep working toward your goal of earning the PMI-ACP credential. You've already done more than many who say they want to earn the PMI-ACP: you've read the first chapter of the guide that aims to get you there. Keep working smart, stay focused, stay confident. You can do this!

Key Terms

Agile life cycle   The agile life cycle works with dynamic requirements for the development team to deliver working software frequently through small releases.

Agile Manifesto   The Agile Manifesto is a broad document that establishes the values of agile project management. The four values are individuals and interactions over processes and tools; working software over comprehensive documentation; customer collaboration over contract negotiation; responding to change over following a plan.

Agile mindset   The agile mindset is a way of thinking about and doing agile projects. Having the agile mindset means you exemplify the values and principles of agile in how you work, how you lead a project, and how you share a passion for agile with others.

Backlog refinement meeting   A backlog refinement meeting is a Scrum event where the product owner, the ScrumMaster, and the development team work together to discuss the backlog items and prioritize the items.

Coach   This is an XP role that is like a project manager but is more of a mentor and facilitator. The coach mentors people on the project team, helps get things done, and serves as the hub of communications for the project stakeholders.

Code standards   An XP concept is that all programmers on the development team follow defined and communicated standards for developing the code.

Collective code ownership   An XP concept is that any pair of programmers on the development team can edit anyone's code.

Crystal   Crystal is an agile approach that uses eight different schemes of agile project management based on several factors, such as the complexity of the project, the number of project team members, and the criticality of the project.

Daily Scrum   This is a daily 15-minute meeting during which the team members share progress updates; it is sometimes called a standup meeting because everyone stands for the duration. The Daily Scrum happens every day at the same time, in the same place.

Development team   The development team is responsible for sizing the requirements of the product backlog and getting work done in each sprint. The development team is self-organizing and self-led, and its members are called generalizing specialists because they can often do more than one function on the team. An ideal Scrum team has no less than five people and no more than eleven people.

Dynamic Systems Development Method (DSDM)   DSDM is one of the predecessors of today's agile project management and relied on a business case to show value and a feasibility study to determine if the development team could create the architecture and requirements the customer identified.

Empirical processes   Empirical processes are based on observation, trial and error, and the experience of the person doing the work. Agile projects rely on the knowledge worker to be creative, innovative, and to figure out the work to reach the desired results.

Feature-Driven Development (FDD)   FDD is an iterative approach to software development that bases its progress on the client's values of features the software will provide.

Incremental life cycle   The incremental life cycle works with dynamic requirements for the development team to quickly deliver working software through increments of product releases.

Industrial-work projects   Industrial-work projects utilize defined approaches to complete processes and tasks; the project team members know exactly what to do and what to expect in the project and in the project management approach. Construction is an example of an industrial-work project.

Inverted triple constraint   Agile projects invert the traditional triple constraints (or iron triangle) so that time and cost are fixed, but the scope is now flexible.

Iterative life cycle   The iterative life cycle works with dynamic requirements for the development team to create a single delivery of the software solution at the end of the project.

Kanban   Kanban is a Japanese word that means signboard. This approach started at Toyota and it helps to visualize the flow of the work through a system.

Knowledge-work projects   Agile projects are knowledge-work projects and are driven by creativity and brain power, rather than brawn and effort applied to defined processes and tasks. Software development is an example of a knowledge-work projects.

Lean Product Development   Commonly called Lean, this agile approach uses a visualization of what needs to be done, creates requirements based on the customer's definition of value, and includes opportunity for learning and process improvement throughout the project.

Little's Law   A theorem that states "the average number of items in a queuing system equals the average rate at which items arrive multiplied by the average time that an item spends in the system." In other words, the more items that are in the WIP queue, the longer it will take the team to complete the items in the queue.

Metaphor   An XP practice is to create a metaphor for the project. A metaphor explains the goal and function in plain, understandable language for all stakeholders.

Pair programming   This is an XP approach where developers work in pairs; one person codes while the other checks the code. The pair switches roles periodically.

Predictive life cycle   The predictive life cycle works with fixed requirements for the project team to create a single delivery of the product, manage costs, and manage the project schedule.

Product backlog   The product backlog is the long list of prioritized project requirements. The product owner is responsible for maintaining the product backlog.

Product owner   This is a role in the Scrum agile methodology that describes the individual that manages the product backlog for the project.

Refactoring   Refactoring involves cleaning up the code to remove waste, redundancy, dependent connections, and shortcuts.

Scrum of Scrums Scrum   This is a meeting for larger Scrum projects where multiple teams are working together. Rather than having a huge Daily Scrum, the teams meet separately and then a representative from each team meets in a Scrum to report on each team's progress. The team representatives answer the same questions as in the Daily Scrum, but for the team rather than individuals. In addition, a fourth question is often posed: Will our team be putting something in another team's way?

ScrumMaster   The ScrumMaster ensures that everyone understands the rules of Scrum, removes impediments for the team, facilities Scrum meetings, helps the product owner groom the backlog, and communicates the vision of the project to everyone that's involved.

Sprint planning meeting   In this Scrum event, the development team determines how much work they can take on from the prioritized backlog for the next sprint. This determination is based on estimates of the items in the product backlog and past sprints. The selected items from the product backlog become the sprint backlog and the goal of the sprint.

Sprint retrospective   This Scrum event is held after the sprint review and before the next sprint planning meeting. The team discusses what's worked well with people, product, and processes in the project, what needs improvement, and the feedback from the product owner from the sprint review meeting.

Sprint review   This Scrum meeting is held at the end of each sprint. The development team demonstrates for the product owner, the ScrumMaster, and other key stakeholders the work they've accomplished in the past sprint. This review is for the product owner to offer feedback on whether the work has reached the done stage, and, if it hasn't, describe what's missing and elaborate on corrections or modifications for the increment of work created.

Sprints   Scrum uses timeboxed iterations, called sprints, to create prioritized requirements for the customer. Sprints last from two to four weeks to complete the selected requirements for the current iteration.

Technical debt   Technical debt is sloppy code, shortcuts, and redundancies that need to be cleaned up as the project moves forward. Technical debt can accumulate and cause the project code to become more complex.

Test-driven development   In test-driven development, an acceptance test is written before the code is written so the developers know what it takes to pass the acceptance test and can program accordingly.

The Declaration of Interdependence   This agile methodology document serves as a value system for agile project managers. The idea behind this document is that all participants in an agile project are interdependent on one another: the project manager, development team, customers, and other stakeholders.

WIP (Work in progress)   The work in progress is what the team is working on right now.

XP   XP is short for eXtreme Programming and is an agile approach that is focused on software development. XP also uses iterations of development, but these iterations last for two weeks in a typical project.

Questions

1. You are the agile project manager for your organization and your current project is to manage a team developing software that will affect the business practices of the organization. When working on an agile project, processes, tools, documentation, and plans are necessary. However, which of the following should be the initial focus?

   A. Scope of the project

   B. People involved in the project

   C. The individuals and interactions involved

   D. Definition of success as defined by the project manager

2. A diverse agile team has been assembled by upper management, and there is confusion about the requirements and definition of success of the project. What might have been a better method of creating the team?

   A. Select a person from each team with interest in the project

   B. Allow a self-organizing team from the people that helped create the requirements and definition of success

   C. Have the business partner select the members she wants on the project

   D. Have the business partner hire a team of contractors that have to be "sold" on the project

3. What is one item that should be accomplished during a sprint planning meeting?

   A. The product owner shares the updated backlog, and the team discusses it to ensure a shared understanding.

   B. Three questions—what have I accomplished?, what do I plan to accomplish?, and are there any roadblocks?—are answered by each participant.

   C. The product owner decides if the product is done.

   D. The scope and costs of the project are renegotiated.

4. A good practice in keeping a project on track is to minimize waste. Which of the following could be eliminated from a project to maximize value?

   A. Daily meetings

   B. Unnecessary features

   C. Testing

   D. Sprint reviews

5. Tom is the project manager for his organization and he's educating the project team and key stakeholders about Scrum. Some of the team members are confused about the activities that happen after the sprint review. What activity should Tom indicate is completed after the sprint review?

   A. Product backlog refinement

   B. Sprint planning meeting

   C. Daily Scrum

   D. Sprint retrospective

6. Samantha is the ScrumMaster for her organization and she's working with the team and the product owner to refine the product backlog. What is the role of the team in this meeting?

   A. Prioritize the work items

   B. Add features to the project backlog

   C. Estimate and refine the work items

   D. Identify fixes

7. Which of the following describes how Kanban differs from agile?

   A. Kanban teams plan their work in sprints or iterations.

   B. Kanban teams work on a project as a whole.

   C. Kanban teams employ a pull system.

   D. There are no WIP limits in Kanban.

8. Pat has been selected to lead the RGW Project with Scrum methodologies. The project team is excited about this decision. Select which trait has made the team happy about this decision.

   A. Pat likes to work within the box.

   B. Pat has been with the company for 12 years.

   C. Pat is honest and explains why decisions are made.

   D. Pat will lead according to the project plan.

9. You are the project manager of the JLK Project utilizing Scrum. Several stakeholders have lost interest in the project and rarely attend meetings, offer input, or give feedback. What is a good practice to avoid this pitfall going forward?

   A. Making project meetings mandatory

   B. Meeting with each business partner on a one-on-one basis

   C. Proving that everyone's ideas have value and taking advantage of small-scale experiments

   D. Sticking strictly to the project plan

10. You happen to bump into a business partner of the project you are working on, and he asks you how many defects were found in the prior week. Since you don't know the exact answer, what should you do?

   A. Take a guess

   B. Tell the business partner you will send an e-mail to him with the information when you get back to your desk

   C. Take him into the team area, where much information regarding the project is displayed

   D. Ask the business partner to call the team leader to get a correct answer

11. The agile team you are working with encourages each other to suggest innovative ideas. Most ideas are tested to determine whether they will be successful or may not work very well. How is this accomplished without delaying the project?

   A. The new ideas are only tested if there is sufficient time in the project plan.

   B. The ideas are tested during short iterations and end before the next iteration.

   C. Only one idea is accepted by the leader during an iteration.

   D. Only the leader determines what ideas to test and what to put aside.

12. What does the term *emergent leadership* mean in an agile environment?

   A. A new leader is assigned for each iteration.

   B. A team member takes over the leadership role.

   C. A team member tries a new approach after getting approval from the team.

   D. A leader isn't in place until the team selects one of the team members.

13. How is an agile team better prepared to suggest solutions to a business request versus a team that is not using an agile methodology?

   A. The agile team is made up of business people.

   B. The agile team worked with the business partner to prepare the project plan.

   C. The agile team and business partners work together throughout the project life cycle.

   D. The business partners review statuses and ask for recommendations.

14. As a PMI-ACP candidate you need to recognize the terms and techniques utilized in agile projects. Which one of the following is the best example of an empirical process?

   A. Following a plan

   B. Observing results and adapting the code

   C. Making collaborative decisions

   D. Working alone on a project requirement

15. You are the agile project manager for your organization and you're helping your development team better understand agile. You have reviewed the Agile Manifesto with your team. Which one of the following is not an attribute of the Agile Manifesto?

   A. Promoting collaboration

   B. Expecting changes to the product backlog

   C. Documenting how the code is to be developed

   D. Accepting tradeoffs with the vendor

16. Elizabeth is the project manager of an XP project. Her manager stops by to check on the progress and notices that the developers are working in groups of two rather than individually. What is this approach called?

   A. Pair programming

   B. Pared programming

   C. People-People Programming

   D. P2P (Programmer-to-Programmer)

17. Jane is a senior project manager in your company. Wally is a new project manager who is not familiar with the Scrum methodology. Jane explains the five Scrum values to Wally. Which one of the following is not one of the five values of Scrum?

   A. Commitment

   B. Focus

   C. Respect

   D. Innovation

18. Erin is a new project manager who is working on a Scrum project. She's confused on the difference between a sprint review and a sprint retrospective. What's the difference?

   A. Sprint reviews are demonstrations of the work completed in the sprint. Sprint retrospectives are demonstrations of all the compiled work completed in the project.

   B. Sprint review are for lessons learned. Sprint retrospectives are for product demonstrations.

   C. Sprint reviews are for product demonstrations. Sprint retrospectives are for lessons learned.

   D. Sprint reviews discuss what's worked in the sprint. Sprint retrospectives are done at the end of the project for a lessons learned opportunity.

19. You are the project manager of the BNK Project for your organization. This project is utilizing the XP framework. What is your title in this XP project?

   A. Project manager

   B. Product manager

    C. Coach

    D. Team leader

20. Your organization uses the Lean agile project management approach. One of the principles of Lean is to remove waste. Which one of the following is an example of waste in a Lean project that should be removed?

    A. WIP

    B. Bottleneck identification

    C. Motion

    D. Colocation

Questions and Answers

1. You are the agile project manager for your organization and your current project is to manage a team developing software that will affect the business practices of the organization. When working on an agile project, processes, tools, documentation, and plans are necessary. However, which of the following should be the initial focus?

    A. Scope of the project

    B. People involved in the project

    C. The individuals and interactions involved

    D. Definition of success as defined by the project manager

    C. While processes and tools will likely be necessary on the project, the focus of the agile team's attention should be on the individuals and interactions involved. Projects are accepted by people, people debate scope, and people negotiate the definition of done. Focusing early on developing the individuals involved in the project and emphasizing productive and effective interactions help set up a project for success.

    A is incorrect because the scope of the project will likely change throughout the project. B is incorrect because this choice isn't the best answer. People involved in the project can include all the stakeholders, rather than only interactions of the individuals involved. D is incorrect because although the definition of success is important, it's not the initial focus of the project manager.

2. A diverse agile team has been assembled by upper management, and there is confusion about the requirements and definition of success of the project. What might have been a better method of creating the team?

    A. Select a person from each team with interest in the project

    B. Allow a self-organizing team from the people that helped create the requirements and definition of success

    C. Have the business partner select the members she wants on the project

    D. Have the business partner hire a team of contractors that have to be "sold" on the project

B. A self-organizing team composed of the people who created the requirements and defined success has a higher level of ownership and pride in the requirements and design, so the members don't have to be "sold" on the project. Ideas that come from outside resources need to be sold to the team for the implementation to be successful, which sometimes creates a challenging task.
A is incorrect because although people on teams that were not part of the requirements gathering may have more merit on paper, they may want to implement the project differently than what was originally envisioned. C is incorrect because this solution creates the same problem of choosing people who are already invested in the value and understanding of the project goals. D is incorrect because it's best to utilize internal resources that already understand the project goals rather than to hire contractors who have to be sold on the value of the project.

3. What is one item that should be accomplished during a sprint planning meeting?

   A. The product owner shares the updated backlog, and the team discusses it to ensure a shared understanding.

   B. Three questions—what have I accomplished?, what do I plan to accomplish?, and are there any roadblocks?—are answered by each participant.

   C. The product owner decides if the product is done.

   D. The scope and costs of the project are renegotiated.

   A. The product owner should share the updated backlog items and ensure the entire team has a good understanding of how to move forward.
   B is incorrect because the questions regarding accomplishments and roadblocks are answered during Daily Scrums to uncover any obstacles. C is incorrect because the sprint planning meeting is not where the project's success is discussed. D is incorrect because the scope of the project is based on the prioritized requirements.

4. A good practice in keeping a project on track is to minimize waste. Which of the following could be eliminated from a project to maximize value?

   A. Daily meetings

   B. Unnecessary features

   C. Testing

   D. Sprint reviews

   B. In addition to eliminating the introduction of unnecessary features, value can be maximized by eliminating partially done work, delays, extra processes and features, task switching, waiting, moving information or a deliverable, defects, and handoffs. A, C, and D are incorrect because daily meetings, testing, and sprint reviews are just a few of the activities required for a successful project.

5. Tom is the project manager for his organization and he's educating the project team and key stakeholders about Scrum. Some of the team members are confused about the activities that happen after the sprint review. What activity should Tom indicate is completed after the sprint review?

A. Product backlog refinement

B. Sprint planning meeting

C. Daily Scrum

D. Sprint retrospective

D. After a sprint review but before the sprint planning meeting, a sprint retrospective should be held to gather lessons learned and look for opportunities for improvement. This allows the team to consider the owner's feedback and implement improvements before the next sprint.
A is incorrect because product backlog refinement is done in product refinement meetings. B is incorrect because sprint planning meetings happen after the product refinement meeting. C is incorrect because the Daily Scrum is hosted every day at the same time and same location.

6. Samantha is the ScrumMaster for her organization and she's working with the team and the product owner to refine the product backlog. What is the role of the team in this meeting?

A. Prioritize the work items

B. Add features to the project backlog

C. Estimate and refine the work items

D. Identify fixes

C. The team is responsible for estimating and refining work items. Each time the team refines their estimates with a higher level of detail, the product owner might need to adjust the priority of those items.
A is incorrect because the product owner and the team collaborate on prioritizing the requirements; ultimately, the prioritization is the responsibility of the product owner. B is incorrect because the team doesn't add features to the backlog. D is incorrect because the team doesn't identify fixes to the project in the refinement of the product backlog.

7. Which of the following describes how Kanban differs from agile?

A. Kanban teams plan their work in sprints or iterations.

B. Kanban teams work on a project as a whole.

C. Kanban teams employ a pull system.

D. There are no WIP limits in Kanban.

C. The main difference is that Kanban teams employ a pull system, which means that when an item of work is completed, it triggers a pull to bring in the next item in the queue to work on. Kanban teams also work off a Kanban board that displays columns of processes, each with a work in progress (WIP) limit. A is incorrect because agile teams, not Kanban teams, work in sprints before moving on to the next sprint backlog. B is incorrect because Kanban teams don't work on the whole project at once, but in chunks of requirements. D is incorrect because there is a WIP limit in Kanban.

8. Pat has been selected to lead the RGW Project with Scrum methodologies. The project team is excited about this decision. Select which trait has made the team happy about this decision.

   A. Pat likes to work within the box.

   B. Pat has been with the company for 12 years.

   C. Pat is honest and explains why decisions are made.

   D. Pat will lead according to the project plan.

   C. Because Pat is honest and will communicate to the team the reasons for his decisions, he is a suitable ScrumMaster and will be less focused on command and control and more focused on being a servant leader.
   A is incorrect because agile calls for flexibility and adaptability in a project. B is incorrect because Pat may be with the company for many years and may be very competent, but may not know enough about the project to move it to success. D is incorrect because the leader must be able to accept changes and be willing to adjust plans.

9. You are the project manager of the JLK Project utilizing Scrum. Several stakeholders have lost interest in the project and rarely attend meetings, offer input, or give feedback. What is a good practice to avoid this pitfall going forward?

   A. Making project meetings mandatory

   B. Meeting with each business partner on a one-on-one basis

   C. Proving that everyone's ideas have value and taking advantage of small-scale experiments

   D. Sticking strictly to the project plan

   C. Allowing stakeholders to suggest new ideas, and then giving them a chance to experiment with new concepts, proves that everyone's ideas have value. Nothing is more discouraging than having a good idea disregarded. Keeping stakeholders engaged allows the opportunity that agile projects present for small-scale, localized experiments in a supportive, low-risk environment.
   A is incorrect because mandatory meetings won't bolster stakeholder engagement. B is incorrect because meeting with each business partner one-on-one may be a good way to communicate, but it's not the best choice available. D is incorrect because agile plans change based on the product backlog.

10. You happen to bump into a business partner of the project you are working on, and he asks you how many defects were found in the prior week. Since you don't know the exact answer, what should you do?

  A. Take a guess

  B. Tell the business partner you will send an e-mail to him with the information when you get back to your desk

  C. Take him into the team area, where much information regarding the project is displayed

  D. Ask the business partner to call the team leader to get a correct answer

  C. A core task of the agile leader is to be transparent, not only about progress, but also about issues and roadblocks. It is normal to walk into an agile team's area and see graphs showing velocity, defect rates, and results of retrospectives including what is working well and what needs improvement. When the leader is open and honest, it fosters openness where people can be less guarded and focus on improvements.
  A is incorrect because guessing isn't an accurate or transparent way to communicate the project status on defects. B is incorrect because e-mailing the answer may be viable, but it's not the best way to be open and transparent about the project. D is incorrect because asking the business partner to call the project team lead can be a disruption and doesn't provide the readily available information.

11. The agile team you are working with encourages each other to suggest innovative ideas. Most ideas are tested to determine whether they will be successful or may not work very well. How is this accomplished without delaying the project?

  A. The new ideas are only tested if there is sufficient time in the project plan.

  B. The ideas are tested during short iterations and end before the next iteration.

  C. Only one idea is accepted by the leader during an iteration.

  D. Only the leader determines what ideas to test and what to put aside.

  B. New processes or techniques are tested during short iterations, enabling the team to either implement the successful idea or not, and before the next iteration. This is part of the concept of being innovative, and if necessary, failing fast, learning from the experiment, and moving on.
  A is incorrect because additional time doesn't need to be accounted for when iterations are typically between two and four weeks, and a decision will be made quickly. C is incorrect because there is no limit to good ideas and the team should decide whether to move forward with a concept. D is incorrect because the team is self-led and can determine what ideas should be tried and implemented.

12. What does the term *emergent leadership* mean in an agile environment?

   A. A new leader is assigned for each iteration.

   B. A team member takes over the leadership role.

   C. A team member tries a new approach after getting approval from the team.

   D. A leader isn't in place until the team selects one of the team members.

   C. An emergent leader is a team member who takes the initiative to try a new process or idea once they have the team's approval.
A is incorrect because emergent leadership allows a leader to emerge at any point in the project, not by assignment. B is incorrect because emergent leadership is not about a formal role and assignment as leader. D is incorrect because leaders emerge based on conditions in the project, not by assignment or voting.

13. How is an agile team better prepared to suggest solutions to a business request versus a team that is not using an agile methodology?

   A. The agile team is made up of business people.

   B. The agile team worked with the business partner to prepare the project plan.

   C. The agile team and business partners work together throughout the project life cycle.

   D. The business partners review statuses and ask for recommendations.

   C. Working with business partners almost daily throughout the project life cycle is far more valuable and collaborative than meeting occasionally. The team hears what the business would like the results to be, and meeting face-to-face is far better than reading requirements, documents, and e-mails, or even a conference call. Another benefit of daily interactions is that the business partners will learn what task or activity might be far more expensive than another solution or take far longer than they expect.

   A is incorrect because the team is made up of developers, not just business people. B is incorrect because while the team collaborates with the business partner, the team creates a plan based on the sprint backlog. D is incorrect because the business partners may review statuses and ask for recommendations, but this isn't the best option available. For your PMI-ACP exam, you must always choose the best answer, even if more than an one answer is acceptable.

14. As a PMI-ACP candidate you need to recognize the terms and techniques utilized in agile projects. Which one of the following is the best example of an empirical process?

   A. Following a plan

   B. Observing results and adapting the code

C. Making collaborative decisions

D. Working alone on a project requirement

B. Empirical processes require observation, creativity, and trial and error, so observing results and adapting the code is the best answer.
A is incorrect because following a plan describes a defined process. C is incorrect because making collaborative decisions isn't an empirical process. D is incorrect because working alone can involve utilizing either an empirical process or a defined process.

15. You are the agile project manager for your organization and you're helping your development team better understand agile. You have reviewed the Agile Manifesto with your team. Which one of the following is not an attribute of the Agile Manifesto?

A. Promoting collaboration

B. Expecting changes to the product backlog

C. Documenting how the code is to be developed

D. Accepting tradeoffs with the vendor

C. One of the values of the Agile Manifesto is that we value working software over comprehensive documentation. Documentation should be light and minimally sufficient.
A is incorrect because team collaboration is an aspect of the Agile Manifesto. B is incorrect because responding to changes over following a plan is also a value of the Agile Manifesto. D is incorrect because customer collaboration over contract negotiation is a value of the Agile Manifesto.

16. Elizabeth is the project manager of an XP project. Her manager stops by to check on the progress and notices that the developers are working in groups of two rather than individually. What is this approach called?

A. Pair programming

B. Pared programming

C. People-People Programming

D. P2P (Programmer-to-Programmer)

A. XP utilizes pair programming where one developer codes and the second developer checks the code.
B, C, and D are incorrect choices as these are not valid descriptions of pair programming in XP.

17. Jane is a senior project manager in your company. Wally is a new project manager who is not familiar with the Scrum methodology. Jane explains the five Scrum values to Wally. Which one of the following is not one of the five values of Scrum?

A. Commitment

B. Focus

C. Respect

D. Innovation

D. Innovation, while encouraged, is not one of the five values of Scrum. The five values are commitment, focus, openness, respect, and courage.
A, B, and C are incorrect because these choices are part of the five values of Scrum.

18. Erin is a new project manager who is working on a Scrum project. She's confused on the difference between a sprint review and a sprint retrospective. What's the difference?

A. Sprint reviews are demonstrations of the work completed in the sprint. Sprint retrospectives are demonstrations of all the compiled work completed in the project.

B. Sprint review are for lessons learned. Sprint retrospectives are for product demonstrations.

C. Sprint reviews are for product demonstrations. Sprint retrospectives are for lessons learned.

D. Sprint reviews discuss what's worked in the sprint. Sprint retrospectives are done at the end of the project for a lessons learned opportunity.

C. Sprint reviews are for product demonstrations. Sprint retrospectives are for lessons learned.
A, B, and D are incorrect descriptions of the sprint reviews and sprint retrospectives.

19. You are the project manager of the BNK Project for your organization. This project is utilizing the XP framework. What is your title in this XP project?

A. Project manager

B. Product manager

C. Coach

D. Team leader

C. A project manager in an XP environment is called a coach.
A, B, and D are incorrect as XP calls the project manager a coach, not a project manager, product manager, or team leader.

20. Your organization uses the Lean agile project management approach. One of the principles of Lean is to remove waste. Which one of the following is an example of waste in a Lean project that should be removed?

A. WIP

B. Bottleneck identification

C. Motion

D. Colocation

C. Motion is a waste in Lean projects. Moving items from person to person is motion and that takes time and creates waste. If there's not a clear workflow of how items move through the project processes, then there's waste.

A is incorrect because work in progress (WIP) is needed in Lean and is not waste. B is incorrect because bottlenecks are wasteful, but the identification of a bottleneck is not waste. D is incorrect because colocation is a desirable aspect for the project team.

Value-Driven Delivery in Agile Projects

In this chapter, you will

- Define the 14 exam tasks of value-driven delivery
- Embrace the goal of delivering value quickly for stakeholders
- Define value in organizations
- Prioritize value in agile projects for stakeholders
- Create an incremental approach to value delivery
- Tackle the Theory of Constraints
- Validate value in project deliverables for stakeholders

While I like to think I have a good diet, I sometimes have pie for breakfast. And sometimes, I like to eat my dessert first—and sometimes that's all I eat. What does my sweet tooth have to do with agile project management? In agile projects, we want to eat our dessert first. In agile, our dessert—technically our stakeholders' dessert—is the value of the project. We want to give the stakeholders the value of the project as quickly as possible. While the value of the project is more than just dessert, the concept is that we don't have to wait for months, or even years, in an agile project to create and show value for the work we're doing.

In a predictive project, like building a new house, we can't use the house until the house is all done, approved by the city inspectors, and we're given the keys to the front door. All the time we're waiting and waiting for the construction crew to finish the house is full of anxiety as we're paying for something we can't yet use. Now shift that scenario into a huge project in your organization: creating software, building a website, or building a mobile app. In a predictive environment all the deliverables are held back until everything is done. In agile, we create the most valuable thing first and then deliver that thing to the customer. We eat dessert first!

 For a more detailed explanation, watch the *Creating Value in Agile Projects* video now.

The second exam domain, on value-driven delivery, is the largest exam domain for the PMI-ACP exam. This exam domain is worth 20 percent of your exam score and you can expect 24 questions on this topic. While this is the largest exam domain, the good news is that the information is direct: know what value is, create the value, and then deliver the value as soon as possible. Value, however, is an ambiguous term. You must work with the product owner or project customer to define value for the project, and then you must clearly communicate that definition to the development team.

Introducing the Agile Principles of Value Delivery

In your early conversations with the product owner or customer, you'll discuss value. You might not come right out and ask what's valuable in the project, but the customer will certainly tell you. If the customer states that it wants the project team to create an app that'll allow employees to track their time for purposes of payroll, the customer is discussing the value the app provides. And if the customer is talking about updating existing software to remove some glitches and bugs, they're talking about creating value by improving an existing product. The initial conversations go to the heart of the project—not all the nice-to-haves, but the must-haves for the project to be successful. And when you're talking about success, you're talking about value. The customer determines what the value of the project is.

Value stems from the foundation of agile: the Agile Manifesto. Recall that the Agile Manifesto is all about value in its four principles:

- We value individuals and interactions over processes and tools.
- We value working software over comprehensive documentation.
- We value customer collaboration over contract negotiation.
- We value responding to change over following a plan.

The entire thrust of agile project management is about creating value as quickly as possible. Value is in the deliverable, not in the busyness that some project managers seem to love. Value is not in the rules, reading the minutes, or writing long, windy reports that no one is going to read. Value is not in meetings or negotiating over what can or can't be done. Nope. Value is in the team getting to work and creating results that can be used as quickly as possible. It's the exact opposite of that predictive home construction project—you want the stakeholders to have their value fast while the team continues to work on the less-valuable items that'll come later in the project delivery. For your exam, look for every opportunity to give the customer value as quickly as possible.

Reviewing the 14 Tasks for Exam Domain II

You'll need to know 14 tasks for this domain, all centered on value-driven delivery within projects. This second domain of the exam has four subdomains, something different than the first domain we looked at in Chapter 1. The goal of this domain is to deliver value through increments early and often based on the stakeholders' priorities. Stakeholders, as in the product owner or customer, will review the work and offer feedback for acceptance or improvements.

Here are the four subdomains and the 14 tasks based on what PMI offers as guidance for the PMI-ACP exam.

Define Positive Value

- Define deliverables by identifying units that can be produced incrementally in order to maximize their value to stakeholders while minimizing non-value-added work.

- Refine requirements by gaining consensus on the acceptance criteria for features on a just-in-time basis in order to deliver value.

- Select and tailor the team's process based on project and organizational characteristics as well as team experience in order to optimize value delivery.

Avoid Potential Downsides

- Plan for small releasable increments by organizing requirements into minimally marketable features/minimally viable products in order to allow for the early recognition and delivery of value.

- Limit increment size and increase review frequency with appropriate stakeholders in order to identify and respond to risks early on and at minimal cost.

- Solicit customer and user feedback by reviewing increments often in order to confirm and enhance business value.

Prioritization

- Prioritize the units of work through collaboration with stakeholders in order to optimize the value of the deliverables.

- Perform frequent review and maintenance of the work results by prioritizing and maintaining internal quality in order to reduce the overall cost of incremental development.

- Continuously identify and prioritize the environmental, operational, and infrastructure factors in order to improve the quality and value of the deliverables.

Incremental Development

- Conduct operational reviews and/or periodic checkpoints with stakeholders in order to obtain feedback and corrections to the work in progress and planned work.

- Balance development of deliverable units and risk reduction efforts by incorporating both value producing and risk reducing work into the backlog in order to maximize the total value proposition over time.

- Re-prioritize requirements periodically in order to reflect changes in the environment and stakeholder needs or preferences in order to maximize the value.

- Elicit and prioritize relevant non-functional requirements (such as operations and security) by considering the environment in which the solution will be used in order to minimize the probability of failure.

- Conduct frequent reviews of work products by performing inspections, reviews, and/or testing in order to identify and incorporate improvements into the overall process and product/service.

Applying the Four Value-Driven Delivery Principles

On the PMI-ACP exam you'll be faced with scenarios of how to best act in light of these value-driven delivery goals. The PMI-ACP exam won't test simple recall of these tasks; instead, it will present short case studies and ask you to select the best way to respond or behave in a given scenario. A key for the PMI-ACP exam, and for agile projects, is to take every opportunity to deliver value to the project customer. Consider the themes of the four subdomains of value-driven delivery:

- **Define positive value** The project requirements are prioritized based on value and then the development team works to deliver the most-valuable items first, working down the backlog to the least-valuable items.

- **Avoid potential downsides** Rather than having one final product, the development team creates increments of value with opportunity for the customer to provide feedback, changes in priority, and address risks in the project.

- **Prioritization** The prioritized backlog of requirements is periodically updated and reprioritized with the customer or product owner. The goal is to ensure that the team is always working on the most valuable items from the list of requirements.

- **Incremental development** This is the engine of agile software development. By working in increments the team addresses the most valuable requirements first, incorporates risk management into the project approach, and offers reviews and continued prioritization of the requirements.

These four domains are what you *really* want to know for the exam. Understand that the goal is to identify value, rank the value based on the customers' needs, protect the value, and deliver value through increments. That's the gist of this whole chapter, and this whole PMI-ACP exam domain.

Delivering Value in Agile Projects

Your goal, as a project manager, is to get things done. Your goal as an agile project manager is to deliver value to the customer as quickly as possible. In agile projects, the project manager isn't at the hub of command and control, but rather serves more as a coach or facilitator. The project customer defines the value of the project—the working product—and the project team aims to deliver that value quickly. That's the whole point of a prioritized backlog: let's find the most valuable items and then let's create them. By delivering value first, by eating your dessert first, you've accomplished the big goal of the project—delivering value to the customer. And by "you" I mean the project team. In agile, you're there to make certain the team has the tools and framework to get the value to the customer.

I don't mean to imply that the project manager isn't an important role in the agile project management world—it certainly is. I want to stress, however, that all stakeholders are involved in the value equation. You need the product owner or customer to tell you what's valuable to them by prioritizing and grooming the product backlog. Then you need the development team to do their part and create the most valuable items first. The project manager makes certain things are humming along, that people are following some framework and rules, and that the project team has the items and information they need to create the value as planned.

Everything in agile is about creating value.

Delivering Value ASAP

Projects have the most risk at their launch. The closer a project gets to its completion, the better the odds of its success. Agile inverts this idea and goes for the gold up front—why wait for the good stuff? Why wait for dessert? The product owner, the project team, and the project manager work together to create the prioritized backlog of requirements. The items at the top of the list are top priorities for the team. The team selects a chunk of work they can deliver in the next several weeks, and then they create an attack plan of who'll do what and how they'll get it done.

By delivering on the items that the customer needs and wants first, you're accomplishing a goal of agile project management: deliver value quickly. If you've managed projects for very long, you know that short, precisely scoped projects are super-easy to do. Everyone on the project team knows exactly what needs to be accomplished, there's a doable schedule, and there's clarity on getting to the desired future state. In a sense, an iteration in an agile project is like that short, precisely scoped project. The team selects the most important items from the backlog, plans and attacks the items, and gets things done quickly to deliver the results, the value, to the product owner.

Quick wins keep people excited, motivated, and happy. The product owner and customer are wowed at the work the team has accomplished. The first deliverable of the project is the most important deliverable of the project, and the development team feels a sense of accomplishment and they know they can deliver more. Of course, I'm speaking in a perfect world, but that's our goal—to deliver value, to build rapport and synergy with the product owner and customers, and to be happy in the project. That's all about valuing people, getting people what they want and need quickly. That's the really beautiful thing about agile project management.

Combating Waste in Agile Projects

Have you ever worked on a project that just wouldn't end? Issues, risks, and changes kept popping up into the project and slowing things down. Or maybe you experienced a group of stakeholders that couldn't make up their minds on what they wanted the project to accomplish. Waiting for requirements, information, and resources is all waste in any project. For most projects, waiting time is billable time—that's money spent for people to sit around and wait. And it's also time lost to getting work done and creating value.

A few years ago, I was managing a sizeable project for a large, bureaucratic organization and the project fell into limbo over some legal mumbo-jumbo. My team wasn't allowed to work on the project content until the attorneys sorted everything out. So, we shifted priorities to other projects, other work. Eventually, several months later, we got the green light to move ahead. Of course, people on the original team weren't available, new people had to be brought up to speed, rework had to be done—it was an expensive mess that killed any value the project aimed to provide.

While that scenario is a bit out of the norm of most agile projects I've led, it's a valuable lesson that planning and execution can still succumb to risks external to the project. Most agile projects aim to identify and remove waste as soon as possible to help the project move along and get the valuable items out to the customer. The longer a project churns without creating value, the less value the project is likely going to create. The longer a team takes to create value, the less support, excitement, and stakeholder engagement there's going to be. For your PMI-ACP exam, keep the goal of delivering value quickly and protect the value by removing waste.

Waste is anything that threatens the value of the project, slows down the progress, or creates impediments for the project team. By minimizing waste we're maximizing value. Recall Poppendieck's Seven Wastes from Chapter 1:

- Partially done work
- Extra processes
- Extra features
- Relearning
- Task switching
- Motion
- Defects

These items rob the project of creating value. Time and energy spent on these items are time and energy lost from working on value. Know these seven wastes for your PMI-ACP exam.

 EXAM COACH   Delivering value is all about creating results as quickly as possible. However, rushing to get to results can generate senseless motion and create defects. While we want results, we really want working software.

Defining Value in Organizations

Agile project managers need to define value in organizations. When discussing value in organizations, I'm talking about defining the business value. Business value means you're identifying the links between your project and the missions, goals, vision, strategy, and tactics of the organization. You're aiming to identify what the organizations wants from the project to bolster the business value of the entity.

Tangible business value is easy to see: monetary assets and return on investment are the two big business value examples. But tangible assets can also include stockholder equity, fixtures and tools your project creates or acquires, and the market share your project captures. Intangible business value is a bit harder to quantify, but these items directly support the goal and purpose of your organization. For intangible business value, look to how your project will create goodwill, improve your organization's reputation, provide brand recognition, provide public benefit, offer trademarks, and improve the strategic alignment of your organization.

It's important to see the business value your project will provide because then you can better link the day-to-day tasks of the project team to the importance of the organization. It's easy to be short-sighted on a project and only see the big list of requirements without really seeing why the requirements are important to the project customer. When the members of a project team understand the value of the project, they're more likely to work diligently to deliver on the important objectives as defined by the product customer.

Exploring the Time Value of Money

While the PMI-ACP might have only one or two questions on the time value of money, it's important for you to grasp this concept. An organization that invests funds in your project expects a return on investment (ROI). One of the reasons a project teams delivers value quickly is to enable the organization to begin recouping its investment and feel confident in the commitment that it made to the project. The faster the organization can realize benefits and business value, the faster the project can pay for the investment.

Payback Period

An organization will want to know how long it will take the project to "pay back" the investment. For example, if your project will cost the organization $500,000 to deliver the set of requirements, how long will it take to recover those costs and become profitable? As soon as your project delivers value in working software, the organization can expect cash inflow on the project deliverable. With each increment of the product, the value of the deliverable can increase, and the payback period diminishes. At some point, the investment is paid back to the organization by the cash inflow, and the deliverable of the project is profitable.

This value analysis method, while one of the simplest, is also the weakest. This approach shows the management horizon, the breakeven point of the project, but it doesn't really consider the time value of money. The longer the project takes to return the $500,000 investment, the less value there actually is on the investment; $500,000 five years from now is worth less than $500,000 in the bank today.

Considering the Future Value and Present Value

If you were to borrow $500,000 for five years from a bank, you'd be paying interest on the money. If the $500,000 were invested for five years and managed to earn a whopping

6 percent interest per year, compounded annually, it'd be worth $669,112.79 at the end of five years. This is the future value of the money in today's terms.

The formula for future value is $FV = PV(1 + i)^n$, where:

- FV is future value
- PV is present value
- i is the interest rate
- n is the number of periods (years, quarters, etc.)

Here's the formula with the $500,000 in action:

$FV = 500,000(1 + .06)^5$
$FV = 500,000(1.338226)$
$FV = \$669,112.79$

The future value of the $500,000 five years from now is worth $$669,112.79. So how does that help define value for the organization? In this example, with a long, five-year project, your project must be worth more than $669,112.79 in five years. If it's not worth that amount, then the project isn't a good investment from a financial point of view.

If you can predict the future amount for a known investment, you can also do the inverse and see what's the most an organization should invest in a project based on predictions for value in the future. We're looking for the present value of future cash flows: $PV = FV / (1 + i)^n$.

In other words, if a project is projected to earn the organization $250,000 in two years, that's great, but what's $250,000 two years from now worth today? This puts the amount of the promised value in perspective with what the projections are in today's money. Let's plug it into the formula and find out (assuming the interest rate is still 6 percent):

$PV = FV / (1 + i)^n$
$PV = 250,000 / (1.1236)$
$PV = \$222,499.11$

Thus, $250,000 in two years is worth $222,499.11 today, assuming we'd earn 6 percent return somewhere else. So, this means that an organization shouldn't invest more than $222,499.11 in a project that'll last for two years. Of course, there are other factors to consider, such as the risk within the project, the obligation to do the project, other opportunities to consider, and actually earning a 6 percent ROI. But this formula does give some insight into the value of the project in ratio to the needed investment of the project.

 EXAM COACH   You should be able to look at the present value of two proposed projects and determine which one an organization should invest in. The project with the highest financial value is the best choice if the question is from a purely financial perspective.

Calculating the Net Present Value

Another time value of money calculation is net present value (NPV). NPV allows you to predict a project's value more precisely than the present value formula. NPV evaluates the monies returned on a project for each period the project lasts. As agile projects can, and often do, have increments of value delivered, the project will likely have a return on investment for each time period an increment is deployed from the project.

Here are the NPV formula steps:

1. Calculate the project's cash flow for a time period (typically quarters or years).

2. Calculate each time period into present value.

3. Sum the present value of each period.

4. Subtract the investment for the project.

5. Examine the NPV value. An NPV of zero or higher is good, and the project should be approved. An NPV less than zero is bad, and the project should be rejected.

When comparing two projects, the project with the greater NPV is typically better than the project with the lower NPV value. Table 2-1 provides an example of an NPV calculation.

 EXAM COACH   You likely will not have to calculate NPV for your PMI-ACP exam. I've included the whole scenario here to provide an understanding of the formula.

Tracking Performance with Earned Value Management

Earned value management (EVM) is a suite of formulas that show project performance. EVM is traditionally used in predictive projects, but you can, if you really want to, use

Period	Cash Flow	Present Value
1	$15,000.00	$14,150.94
2	$25,000.00	$22,249.91
3	$17,000.00	$14,273.53
4	$25,000.00	$19,802.34
5	$18,000.00	$13,450.65
Totals	**$100,000.00**	**$83,927.37**
Investment		**$78,000.00**
NPV		**$5,927.37**

Table 2-1   Net Present Value Calculation

these formulas in an agile project too. The PMI-ACP exam won't target EVM in depth, but I'd expect maybe a question or two, as EVM can show performance of the project—and performance directly affects the overall value of the project.

Earned value management measures the performance of project work—what your team has created—against what was planned as a way to identify variances, find opportunities to improve the project, or check the project's health. EVM can also be used to predict future performance of the project and create expectations for how the project will conclude financially. EVM is a suite of linked mathematical formulas that compares work performed against work planned and measures the actual cost of the work your project has performed. EVM helps the project manager monitor and control costs in relation to the number of requirements the team is creating. I'll talk a bit more about agile project performance in Chapter 4, which covers team performance.

EVM is based on three formulas that reflect project performance for time and cost. Figure 2-1 demonstrates the connection between the following EVM values, all based on the project's budget, which EVM calls the budget at completion (BAC) even though the project isn't yet completed.

- **Earned value (EV)** This is the amount of work completed to date and the authorized budget for that work. For example, if your project has a budget of $450,000 and your project is 35 percent complete, your earned value is 35 percent of $450,000, or $157,500. In other words, the work completed is 35 percent of the project's budget. EV is percent complete times the budget at completion.

- **Planned value (PV)** Planned value is where you're supposed to be in the project. Continuing with the example project, let's say you're supposed to be 40 percent complete by this time, though you're only 35 percent complete. Planned value is what you're supposed to be worth; in this case, it's 40 percent of the budget at completion: 40% × $450,000 = $180,000.

- **Actual cost (AC)** Actual cost is the actual amount of monies spent on the project so far. In knowledge-work projects, that might all be labor of the project team. In this scenario, the BAC is $450,000, and your earned value is $157,500. As it turns out, your project team had some waste, and you spent $165,000 in actual monies to reach the 35-percent-complete milestone. Your actual cost is $165,000.

Figure 2-1 Earned value management shows project performance.

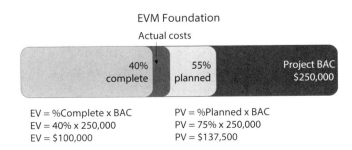

EVM Foundation

Actual costs

40% complete | 55% planned | Project BAC $250,000

EV = %Complete x BAC
EV = 40% x 250,000
EV = $100,000

PV = %Planned x BAC
PV = 75% x 250,000
PV = $137,500

Those are the fundamentals of earned value management. All of our remaining formulas center on these simple formulas. Just remember that earned value is always the percent of work complete times the given budget at completion. On your exam, you'll always be provided with the actual costs, which is the money that has already been spent on the project. You'll have to do some math to find the planned value, which is the value your project should have by a given time.

Finding Cost and Schedule Variances

Let's continue our study with the project that has a BAC of $450,000. Assume you've completed 35 percent. You have spent, however, $165,000. To find the cost variance, you'll find the earned value, which is 35 percent of the $450,000 budget. As Figure 2-2 shows, this is $157,500. In this example, you spent $165,000 in actual costs. The formula for finding the cost variance is earned value minus actual costs (EV – AC). In this instance, the cost variance is –$7,500.

This means you've spent $7,500 more than what the work the development team has completed is worth. A $7,500 cost variance is waste due to defects, rework, or overestimating the amount of work the team could complete in an iteration. That's antivalue and chips away at the confidence of the project team and the value of the project deliverables.

Can you guess how the schedule variance works? It's basically the same as cost variance, only this time, we're concerned with planned value instead of actual costs. Let's say your project with the $450,000 budget is supposed to be 40 percent complete by today, but you're only 35 percent complete. We've already found the earned value as $157,500 for the project and the planned value is $180,000.

The schedule variance formula is earned value minus the planned value (EV – PV). In this example, the schedule variance is $22,500. Though, in reality, you won't need to do a mathematical formula to already know the project is running later than expected.

Finding the Performance Indexes

An index is an expression showing a ratio—a ratio of work performed to the value of the work performed. We'll also show an index of the value of the planned work to

Figure 2-2   Schedule variance is the difference of earned value and planned value.

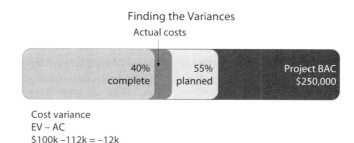

Finding the Variances

Actual costs

40% complete

55% planned

Project BAC $250,000

Cost variance
EV – AC
$100k –112k = –12k

Schedule variance
EV – PV
$100k –137,500 = –37,500

the value of what's been completed. These indexes in earned value management show the health of the project's time and cost. The index is measured against 1: the closer to 1 the index is, the better the project is performing. You don't want to be less than 1, because that's a poorly performing project. And, believe it or not, you don't want to be too far above 1 in your index either, as this shows estimates that were bloated or overly pessimistic.

The first index we'll look at is the cost performance index (CPI). CPI measures the project based on its financial performance. It's an easy formula: earned value divided by actual costs (EV / AC). Your project, in this example, has a budget of $450,000 and you're 35 percent complete with the project work. You've spent $165,000 in actual costs. So, the formula is $157,500 / $165,000 for a CPI of .95.

Another way to consider the .95 CPI value is that you're actually losing five cents on every dollar you spend on the project. Yikes! That means for every dollar you spend for labor, you actually only get 95 cents' worth of value. Not good for the project and the customer. As stated earlier, the closer to 1 the number is, the better the project is performing.

Now let's find the schedule performance index (SPI), which measures the project schedule's overall health. The formula is earned value (EV) divided by planned value (PV). In other words, you're trying to determine how close to the project schedule your project work is being completed. Let's try this formula.

Your project with the $450,000 budget is 35 percent complete, for an earned value of $157,500, but you're supposed to be 40 percent complete by today. That's a planned value of $180,000. The SPI for this project at this time is determined by dividing the earned value of $157,500 by the planned value of $180,000, for an SPI of .88. This tells you that this project is 88 percent on schedule, or, if you're a pessimist, the project is 12 percent off track.

Finding the Estimate to Complete

I admit we're getting a little deep into EVM in this discussion, and I don't expect that you'll encounter many questions about EVM on the PMI-ACP exam, but I want you to be fully prepared to pass the test, so, since there's a chance you might see this on your exam, I'm including it in our conversation. The formula for calculating the estimate to complete (ETC) is needed when management wants to know how much more your project is going to cost. There are three flavors of this formula, based on conditions within your project.

ETC Based on a New Estimate Sometimes you just have to accept the fact that all the estimates up to the current point in the project are flawed, and that you need a new estimate. Agile projects work with a fixed estimate, a fixed schedule, and a flexible scope, but agile projects also work out there in the real world. Agile projects have project budgets that are often based on guesses and assumptions and can be wildly inaccurate depending on the scope and requirements. Imagine a project where the project manager and the project team estimate that the work will cost $200,000 in labor, but once they get into the project, they realize it'll cost $275,000 in labor because the work is much more complex than originally anticipated. That's a reason for the ETC based on a new estimate.

ETC Based on Atypical Variances   This formula is used when the project has experienced some unusual fluctuation in costs, and the project manager doesn't believe the variances will continue within the project. For example, the project team took some additional time to set up a system, build out the architecture, and try some innovations that didn't work out. This fluctuation represents the cost of the work that has changed, but the project manager doesn't believe the cost variance will affect the cost to deliver the other requirements in the product backlog. Here's the formula for atypical variances: ETC = BAC – EV.

Let's say that this project has a BAC of $450,000 and is 35 percent complete. The earned value is $157,500, so our ETC formula would be ETC = $450,000 – $157,500, for an ETC of $292,500. This formula is based on some assumptions and won't be the best forecasting formula for every scenario. If the cost of the work has changed drastically, a whole new estimate would be more appropriate or the product owner or customer would need to trim the scope.

ETC Based on Typical Variances   Sometimes in a project, a variance appears and the project management team realizes that it is going to continue through the rest of the project. The formula is ETC = (BAC – EV) / CPI. For example, consider a project to create a new application using new technology the team hasn't worked with before. The initial cost estimate for the project was $450,000, but once the team got going they realized the complexity of the project is much higher than they expected. They're working with new technology and trying to complete a project they've not done before. While some may argue a new estimate is better for this scenario, you might choose to use this ETC formula instead.

The ETC in this formula requires that the project manager know the earned value and the cost performance index. Let's say that this project is 35 percent complete, so the EV is $157,500. Recall that the CPI is found by dividing the earned value, $157,500, by the actual costs of $165,000. The CPI for this project is .95.

Now let's try the ETC formula: (BAC – EV) / CPI, or ($450,000 – $157,500) / .95, which equates to $306,428.57. That's $306,428.57 in additional funds that the project will need to deliver based on current project performance.

Finding the Estimate at Completion

Sometimes management or the customer will want to know the estimate at completion if you go ahead and include everything in the product backlog, based on current performance, how much the project is likely going to cost. This calls for the estimate at completion (EAC). This formula accounts for all those pennies you're losing on every dollar if your CPI is less than 1. It's an opportunity for the project manager to forecast what the total final costs for the project will be at the end of the project.

There are several different formulas you can use for the EAC, but I'm going to share the most common approach to finding it. Let's continue with our project case study. If this project has a CPI of .95, you could say the project is losing a nickel on every dollar. Those five pennies are going to add up over time. This formula, as Figure 2-3 demonstrates, is EAC = (BAC) / CPI.

Let's try this one out. Our BAC for the project is $450,000 and the CPI is .95. The formula for the EAC is $450,000 / .95, for a value of $471,429. That new value is if we change the agreed-upon cost of the project from $450,000 to $471,429.

Figure 2-3 The estimate at completion is usually based on the original project budget.

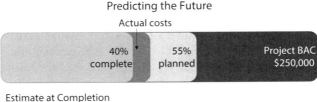

Predicting the Future

Actual costs

40% complete | 55% planned | Project BAC $250,000

Estimate at Completion
Standard formula
BAC / CPI
$250k / .89 = $280k

EXAM COACH   I don't believe you'll have many EVM questions on your exam, but you might. I've elected to share the most common EVM formulas with you here. Some people might argue that EVM is fine for predictive projects, but agile uses story points, something we've not yet discussed, to predict progress, instead of dollar amounts. You could, if you wanted to, use story points instead of dollars in these formulas and the math would work the same.

Agile Project Accounting

In a predictive project, accounting and reconciliation of the project funds is easy to track. You predict how much it costs to do the project activities, then you measure the actual costs of doing the project activities, and then you calculate the difference. Project team members in a predictive environment bill their time against categories of work, such as framing, plumbing, or landscaping. In an agile environment, things are not so clear cut. Agile is knowledge work, and some things are going to take longer than others to complete. Your team will have good days and bad days, and costs will fluctuate from project to project.

Even in a waterfall software development life cycle project, requirements are known up front in the feasibility and requirements analysis phases. There are assumptions in waterfall that the requirements are stable and that the team can code, test, and deploy as planned with a predicted cost for the different stages and activities. Waterfall does have the advantage of stability, assuming the requirements are stable, and it's much easier to predict cost and time in waterfall than in an agile environment. Agile, however, has many more advantages over waterfall, but needs an approach to track and predict costs with more accuracy.

Another challenge that agile faces is the use of incremental deliverables, as opposed to waterfall, where the deliverable happens once—at the end of the project. Because agile works closely with the business people throughout the project, the team gets quick feedback, makes adjustments and corrections, and adds value to the software that's not as distinct as processes in traditional software project management.

The idea of agile project accounting is to tie financial accountability to the deliverables the team creates. The goal in agile project management is to be nimble and not bogged down in accounting, tracking every movement, and to minimize waste. Agile project accounting, at its most basic approach, tracks the cost and ROI of the project and the iterations of the project. There's another complexity when dealing with vendors in an agile project. Later in this chapter, I'll talk about the Dynamic Systems Development Method (DSDM) as an approach for better management of vendors' involvement in the project.

Creating Key Performance Indicators

When you're talking with management or customers about creating software, they always want to know how much this thing will cost and when will this thing be done. Those are two common key performance indicators (KPIs) in a typical project, but they're not necessarily the best indicators of an agile project performance. Tracking time and cost in predictive environments is an excellent method to see the work that's been completed in ratio to the cost of the work completed.

Agile projects, however, can use different KPIs to show project performance. You already know about the inverted triangle of cost constraints from Chapter 1. Recall that with agile projects we work with a fixed schedule and fixed costs and allow scope to change as much as the customer likes. So, what should we track for performance? There are four metrics you should know when it comes to tracking KPIs in agile:

- **Rate of progress** The development team will size the product requirements through elements called story points. I'll talk more about story points coming up, but it's a way of sizing the user requirements to communicate the effort, complexity, and relative sizing to other elements in the backlog. Over time, you'll be able to track how many story points are accomplished per iteration, or even per week, to show the customer how quickly you're moving through the stack of requirements.

- **Remaining work** If you know the rate of progress, you can also deduce the amount of work remaining to do in the project. For example, let's say there are 230 story points total in the backlog. If the team has knocked out 60 story points in eight weeks, there are 170 story points left in the backlog to tackle.

- **Completion date** When you know the rate of progress and the amount of remaining work to do, you can predict a rough completion date. In our example, the team's rate of progress is 30 story points per four-week iteration. With 170 story points remaining, the team will need six more iterations, or 24 weeks, to complete the project. It's a rough guess for sure, as the team may uncover additional work, have defects, and encounter other variables they'll need to manage, but it's a good KPI to track.

- **Cost remaining** Because knowledge work is typically billed at an hourly rate, this is straightforward math. Let's say your project has 10 project team members and their billable rate is $75 per hour per person, for a project rate of $750 per hour. That's $30,000 per week. Now let's say there are 24 weeks until your completion date. That's a predicted cost of $720,000. So, you'd compare that amount to the project budget to identify the cost remaining—hopefully on the positive side. You might also have to consider other project expenses, such as consultants, training, special hardware, or software purchases, too.

These are some KPIs you should know for the PMI-ACP exam, but a KPI is technically anything the customer or project manager wants to track that can show performance. You could track defects, time for defect resolution, or even total number of hours worked in the project in ratio to the story points. If you want to get overly complicated, which I wouldn't, you could track EVM for earned value and planned value to show performance.

Managing Risk in Agile Projects

Risk is anti-value in agile projects. In an agile project, risk is anything that threatens the success of the project, and we must address risks sooner rather than later. Risk is an uncertain event that can have a negative effect on an agile project. Traditional, predictive project management moves through a series of risk management processes:

- Risk identification
- Qualitative risk analysis
- Quantitative risk analysis
- Plan risk responses
- Do risk responses
- Continuously monitor risks

These processes are repeated over and over in predictive projects. Agile takes a condensed approach: examine the product backlog and identify risks that need to be addressed. Rather than allow a risk to be lurking in the backlog for discovery and management later in the project, the agile team, the project manager, and the product owner create a risk-adjusted backlog. The items that carry large risk impact and probability are shifted up in priority to be dealt with at the start of the project, rather than later in the project when their impact can be even larger than at the onset.

By taking on risks that threaten the project early in the project timeline, the development team is removing the risk events, proving that the project can move forward, and building confidence with the project customers. I'll talk more about risk management in Chapter 6 in the context of adaptive planning. For now, and for your exam, know that we prioritize the requirements non only on value, but also based on risk events that can threaten the project's success.

Considering Regulations as Requirements

Regulations are the laws and rules that a government agency has enacted for your discipline. Consider, for example, the laws and rules for healthcare organizations, banks, and other financial institutions. Regulations are requirements that must be followed. This means that you, the project manager, and the product owner need a good grasp on what regulations exist for your industry and how to apply them to the project. This might mean you work with subject matter experts or consultants to identify the regulations and map them to the requirements in the product backlog.

Regulations for software development will also mean that the development team understands the regulations and how the project solution meets regulatory compliance.

When you consider the long list of requirements in the backlog, regulations might affect some or all of the requirements, so the development team needs a clear understanding of the regulations, how they'll create the product to meet regulations, or if they'll treat the regulations as a standalone requirement. For example, a regulation that deals with user data and security could be managed through multiple components in the project.

Whatever approach your team comes up with, you'll likely need some evidence that the team's solution meets the regulatory compliance and has been tested, and validation that the scope satisfies the requirements. You don't want to publish a software solution that doesn't meet regulations—that's anti-value and can introduce all sorts of negative consequences for your organization and customers.

Prioritizing Requirements

Have you ever worked with a customer who said everything was top priority? All the requirements are of the same value—there's no flexibility for prioritizing anything over the others. Well, that approach doesn't work well in agile project management, but there are some strategies to combat that mindset. Agile project management is largely based on the development team completing the requirements from most important to least important. The product backlog is a long list of requirements, and the project team can only work on so many requirements at a given time. So, the question is, which requirements should you work on first?

That's the thrust of prioritizing requirements: the customer picks what's the most important requirement, then the next, and the next, and so on. The team will decide how much they can complete in the next iteration, plan the iteration work, and then deliver. And then the process repeats. Project customers, or the product owner, may need a little training on how agile works to get a feel for the approach. The product owner, the project manager, and the project team can work together to help prioritize the requirements, but the decision on priorities is largely left to the product owner.

In this section I'll explore several different approaches you, the team, and the product owner or customer can use to sort and prioritize the requirements. You should know these approaches for your PMI-ACP exam—you'll likely see them all, as they all relate to scoring value for agile projects.

Using the MoSCoW Approach

Hello, comrade—let's visit Moscow! Wait, it's not that Moscow, but MoSCoW—note the capitalization of MSCW. This approach is a simple way to filter the requirements based on value to the customer. MoSCoW means:

- **Must have**   Needs to be included for the project to be successful
- **Should have**   Needs to be included for the solution to work
- **Could have**   Needed to add some additional value for the solution
- **Would like to have but not at this time**   Nice ideas, but not necessary for the project to be successful

Each requirement in the product backlog is sorted into these four categories. This approach helps the stakeholders filter out the bells and whistles that don't necessarily add value and sort the requirements by which ones ("must have" and "should have" requirements) are linked directly to the overall value of the project. The "must have" requirements are the first requirements the team will attack in their initial iterations.

The product owner or customer, the project manager, and the development team examine these requirements and continue to size, prioritize, and rank the requirements to choose how much work the team can do from this set of requirements in the first iteration of the project. When the next iteration is about to begin, the process can repeat and the project moves forward over and over until the team reaches the definition of done.

Prioritizing with Kano Analysis

Kano analysis is an approach developed by Noriaki Kano, a professor at Tokyo University of Science, to sort customer requirements into five categories. The five categories of Kano are as follows:

- **Must-be quality**   Attributes that must exist and are expected. If these attributes are not present, then the customer will be very dissatisfied. These are core requirements that must exist in the product to make it complete. For example, a video game needs to install, launch, and not crash so the customer can play and enjoy the experience.

- **One-dimensional quality**   Attributes that will satisfy the customer expectations when present, but will create dissatisfaction when absent from the product. The product must operate as advertised or the customer won't be happy. Continuing the example, a video game needs to follow some rules and logic and function properly; pressing Button A must make the player jump consistently, not switching Button A in the next level to make the player crawl.

- **Attractive quality**   Attributes that will satisfy customer expectations when present but don't create dissatisfaction when not present. For example, showing your score from previous launches of the video game is an attractive feature.

- **Indifferent quality**   Attributes that won't satisfy or dissatisfy the customer when present or missing. The customer often doesn't even know about these attributes. For example, the video game offers the player the choice to change the brightness of the sun in the software experience.

- **Reverse quality**   Attributes that may make the customer very satisfied or very dissatisfied if the attribute is present. For example, some customers like the controller in the game to vibrate with actions on the screen, whereas other customers hate the vibrations in the game controller. Not all customers are alike.

These attributes are mapped against a satisfaction and achievement axis as shown in Figure 2-4. The attributes are plotted with three terms for the overall performance of the product: exciting quality, normal quality, and expected quality. These are also known as delighters and satisfiers in Kano analysis.

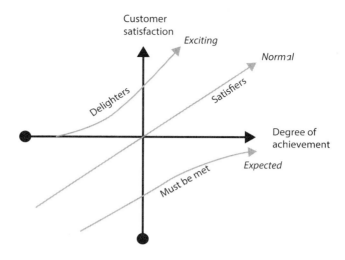

Figure 2-4 Kano analysis maps out the performance of the deliverables based on satisfaction and achievement.

Voting with Dots

Voting with dots, sometimes called multivoting, is exactly what it sounds like. Participants vote on the requirements priority with dots, check marks, or even little sticky notes. Participants are given a limit amount of dots; the more dots next to a requirement equates to higher priority. You can buy rolls of dot stickers online or from an office supply store.

Here's how it works:

1. You first sum up the number of requirements to vote on and then give each person 20 percent of that number in dots. For example, if you have 50 potential items to vote on, each participant receives 10 dots.

2. Participants then put a dot next to the items they think are most important.

3. You then sum up the dots for each requirement and rank the requirements by their votes.

You can also make the second step private, so people won't follow the crowd or be afraid to vote on items that have received smaller numbers of votes. Some organizations can make this more complex by giving different colors of dots to represent different values. You can also, if so inclined, give stakeholders different colors of dots to help weigh who's voting on what in the process.

Spending Monopoly Money

Growing up with four brothers, we'd occasionally play the classic board game Monopoly. Of course, after a few hours of fun, the game would wind down into a wrestling match, somebody would be crying, and my parents would send us to our rooms for a little cooling off and some peace and quiet for them. Fun times!

Well, voting with Monopoly money is nowhere as fun as the board game, but people probably aren't going to get into fights and break down in tears. Voting with Monopoly money gives each stakeholder an equal amount of pretend cash to spend on the different items in the requirements backlog. Participants spend their money on the requirements based on how valuable they perceive the items to be in the project. You then sum up the amount spent on each feature and rank them accordingly.

Voting with 100 Points

This simple approach assigns each stakeholder in the requirements prioritization meeting 100 points to vote on requirements as they see fit. A stakeholder can distribute their points equally among the requirements, in big 25-point chunks, or even spend all 100 points on one single requirement. There's no rule on how the points are spent or distributed, but it's a good idea to explain the process and the importance of assigning points based on their priorities for the list of project requirements.

Prioritizing with a Requirements Prioritization Model

This model is ideal for requirements that haven't quite made the "must have" category of project requirements. You might have a long list of requirements that still needs to be prioritized to determine which requirements will be in the project, and which requirements are basically trimmed from the project's backlog of requirements.

In the requirements prioritization model, stakeholders vote on the following four factors of each proposed requirement on a scale of 1 to 9:

- **Benefit**   What the customer receives for having the requirement
- **Penalty**   Penalty experienced if the customer doesn't receive the requirement
- **Cost**   How costly is it to create the requirement
- **Risk**   Perceived risk exposure to create the requirement

Once stakeholders have voted on each requirement with the four categories, you plug the values into a spreadsheet to find the total points for each category and the overall percentage for each requirement, and then, based on costs and risks, you determine the overall priority of each requirement. Figure 2-5 is a screenshot of the formulas in action to show the results and prioritization of the model. It's a somewhat complicated formula, and certainly not one you'll need to know for your exam, but do be familiar with the idea of voting on the four factors for each requirement presented.

Delivering Value Incrementally

On the PMI-ACP exam there is a distinction between iterative projects and incremental projects. Iterative projects repeat iterations until the project is done. Each iteration builds on the previous iteration all the way through the entire project life cycle. Incremental projects, however, deliver value in increments—short pieces of functional deliverables that the business can take advantage of while the project is still in motion.

Consider the prioritized backlog. If the project team selects a chunk of work to deliver, that chunk of work represents the most valuable items, at that time, that the customer

Requirement	Benefit	Penalty	Value	Value %	Cost	Cost %	Risk	Risk %	Priority
A	2	4	8	5.2	1	2.7	1	3.0	1.22
B	5	3	13	8.4	2	5.4	1	3.0	1.21
C	9	7	25	16.1	5	13.5	3	9.1	0.89
D	5	5	15	9.7	3	8.1	2	6.1	0.87
E	9	8	26	16.8	3	8.1	8	24.2	0.83
F	3	9	15	9.7	3	8.1	4	12.1	0.63
G	4	3	11	7.1	3	8.1	2	6.1	0.64
H	6	2	14	9.0	4	10.8	3	9.1	0.59
I	3	4	10	6.5	4	10.8	2	6.1	0.47
J	7	4	18	11.6	9	24.3	7	21.2	0.33
Totals	53	49	155	100.0	37	100.0	33	100.0	

Figure 2-5 Requirements prioritization models score four factors for each requirement—benefit, penalty, cost, and risk.

wants. If the development team can create an increment of deliverables with these valuable items as stable software, then the business can start using the deliverables while the team returns to the product backlog for the next chunk of requirements to create the next increment of product deliverables. Each increment can build upon the existing product, so the product just keeps getting better and better.

Okay, that's the dreamy and simple way to explain incremental value. The truth is that development teams usually create an increment that will go into a test environment and then build the next increment upon the prior increment still in a test environment. At some point, based on release planning, the collection of increments is stable enough and offers enough value to be deployed to the customer. The development team continues to work on the next release by continuing their increments of work into a test environment for the next release.

 EXAM COACH Iterative projects build on previous work until the project is done. Incremental projects append to existing work and offer increments of value and deliverables to the project customers. The timeboxed period to create the code or deliverables is often called an iteration regardless of the project life cycle being iterative or incremental.

Considering the Cost of Change

You already know that agile projects expect change to happen; however, some changes can have dramatic effects on the project work. As we discuss iterative and incremental projects, we have to consider the cost of change for these types of projects. First, change can enter the product backlog whenever the customer wants. Changes to the current iteration or increment are not considered until the current iteration or increment is complete—unless there's serious reason to do so, such as that the change is so drastic it'll wipe out the current iteration's work. Changes to requirements go into the prioritized backlog and are then considered during the next iteration planning session.

When changes are added to the product backlog, the project manager, development team, and customer have to ask several questions:

- What's more important than this change?
- What existing requirements that the team has already completed will be affected?
- What requirements will shift out of scope due to time and cost constraints?
- What risks are introduced because of this change?
- What effect will the change have on existing requirements?

Usually, the later in the project the change is introduced, the more expensive the change is to incorporate. While agile projects do welcome change, the change may cause rework, introduce risk, and cause other requirements to be dropped from the project because time and costs are fixed constraints in agile. A serious conversation must happen when considering change requests in an incremental project as the change can affect existing deliverables that the organization is already using. Changes can pull the solution back into development, cause risks or issues, and require the code to pass through testing once again. While change is welcome, change can also be expensive.

Creating the Minimal Viable Product

The minimal viable product (MVP) is the smallest thing you can build that delivers value to the customer. You might also see the MVP described as the minimal marketable features (MMF), but it's the same idea. The MVP is all about delivering value from the project to the customer as soon as possible. The MVP doesn't represent the entire project and all the requirements, but it offers some value to the customer and early adapters of your project deliverables. The MVP is one of my favorite agile project management concepts: don't wait until the end of the project to deliver some value to the customer. By delivering value early in the project, the customer buy-in and support of the project will increase.

The MVP is a quick win for the project team and the customer—and it can also help management see the ROI of the project sooner rather than later. The MVP is an incremental approach to project delivery. The first release has a limited set of features, but they are features pulled from the requirements backlog and are top priority for the customer. The next release builds on the first release, appending to the MVP and continuing to garner support for the project, provide faster ROI, and help the customer receive the benefits of the agile approach.

Embracing Low-Tech/High-Touch Tools

One of the biggest mistakes I see organizations make when beginning to implement agile is to computerize their approach. There are lots of really cool software programs to help manage an agile project. There are apps for voting with dots, apps for planning agile, apps for icebreakers, and apps to visualize the project. Icebreakers are games for quickly learning about about project team members. Too much technology goes against the idea of keeping things simple. I see too many agile project managers managing the technology rather than managing the project.

Okay, rant over.

My rant is relative to what you need to know for your exam (and really what you need to have for your project): low-tech/high-touch tools are so much better for a project than all the doodads you'll find in software packages. Agile is simple, clean, direct. You and the team don't need technical solutions to manage a technical project. Too much time (and reliance) on technology can actually slow down some really simple activities in agile. For example, do you really need an app to vote with dots when you can just vote with dots?

Let's discuss three low-tech/high-touch tools you should know for your PMI-ACP exam:

- **Kanban board**   I talked about Kanban boards in Chapter 1, but this is a great example of a low-tech/high-touch tool. Requirements are written on sticky notes or cards and are moved from the backlog to the different phases of the project to represent where the requirement currently is in the project life cycle. It's easy to create and to understand.

- **Task board**   This board, like a Kanban board, represents the project tasks and their status. A task board is more closely associated with Scrum and it shows the status of the requirements in the sprint backlog rather than the requirements for the whole project.

- **WIP limit**   WIP means work in progress. Kanban boards, task boards, and any hybrid approach to agile project management should set a limit on the number of requirements in the WIP. You want the team to select activities or requirements, complete them, and then move on to the next item to be created. Too many items in WIP creates waste, such as task switching and waiting. Focus on one thing at a time and get it done.

Introducing the Theory of Constraints

You've likely heard the old adage that a chain is only as strong as its weakest link. Eli Goldratt expounded upon that concept in his book *The Goal* and introduced his theory of constraints. The theory of constraints posits that there's always at least one constraint that is holding back the system, or project management approach, from reaching its maximum potential. A constraint is anything that limits your options: time, costs, scope requirements, people, software, hardware, and any number of other factors. The basic idea is that you attack the constraint that is most restrictive until it's no longer the most restrictive constraint and then repeat the process with the next most restrictive constraint.

Bottleneck is a way to describe when work comes to a slowdown, just like water pouring out of a bottle slows down when it reaches the neck. For example, testing may be a bottleneck if the testing team can't keep up with what developers are creating. If work is piled up in testing, that can affect the deployment, cause rework for the developers, and put pressure on the testing team. In addition, the testing team might be tempted to take shortcuts to buzz through the work quicker, allowing escaped defects to enter production, which will reduce overall quality, stakeholder investment in the project, and the morale of the project team.

Testing is just one example of a bottleneck—it can be any area of the project where work stacks up in a queue.

Addressing Bottlenecks

In Goldratt's book, the most restrictive constraint is commonly called a bottleneck. Bottlenecks need to be addressed and managed or, like in the testing example described previously, quality and overall production will suffer. The theory of constraints provides five focusing steps:

1. *Identify the constraint.* You must identify the constraint before you can deal with the constraint.

2. *Determine how best to exploit the constraint.* This means to first confirm that you are getting the most from the existing constraint. For example, before purchasing new hardware, configure the existing hardware to get the most from what's already in place.

3. *Subordinate everything else to the constraint.* This means you keep the constraint at its capacity—never overloaded or underutilized. With the hardware example, you make certain that the hardware is being utilized at its capacity without a long backlog or queue of items for the constraint to work through.

4. *Elevate the constraint.* Once you've confirmed that the identified constraint is at its capacity and it's still a bottleneck, then you can replace the constraint or elevate the bottleneck for additional throughput by adding labor or other resources. Remember, the constraint isn't always equipment, it could be an individual. A project team member may be replaced or educated, or additional help added to the tasks.

5. *Prevent inertia from becoming a constraint.* After you eliminate the bottleneck, other components of the system will need to keep up with the new component or the entire process is repeated on the next bottleneck in the project.

The theory of constraints is something that you should be familiar with for your PMI-ACP exam. While you likely won't have to actually solve a bottleneck on the exam, you'll likely need to recognize the steps involved to address a constraint and make corrections to your project management approach.

Creating a Cumulative Flow Diagram

A cumulative flow diagram (CFD) can help identify and track bottlenecks in an agile project, as shown in Figure 2-6. CFDs show how many work items are in the different stages of the project, how long each item stays in a stage or queue, when items move into

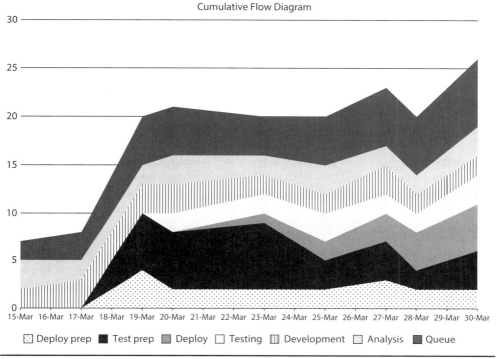

Figure 2-6 Cumulative flow diagrams help reveal bottlenecks.

the next queue of the project, and when items leave any stage of the project. Think of the cumulative flow diagram as a way to illustrate the accumulation of work to enter a phase. The longer the queue of the work to enter or exit a phase of the project, the more likely there's a bottleneck that needs to be addressed.

A great project will have a CFD with even bands for each stage of project work, such as backlog, approved items, work in progress, testing, and done. Note that the category of done should grow and grow, as the accumulation of done items means that the work is efficiently making its way through each stage of the project and the finished items are accumulating.

A not-so-great project will have one or more bands in the CFD where work is stacking up in any one area of the phase. A fat band in the CFD represents where work is stalling and a bottleneck is present—except for the final stage of done. A CFD is a great component to include as part of your project's information radiator—it's honest, tells a story of how the project is performing, and helps the team remain transparent in its work and where improvements are needed.

Exploring Little's Law

John Little observed that when work is introduced into a system faster than the work is being completed, the queue time will increase for the work. You've probably experienced this at the airport or grocery store. As more and more people get in line, the queue continues to grow faster than the person managing the line can handle. And you, and other customers, get aggravated, might leave the line, or be frustrated with the employees.

Employees feel this aggravation too—that's when people doing the work, your development team, will feel overwhelmed, switch from task to task, and allow technical debt to pile up because there's so much work to get done, who has time for refactoring code? Too much work in the system, too much work in the WIP, leads to a breakdown in efficiency and effective development.

The overall goal of Little's Law is to reduce the WIP while maintaining the efficiency of work completed per time period. The fewer items that the team has to work on at any given time, the faster they'll complete the items in WIP. Get rid of long queues, focus on fewer items, and avoid multitasking (task switching) to add value and reduce frustration.

Working with Vendors in Agile Projects

Hiring a vendor to complete a portion or even all of a project with an agile mindset can create challenges. Consider that vendors, and customers, usually want to know all the work that they will be obligated to complete before signing on the contract's dotted line. Agile projects, as you know, often work with an ambiguous and changing product backlog, something that doesn't mesh well with traditional vendor contracting. Vendors want to know upfront everything they're expected to deliverfor the project, and that goes against the primary concept of agile.

In the *PMBOK Guide, Sixth Edition*, the flow of the procurement processes follows a rigid path for predictive projects:

- **Statement of work**   Defines what the project must have.
- **Creation of request for quotes, bids, or proposals**   Bids and quotes are essentially the same type of document as these documents just provide a price, while proposals are an in-depth offer that includes ideas and approaches for project solutions.
- **Bidder conference**   Vendors attend this meeting to ask questions about the statement of work.
- **SOW update**   The buyer updates the SOW to reflect all of the new information gathered from the bidder conference
- **Review and negotiation**   The buyer reviews the bids, quotes, or proposals and enters negotiations with the vendor to define the terms of the contract. The seller and the buyer both know exactly what's included in the contract and who's responsible for what in the project.
- **Contract**   The seller and the buyer sign a contract that kicks off the contractual relationship between the two parties.

In agile environments, much of that defined flow of the procurement processes doesn't work because requirements aren't fully known at the launch of the project. This makes it difficult for the vendor to create an accurate bid and may even cause the vendor to bloat their costs to accommodate the potential for changes and unforeseen work in the project. There are some tactics, however, that you can use to bring vendors into the agile project without wrecking their profit margins and still getting the deliverables done with value for the organization.

Working with DSDM Contracting

Recall from Chapter 1 that DSDM flows through exploration, engineering, and incremental deployment. DSDM aims to accomplish the prioritized requirements that fit within the defined constraints of time and money. DSDM contracting is a contracting methodology that sizes the project work to fit the amount of time and money the organization has available. For example, if the customer has a budget of $500,000 and six months to complete a project, the vendor would negotiate the size of the scope that fits the fixed constraints of time and costs.

Requirements are prioritized using the MoSCoW approach introduced earlier in the chapter (must have, should have, could have, and would like to have but not at this time). When requirements won't fit the amount of funds or time available, negotiation takes place to either increase time and funds or, more likely, trim scope. Changes are still allowed to the product backlog as long as there's a tradeoff with other, less-valuable requirements. Those less-valuable requirements are usually shifted out of scope for the project.

DSDM contracting follows eight principles for agile projects:

- Continually focus on the business need
- Deliver on time as promised
- Collaborate with the customer
- Never compromise quality of the product
- Build through increments
- Develop the solution iteratively
- Communicate with all parties clearly and continuously
- Demonstrate control throughout the project

While you don't need to know much about DSDM for the PMI-ACP exam, you should be topically familiar with the approach and how it allows organizations to still utilize agile project management while getting vendors involved in the process. DSDM contracting still adheres to agile principles, such as timeboxing, using prototypes, testing code, and configuration management, to ensure consistency in the features and functions of the software and project deliverable.

Using a Graduated Fixed-Price Contract

A graduated fixed-price contract allows the buyer and the seller to share some risks in an agile project. With this model the hourly rate of the contracted work varies based on performance within the project. For example, the vendor's hourly rate for software development could be $120 if they finish the project on time and as planned. If the vendor is late, however, the hourly rate decreases to $110. If the vendor completes the project ahead of schedule, the hourly rate increases to $130.

With this model, the vendor can participate in the agile model and work as efficiently as possible to maximize their hourly rate and profit margin. If the vendor makes mistakes, can't keep pace, or encounters some other issue and they're late, then their hourly rate goes down and so too will their profit margin on the project. Of course, if they finish right on time, their hourly rate remains consistent. Both parties share some risk in the approach, but performance is up to the vendor to deliver value as quickly as possible to achieve their milestones and goals in the project.

Creating a Fixed-Price Work Package

A work package is a deliverable and is technically the name of the smallest items in a work breakdown structure (WBS). The WBS is a visual decomposition of the project scope; while we typically don't have a WBS in agile, a work package can describe a chunk of the project work that you want a vendor to complete for the project. Your contractual agreement with the vendor can be for many work packages or just one, though it's often several.

The vendor will examine each work package and estimate their costs and time to deliver the item. As more information becomes available, such as detailed requirements, risks, and shifting priorities, the vendor can modify their estimate based on the new information. This approach allows the vendor to take one portion of the project and manage that portion as they see fit—as long as they deliver value on time and as promised. Rather than creating one large estimate for the entire project, the vendor will create individual estimates for portions of the project with the agreed-upon option to adjust estimates as new information becomes available.

Validating Value in Agile Projects

One of the problems with agile projects is that the work is invisible. Look at a developer coding—how do you know what he's developing is actually good and reliable, or even if he's coding at all? He could be writing love sonnets in his private, made-up language. Alright, probably not that extreme, but the idea is that you don't know if knowledge work is valuable until you can show that value has been created, that the development team has created the requirements that were asked for with the correct conformance to requirements and that the deliverable is fit for usage.

Projects, I like to say, fail at the beginning, not the end. Having a poor set of requirements or a misunderstanding of requirements will result in the team creating something likely different than what the customer had in mind. That's why prototypes—even sketches on a whiteboard—help to clarify the functions of the product and make certain that everyone on the team has a common understanding of what constitutes value and what the goals of the project and of the iteration are.

Agile project management has some validation built into the process. Scrum, for example, finishes each sprint with a sprint review where the team can demonstrate for the product owner and the ScrumMaster what has been created in the last iteration. The demonstration is an opportunity for the customer to review the work and confirm, or deny, that the team is on track and creating what was requested. It may be frustrating when the product owner isn't pleased with what the team has created, but that's part of the process. It's better to catch mistakes and misunderstandings early in the project than in the final release.

XP also has some built-in reviews to confirm value before the product is released. Remember XP uses pair programming, where two programmers work together. One programmer is programming while the other is checking the code. XP also has its teams run unit tests frequently to confirm that the code works as intended. Continuous integration is also a theme in XP (and other agile approaches) to confirm that the developed code will be integrated seamlessly without breaking the existing code.

Implementing Continuous Integration

Considering that your agile team may have several developers working on the software, you'll need a mechanism to pull all that code together into a uniform, stable result; that's where continuous integration comes into play. Continuous integration (CI) is a way to merge all the code from different developers to confirm that the compiled code is still working successfully. CI aims to build and test the code several times a day from a shared repository.

Rather than waiting days, weeks, or even months to integrate all the code (and all the bugs and messes), CI requires the team to integrate the code several times throughout a workday. This approach originated in XP, but many flavors of agile now work with CI. CI utilizes build servers that are dedicated to the tasks of integrating and testing the code and reporting the results back to the development team. Creating a build server requires both time and a financial commitment for a server that's only used for testing and integrating code.

CI also provides versioning through hosting a code repository—this makes it easier to roll back changes. Versioning, while handy, needs to be managed so that there aren't multiple versions of the software being integrated at once. The build process can be automated with third-party tools. Once the build happens, testing should be implemented on the latest build as part of the CI process. No development team member should hold back commits to the code—integration should happen several times throughout the day by everyone. Holding back on integration, even by one person, can cause huge issues in the code, create duplicity, and create risks with future builds. If the results of CI fail, problems are addressed immediately and then CI happens once again.

 EXAM COACH   Iteration Zero, something I'll discuss in detail in Chapter 5, is a special iteration just for setting up the project environment. This is a good example of where Iteration Zero is needed. The setup time for continuous integration can be lengthy, so an iteration may be dedicated to set up the server and the suite of automatic testing tools.

Working with Test-Driven Development

Test-driven development begins with the developers writing the tests before writing the code. They write the tests with an understanding of what it'll take for the code to pass the tests. Tests are written through unit testing, typically JUnit or NUnit—these are frameworks to write repeatable tests (you won't need to know much about JUnit or NUnit for the exam). Once the tests have been written, the development team writes the code to pass the tests. If the code doesn't pass, then the developers make adjustments to the code and run the tests again, and repeat the process until the code passes. Figure 2-7 is a flowchart of test-driven development.

Before moving onto the next chunk of work after code passes the tests, the development team needs to clean up all the code and run the tests once more; if the code passes, then they can move on to the next task. This cleanup of the code is called *refactoring*. Refactoring should be done often to keep code consistent, clean, and easy to maintain. If messy code piles up, it becomes technical debt, as discussed in Chapter 1.

Red-Green-Clean is a way to describe test-driven development: First, develop a test that's going to fail because the code isn't yet written (red). Next, write code that'll pass the test (green). Finally, clean up and refactor the messy code. You might also see this as Red-Green-Refactor, but it's not as much fun to say.

Another type of test-driven development is acceptance test–driven development (ATDD). This approach has the entire team writing tests before developing the code. ATDD is sometimes called the "three amigos" as it addresses three perspectives and their respective questions:

- **Customer perspective**   What problem are we trying to solve?
- **Development team perspective**   How will we solve this problem?
- **Testing staff perspective**   What about this hypothetical scenario?

The primary point of ATDD is that the whole team participates in writing the tests to confirm if the expectations of the three perspectives and, ultimately, the customer were met. If any of the tests fails, then the process is repeated. ATDD follows the same pattern as test-driven development: write a test that will fail, create code that will pass the test, and clean up the code before moving on.

Confirming Value with Exploratory Testing

The term "software testing" often conjures up thoughts of automated scripts that bang up against the code to see what will break. Test cases and scripts are created in advance of the code and are all based on logic, prediction, and control. While automated testing suites can save lots of time, they do have one major drawback: they cannot think. Combined with automated testing, not in lieu of it, teams should implement exploratory testing.

Exploratory testing is based on the tester trying different things in the software, exploring the different parts of the application, and playing "what if" with combinations of commands. In other words, the exploratory tester is free to try anything and everything in the software to see what conforms, or does not conform, to requirements.

Figure 2-7
Test-driven development follows a logical workflow.

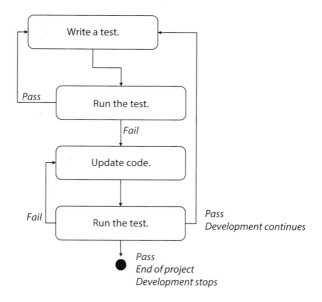

Exploratory testing is more freewill, ad hoc, and spontaneous than scripted testing—it's more fun, too. Exploratory testing acts like a typical user, and we know a typical user will find things to break that a scripted test won't ever encounter.

Exploratory testing does follow some general guidelines:

- The purpose of the testing should be well-defined.
- The tester must keep accurate notes on what's being tested.
- Documentation of questions, issues, and bugs is mandatory.
- Exploratory testing works best when completed in pairs of testers.

Exploratory testing shouldn't be rushed but is also timeboxed to allow the tester to fully explore the software. A rushed testing session will likely result in escaped defects and the diminishing of value. Testing is an important part of the process—it's always better to catch mistakes through the testing process than to have users find the mistakes for you.

Completing Usability Testing

Usability testing is an approach that observes participants using the software. The participants try to complete certain tasks in the software while the project team or a few developers watch, listen, and take notes. The goal is to identify usability problems, collect data, and gauge how satisfied the users are with the software. Ideally, usability testing has the participants in one room and the development team or observers in another room so as not to affect the participants as they try to complete the tasks in the software.

Usability testing has several key goals:

- See if participants can use the software to accomplish the given tasks
- Track the time for participants to complete tasks
- Rate the satisfaction level of participants with the software
- Determine what changes, if any, are needed to improve value in the software

Usability testing can take time as you'll have to configure the hardware and software, recruit participants, and create a schedule of when the testing can take place. While there may also be a financial commitment for the testing, this approach doesn't have to be costly. The value of usability testing is to gather data about the key elements of the software to see how the smaller population of user participants work with and through the software as a reflection of how the greater population will likely react to the software provided.

Chapter Summary

In this chapter we talked all about value-driven delivery. This is the largest PMI-ACP exam domain at 20 percent of your test, so make sure you really know this chapter's contents. We started off our conversation by discussing the 14 exam domain tasks and the types of activities you'll be asked questions about—all related to value. Right at the beginning of the chapter, we also discussed what it means to deliver value and how we want to give the customers value right away while also looking for opportunities to remove waste.

Recall that value can be tangible, such as financial returns, equipment, and the software your team is creating. Value can also be intangible through brand recognition, goodwill, and reputation. Know both of those concepts for your exam and how an agile project can deliver value in either or both categories. Value is most often associated with financial returns on the project, and that's why we spent some time detailing the time value of money. While you may have just one or two questions on present value and future value, it's a good idea to know these formulas to show expectations for value in project selection. In this section we also talked about anti-value: risk. Risks are uncertain events that can threaten the project success, and that's why we consider risk-laden items in the backlog and prioritize to take on risks sooner rather than later in the project timeline.

Prioritizing requirements is the responsibility of the product owner, but the whole team is likely involved in the exercise. We looked at several prioritization schemes, such as dot voting, monopoly money, Kano analysis, and MoSCoW. It's a great idea to be able to recognize all of these prioritization schemes and how they work for the PMI-ACP exam—you'll likely see these approaches on the test. The whole point of prioritization is for the team to develop the most important requirements first and then work their way down the list of requirements to less-valuable requirements. This gets the good stuff, the dessert, to the customers first.

Once a chunk of work has been selected based on its prioritization and the capacity of the project team, the team manages the work through a sprint or iteration backlog. A self-directed team decides who'll do what, manages the work in progress, and visualizes the work through Kanban or signboards as part of transparency. Within the iteration or increment the work may succumb to the theory of constraints. Recall that this theory is that the work can only move as fast as the bottleneck in the project allows. The theory of constraints aims to remove or improve the bottleneck to keep the work moving along.

In this chapter, we also talked about working with vendors and the challenge vendors may have participating in an agile environment. To resolve this issue, organizations can use DSDM contracts, graduated fixed-price contracts, and fixed-price work packages. Contracting, while not a huge component of the PMI-ACP exam, is important as many organizations hire IT firms to develop software or at least be part of the agile teams. We value collaboration over negotiation.

Finally, we discussed testing in an agile environment and why that's so important: escaped defects diminish stakeholder buy-in, are embarrassing, and can cause lots of rework. Testing is a phase of software development, but there are different strategies for how the testing can be completed. Exploratory testing allows testers to explore the software and think through actions. Usability testing requires participants to use the software as a testing approach. Test-driven development and acceptance test–driven development both create tests before the code is written. Then the development team writes the code, passes the test, refactors the code, and repeats the process.

You're making great progress! Keep going—you can do this!

Key Terms

100-point voting Each stakeholder in the requirements prioritization meeting has 100 points to vote on requirements as they see fit. A stakeholder can distribute their points equally among the requirements, in big 25-point chunks, or even spend all 100 points on one single requirement.

Acceptance test–driven development (ATDD) This approach has the entire team writing tests before developing the code. ATDD addresses three perspectives and their respective questions:

Customer perspective: What problem are we trying to solve?
Development team perspective: How will we solve this problem?
Testing staff perspective: What about this hypothetical scenario?

Actual cost (AC) Actual cost is the actual amount of monies the project has spent so far.

Agile project accounting This methodology ties financial accountability to the deliverables the team creates. It tracks the cost and ROI of the project and the iterations of the project.

Continuous integration (CI) Continuous integration is a way to merge all the code from different developers to confirm that the compiled code is still working successfully. CI aims to build and test the code several times a day from a shared repository.

Cost performance index (CPI) CPI measures the project based on its financial performance. The formula is earned value divided by actual cost (EV / AC). The closer to 1, the better the project is performing financially.

Cost variance The earned value of the project minus the actual cost spent reveals the cost variance. The formula is EV – AC.

Cumulative flow diagram (CFD) A CFD can help identify and track bottlenecks in an agile project. A CFD shows how many work items are in the different stages of the project, how long each item stays in a stage or queue, when items move into the next queue of the project, and when items leave any stage of the project.

Earned value (EV) This formula measures the amount of work completed to date and the authorized budget for that work. Earned value is the percent complete times the project's budget.

Estimate at completion (EAC) This formula predicts where the project is likely to end up financially based on current performance. The formula is EAC = budget at completion (BAC) / cost performance index (CPI).

Estimate to complete (ETC) ETC shows how much more money will be needed to complete the project. The most common ETC formula is budget at completion (BAC) – earned value (EV).

Estimate to Complete based on Atypical Variances This formula is used when the project has experienced some unusual fluctuation in costs, and the project manager doesn't believe the variances will continue within the project. The formula is ETC = BAC – EV.

Estimate to Complete based on Typical Variances This formula is used when the project has experienced some fluctuation in costs, and the project manager believes the variances will continue within the project. The formula is ETC = (BAC – EV) / CPI.

Exploratory testing Combined with scripted tested, exploratory testing is based on the tester trying different things in the software, exploring the different parts of the application, and playing "what if" with combinations of commands. The exploratory tester is free to try anything and everything in the software to see what conforms, or does not conform, to requirements. Exploratory testing is more freewill, ad hoc, and spontaneous than scripted testing.

Fixed-price work package This agile approach to contracting enables the vendor to examine each work package and estimate their costs and time to deliver the item. As more information becomes available, such as detailed requirements, risks, and shifting priorities, the vendor can modify their estimate based on the new information. This approach allows the vendor to take on a portion of the project and manage that portion as they see fit—as long as they deliver value on time and as promised.

Future value (FV) Future value is what a present amount of funds will be worth in the future. The formula for future value is $FV = PV(1 + i)^n$, where i is the given interest rate and n is the number of time periods (years, quarters, etc.).

Graduated fixed-price contract A graduated fixed-price contract allows the buyer and the seller to share some risks in an agile project. With this model the hourly rate of the contracted work varies based on performance within the project. For example, the vendor's hourly rate for software development could be $120 if they finish the project on time and as planned. If the vendor is late, however, the hourly rate decreases to $110. If the vendor completes the project ahead of schedule, the hourly rate increases to $130.

Incremental development   By working in increments the development team addresses the most valuable requirements first, incorporates risk management into the project approach, and offers reviews and continued prioritization of the requirements.

Incremental project   An incremental project delivers value in increments—short pieces of functional deliverables that the business can take advantage of while the project is still in motion.

Intangible business value   Intangible business value is derived from the invisible elements that a project creates, such as goodwill, reputation, brand recognition, public benefit, trademarks, and strategic alignment for your organization.

Iterative project   An iterative project repeats iterations until the project is done. Each iteration builds on the iteration before all the way through the entire project life cycle.

Kanban board   Requirements are written on sticky notes or cards and are moved from the backlog to the different phases of the project to represent where the requirement currently is in the project life cycle.

Kano analysis   Kano analysis is an approach to sort customer requirements into five categories: must-be quality, one-dimensional quality, attractive quality, indifferent quality, and reverse quality.

Key performance indicators (KPIs)   KPIs are factors that show project performance. Agile uses four KPIs: rate of progress, remaining work, completion date, and costs remaining.

Little's Law   A theorem that states "the average number of items in a queuing system equals the average rate at which items arrive multiplied by the average time that an item spends in the system." In other words, the more items that are in the WIP queue, the longer it will take the team to complete the items in the queue. When work is introduced into a system, such as your workflow, faster than the work is being completed, the queue time will increase for the work.

Low-tech/high-touch tools   Tools for agile project management that are not technology based are preferred because they are simple, clean, and direct like agile itself. Examples are Kanban boards and the WIP limit.

Minimal viable product (MVP)   The MVP is the smallest thing you can build that delivers value to the customer. You might also see the MVP referred to as the minimal marketable features (MMF).

Monopoly money   Using Monopoly money is a requirements prioritization technique where participants "spend" pretend money on requirements. Participants spend their money on the requirements based on how valuable they perceive the items to be in the project. You then sum up the amount spent on each feature and rank them accordingly.

MoSCoW   MoSCoW is a prioritization schema for the product backlog. MoSCoW stands for Must have, Should have, Could have, and Would like to have but not at this time.

Net present value (NPV)   This calculation of the time value of money predicts a project's value more precisely than the present value formula. NPV evaluates the monies returned on a project for each period the project lasts and considers the investment into the project.

Payback period   The payback period is the duration it will take for the return on the investment to equal, or pay back, the project investment. This approach shows the management horizon, the breakeven point of the project.

Planned value (PV)   Planned value represents the percent of project completion the project should be at this time. Planned value is found by finding the percentage of planned completion times the budget at completion.

Present value (PV)   Present value is what a future amount of funds is worth today. The formula for present value is $PV = FV / (1 + i)^n$, where i is the given interest rate and n is the number of time periods (years, quarters, etc.).

Prioritized backlog   A backlog of prioritized requirements based on the customer's opinion of what's the most important requirement, then the next, and the next, and so on. The team decides how much they can complete in the next iteration, plan the iteration work, and then deliver.

Requirements prioritization model   In the requirements prioritization model, stakeholders vote on four factors of each proposed requirement on a scale of 1 to 9. The four factors voted on are benefit, penalty, cost, and risk.

Risk   Risk is anti-value in agile projects. In an agile project, risk is anything that threatens the success of the project and must be addressed sooner rather than later.

Schedule performance index (SPI)   SPI measures the project based on its schedule performance. The formula is earned value (EV) divided by planned value (PV). The closer to 1, the better the project is performing on schedule.

Schedule variance   The schedule variance is determined by calculating the earned value (EV) of the project minus the planned value (PV) of the project.

Tangible business value   Tangible business value are derived from items like monetary assets, return on investment, stockholder equity, fixtures and tools your project creates or acquires, and the market share your project captures.

Task board   This board, like a Kanban board, represents the project tasks and their status. A task board is more closely associated with Scrum and it shows the status of the requirements in the sprint backlog rather than the requirements for the whole project.

Test-driven development   Test-driven development begins with the developers writing the tests before writing the code. They write the tests with an understanding of what it'll take for the code to pass the tests. Once the tests have been written, the development team writes the code to pass the tests. If the code doesn't pass, then the developers make adjustment to the code and run the tests again, and repeat the process until the code passes. Once the code passes, the developers refactor the code and try the test once more.

Theory of constraints   The theory of constraints posits that there's always at least one constraint that is holding back the system, or project management approach, from reaching its maximum potential. A constraint is anything that limits your options: time, costs, scope requirements, people, software, hardware, and any number of other factors. You attack the constraint that is most restrictive until it's no longer the most restrictive constraint and then repeat the process with the next most restrictive constraint.

Usability testing   Usability testing is an approach that observes participants using the software. The participants try to complete certain tasks in the software while the project team or a few developers watch, listen, and take notes. The goal is to identify usability problems, collect data, and gauge how satisfied the users are with the software.

Voting with dots   Voting with dots, sometimes called multivoting, is a requirements prioritization approach where participants are given a list of requirements and vote on which ones they think deserve the highest priority by labeling them with dots, checkmarks, or even little sticky notes.

WIP limit   WIP means work in progress. Kanban boards, task boards, and any hybrid approach to agile project management should set a limit on the number of requirements in the WIP.

Questions

1. You have been identified as a team member on a project. When you begin gathering requirements, what is a logical first question that should be asked and answered?

    A. How much is in the budget?

    B. How long will the project last?

    C. What is the business value?

    D. How many team members will participate?

2. You are the project manager of an agile project. An agile team's focus is to maximize value. When the team needs to make a decision , what question should be the first to be asked?

    A. How long will it take to test?

    B. Will the decision made derail the project?

    C. What will it cost in man hours?

    D. What is the value to the customer?

3. Most agile software developers use continuous integration tools to test code. These tools tell them whether the code passed or failed by communicating what status?

   A. Red-Yellow-Green

   B. Pass/Fail

   C. Go/No Go

   D. Red-Green-Refactor

4. The agile team for which you are the project manager has determined several key values to deliver to the customer. How should these tasks be tackled by the team?

   A. The tasks should be prioritized, tested, and delivered incrementally.

   B. The tasks should be delivered while in progress, whether tested or not, to gather feedback.

   C. The tasks should be delivered according to the project plan.

   D. All deliverables should be presented at the end of the project.

5. The agile team for which you are the project manager has identified the highest-value features of the project and wants to deliver them as soon as possible. Why is this a good idea?

   A. It gets the features out of the way.

   B. The longer the project goes on, the value of a feature may be compromised.

   C. Delivering the most intense tasks could shorten the project duration.

   D. It proves the team's understanding of value.

6. As a member of the PMO, you have been analyzing upcoming projects and have identified one particular project that you believe project teams will push back on. You understand this project is meant to implement safety standards for an off-shore manufacturing plant. Some project teams may not understand the value of this project. How do you avoid a long, drawn-out process of getting this project approved to move forward?

   A. Attempt to make the teams understand why it is important

   B. Have the project outsourced to avoid the pushback

   C. Make the project mandatory

   D. Take the project off the list of projects for the year and try to implement it at a different time

7. You have been tasked to evaluate the financial metrics of a potential project. You plan to evaluate the percent of the benefit of the investment to the money invested. This is which of the following financial assessment metrics?

   A. Net present value (NPV)

   B. Return on investment (ROI)

   C. Internal rate of return (IRR)

   D. Future value (FV)

8. A great visual to see your project's progress is an earned value management (EVM) chart. Knowing that an agile project is different than a non-agile project in that the initial plan is likely to change, you still see a benefit in using this visual since an EVM chart is a forward-looking indicator and could be used to assist in predicting which of the following?

   A. Number of team members required

   B. Completion dates and final costs

   C. Quality of deliverables

   D. Timings to begin new iterations

9. When working on an agile project, "risk" most likely means something different than it does on a traditional project. Agile sees risks as potential events or circumstances that could have a negative impact on the project, whereas a non-agile project may define a risk as a "good risk" that could present opportunities for the project. How does an agile project deal with risk?

   A. The team identifies risks and then tackles them at the end of the project so that they can all be addressed at once in a separate task.

   B. The iterative nature of agile allows the team to schedule the high-risk activities early in the project so that they are tackled sooner rather than later.

   C. The team keeps the risk-finding results within the team so that the team can address the risk without any outside interference.

   D. Early in the project planning, to ensure that the project won't be cancelled, the team does not relate risks to value, so that there is no chance of showing how the project could be delayed or cost more than planned.

10. The agile team you are working with has just finished an iteration and all tasks are completed. You are ready to move to the next iteration. How do you determine which iteration should be next?

    A. The team follows the project plan developed early in the project.

    B. The PMO has already determined how the project should progress.

    C. The customer continuously prioritizes the backlog.

    D. The team leader determines the next iteration.

11. While meeting with the customers or business owners, they introduce several pieces of new functionality into the priority list. Since the deadline date cannot be moved out, how should the team react to these additions?

    A. Stand firm and tell the customers the project will not be delivered on time

    B. Be sure the customers understand that lower priority tasks or functionality may drop off the project completely

    C. Cancel all vacations and days off and let the team know there will be many long days of work ahead to deliver the project on time

    D. Agree with the customers to have all new items put into a separate category that will be completed if time allows

12. You are working with an agile team that is developing and delivering a software solution to your company's HR group. Several minimum viable product (MVP) releases are scheduled throughout the duration of the project. Why is this a good idea?

    A. To show the progress being made by the development team

    B. To enable the users to test the product for the development team

    C. To enable the business to begin to get value from the project prior to the project ending

    D. To shorten the duration of the project

13. The agile team you are working with utilizes a whiteboard and writes tasks on sticky notes. Initially, you feel like they've taken a step backward by not utilizing an electronic project planning tool. After a period of time, you come to value the whiteboard system more and more. Why do you think this method is beneficial?

    A. It is easy to disregard a sticky note and bypass a task.

    B. No one takes sticky notes seriously.

    C. It is visual, and at a glance shows the progress of the project.

    D. Many people have access to the board and can move notes to their advantage.

14. Agile teams practice frequent verification and validation during and at the end of each iteration. Which one of the following is not a benefit of this method?

    A. It enables the team to catch mistakes and mismatched expectations early.

    B. It keeps everyone busy.

    C. It is easy to manage since there are multiple feedback loops.

    D. It reduces project cost overruns since mistakes are found early prior to additional tasks being built upon a faulty foundation.

15. You are on an agile software implementation project with a very short deadline. How do agile teams shorten the time between identifying a defect and resolving the defect?

    A. Daily build and smoke tests

    B. Continuous integration

    C. Usability testing

    D. Exploratory testing

16. With all the different methods of testing, either a software or product deliverable, when should the team determine what method of testing should be performed?

    A. When the first iteration is complete

    B. When a deliverable is available for testing

    C. Before the product is developed

    D. At the end of the project

17. You've just completed a requirements-gathering session for an agile software implementation team. It became apparent that an outside vendor team must be brought onto the project. You are working with the legal department to draw up a contract for the vendor. What type of contract is best for an agile project?

    A. A contract that accommodates changes

    B. A fixed-price contract

    C. A graduated fixed-price contract

    D. A time and materials contract

18. Approximately midway through an agile project, the business partner asks, "If we stick to the agreed-upon scope, when do you think the project will be done, and how much will it cost?" How will you gather the information necessary to answer the business partner?

    A. By reviewing the Kanban board

    B. By checking progress on the backlog

    C. By analyzing the key performance indicators

    D. By having a team meeting and logging everyone's status

19. You are attending the kick-off meeting with the agile team and the business owners. The business owners have decided to use MoSCoW as a priority tool. What are the categories for this method?

    A. Priority 1, Priority 2, Priority 3, Priority 4

    B. Low, medium, high

    C. Must have, should have, could have, would like to have

    D. Point method, assigning the most points to the highest priority item

20. Agile teams use different methods to manage work in progress (WIP). What is a drawback of not having limits to WIP?

    A. There is typically enough work to keep everyone busy.

    B. It keeps the project moving forward.

    C. Too many tasks are taken on all at once.

    D. Fail to fully utilize everyone's availability.

Questions and Answers

1. You have been identified as a team member on a project. When you begin gathering requirements, what is a logical first question that should be asked and answered?

    A. How much is in the budget?

    B. How long will the project last?

    C. What is the business value?

    D. How many team members will participate?

C. The reason projects are carried out is to generate business value. The business risk and the impact of not undertaking the project must be considered. A, B, and D are incorrect because the budget, duration, and member participation will be determined once the value-driven delivery is identified.

2. You are the project manager of an agile project. An agile team's focus is to maximize value. When the team needs to make a decision , what question should be the first to be asked?

   A. How long will it take to test?

   B. Will the decision made derail the project?

   C. What will it cost in man hours?

   D. What is the value to the customer?

   D. The focus on delivering value drives many of the activities and decisions on an agile project. This is the crucial goal of many practices in the agile toolkit. A, B, and C are incorrect because answers to questions regarding duration, impact, and cost of the decision will be determined after the value to the customer is defined.

3. Most agile software developers use continuous integration tools to test code. These tools tell them whether the code passed or failed by communicating what status?

   A. Red-Yellow-Green

   B. Pass/Fail

   C. Go/No Go

   D. Red-Green-Refactor

   D. The process of writing a test that initially fails, adding code until the test passes, then refactoring the code is known as Red-Green-Refactor (or Red-Green-Clean).
   A, B, and C are incorrect because CI tools do not use these terms to communicate status.

4. The agile team for which you are the project manager has determined several key values to deliver to the customer. How should these tasks be tackled by the team?

   A. The tasks should be prioritized, tested, and delivered incrementally.

   B. The tasks should be delivered while in progress, whether tested or not, to gather feedback.

   C. The tasks should be delivered according to the project plan.

   D. All deliverables should be presented at the end of the project.

   A. One of the most important agile themes ties together many fundamental concepts, such as prioritization, incremental delivery, and test-driven development. This is an essential component of agile methods, and lends credence to the early delivery of business value.

B is incorrect because tasks should never be delivered before being tested. C is incorrect becauseagile projects don't utilize a project plan like predictive projects. D is incorrect because presenting all deliverables at the end of a project is setting up the entire project for failure.

5. The agile team for which you are the project manager has identified the highest-value features of the project and wants to deliver them as soon as possible. Why is this a good idea?

   A. It gets the features out of the way.

   B. The longer the project goes on, the value of a feature may be compromised.

   C. Delivering the most intense tasks could shorten the project duration.

   D. It proves the team's understanding of value.

   B. The longer high-value features take to deliver, the longer the horizon becomes for risks that can reduce value. Maximize success by delivering as many high-value features before things change. Value-driven delivery means making decisions that prioritize the value-added activities and risk-reducing efforts of the project, then accomplishing the tasks based on the priorities.
   A is incorrect because the goal isn't to simply get features out of the way, but to deliver value based on the prioritized backlog. C is incorrect because delivering intense tasks first doesn't support completing the requirements with the most value and won't necessarily shorten the project duration. D is incorrect because while understanding value is important, this doesn't best answer the question as delivering value.

6. As a member of the PMO, you have been analyzing upcoming projects and have identified one particular project that you believe project teams will push back on. You understand this project is meant to implement safety standards for an off-shore manufacturing plant. Some project teams may not understand the value of this project. How do you avoid a long, drawn-out process of getting this project approved to move forward?

   A. Attempt to make the teams understand why it is important

   B. Have the project outsourced to avoid the pushback

   C. Make the project mandatory

   D. Take the project off the list of projects for the year and try to implement it at a different time

   C. Assessing the value in financial terms is usually where a project begins. The organization would look at the financial ramifications of not undertaking a project, such as fines that might be assessed, lawsuits the business may be subjected to, and the risk of the business shutting down. To avoid spending time trying to make teams understand the project's importance (A), spending money to outsource (B), or worse, deferring the project to another time (D), the project should be marked as mandatory.

7. You have been tasked to evaluate the financial metrics of a potential project. You plan to evaluate the percent of the benefit of the investment to the money invested. This is which of the following financial assessment metrics?

   A. Net present value (NPV)

   B. Return on investment (ROI)

   C. Internal rate of return (IRR)

   D. Future value (FV)

   B. ROI measures the amount of return on an investment relative to the investment's cost. A is incorrect because NPV is defined as the present value of cash flow over a series of time periods. The drawback to using the NPV approach is that designating what the inflation rate and interest rate will be in the future is just a best guess. C is incorrect because IRR is the discount rate at which project revenues and project costs equal zero. When a company is selecting which project to invest in, it will calculate the expected rate of return for each project and select the one that is projected to yield the highest IRR. D is incorrect because future value determines what a present amount of funds today is worth in the future.

8. A great visual to see your project's progress is an earned value management (EVM) chart. Knowing that an agile project is different than a non-agile project in that the initial plan is likely to change, you still see a benefit in using this visual since an EVM chart is a forward-looking indicator and could be used to assist in predicting which of the following?

   A. Number of team members required

   B. Completion dates and final costs

   C. Quality of deliverables

   D. Timings to begin new iterations

   B. EVM looks forward, trying to predict completion dates and final costs, in addition to scope, schedule, and cost performance.
   A and D are incorrect because the number of team members and when iterations will start and stop are fluid dimensions and not easily tracked. Answer C is incorrect because quality of deliverables can be tracked, but not in an EVM chart.

9. When working on an agile project, "risk" most likely means something different than it does on a traditional project. Agile sees risks as potential events or circumstances that could have a negative impact on the project, whereas a non-agile project may define a risk as a "good risk" that could present opportunities for the project. How does an agile project deal with risk?

   A. The team identifies risks and then tackles them at the end of the project so that they can all be addressed at once in a separate task.

   B. The iterative nature of agile allows the team to schedule the high-risk activities early in the project so that they are tackled sooner rather than later.

C. The team keeps the risk-finding results within the team so that the team can address the risk without any outside interference.

D. Early in the project planning, to ensure that the project won't be cancelled, the team does not relate risks to value, so that there is no chance of showing how the project could be delayed or cost more than planned.

B. Iterative development allows high-risk work to be addressed early in the project, to avoid problems further down the road. Agile teams engage the development team, business partners, customers, and other relevant stakeholders to draw on lessons learned, risk logs, and likely risks for the project from multiple views. Risks are directly related to the value of the project, since negative risks will most likely add time, which relates to the cost of the project. A is incorrect because risks are reserved for the end of the project; in fact, high-risk items are often prioritized to determine project feasibility. C is incorrect because outside subject matter experts and stakeholders are often needed to contribute to risk management. D is incorrect because risks are assessed as anti-value, not ignored. A failure to address risk can actually cause project costs to increase.

10. The agile team you are working with has just finished an iteration and all tasks are completed. You are ready to move to the next iteration. How do you determine which iteration should be next?

A. The team follows the project plan developed early in the project.

B. The PMO has already determined how the project should progress.

C. The customer continuously prioritizes the backlog.

D. The team leader determines the next iteration.

C. The teams works through a list of items that have identifiable value and have been prioritized by the customer.
A is incorrect because agile teams understand that the plan developed in the beginning of the project is fluid and is subject to change, so trying to follow an early developed plan is probably not feasible. B is incorrect because the project management office doesn't determine how the project should progress. D is incorrect because the team leader doesn't determine the next iteration.

11. While meeting with the customers or business owners, they introduce several pieces of new functionality into the priority list. Since the deadline date cannot be moved out, how should the team react to these additions?

A. Stand firm and tell the customers the project will not be delivered on time

B. Be sure the customers understand that lower priority tasks or functionality may drop off the project completely

C. Cancel all vacations and days off and let the team know there will be many long days of work ahead to deliver the project on time

D. Agree with the customers to have all new items put into a separate category that will be completed if time allows

B. The agile team can certainly accept changes either early or late during the project duration because of the iteration methodology. But the team still needs to work within the timeframe and budget of the project, so the customer must understand that although the new pieces of functionality can be added to the project, it can only be done at the expense of a lower-priority work item. Agile teams are committed to being "agile," so dictating timeframes or lack of work/life balance are not part of the agile methodology. Project managers must not overwork the project team to maintain the pace of the project work. A is incorrect because lower-priority requirements should be dropped from the project scope to accommodate higher-priority items to balance the fixed constraints of time and costs. C is incorrect because it's poor management to cancel vacation days and time off as this will affect team morale and team support of the project. D is incorrect because requirements should be prioritized into the product backlog, not a separate list of requirements. The existing product backlog will already map to the fixed time constraint.

12. You are working with an agile team that is developing and delivering a software solution to your company's HR group. Several minimum viable product (MVP) releases are scheduled throughout the duration of the project. Why is this a good idea?

   A. To show the progress being made by the development team

   B. To enable the users to test the product for the development team

   C. To enable the business to begin to get value from the project prior to the project ending

   D. To shorten the duration of the project

   C. Incremental releases can allow for some ROI while the team develops the remaining functionality.
   A is incorrect because releasing the MVP is to deliver value, not to show the project progress is being made. B is incorrect because the software should be fully tested and functional before being released to the user community. D is incorrect because utilizing MVP releases will not shorten the duration of the project, since the MVPs are defined in the project life cycle.

13. The agile team you are working with utilizes a whiteboard and writes tasks on sticky notes. Initially, you feel like they've taken a step backward by not utilizing an electronic project planning tool. After a period of time, you come to value the whiteboard system more and more. Why do you think this method is beneficial?

   A. It is easy to disregard a sticky note and bypass a task.

   B. No one takes sticky notes seriously.

   C. It is visual, and at a glance shows the progress of the project.

   D. Many people have access to the board and can move notes to their advantage.

C. Since the whiteboard is usually located in the team's area, meetings can be held around the whiteboard and the team's WIP is easily visible along with any tasks that may be falling behind. It is also valuable to the business partner to see a growing collection of completed work. This is an example of a high-touch/low-tech tool.

A is incorrect because the whiteboard approach will utilize a pull system to pull the next prioritized item into WIP, not bypass the item. B is incorrect because agile teams consistently use sticky notes as part of the high-touch/low-tech tool. D is incorrect because the team follows the rules of the pull system and does not reorder the requirements or identified tasks.

14. Agile teams practice frequent verification and validation during and at the end of each iteration. Which one of the following is not a benefit of this method?

    A. It enables the team to catch mistakes and mismatched expectations early.

    B. It keeps everyone busy.

    C. It is easy to manage since there are multiple feedback loops.

    D. It reduces project cost overruns since mistakes are found early prior to additional tasks being built upon a faulty foundation.

    B. Busywork does not add value to the project.
    A, C, and D are incorrect because a key practice on an agile team is frequent verification and validation. Having a gap between requested and delivered features will lead to rework, project delays, and cost overruns. It is important to discover the discrepancy early to adjust the direction of the development. This method enables the team to catch mistakes and mismatched expectations early, is easy to manage because it provides multiple feedback loops, and reduces project cost overruns since mistakes are found before tasks are built upon a faulty foundation.

15. You are on an agile software implementation project with a very short deadline. How do agile teams shorten the time between identifying a defect and resolving the defect?

    A. Daily build and smoke tests

    B. Continuous integration

    C. Usability testing

    D. Exploratory testing

    B. Continuous integration executes far more tests per day than the other options, and less time passes before a problem is identified.
    A is incorrect because daily build and smoke tests don't shorten the resolution of a defect. C is incorrect because usability testing requires planning and participants to test the software. D is incorrect because exploratory testing allows testers to explore and test different facets of the software. Continuous integration is done several times throughout the day.

16. With all the different methods of testing, either a software or product deliverable, when should the team determine what method of testing should be performed?

   A. When the first iteration is complete

   B. When a deliverable is available for testing

   C. Before the product is developed

   D. At the end of the project

   C. If acceptance tests are designed before the development of a deliverable, you are more likely to end up with tests for the majority of the work.
   A, B, and D are incorrect because determining the method of testing after the project has started means you are trying to fit the developed product into a test scenario.

17. You've just completed a requirements-gathering session for an agile software implementation team. It became apparent that an outside vendor team must be brought onto the project. You are working with the legal department to draw up a contract for the vendor. What type of contract is best for an agile project?

   A. A contract that accommodates changes

   B. A fixed-price contract

   C. A graduated fixed-price contract

   D. A time and materials contract

   A. Agile contracts need to accommodate changes that take into account the difficulty of defining the requirements in advance.
   B, C, and D are incorrect because agile contracts can also be used with fixed-price, graduated-fixed price, and time and materials contracts, but with the understanding that they have some sort of limits, whether it be a fixed timeframe or dollar amount.

18. Approximately midway through an agile project, the business partner asks, "If we stick to the agreed-upon scope, when do you think the project will be done, and how much will it cost?" How will you gather the information necessary to answer the business partner?

   A. By reviewing the Kanban board

   B. By checking progress on the backlog

   C. By analyzing the key performance indicators

   D. By having a team meeting and logging everyone's status

   B. The most reliable metrics to use are the key performance indicators (KPIs). This will give you the rate of progress, remaining work to be completed, the likely completion date, and the likely costs remaining.
   A, C, and D are incorrect because the Kanban board, backlog, and statuses will give you only bits of information, whereas the KPIs will provide a broader picture of the project at any given time.

19. You are attending the kick-off meeting with the agile team and the business owners. The business owners have decided to use MoSCoW as a priority tool. What are the categories for this method?

A. Priority 1, Priority 2, Priority 3, Priority 4

B. Low, medium, high

C. Must have, should have, could have, would like to have

D. Point method, assigning the most points to the highest priority item

C. The MoSCoW method of prioritization labels tasks as must have, should have, could have, and would like to have but not at this time. Any method can be used on an agile project, but the MoSCoW labels are clear in many members' opinions.
A, B, and D are incorrect because they are not the MoSCoW categories. MoSCoW is a good method to avoid the tendency to label too many items as priority 1 or high priority or the most points assigned, which becomes ineffective. A business partner will rarely ask for a new feature to be assigned a lower priority, because they know it most likely won't get done. While point systems can be effective, MoSCoW challenges the stakeholders to identify priorities rather than assigning points.

20. Agile teams use different methods to manage work in progress (WIP). What is a drawback of not having limits to WIP?

A. There is typically enough work to keep everyone busy.

B. It keeps the project moving forward.

C. Too many tasks are taken on all at once.

D. Fail to fully utilize everyone's availability.

C. Without limits on WIP, a project team may undertake too many different tasks at once.
A is incorrect because there is typically enough work for everyone to contribute. B is incorrect because not setting a limit on WIP can cause too many tasks to be in motion at one time. D is incorrect because setting the WIP limit doesn't prevent everyone from contributing, but encourages the idea of generalizing specialists.

Managing Stakeholder Engagement

In this chapter, you will
- Define the nine exam tasks of stakeholder engagement
- Get stakeholders involved and engaged in the project
- Share the project vision for stakeholders
- Model an agile project with stakeholders
- Collaborate and communicating with stakeholders
- Define soft skills for stakeholder engagement
- Make effective project decisions

Think of all the people who are affected by your project and all the people who your project will affect: customers, the project team, management of your organization, the different employees in the organization that'll use your solution, vendors, and possibly many more types of people. All these people that are affected by your project and that can affect your project are *stakeholders*. Stakeholders have a stake in the project because it'll affect their lives, and some stakeholders have a stake in the project because they're involved with the project decisions and actions that'll affect the project's outcome. Stakeholders are the people that project managers and the development team communicate and collaborate with.

Stakeholder engagement, the primary topic of this chapter, is about getting stakeholders involved in the project and keeping them interested and excited about the project work. Stakeholders want information about your project, and often they'll be providing information to your project. In this chapter we'll explore everything about stakeholder engagement. Much of this chapter is related directly to the *PMBOK Guide, Sixth Edition*, and its chapter on stakeholder management. The big difference, of course, is that stakeholder engagement in agile projects is a bit different than in predictive projects.

For a more detailed explanation, watch the *Stakeholder Engagement in Agile Projects* video now.

This third exam domain, on stakeholder engagement, is the second largest exam domain for the PMI-ACP exam. This exam domain is worth 17 percent of your exam score, and you can expect about 20 questions on this topic. On your PMI-ACP exam look for any opportunities to get stakeholders involved, to communicate directly with stakeholders, and to keep stakeholders excited and happy about the project: that's the thrust of stakeholder engagement. Much of stakeholder engagement centers on project communications, so you'll see a good deal about communicating with people in agile projects too. This isn't a difficult topic to grasp, but there are a few terms and concepts I'll point out as you prepare to pass the PMI-ACP exam.

Introducing the Stakeholder Engagement Principles

One of the key principles of agile project management is that you work to keep stakeholders involved in the project. Stakeholders are represented by and work with the development team and the project manager. It's not an us-against-them mentality that sometimes creeps into predictive projects, but more of a sense of teamwork, partnership, and collaboration. We need the stakeholders, particularly the project customers (sometimes called the business people), involved to give quick feedback, provide insight, and keep the backlog of requirements prioritized.

For your PMI-ACP exam, this is the one exam domain that clearly overlaps with the *PMBOK Guide, Sixth Edition*. Chapter 13 in the *PMBOK Guide* is all about stakeholder management. There are four processes from project stakeholder management that you should be topically familiar with for this exam domain:

- **Identify stakeholders** This is an initiation process and aims to identify and document stakeholders in a stakeholder register. The stakeholder register helps you to know who's interested or concerned about what, their role and responsibility in the project, and to whom you'll communicate what information.

- **Plan stakeholder engagement** This is a planning process. While agile discourages lengthy planning documents, you still need a plan for how and when stakeholders will be engaged. While a predictive project may have an in-depth plan for every action and stakeholder objective, agile is more likely to have intent and a cadence defined for stakeholder engagement. Agile is more fluid when it comes to stakeholder engagement because of the agile mindset I discussed back in Chapter 1.

- **Manage stakeholder engagement** This is an executing process. Managing stakeholder engagement is about communicating with, not just to, stakeholders. It's getting stakeholders involved, being transparent about all project news, sharing the project vision, and building energy and interest by delivering value in the project.

- **Monitor stakeholder engagement** This is a monitoring and controlling process. You'll need to monitor stakeholder engagement to identify stakeholders who may have fading interest or are drifting away from their responsibilities. It's your job, as the project manager, to keep stakeholders engaged, but you'll also want the team to work with stakeholders to keep them interested and supportive of the project work.

The goal of managing stakeholder engagement is to keep stakeholders interested, excited, and involved in the agile project to bolster project success. When stakeholders don't live up to their obligations or if they lose interest, the project can stall or the team can move ahead without clear directions—and that's a formula for failure. One of the best ways to keep stakeholders engaged is to delivering value early and consistently.

Reviewing the Nine Tasks for Exam Domain III

The stakeholder engagement domain for the PMI-ACP exam has nine tasks divided into three subdomains. You'll want to look for answers that keep stakeholders engaged by creating a trusting environment, balancing their requests with value, costs, and efforts needed for the requests, and having a cooperative, agile spirit. Collaboration is key to the exam domain—work with the stakeholders, especially the customers, throughout the project life cycle to deliver value, be transparent with good and not-so-good news, and share information through tools like the information radiator. You'll also be tasked with making effective and informed decisions that will affect stakeholders.

Let's look at the three subdomains and nine tasks.

Understand Stakeholder Needs

Identify and engage effective and empowered business stakeholder(s) through periodic reviews in order to ensure that the team is knowledgeable about stakeholders' interests, needs, and expectations. Identify and engage all stakeholders (current and future) by promoting knowledge sharing early and throughout the project to ensure the unimpeded flow of information and value throughout the lifespan of the project.

Ensure Stakeholder Involvement

Establish stakeholder relationships by forming a working agreement among key stakeholders in order to promote participation and effective collaboration. Maintain proper stakeholder involvement by continually assessing changes in the project and organization in order to ensure that new stakeholders are appropriately engaged. Establish collaborative behaviors among the members of the organization by fostering group decision-making and conflict resolution in order to improve decision quality and reduce the time required to make decisions.

Manage Stakeholder Expectations

Establish a shared vision of the various project increments (products, deliverables, releases, iterations) by developing a high-level vision and supporting objectives in order to align stakeholders' expectations and build trust. Establish and maintain a shared understanding of success criteria, deliverables, and acceptable tradeoffs by facilitating awareness among stakeholders in order to align expectations and build trust. Provide transparency regarding work status by communicating team progress, work quality, impediments, and risks in order to help the primary stakeholders make informed decisions. Provide forecasts at a level of detail that balances the need for certainty and the benefits of adaptability in order to allow stakeholders to plan effectively.

Identifying and Engaging Project Stakeholders

Stakeholders need to be identified as early as possible in the project. It's no fun to overlook a stakeholder in the early stages of the project, make project decisions, even make some progress on the project work, and then discover you've missed involving a key stakeholder. Stakeholders that are overlooked in the project are probably not going to be happy about being overlooked and not being involved in project decisions, and you'll need to spend time catching them up on the project and explaining how the project will affect them.

You, the project manager, have the responsibility of identifying stakeholders. Sure, the project team and other stakeholders can help with the process, but determining who should be involved in the project is squarely on the project manager's shoulders. You'll also be constantly on the lookout for new stakeholders. Changes to the organization can certainly introduce new stakeholders that you'll need to quickly engage about the project and get them involved. You might also have new requirements added to the product backlog that will inadvertently introduce new stakeholders—that's another opportunity to identify and engage the right people.

Typical stakeholders in a project include

- **Customers** Anyone who will pay for and/or use the results of the project.
- **Project sponsor** The person with the authority to make big project decisions and authorize the project and grant the project manager control over the project resources.
- **Project leaders** Obviously this includes you, the project manager, but also includes people on the project team, consultants, and subject matter experts who'll make key decisions on the project work.
- **Development team** The people writing the code, also known as the project team.
- **Vendors** Any vendors who'll provide resources to the project are key stakeholders that need to be engaged and communicated with.
- **End users** Like the project customers, but they are ultimately the people who'll use the product your project is creating.

All of these stakeholders need representation in the project. Sometimes, like in big groups of users, a representative of the group will work with the project manager and the development team in the project. You might know the representative as the product owner, a proxy, or ambassador for the group of stakeholders. This person will make decisions on behalf of the group they represent, and they must be involved throughout the project—from initiating to closing.

 EXAM COACH Stakeholders need to be identified as early as possible in the project. If you identify stakeholders late in the project schedule, you're introducing risk to the project.

Starting at the Beginning

Stakeholder identification happens as early as possible in an agile project. Once you've identified the stakeholders, then you immediately work to engage the stakeholders. You want the stakeholders engaged and excited (both the customer and the development team) because they'll have a huge effect on the likelihood of project success. You must work to keep stakeholders engaged, not only to keep them excited and invested in the project, but so you'll know about change requests to the product backlog as soon as they happen. You don't want stakeholders, like the customer, to drift away and then rush back with a change to requirements that'll wreck weeks of work the team has completed.

At the beginning of the project you need to understand the customer's vision of the project result. Then you'll work with the customer to prioritize the requirements—this helps everyone involved understand what's important and how the requirements support the value the customer expects from the project. It's a simple formula: arrange requirements by value, then deliver those requirements.

Agile projects also aim to keep stakeholders involved throughout the project—not just during planning sessions. Consider in Scrum the sprint reviews, retrospectives, and planning meetings that take place. Key stakeholders can, and often should, be present to see how the project works, how the project team and the stakeholders collaborate on the project, and how everyone shows respect for one another. That's all part of the agile mindset, part of being agile, not just doing agile. With these meetings and participation also comes the need for courage to share ideas, share failures, and share a lack of knowledge and a desire to learn. Collaboration is paramount—we don't judge, but educate, seek to understand, and continue to be respectful of each other.

From the beginning of the project we also aim to combat the difference between what a stakeholder wants and what the project manager or project team understands. This misunderstanding is called the *gulf of evaluation*. When a customer has a vision in their mind's eye of what the deliverable will do, but the team misunderstands the deliverable, the team is likely to create something different than what the customer wanted. Upfront planning, interviewing, and modeling help to clarify the customer's wants and needs and convey that information so everyone has a clear understanding of what the result of the project must be.

Building Stakeholder Synergy

Synergy is a word we use a lot in agile project management. Synergy means that two or more organizations or people cooperate to create something greater than the parties could do on their own. Synergy means we, the project team and the project customer, work together to create something unique, effective, and powerful to gain value. In order to have synergy, the two parties have to trust one another, believe in one another, and be willing to have courage, respect, and collaboration.

I'm sure you've heard customers and project team members privately criticize one another, grumble about the other party, and have a "throw it over the wall" mentality. That's not agile and that mindset certainly won't help you on the PMI-ACP exam. Promoting synergy and stakeholder engagement doesn't mean that the project team and the project manager bow down and worship the project customer, but that all parties show respect for one another. However, for your exam, have the attitude that the team and the project manager are working to keep the customer happy while balancing the realities of what can be done within the fixed time and cost constraints.

One of the most effective ways to create synergy is to deliver value quickly to the customer. Once the customer sees that the team attacks the highest priorities first, creates value, and is producing a quality product that's in alignment with the customer's vision, they'll become excited and invested in the continued work of the project. With each increment, sprint review, or release, the customer's trust and belief in the project will continue to increase. This is a golden rule for the PMI-ACP exam: value is in working software, in the result we provide to customers. Value creates synergy and better cooperation.

Keeping Stakeholders Involved

Stakeholder engagement begins with identifying the stakeholders and then continues with stakeholder involvement throughout the project. The project manager and the agile project team collaborate with stakeholders, unlike the old command-and-control mentality of predictive projects. Stakeholders really become part of the effort—need to be involved in the project—for the project to be successful. Some stakeholders might resist this change and will need to be educated on how agile is different than predictive project management. Many stakeholders, however, will welcome this involvement and opportunity to see true progress and insight into the workings of an agile project.

The nature of agile projects aims to keep stakeholders involved through short iterations, frequent reviews, and demos of the work results. Stakeholders meet with the team and not through an intermediary project manager—and stakeholders need to be available for the project team to ask questions and get clarifications on requirements. It's a symbiotic relationship between all the project stakeholders: collaboration, communication, and participation. In the initial stages of the project, the project manager may have to facilitate the involvement, but over time (and with success) the collaboration will become second nature among the project team and the stakeholders.

There is a fine balance, however, between collaboration and customers getting in the way of project work. We don't want stakeholders interrupting the team for updates, but we do want the team available for input and feedback. That's part of the role of the project manager, to protect the project team, to provide information to stakeholders, but to allow stakeholders and the project team to communicate when needed. You'll need to caution everyone involved to avoid adding changes directly to the iteration or sprint backlog—something that's tempting to do when customers and stakeholders can chat at will. Changes are allowed, but only to the prioritized backlog, not to the work in progress.

Leading Stakeholder Conversations

Much of stakeholder engagement is communicating. Communication is paramount to all types of project management, not just agile, but agile has a different take on communications than does predictive project management. Predictive project management requires a communications management plan that defines who needs what information, when the information is needed, what's the expected modality, and how to secure and recall the communications. This involves lots of planning and more formality than in agile.

Agile project management communications still answer those questions, but much of the information is readily available for the customers to see through information radiators, sign boards, and the prioritized backlog. This doesn't mean the project manager gets to ignore stakeholders, but rather that stakeholders can visit the information radiator at any time to see what's happening in the project. The project manager still communicates with stakeholders through sprint reviews, product backlog prioritization meetings, and planning sessions. The project manager works with the stakeholders to regularly discuss the project vision, the definition of done, and the overall progress of the project. The conversations can be more ad hoc than the planned and staged communications in predictive project.

 EXAM COACH   Agile project managers may need to physically take stakeholders to the information radiator and explain that they can come see the information at any time.

Sharing the Project Vision

It's so important that all members of the project team and the project's customers have the same vision of what the project is creating. Everyone needs to participate in sharing the project vision—and that needs to be a centered, common message. There shouldn't be surprises at the end of an iteration—and certainly not at the end of a project. The customer and the development team will communicate with each other as well as with the project manager and consistently discuss the definition of done, the goals of the project, and the specifics the project will create.

As more and more information becomes available in the project, more and more detail can be discussed—that's progressive elaboration once again. Early in the project the team can help the product owner, or the customers, formulate what the solution will be. The customer may need your insight to better enunciate the goals, and this means that you, the development team, and a business analyst may get involved in eliciting the requirements. You may need to go and see the problem, experience the problem, to have a better insight as to what the project is aiming to solve or the opportunity the project should be creating.

Creating the Project Charter

In predictive projects the project charter is a document that comes from the project sponsor and authorizes the project and grants the project manager control over the project resources. It has some high-level goals, presents a summary budget, and really gets the project moving. In an agile project, the project charter is bit different. An agile project charter allows more flexibility than in a traditional project—and that makes sense, right? A predictive project charter already has a clear vision of what the project will create, while an agile project is more ambiguous and subject to change as requirements are developed and prioritized.

An agile project charter embraces the idea of change and that the value of the project is working software and in the creation of the shared project vision. The agile project charter does summarize the project's key success factors and should be displayed on a team wall for everyone to see daily. The project charter also defines any boundaries of the project and any agreements in place between the project team and the stakeholders. The project charter, at a minimum, should define:

- Who are the engaged stakeholders?
- What is the central goal of the project?
- Where will the project work take place?
- What are the project start and end dates?
- Why are we doing this project?
- What's the project methodology?

The project charter shouldn't be very long at all—short and sweet with room to change. A poorly written project charter can box in the development team and the product customer from solutions that'll work. The project charter can use these guidelines and formulate a quick "elevator statement" about the project, meaning the project goals, purpose, and characteristics are defined in the amount of time an elevator ride takes, about a minute or less. Other trends include creating a project tweet—like something you'd post on Twitter. A project tweet defines the project in 280 characters or less.

Defining Done in Agile Projects

A question I always ask in any project is "How will we know when we're done?" And then I ask "What does success look like for this project?" In an agile project, and for your PMI-ACP exam, you'll need to know the definition of done. Done means that the requirements have been met in alignment with the amount of time and the amount of monies available for the agile work. Done also means that there's a definition of finality to the project, the individual requirements, and all of the work that must happen in the project to satisfy the stakeholders' requests. This means the releases have been released, the deliverables have been transferred to operations, and all of the final reports and communications have also happened.

Agile projects move through phases of work, so there's a definition of done for each phase too. Consider the planning, the design, development, testing, continuous integration, builds, releases, resolution of bugs, limited support, and the stakeholder acceptance. Your organization may have different phases or terminology in the project, but each phase has its definition of done that must be met.

While it's easy to talk about the big picture of done in an agile project, you're also addressing that each user story, each requirement, passes the test of done. Done means that the entire user story or requirement is completely done so that the product owner can review the result and confirm that the result is acceptable. Agile teams should work through the definition of done on each requirement and then work to meet the definition of done throughout the project—not a mad rush at the end of an iteration to satisfy the definition of done. Teams should use a methodical approach to move to the definition of done throughout the iteration, not just at the end of the iteration.

Modeling in Agile Projects

Modeling means that you create a model of what the solution will look like. Rather than invest hours of developing and testing solutions, you, the development team, and the product owner work together to create a model or mockup of the solution. It's much faster (and easier) to draw and tinker with a solution on a whiteboard than to create code to find a solution that works. Agile modeling is not unlike the models you might see of a skyscraper an architect makes before the building is built. It's cost effective, saves time, and helps to solidify the vision of the project.

Agile modeling embraces the idea of barely sufficient and lightweight. Agile models are part of the project artifacts, so even a whiteboard sketch should at least have a photo to keep record of what's been agreed to or discussed. Models should be just barely good enough, simple, and follow the idea of just-in-time (JIT) when planning the project work. Architecture modeling or envisioning is best done at the start of the project and helps to reduce overall risk and waste in rework.

Agile project managers don't need to overcomplicate their models. Keep it simple. Agile modeling follows five principles:

- **Communicate**   Agile models help communicate ideas and solutions.
- **Simplify**   Take a complex idea and make it easier to understand.
- **Feedback**   It's a group activity, so feedback and conversation are part of the value.
- **Courage**   It takes courage to state ideas, be involved, and to try new ideas and let go of old ideas.
- **Humility**   Everyone, even the best developers, needs to acknowledge that they don't know everything and that we respect one another's opinions.

You'll typically work with stakeholders early in the project to do modeling. This builds a good foundation and creates shared ownership of the project. It enables people to see the concepts of the project and lets the team and the stakeholders work through the challenges, risks, and priorities of what the project aims to accomplish. Modeling can be done for the entire project, but it also can be done for just challenging portions of the project. Of course, the bigger the model the longer it'll take to create and work through the solution.

Creating Personas for Modeling

One of my favorite approaches to agile modeling is to think about the end user of the software or thing the development team is creating. A persona represents the typical user of the system and addresses that individual's needs, expectations, and how they'll use what you're creating. It's a fictional character description of real people and it addresses their needs, wants, and concerns about the solution. Here's a persona example for a mobile banking software:

Charlie Hertz   Charlie is a 50-year-old insurance salesman in Detroit, Michigan. He's been married for 20 years, has two kids, and is active in his community. He's a casual runner, plays golf, and likes to be outside as much as possible. Charlie doesn't want to be visiting the bank or stuck indoors on his computer to do some routine banking tasks. He wants to be mobile and do things on the go. Specifically, Charlie wants to be able to check his bank balance, track transactions, pay bills, make deposits, and review his bank statements all from his phone. It's all about convenience for Charlie—take care of banking tasks wherever he is located with a simple application. Charlie is concerned that his data and access to his accounts are secure—hackers and identify thieves scare him a bit from completely trusting mobile banking apps.

That's it. A persona gives a little sketch of the typical user's background, why they want the solution, how they'll use the solution, and what their primary concerns are. You can get as creative as you like with these—some teams even add a photo and more information, like the names of the persona's kids, what the family dog is like, and the type of car the persona character drives. You don't have to get that detailed with the persona, but it helps to understand who the solution is for and how the typical user will utilize the project deliverables.

 EXAM COACH   Personas help the project team and product owner identify requirements, not replace the requirements.

Utilizing Screen Designs and Wireframes

Screen designs are mock-ups of what the screen and interface will look like. It's nothing complicated—just a visualization of how the end result is going to look. The screen design can be created in PowerPoint or other software to show the product interface the end user will see. The screen design can have limited functionality so that the product owner can interact with the screen elements to an extent, but most of the time a quick sketch or mock-up of the solution is all that's needed.

Some development teams keep things simple and just create a screen sketch on a whiteboard or piece of paper. This approach is fast, easy to change on the fly, and accomplishes the same result as building out a crisper mock-up in software. During planning the team can draw the screen on a whiteboard, move things around, talk through the solution and user interface, and then, once everyone agrees on the design, take a photo to capture the requirements and agreements. There's nothing complicated about this approach.

Wireframes are a way of showing, not just telling. A wireframe is a simple, straightforward diagram that shows your solution. Wireframes often address:

- The different elements in the user interface
- Organization of screen and system components

- Navigation paths
- Feel of the user interface
- User interaction with the solution

Wireframes are just a quick mock-up of your solution, what you're creating the product. You could have actual screens and data flow between the screens be somewhat functional, but typically a wireframe is just a quick sample or even just a printout. It doesn't have to be anything fancy. The goal here is to ensure everyone understands what we're creating, so it's a low-fidelity prototype. (Know that wireframes are a low-fidelity prototype.)

Again, a wireframe doesn't have to be fancy, as in Figure 3-1, a little sketch of what you're creating. Now, I know some of you are saying, "Well, that's not how I do a wireframe. I draw out the screens and make it so you click around." That's fine, but for your PMI-ACP exam, wireframes don't have to be complex. Just a sketch could be a wireframe, and that's all you need to convey your idea.

Figure 3-1 Wireframes are just quick sketches to communicate a solution.

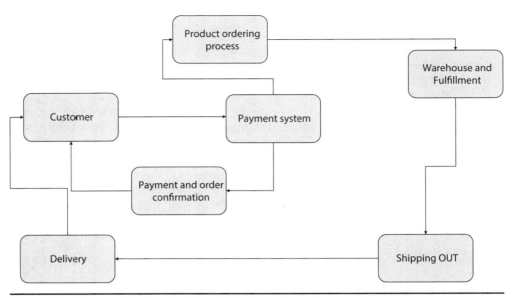

Figure 3-2   Data models show the flow of data through a system.

Working with Data Models

A data model is a data structure. It's just a way to organize your data. Consider making a data model of a new car: you have the engine, the exhaust system, four tires, and so on. Then you'd get more precise with the interior. You've got the front seat, the back seat, the trunk, and you can break those down even more. It's not about breaking down a product; it's just how you're organizing your data, how you're structuring data.

A sample data model is presented in Figure 3-2. This data model tracks the flow of data for a customer who's placing an order. There's lots of activity, lots of data moving around. When a customer orders the product, different roles and different systems are involved, such as the item inventory and the payment system. Then the item is packaged and delivered to the customer. A data model shows how data flows through the system.

Part of the purpose of a software data model is to help the designers think about how the user will interact with the solution. The designers must think of how the user interacts with the solution. User stories are product-focused, so we're promoting cooperation between the team and the product owner to understand what should go on the screen design.

The product owner and the team don't want to add cool features without thinking through the effect on the user. That would be scope creep—tiny changes that don't follow the agile project management approach. We don't want to get into these design black holes, where we add features without thinking through the value and effect on the user. Keep it simple, and only create value for the customer.

Exploring a Use Case Diagram

The whole point of a use case diagram is to model how the system works, including how people interact with the system. The team models the functionality of a system; use case diagrams use actors—the term for people in use cases—to show the activities that people involved with the system will do in their roles.

Use cases represent the actions, the services, and the functions of the system. Actors are the people and entities interacting with the system. A use case may show two systems talking to one another (for example, how a database communicates with a website or how an application sends messages between components), but for the most part, we're concerned with how people interact with the solution.

Figure 3-3 is a use case diagram. The main component of the use case diagram is the system, and it is a large rectangle. The actors are outside the boundaries of the system. Circles represent the usage of the system, functions, and activities. Actors are the users of the system, so one system could be an actor of another system. The relationships between the actors and systems are shown by a line between the actor and system.

In Figure 3-3, one actor is an hourly employee, another is a salaried employee, and a third is a commission-based employee. Each actor enters their time in the time management system, which in turn communicates with the payroll system. The commissioned employee interacts with the time management system to track his time, but also interacts with the purchase order management system because this employee gets a commission as part of sales.

Other actors include the payroll administrator and the bank. Although the bank is a whole system, not an individual, it interacts with the employee payroll system, so it's an actor too. The payroll administrator maintains the employee info and works with the activities, such as the payroll software and the banking system, to create payroll. That's a use case diagram. It's a robust drawing of all the components that interact with a system to capture requirements from each perspective of the people and other systems that will interact with each other.

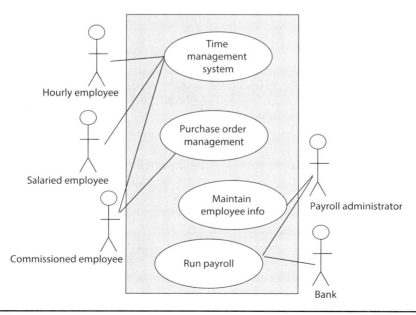

Figure 3-3   Use case diagrams show how people and systems will interact with a solution.

Managing Stakeholder Communication and Engagement

By now, you already know that communication is paramount in agile projects. We've reiterated this idea throughout this chapter. As an agile project manager, you must be honest and transparent in your communication. This requires you to do a little bit of planning when it comes to communicating with stakeholders. This communication approach is based on Chapter 10 in the *PMBOK Guide*.

While communications planning is not going to be to the same depth in an agile project as in a predictive project, you still need to plan some communication. Consider these planning concerns:

- What are the communication requirements?
- What do stakeholders expect when it comes to communication?
- What's the technology that will be used to communicate?
- How will you communicate?
- What are the different methods of communicating?

First up, consider formal and informal communication. Think about your different communication methods: hallway meetings, colocated versus non-colocated, face-to-face conversations, and written messages. Your avenues of communication affect how productive you may communicate. The modality of the message affects the effectiveness of the message, the meaning of the message. Obviously, we're going to have lots of meetings, so determine what regular meetings you can go ahead and schedule, and begin to create a cadence and a routine for these meetings. A schedule and a routine help you set expectations and get everyone involved.

You might be required to create a communications management plan. I say "might" because we know from earlier discussion that documentation is of little value in agile projects, but you might need a plan just to organize communications, especially if you're on an extensive project with many stakeholders that have different communication needs. Then, of course, you'll be updating your project documents as part of communication because agile requires transparency.

Technology also affects how effectively you can communicate. You don't want some people using text messaging if that communication isn't allowed based on the project, your enterprise, or because of enterprise environmental factors. So you and the team, especially a non-colocated team, will need to know which communication technology is approved. You'll define the e-mail or other messaging systems that the team should be using. You'll also have to specify if you're required to do reports and use specific forms in your organization.

 EXAM COACH   You can use the formula of N(N − 1)/2, where N represents the number of stakeholders, to identify the communication channels. For example, a project with 10 stakeholders would be 10(10 − 1)/2 for 45 communication channels. The bigger the project, the more complex the communication will be.

Planning Project Communications

Part of communicating with project stakeholders is performance reporting. Consider these questions when it comes to planning your stakeholder communications:

- Will you be required to do status reports?
- Are you using earned value management or other performance measurement approaches?
- Are there forms and templates you're required to use in your organization?
- How and how often will you communicate with stakeholders?

Communication in agile should not be complicated. If two people want to text one another because it's a quick way to get the answer to a question, they should go ahead—if your organization allows it. For your PMI-ACP exam, however, remember that face-to-face communication is always preferred. In an agile project, the team is ideally within 33 feet of one another. The team is all colocated, so they are face to face and can hear what others are saying, leading to osmotic communication.

Yes, this is a bit formal for your exam, but the common theme here, the overwhelming theme for your exam, is that you want transparent communication. We don't have to over complicate this; embrace transparency and openness, and the idea that a colocated team helps with communication.

You do have to control communication, and the information management system can help. An information management system is just a way of collecting, storing, archiving, retrieving, and searching all of what we've created in the project when it comes to communication.

Part of controlling communications is to utilize expert judgment. This is particularly appropriate when you have a project that has external stakeholders and there are regulations or laws that affect the project work, such as building a website for a government entity. Subject matter experts can consult with you about those regulations or laws, about what you can and can't communicate, or the security required for the website. There might also be complicated regulations in your industry where expert judgment can help you and the team make the best project decisions.

Obviously, meetings are a great way to control communications. If you have rumors and gossip surrounding your project, these are a distraction from value, and you'll have incorrect information being spread about the project. You'll need to bring everyone together and clear things up. This is part of being open and transparent, and though it may not always be pleasant, it's best to address issues head-on.

We know that in an agile project we welcome change. The product owner can add requirements to the product backlog. A change to the project can also stem from a change request on how you communicate. Stakeholders may tell you that they don't need a report every week, or that they want you to keep them updated on the WIP, number of defects, cumulative costs, or any other factor of the project. Such a request would require you to update your communication approach.

For your exam, you might encounter a question or two on the communication model. Figure 3-4 is the communication model you should know for your exam. We're going back in time here with the idea of a fax machine. Instead of a fax, it could be an e-mail, a

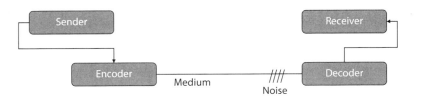

Figure 3-4 The communication model demonstrates how a message moves from the sender to the receiver.

text message, whatever you want, but the figure depicts the primary premise you need to know. In the communication model, we have a sender and a receiver. Suppose I'm going to fax something to you. I'm the sender, and I put my document in the fax machine, so my fax machine encodes it. Then the medium is the telephone line. Your fax machine's the decoder. It hears that analog signal over the medium and then it decodes it and puts it back into a readable format for you, the receiver. There are some other elements to consider. Noise could be static or a distraction. For example, we're having a face-to-face conversation and other people are talking around us, and I get distracted and I miss what you said. That's noise. Anything that distracts from the message or garbles up the message is noise.

A barrier prevents communication. For example, you and I are mad at each other and refuse to communicate. That's a barrier. Or, I speak only English and you speak only French. We may have trouble communicating, or not be able to communicate at all, because we don't speak the same language. Or your fax machine is out of paper, or you don't have a fax machine. That could be a barrier to that communication.

Leading Face-to-Face Communications

For your exam and your agile projects, remember that the best type of communication is face-to-face communication. Face-to-face communication is what's preferred. It has the highest "bandwidth" of all communication types, meaning it's the easiest and the most acceptable way to communicate ideas and messages. Face-to-face conversations provide verbal communication, nonverbal feedback, and opportunities for instant clarifications.

Let's consider the different types of communication channels and their effectiveness:

- **Face-to-face** This is the most effective communication.
- **Video conferencing** While video conferencing is good, it's not as effective as face-to-face.
- **Telephone calls** While not a poor way to communicate, you lose nonverbal clues and body language.
- **Two-way radios** These gadgets, like a walkie-talkie or a CB, aren't incredibly effective for communication. Not many agile projects use them.

- **Written documentation**   Letters, reports, and e-mail are somewhat effective, but can be time-consuming, can be easily misconstrued, and have no nonverbal clues and feedback on the message.
- **Unaddressed documents**   These are junk items, like spam e-mails, bulk e-mails, or even bulk mail, that are not effective.

The closer you are to the top of this list, the more effective your communication will be. Obviously, face-to-face communication is ideal and what we want in agile (and what your first choice should be on the PMI-ACP exam). If your team is not in the same room, then choose video conferencing, and if that's unavailable, then perhaps a teleconference would be your best bet.

EXAM COACH   Always consider that if you have a non-colocated team but you want to take advantage of face-to-face communication, you should rely on video conferencing first.

When it comes to two-way communication, there are two different models to consider: First is a dispatching model, also called top-down communication—for example, a memo from management to employees. Then there's the collaborative model, which is interactive; you are in the same room with your team and you're conversing with one another in a daily standup. The collaborative model, naturally, is more about collaboration. It's interactive communication between the sender and the receiver.

Sharing Project Knowledge

When we talk about communicating with stakeholders, we're specifically interested in learning what information they need and what's important to them. We're talking about sharing knowledge, about useful information, about being transparent. Well, that's what knowledge sharing is when it comes to your exam. It's directly tied to communications, but also to stakeholder engagement.

Knowledge sharing is critical to the success of the project. We're sharing that information with everyone involved, and we aren't trying to hide it. Transparency is something that we see in XP in the idea of collective code ownership. Collective code ownership means that any developer can edit any code at any time.

EXAM COACH   Agile practices, overall, promote knowledge sharing—embrace that concept for your exam.

We've talked about Kanban boards, information radiators, personas, and wireframes. Those are all means of knowledge sharing. Knowledge sharing means keeping things accessible and easy to understand; remember the mantra of low-tech/high-touch tools.

We want to keep things simple, not complex. I don't want a bunch of software to do a simple task. For example, you can get software for your phone to help manage the project, but for your exam, and really in your agile projects, you want low-tech/high-touch.

Another example of simple knowledge sharing is your daily stand-up meeting. This meeting is precise and should be to the point and face-to-face. Agile projects also promote osmotic communication. Recall that osmotic communication occurs when you hear what others are saying around you and you understand what they're talking about, even if you are peripheral to the conversation. You can learn just by hearing what others are saying. And then tacit knowledge is gained through individual experience and can be shared, but more effort is required. With tacit knowledge you can share individual experience by telling a story or recalling how you did work on a similar project.

Building an Information Radiator

When I was growing up, we had radiators in our old farmhouse. The radiators were hot—if you got too close to one you could burn yourself. Of course, that didn't stop me from sizzling and melting some crayons on these old, clunky radiators (until Mom saw the mess, that is).

Like an old radiator sends out heat, an information radiator sends out communication, but you must get close to it to see the information. An information radiator is a highly visible display of all the information in your project. A project's information radiator could be composed of graphs, bar charts, burndown charts, or your Kanban board. An information radiator is out in the open, and everyone can see it; it's easily accessible, not tucked away in a closet or displayed through some software. An information radiator might also be known as visual controls.

Information radiators can include any relevant information for the team and project stakeholders, such as the velocity, burndown chart, defect count, and the WIP. Information radiators typically include stats on features delivered versus features remaining, the current iteration, and the defect measurements. You can include any relevant information for the project that stakeholders have asked about or that you and the development team feel is vital information to share. This honest, open communication helps to engage the stakeholders—especially when you take the stakeholder to the radiator and show them that this is updated consistently and they're welcome to visit the radiator at any time.

Utilizing Social Media for Agile Projects

For your PMI-ACP exam be aware of the concept that you can utilize social media as part of your project communications and engaging with stakeholders. While you might not create a Facebook post to share specific project information, you might create a private group for your team on Facebook or LinkedIn to share information. Twitter, WhatsApp, Google Hangouts, and other technologies are all feasible ways to share project information—to some extent.

For public projects in your organization, you certainly might work with a communications department, specialist, or consultant to manage your public feed about the project. This is a great way to quickly distribute information to people who want the information. The problem with a public page (or other social media feed) is that it's *pull communication*—people have to visit the page to get the information. Sure, folks can create alerts and notifications of what's been posted, but it's a bit static from two-way communication. And don't forget someone has to maintain the site.

The trouble with using any social media platform for private messaging and project information is the risk of hackers, malicious behavior, and people accidentally sharing information to the whole world rather than only to your small group. Caution must be taken when using any social media platform—and that caution can slow the communication process. So, for your exam, know that social media is a viable option, but some risk avoidance needs to take place when considering sharing information through social media.

 EXAM COACH I doubt you'll see Facebook, LinkedIn, or Twitter on your exam, but you might encounter the generic idea of social media.

Collaborating with Stakeholders

A common theme we've seen throughout this chapter is that collaboration is key to stakeholder engagement. Recall from Chapter 1 that the Agile Manifesto promotes customer collaboration over contract negotiation. Agile projects are a partnership, a team effort. Business people and developers collaborate, and the project manager is not in a command-and-control position, but rather facilitates collaboration. Collaboration is a critical exam concept. Business people and developers work together daily throughout the project.

There are huge benefits to collaboration with all stakeholders. Collaboration generates wiser decisions. Through collaboration, developers understand what the business people want in the project. Collaboration leads to better problem solving, promotes action and synergy, and builds social capital. Social capital in turn helps strengthen a sense of community and encourages teamwork.

Collaboration also brings about united ownership of problems. We're not in separate camps about who's responsible for problems; we're all on the same team confronting a problem and trying to find a solution. Collaboration is also about engaging people. Engagement creates better ideas and promotes conversation. Through conversation we create active problem solving. We act; we have collective ownership not only of problems but also of ideas.

Collaboration also motivates and engages the team, and it shifts the power downward, which is part of the idea of servant leadership. Remember servant leadership from Chapter 1? As a servant leader, you "carry the food and water"; you're there to serve. You are there to help the project team and the stakeholders get what they need to get the project done.

Creating Red and Green Zones

As a project manager in an agile project, your leadership approach with your team should make them feel that they're in a safe environment, that they can explore, be innovative, be creative, and give honest feedback. A concept you'll want to know for your exam is that of a green zone versus a red zone and how each affects the project manager, the team, building consensus, and keeping people engaged.

Let's talk about the green zone first. As individuals in a green zone, we take responsibility for our actions. We respond non-defensively. If there is a problem or mistake, we own up to it and we don't get defensive. People in a green zone do not feel easily threatened. We understand that we're all on the same team, that we must not feel threatened just because someone else has a great idea that may conflict with our own.

In a green zone, the project manager and the dev team work together to build mutual success. The overall goal is to create a solution—not just to be correct, but to find the correct solution. If a team member thinks their idea is best, they are free to try to persuade others why they think it is best. You want people to be firm but not rigid in a green zone environment.

In a red zone, the focus is all about short-term and self-centered goals. A red zone encompasses all the bad stuff that can come with teams that aren't cohesive. People blame others and respond defensively. People feel threatened or wrong when others speak out against their ideas. People hold grudges, shame mistakes, blame everyone but themselves and accuse. People operating in a red zone experience binary thinking, which means they quickly decide that an idea is either all right or all wrong. People are all about the short term, not the long term. People tend to feel victimized, don't want feedback, and have an always-right attitude. People feel that they always must win no matter what.

In a red zone, people are rigid, reactive, and have no room for flexibility. There is a climate of antagonism, disapproval, and discontent. They see other people as the enemy, and do not listen effectively. Those are all things that we want to avoid in agile projects. We want to be in the green zone at all times, and never in the red zone.

 EXAM COACH You may see a question or two about green and red zones on your exam, and the answer should be *common* sense. You want the good attributes of a green zone, not the bad attributes of a red zone.

Hosting a Project Workshop

You may host a workshop in your agile project. A workshop brings people together to focus on how to best get project work done. Have you ever been to a workshop where it's a free-for-all, or everybody's sitting around chit-chatting? Nobody knows who's in charge, and the whole time you're thinking, "I have 100 things to do other than this. This is a waste of time." Or maybe you enjoy that occasionally as a little break from work, but it's not a successful workshop.

A workshop requires clear goals and a schedule. You must have an agenda and time allotments to work through the agenda items. Well-organized, effective workshops are a way to get work done. Some examples of workshops you'll experience in an agile project are the retrospective and planning meetings. You should think about your sprint planning meeting or even your product backlog as a potential workshop. You might also take your estimating sessions and make those workshops. For example, you could think about the duration or the size of user stories and complete that group activity in a workshop.

A good idea for a workshop is to have a diverse group of people. You don't want just the project team in the workshop. You want different stakeholders, including the product owner. People who have different points of view may contribute from their perspective. The workshop needs to be facilitated to ensure participant involvement. Facilitation means that you call on people and bring them into the workshop conversation. You want to get people involved early and keep them involved. One thing you can do is an icebreaker session or quick activity that involves everyone in the room. For example, an ice breaker could be writing your project tweet with the team or discussing about what's happened, good or bad, in the project so far. But your goal is the get people involved early, so they know participation is welcome and encouraged. This isn't a class. This is participation.

Brainstorming Ideas

A term I'm sure you're familiar with is brainstorming. Brainstorming is a collaborative effort where we all get together and try to throw out as many ideas as possible about a solution. One rule of brainstorming is that we don't set a limit. Faulty brainstorming requires that everyone must come up with a set number of ideas. The first problem with this rule is that people typically become fixated on coming up with the minimum number of ideas instead of writing down any and all ideas that occur to them. The second problem is that if an individual can only come up with one or two ideas, they'll create irrelevant ideas that don't contribute.

 EXAM COACH   Avoid the notion that a brainstorming session should set a limit or a minimum on the number of ideas people contribute. You want as many ideas as possible.

Brainstorming can be a free-for-all, but it must be nonjudgmental. When someone throws out an idea, we don't laugh or smirk or say, "That's not going to work." No idea is stupid. You write everything down on a whiteboard regardless of your opinion. Even if something isn't appropriate for the project. An item can trigger other thoughts and good ideas for project solutions. One person's imperfect suggestion or comment can help other people have a perfect comment or suggestion. Brainstorm right now and sort through the ideas later. Write them all on the board without judgment.

There are three different methods of brainstorming you want to be familiar with, described next.

Quiet Writing

Quiet writing is a brainstorming exercise that individual team members perform prior to the group brainstorming session, so that everyone comes into the meeting with ideas that can elicit group input. The advantage to this approach is that it gives you an opportunity to focus on just your own ideas before proposing them to the group. The drawback is that the group brainstorming session tends to be less spontaneous and interactive because everyone is bringing fully formulated ideas to the meeting.

Round-Robin

Round-robin meetings go around the table and each person gives one idea. Each idea is considered, written on the whiteboard, and then the next person offers an idea. This continues around the table until everyone has contributed their ideas and all ideas are documented and discussed. You can also introduce a round-robin hybrid approach by utilizing quiet writing first and then doing the traditional round-robin approach. Participants first write down their ideas in a list, then each person around the table shares one idea until all ideas from each person has been shared, discussed, and documented.

Free-for-All

This is my favorite brainstorming approach. A free-for-all approach is where everyone comes to the meeting and throws out as many ideas as possible. I like that type of session because you can learn from each other and hear what ideas make people think of other ideas.

Playing Collaboration Games

Collaboration games, also known as innovation games, are a way of using games to help your team identify requirements. These are activities to help your team come up with a solution or to identify causal factors, or what's holding the project back.

The first game to know for your exam is called Remember the Future. It involves collaboration with your team and key stakeholders. The participants pretend that the project has been completed and that they are looking back at the project retrospectively. Their task is to take (for example) 20 minutes to write a report about how the project went. The participants should think about what went well, what threatened the project success, and issues that weren't managed well. This game is a way of anticipating what's going to happen in a project. You're pretending like you're in the future looking back on the project.

At the end of the exercise, you document the ideas, both good and bad, on sticky notes. You take the sticky notes and create an *affinity diagram*, a diagram on which you group similar ideas or clusters of ideas together and then remove any duplicates. This is a way of defining success by clearly defining what equates to the project being done (definition of done) and identifying potential risks in the project before the project work gets underway.

Another collaboration game is an activity called Prune the Product Tree. It's not a prune tree or a fig tree, but a drawing of a big tree. The trunk of the tree is what you already know about your project or what you've already built. Then you draw branches off the tree, and you add sticky notes of ideas or new requirements on the branches. For example, new functionalities that are related could be one branch. Another branch could be all about data. Another branch could be all about the Internet. A branch could be about the software itself. The closer the items are to the trunk, the higher the priority. It's just a way of organizing project requirements and concerns on the illustration. This allows you to trade off and organize your thoughts.

Another collaboration game to know for your exam is the speedboat game, sometimes called the sailboat game. In this activity, you pretend that you're on a boat that represents your project. And you say, "Well, what winds are pushing this project along? What anchors are holding our project back? What's the direction of the sailboat? And are there any rocks or other impediments in the way?" It's a game to explore the pros and cons of your project and forces for and against your project.

 EXAM COACH Know these collaboration games for the PMI-ACP exam. You'll probably see at least one type of collaboration game on your exam.

Applying Soft Skills for Agile Projects

Have you ever heard the expression that the soft stuff is the hard stuff? In the context of project management, or management in general, it means that developing good soft skills is often the hardest part of managing. The people skills, the interpersonal skills, are easy to discuss and understand but often difficult to implement. We're talking about emotional intelligence. Emotional intelligence is the ability to understand your own emotions, understand the emotions of others, and control your emotions and influence the emotions of others.

Active listening is a soft skill. It means that when you're in a conversation, you're involved; it requires your participation, and dialogue with your stakeholders. As a project manager of an agile project, you also need some facilitation techniques. We talked about the different meeting types and the need as project manager to be able to facilitate these meetings, keep things on schedule, timebox the event, and keep people involved.

Negotiation is another soft skill you need as an agile project manager. You need to be able to give and take in negotiations with the team and stakeholders, and be able to lead conflict resolution. You'll also want to facilitate decision-making, which means getting the team involved in participatory decision-making, rather than approaching the team with a command-and-control mindset. Agile emphasizes the important responsibility of the project manager to get people involved and get their opinion and feedback.

While you don't need to study all of the characteristics of emotional intelligence for your exam, you'll need to know some topical information to answer questions about interpersonal skills. You likely know that emotional intelligence affects every aspect of your life, not just your project. It's how you behave and how others behave. It's how you understand your emotions and control your reactions. Emotional intelligence also means that you understand the emotions of others, the causes of emotions, and the underlying factors of the emotions. Emotional intelligence helps you to identify who you are and what your values are, which in turn helps you to better interact with others.

Exploring Emotional Intelligence Foundations

To be an effective project manager, you'll need to have emotional intelligence for yourself and for the people you'll deal with. For your exam, you need to know that emotional intelligence has four quadrants:

- Self-management
- Self-awareness
- Relationship management
- Social awareness

First off, self-management means that I can manage my emotions, that I have self-control. I'm conscious of how I'm behaving, and making corrections when needed, so that I'm not offensive, brash, or foolish when interacting with my team or stakeholders. Self-management means that I can adapt my emotions based on the circumstances. Self-management affects my drive and motivation and my ability to get things done in my life.

Self-awareness is related to self-confidence, but also requires emotional self-awareness. It's the confidence to ask questions such as, "Why am I feeling this way? Why am I upset? Why am I angry? Why do I not care?" That type of introspection is all part of emotional self-awareness, and it leads to accurate self-assessment. Self-awareness causes me to pause, to use some logic and reason to understand my current emotion. It's the connection between the head and the heart.

Relationship management is part of emotional intelligence. Agile projects require that you work well with others, so you need social skills to communicate and keep the project moving along. As a project manager, social skills are necessary to help you foster the development of other team members and to express that you're about teamwork, collaboration, and acting as a servant leader.

Having social awareness means you have empathy for others, you understand where others are coming from, and you understand what's important in your organization. You understand the environment that you're operating in as a project manager.

Those are the four quadrants of emotional self, and you can see how those intersect in Figure 3-5. You have awareness of yourself and others and you have the skills to manage yourself and your relationship with others.

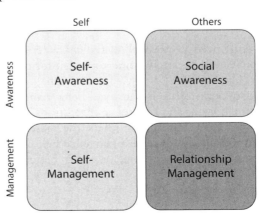

Figure 3-5 There are four quadrants of emotional intelligence.

Listening Actively

You know that effective communication is a very important aspect of being a successful project manager. In fact, it's been said in academic studies that 90 percent of a project manager's job is communicating. But a big portion of communicating is listening. Hearing and listening are not the same thing. Hearing means you hear the noise, the words, without really considering the message. Listening is the reception and understanding of what's being said. Listening is really understanding what someone is trying to say.

There are three levels of listening you want to recognize for your exam:

- **Level one (internal listening)**   You're hearing words, but you're not very attentive. For example, you're watching TV during a phone conversation, or you're in a meeting but are texting on your phone. Internal listening means you listen to what's being said, you interpret the meaning, and you think, "Okay, how is this affecting me?" You're not thinking broader than just about yourself. Level one isn't ideal.

- **Level two (focused listening)**   You're paying attention and listening to the speaker's perspective. We can empathize with the speaker as they are sharing bad news or telling a sad story, or whatever is being said. In a group setting, you take into consideration that the speaker might not be comfortable with public speaking but is in front of this group trying to convey a message. You're listening and picking up on not only the words but also the nonverbal language like facial expressions and gestures. You're paying attention to paralingual aspects such as the speaker's pitch and the tone, the emotional indicators.

- **Level three (global listening)**   Built on top of level two, it's a higher level of awareness. You're looking for subtle clues about the meaning, such as the speaker's posture and energy. The speaker can pause in their message and that can add drama and emphasize a serious point. This variety in speech helps us to understand a fuller context of the message, so that's global listening.

Negotiating with Project Stakeholders

As an agile project manager, you also need to be familiar with negotiation. Negotiation is about both parties working together to get good results. There are different types of negotiation, but ultimately the goal is a win-win resolution. In negotiation, we have to consider the priorities of the customers, the priorities of the product backlog, and the priority of the project. We need to understand what's contributing to the value of the project.

A principle in project negotiations is that we want to avoid any zero-sum type of negotiation in which only one person gets their way. For example, a stakeholder demands that you add a long list of requirements to the project scope. Of course, you're okay with that, but you'll need to either shift some things out of scope or request more time and more money. Now imagine that the stakeholder demands that you add these new requirements to the scope without shifting anything out of scope, and refuses to give you more time or money. That's zero-sum. That's not a healthy negotiation.

A healthy negotiation involves give and take, has tradeoffs, distributes risk, and considers each other's perspective. Think about collaborating with the customer. You create options for the customer, and you don't push everything into one solution. You need some objective criteria from the customer, such as time, cost, and scope, but you discuss the tradeoffs for an agreeable solution. You and the customer define what's valuable, what requirement or change is more important than other requirements. You also can incorporate the MoSCoW approach to consider if the change and the existing requirements are a must have, a should have, a could have, or a would like to have.

Resolving Conflicts

The PMI-ACP exam expects you to understand several conflict resolution methods. You may already know them from studying for the PMP or CAPM exam, but they are applicable to conflict resolution in agile projects too, so you should review them here.

First, is withdrawal. One way to resolve a conflict, at least temporarily, is to *withdraw* from the situation and avoid further discussion. One party simply says, for example, "Let's discuss this later after we've cooled off" and leaves the room. This method requires a healthy level of emotional intelligence. *Smoothing* in conflict resolution means to accommodate. For example, two people are in a heated argument, and the project manager comes in and says, "Hey, let's settle this for a little bit. It's not that big of a difference. I know that you like Oracle, Bob, and that you like SQL, Sally, but they're both databases. For now, let's just agree that we need a database in our solution and we can decide later which one to use." The project manager has downplayed the issue or even delayed the issue to keep things moving on. That's smoothing, and the person exercising the smoothing technique doe not consider the substance of the he disagreement in any depth.

Resolving a conflict through compromising or reconciliation means that both parties agree to give up something. Revisiting the example from the previous section, the customer wants to add more things to project, but won't flex on the scope, time, or cost. You often have to compromise. You can add things to the project, but the customer must agree to shift the scope or add more time and more money. Compromise is both parties give up something. It's a lose-lose.

Forcing or *directing* the resolution of a conflict occurs when a person with authority forces their opinion on a subordinate. Sometimes a project manager has to resort to this authoritarian style of conflict resolution if it is the only way to fulfill a project requirement, such as compliance with a safety regulation that is burdensome to the team. *Collaboration* is the ideal method of conflict resolution. Collaboration means that two people can be in disagreement but still work together peaceably to problem solve. The people are working together for the best solution for the project. To collaborate is a win-win. We don't care who's right or wrong. We want the best solution.

 EXAM COACH   A self-led and self-directed agile team may have a conflict, but it's not immediately up to the project manager to find a resolution. Allow the team to work out the solution; it's part of their responsibility.

Facilitating Project Meetings

As an agile project manager, you have to facilitate meetings. Facilitation is all about running effective meetings—not just running the meeting, but making it effective for the participants. Effective meetings have specific goals and a plan to reach those goals, and they create value for the participants. You'll start with an agenda that defines the goals of the meeting. We want to stay away from waste of time (WOT) meetings. Get people involved, knock out the goals, and move on.

To have an effective meeting, you have to set ground rules. For example, my number one rule of meetings is, we start on time and we're going to end on time, if not earlier. And so if that meeting's at nine o'clock and you're not there at nine o'clock, I'm not waiting. We start at nine o'clock. We have an agenda, we get it done, and we get on with our day. When people are late a few times, they'll quickly learn that you don't wait for them. It's incredibly rude to keep a room full of people waiting. I don't.

Another rule of an effective meeting is to define the timing. A meeting can be 15 minutes, an hour, or whatever's appropriate for your meeting; just set expectations and then live up to them by timeboxing the meeting. Schedule enough time for the contents of the agenda; don't block an hour and then fill your agenda with non-value-added chatter.

Project managers also can make the meeting effective by ensuring that everyone contributes. Facilitation means that when someone's hogging the time in the meeting, you have to gently rein them in: "Okay, I appreciate your input, lots of important things to say. We've got other people who want to talk too, so let's table that for now." Or "We'll talk about that later." Or "I think we've got it." Simply choose a nice way of saying "wrap it up and move on." Sometimes in standup meetings, you get people who want to give a minute-by-minute reenactment of what they did yesterday. You can't allow that. You need to permit only a quick summary and then move on to next person. Facilitation is about keeping things moving and getting everyone involved that needs to be.

There are four types of scrum meetings you want to know for your exam:

- **Daily Scrum or standup meeting**   As introduced in Chapter 1, a 15-minute meeting in which each team member states what they did yesterday, what they're doing today, and whether there any impediments to their work.

- **Sprint planning**   Planning for what we're going to accomplish in this sprint.

- **Sprint retrospective**   Discuss improvements for the next sprint by reviewing what did and didn't work well in the previous sprint. It's not to place blame or accuse people, but an honest review of issues and how we may improve in the project.

- **Sprint review**   A discussion of the actual work results from the previous sprint. Product demonstrations happen in the sprint review.

Making Effective Decisions

To make good decisions, we need to make valuable decisions that create or protect the value of the project. In agile projects, we're all about collaboration, so this means we utilize participatory decision-making, where participants are involved in the decisions.

To make participatory decisions, we have to get stakeholders involved, so this is part of stakeholder engagement. You're going to communicate with the stakeholders that this is a group decision. Invite them to discuss the decision, and get their input and ownership of contributing to the decision.

Decision-making is important. We want people involved; we value stakeholders' opinions. This is part of the collective ownership of our project. Stakeholder involvement and support will increase as they commit to the project. If stakeholders are kept outside of the project, and only the project manager or a few key team members make all the decisions (which is not how agile works), stakeholder excitement and synergy are going to diminish. Effective and valuable decisions mean that you keep all stakeholders involved.

A project manager can take either of two roles when it comes to decision-making. One is an authoritarian role that dominates the project, which is not a role you want to take as an agile project manager. This approach is self-centered, command and control. No one is allowed to question what the project manager has been decided.

The other role is a participatory role, which you do want to take in agile projects. A participatory role is more about team involvement, where everyone contributes. This is especially effective with a smaller team because it makes it easier to work out issues and come to grips with decisions. This is a collaborative approach. People can influence authority, and it's not command and control. It's participatory. As a project manager, you want to keep people involved and create a sense of community, synergy, and involvement. That makes people excited about your project, and they'll take pride in the ownership of their work.

Empowering the Project Team

Empowering the project team contributes to keeping everyone involved in participatory decision-making. An agile team is a self-organizing team. The team comes together and decides who's going to do what in each iteration or each sprint. The team members need to know that they are empowered, especially if they are new to agile. The team needs clarity and needs to understand that they have permission to be self-organizing, to be empowered, to do the work, and to be creative and innovative.

The team also needs the ability to organize the project work and their roles. If they don't have the skills to be self-led and self-organizing initially, then training or coaching needs to happen. Team members need to know that as part of agile they have the authority, sometimes called "the agency," to make decisions. That position of authority is granted to every project team member. The project manager is not in command and control, but rather it's up to the team to get things done.

Agile teams also need to have a sense of safety, meaning that if things don't go well, they know that as project manager you're going to protect them and acknowledge that they already had permission to experiment and possibly fail. Agile teams know that there are not going to be repercussions if they try something and it doesn't work. Agile teams need to have confidence in their abilities, but also confidence in the system and the processes.

That brings us to the subject of shared collaboration and convergent collaboration. Convergent collaboration involves participatory decision-making, as discussed earlier. All opinions and ideas are considered, and the decision converges from several sources. Shared collaboration means people are sharing in the decision-making fairly, where it's not two or three people that are the lead developers, but rather everyone gets to contribute and their opinion matters. This is team empowerment, because the team is leading the conversation, not the project manager.

Leading Participatory Decision-Making

There are several different techniques that you can use to make decisions as a group. The first one is simple voting. You and the stakeholders vote on a topic, such as a requirement or an approach, with a yeah or nay or a show of hands.

An approach I suspect you'll see on your PMI-ACP exam is Fist of Five voting, in which the number of fingers that you show demonstrates your degree of support for a decision. Showing all five fingers means you're really support it, while showing just one finger means your support is minimal. There is a variation of this approach where you show a closed fist if you're strongly opposed to the decision. So if anyone's showing their fist, the project manager should ask why the person is showing their fist. It opens the conversation.

The Fist of Five approach also requires a synchronized vote. Everyone votes on the count of three, for example, then you tally up the score. Having everyone vote at once keeps people from adjusting their show of fingers based on how other people vote.

A similar approach is to vote with a thumbs up to indicate support for the decision or a thumbs down to indicate that you don't like it. This approach also can include the option to show a sideways thumb to indicate that you are neutral or undecided. It provides an option beyond the binary choice of being either for or against a decision. A sideways thumb option also gives the voter the opportunity to voice their concerns or ask for clarifications about the topic.

Another technique for group decision-making is to use the Highsmith Decision Spectrum, which shows a spectrum of possible choices from in favor to opposed. Participants put a check mark on the spectrum to indicate how they feel about a particular idea. People can vote in private so that they aren't influenced by the group; then the project manager tallies the votes.

Chapter Summary

Stakeholders are all of the people that are affected by your project and that your project may affect. Stakeholders include the project manager, project sponsor, project team, product owner, business people, inspectors, government officials, customers, vendors, and all the groups of people your project will interact with at some point. Stakeholder engagement, the theme of this chapter, is about getting the right stakeholders involved with your project to help your project team reach the definition of done. It's about communicating with the stakeholders, sharing information, being transparent, and keeping the project moving along by working with the people responsible for decisions and actions in the project.

In this chapter we discussed the nine tasks and three subdomains for engaging stakeholders in an agile project. Recall that these nine tasks will equate to 17 percent of your PMI-ACP exam—that's roughly 20 questions you'll be faced with for the exam. So, while this concept isn't the largest domain, it's the second-largest domain on the exam. The principles of stakeholder engagement deal with creating and sharing the project vision, collaboration, and communication with stakeholders throughout the project.

Early in the project you'll need to identify stakeholders so that you get these people engaged in the project and contributing their project information, making decisions, and helping to identify and prioritize the project requirements. You'll keep stakeholders engaged through communication, participation, and synergy on the project. Synergy means that the stakeholders feel a sense of project ownership, that they're part of project decision-making and will help contribute to the project deliverables and balance the scope with the amount of time and costs available in the project.

In this chapter, we also discussed the project charter and how it addresses the stakeholders, the goal of the project, where the work takes place, the timing of the project work, and why the project is happening. The project charter in an agile project is different than in a predictive environment. A predictive project charter is about authorizing the project manager and the project, while an agile project charter is more about the vision and acknowledges the ambiguous nature of the project at its onset. The agile project charter summarizes the key factors of success, but leaves room for changes and specifics to be in the prioritized list of requirements.

Modeling in agile projects is an approach that creates a simple and quick model or mockup of the project solution. An agile model communicates the project purpose and simplifies the complexity that may be hidden in the code of the project deliverable. One agile modeling technique utilizes personas, fictional narratives of typical users of the project deliverables. Personas show what the typical user is like, their concerns, and why they'll use the project deliverables. We also discussed wireframes and screen designs as an agile modeling technique to share information through a low-tech/high-touch tool. Other modeling types we discussed include data models and use case diagrams.

So much of managing stakeholders is based on effective project communication. This includes how the project manager and the project team interact with the stakeholders, keep the stakeholders involved in the project, and participate in active listening. Project communication also includes some emotional intelligence—which is the ability to control our emotions, understand the emotions of others, and influence how others may react to project situations. The communication model defines the sender, receiver, encoder, decoder, medium, noise, and barriers—something you should recognize for your exam. The goal of this chapter is to capture and address all of the aspects of stakeholder engagement and project communications. Spend a little extra time becoming familiar with the key terms for this chapter—they're sure to be on your PMI-ACP exam.

Key Terms

Active listening   Active listening is conversational. The message receiver is paying attention to the sender and is involved in the conversation. Active listening means it's a dialogue and the sender and receiver are listening to each other and confirming the understanding of the message being offered. Active listening is to really hear what's being said.

Agile modeling Agile modeling is way to illustrate solutions and ideas. There are five principles of agile modeling: *communicate* ideas and solutions; *simplify* a complex idea and make it easier to understand; give *feedback* to the sender of a message as part of the conversation; foster *courage* to state ideas, be involved, and to try new ideas and let go of old ideas; and express *humility*, as even the best developers need to acknowledge that they don't know everything and respect one another's opinions.

Agile project charter An agile project charter allows more flexibility than a charter in a traditional project because an agile project is more ambiguous and subject to change as requirements are developed and prioritized.

Barrier A barrier is anything that prevents communication from occurring, such as speaking different languages or an error with the technology used in the communication.

Collaboration Collaborate means two people or groups can be in disagreement, but it's not heated and they work together for a good, viable project solution.

Collective code ownership Collective code ownership means that any developer can edit any code at any time.

Communication model The communication model describes how information is transferred between people in any communication modality.

Compromise Compromising means that both parties have to give up something as part of the conflict resolution. Compromising is lose-lose.

Customer A project customer is anyone who will pay for and/or use the results of the project.

Data model A data model is a structure with which to organize your data. The data model designers must think about user interaction in the software.

Decoder A decoder, part of the communication model, is a device, such as the receiver's e-mail system, that decodes a coded message back into useable information.

Definition of done The definition of done describes what constitutes done for any element of the project and for the project as a whole. The project manager and team consider planning, design, development, testing, continuous integration, builds, releases, resolution of bugs, limited support, and stakeholder acceptance when defining done.

Elevator statement An elevator statement is a quick definition of the project goals, purpose, and characteristics that can be expressed in the amount of time of an elevator ride, about a minute or less.

Encoder An encoder, part of the communication model, is a device, such as an e-mail system, that encodes the message to be sent.

End users End users are similar to the project customers but are ultimately the people who'll use the product your project is creating.

Face-to-face communication   Face-to-face communication provides the highest "bandwidth" of all communication types, meaning it's the easiest and the most acceptable way to communicate ideas and messages.

Fist of Five voting   Fist of Five voting is a participatory decision-making technique where participants show their degree of support for a decision by displaying the corresponding number of fingers. Showing all five fingers means total support, while showing just one finger means low support. A variation of this approach allows participants to show a closed fist if they are strongly opposed to the decision.

Focused listening   Focused listening, which is level two of the three levels of listening, is where you're paying attention and listening to the speaker's perspective. You can empathize with the speaker. You are listening and picking up on not only the words but also the nonverbal language like facial expressions and gestures. You're paying attention to paralingual aspects such as the speaker's pitch and tone, the emotional indicators.

Forcing   Forcing the resolution of a conflict occurs when a person with authority forces their opinion on a subordinate. Sometimes a project manager has to resort to this authoritarian style of conflict resolution if it is the only way to fulfill a project requirement, such as compliance with a safety regulation that is burdensome to the team.

Free-for-all approach   A free-for-all approach is a brainstorming technique where everyone comes to the meeting and throws out as many ideas as possible.

Global listening   Global listening, which is level three of the three levels of listening, involves an even higher level of awareness than focused listening (level two). You're looking for the subtle clues about the meaning, such as the speaker's posture and energy.

Green zone   Individuals in a green zone take responsibility for their actions, work collaboratively, and respond non-defensively.

Highsmith Decision Spectrum   The Highsmith Decision Spectrum is a group decision-making technique that presents the group with a spectrum of possible choices from in favor to opposed. Participants then put a check mark on the spectrum to indicate how they feel about an idea. People can vote in private so that they are not influenced by the group; then the project manager tallies the votes.

Identify stakeholders   The first of the four processes in stakeholder management is to identify stakeholders. This is an initiation process and aims to identify and document stakeholders in a stakeholder register.

Information radiator   An information radiator is a highly visible display of all the information regarding your project. A project's information radiator could be composed of graphs, bar charts, burndown charts, or your Kanban board. An information radiator is out in the open, and everyone can see it; it's easily accessible. An information radiator might also be known as visual controls.

Internal listening   Internal listening is level one of the three levels of listening and means you're hearing words but you're not very attentive.

Manage stakeholder engagement The third of the four processes in stakeholder management is to manage stakeholder engagement. This is an executing process. Managing stakeholder engagement is about communicating with, not just to, stakeholders. It's getting stakeholders involved, being transparent about all project news, sharing the project vision, and building energy and interest by delivering value in the project.

Medium The medium, part of the communication model, is the intermediary device(s) that carries the message between the communication parties.

Monitor stakeholder engagement The fourth of the four processes in stakeholder management is to monitor stakeholder engagement. This is a monitoring and controlling process in which you monitor stakeholder engagement to identify stakeholders who may have fading interest or are drifting away from their responsibilities.

Noise Noise, part of the communication model, is anything that distracts from the message, such as static on a phone call.

Persona A persona represents a typical user of the system and addresses that individual's needs, expectations, and how they'll use what you're creating. It's a fictional character description of real people and it addresses their needs, wants, and concerns about the solution.

Plan stakeholder engagement The second of the four processes in stakeholder management is to plan stakeholder engagement. This is a planning process. While agile discourages lengthy planning documents, you still need a plan for how and when stakeholders will be engaged.

Project leaders Project leaders include the project manager, people on the project team, consultants, and subject matter experts who'll make key decisions on the project work.

Project sponsor The project sponsor is the person with the authority to make big project decisions and authorize the project and grant the project manager control over the project resources.

Project tweet Like a Twitter post, a project tweet defines the project in 280 characters or less.

Prune the Product Tree Prune the Product Tree is a collaboration game that uses an illustration of a tree to demonstrate the priorities and requirements of the project. The trunk of the tree is what you already know or what you've already built. Then you draw branches off the tree, and you add sticky notes of ideas or new requirements on the branches. The closer the items are to the trunk, the higher the priority.

Quiet writing Quite writing is a brainstorming technique where participants complete brainstorming as a solo activity before a meeting. Participants then come into the meeting already prepared with their ideas for group discussion.

Receiver A receiver, part of the communication model, is the person who receives the message from the sender.

Red zone   In a red zone the focus is all about short-term and self-centered goals. The red zone encompasses all the negative aspects that may come with teams that aren't cohesive. People place blame and respond defensively. People feel threatened or wrong when others speak out against an idea. People hold grudges, shame mistakes, and accuse. People operating in a red zone experience binary thinking, which means it's all right or all wrong. A red zone is antithetical to the agile mindset.

Relationship management   Emotional intelligence quadrant that requires people to work with others to communicate and keep the project moving along. This means that as a project manager you use your social skills to help develop others, promote teamwork, foster collaboration, and act as a servant leader.

Remember the Future   Remember the Future is a collaboration game involving the project team and key stakeholders in which the participants pretend to look back at the completed project. Participants take (for example) 20 minutes to write a report about how the project went. The participants imagine what went well, what threatened the project's success, and issues that weren't managed well. This game is a way of anticipating what's going to happen in a project.

Round-robin   Round-robin is a brainstorming technique where the facilitator goes around the room and asks each person to give one idea. Each participant offers one idea until all ideas have been given and documented. There can be several rounds of this approach in the process.

Screen design   A screen design is a mock-up of what the screen and interface will look like. It is a visualization of how the end result is going to look. The screen design can be created in PowerPoint or other software to show the product owner the interface the end user will see.

Self-awareness   Self-awareness is an emotional intelligence quadrant that means one has the confidence to ask why they are feeling an emotion, such as being upset or angry or not caring. Self-awareness causes a person to pause and use logic and reason to understand their own emotions.

Self-management   Self-management is an emotional intelligence quadrant that means one can manage their emotions. It requires being conscious of how you are acting and behaving and then making corrections when needed. Self-management means that a person can adapt their emotions based on the circumstances. Self-management affects drive and motivation and the ability to get things done.

Sender   A sender, part of the communication model, is the person who is sending the message to the receiver.

Smoothing   Smoothing in conflict resolution means you accommodate the conflict in order to move forward. A person exercising the smoothing technique does not consider the substance of the disagreement in any depth.

Social awareness   Social awareness is an emotional intelligence quadrant that means you have empathy for others, you understand where others are coming from, and you understand what's important in your organization. You understand the environment that you're operating in as a project manager.

Speedboat game   The speedboat game (or sailboat game) is a collaboration game in which participants pretend that they're on a boat that represents their project. The facilitator asks, "What winds are pushing this project along? What anchors are holding our project back? What's the direction of the sailboat? And are there any rocks or other impediments in the way?" It's a game to explore the pros and cons of your project and forces for and against your project.

Stakeholder register   The stakeholder register is a document that helps you know who's interested or concerned about what, their role and responsibility in the project, and to whom you'll communicate what information.

Synergy   Synergy is the cooperation of two or more organizations or people to create something greater than the parties could do on their own. Synergy means we, the project team and the project customer, work together to create something unique, effective, and powerful to gain value.

Thumbs up/thumbs down   Thumbs up/thumbs down is a participatory decision-making technique in which participants show a thumbs up to indicate support for the decision or a thumbs down to indicate opposition to the decision. An additional option is to allow participants to display a sideways thumb to indicate they are neutral or undecided.

Use case diagram   A use case diagram models how a system works, including how people interact with the system. Use case diagrams include actors, which are the people and other entities, to show the activities that people involved with the system will do. Use cases represent the actions, the services, and the functions of the system.

Vendor   A vendor is any entity that will provide resources to the project. Vendors are key stakeholders that need to be engaged and communicated with.

Wireframe   A wireframe is a simple, straightforward diagram that shows your project solution. Wireframes often address the different elements in the user interface, screen and system organization, navigation paths, user interface look and feel, and user interaction with the solution.

Withdraw   One way to resolve a conflict, at least temporarily, is to withdraw from the situation and avoid further discussion. One party simply says, for example, "Let's discuss this later after we've cooled off" and leaves the room. This method requires a healthy level of emotional intelligence.

Questions

1. You are on an agile team that includes many stakeholders who have not worked with an agile project in the past. Several stakeholders have some valid concerns about some agile methods. How can you make them more comfortable with the process?

   A. Explain that it has worked in the past

   B. Tell the concerned stakeholders that this is how all future projects must be executed

   C. Educate stakeholders, address their concerns, and keep them engaged

   D. Manage their expectations

2. Why is it so important to incorporate multiple touchpoints with stakeholders before, during, and after iterations?

   A. To hear about change requests and identify potential risks and issues

   B. To inform all stakeholders of the development team's direction

   C. To demonstrate the team's value with multiple meetings

   D. So the stakeholders understand everyone is working hard

3. A new stakeholder has joined your team. He is having a hard time focusing on really engaging with the team since his daily responsibilities are taking a lot of time. You've spoken with the team member's manager about this issue, but no solution has yet been proposed. What could the team do to help alleviate the problem?

   A. Pitch in to help the stakeholder get his daily job done

   B. Overload the stakeholder so he can't work on his daily responsibilities until the weekend

   C. Pay for a temp or contractor to take over his daily responsibilities to free him up to work on the project

   D. Go to his boss and explain how this is creating problems for the team

4. How do agile project charters differ from non-agile project charters?

   A. Agile charters set forth high-level goals, whereas non-agile charters are very detailed.

   B. Agile charters name team members, whereas non-agile charters define teams.

   C. Agile charters define the definitive outcome of the project, whereas non-agile charters define the desired outcome.

   D. Agile charters define a stable project plan, whereas non-agile charters outline a high-level project plan.

5. An essential discussion that should take place early in the project is the definition of "done." Why is this critical?

   A. This allows team members to negotiate the meaning of "done" early in the project.

   B. New tasks can be unveiled while discussing the meaning of "done."

   C. All stakeholders must understand fully what "done" means so there are no surprises at the last minute.

   D. To continue to define the meaning of "done."

6. During an agile team meeting, there seems to be a misunderstanding of the requirements of a screen being developed. A team member begins to draw a wireframe of the screen on the whiteboard. What is the purpose of the wireframe?

   A. To test the design

   B. To determine what reports will be included in the output of the design

   C. To get a consensus regarding the content and flow of the design

   D. To understand how long the design will take to develop

7. Agile teams very often create personas to help the team move forward in a project. Which of the following is the best description of a persona?

   A. A persona is a high-level discussion of requirements.

   B. A persona helps the team empathize with the users of the solution.

   C. A persona is a new role developed to engage the stakeholders.

   D. A persona is an image that helps communicate what the result of the project is.

8. Which of the following is the preferred method of communication?

   A. E-mail

   B. Instant messaging

   C. Face to face

   D. Conference calls

9. Your agile team leader encourages knowledge sharing at which of the following points of a project?

   A. When someone shows an interest in a task

   B. At the end of an iteration

   C. Throughout the entire project

   D. At the end of the project

10. You are a new project manager in your organization and your manager has asked you to read the Agile Manifesto. Since working collaboratively is highlighted in several parts of the Agile Manifesto, you find that your leader fosters the practice of engaging stakeholders much more frequently than you have seen in the past. How is this beneficial?

    A. The team receives better input and ideas, develops better problem-solving skills, and becomes more willing to take ownership.

    B. All stakeholders get to know each other better.

    C. The stakeholders stay in their swim lanes rather than being called out from overstepping.

    D. The frequent meetings are a good break from heads-down work.

11. Which of the following is the definition of a workshop?

    A. A gathering where delays are explained

    B. A meeting discussing why the last iteration was a success

    C. A meeting discussing what progress has been made

    D. A meeting defining activities and contributions

12. Why is it important for an agile leader to continuously improve their emotional IQ?

    A. Emotional intelligence enables the agile leader to manage their own emotions and others' emotions.

    B. The leader's emotions have a direct impact on the deliverables.

    C. Agile projects are often changing, so the leader should have the skills to gauge the productivity of the team.

    D. The agile leader should continuously improve their IQ.

13. When your agile leader sends meeting invitations, the goals, rules, timing, and the meeting agenda are all clearly defined. Why is this practice highly beneficial?

    A. You know you can schedule another meeting 15 minutes after this one ends.

    B. There is no ambiguity about why the meeting was scheduled.

    C. You know that at least for this timeframe you won't have any phone calls.

    D. You can ask another team member a question that they have not yet responded to.

14. A disagreement about a project requirement has been brewing on your team. You've noticed that the agile leader is not taking any action to resolve this disagreement. What might be the agile leader's reason for keeping their distance for now?

    A. The leader wants the people involved to try to resolve the difference themselves.

    B. The leader doesn't know the answer or where to find the answer.

    C. The leader's friend is on one side of the disagreement.

    D. The leader is waiting for the point at which the team blows up to intervene.

15. Since agile leaders are not project dictators, how are decisions made?

    A. The most senior member of management makes the decisions.

    B. The stakeholders collectively agree on and share decisions.

    C. The business partners make decisions.

    D. The development team typically makes decisions.

16. A decision needs to be made by the agile team. Someone on the team suggests saving time by skipping discussion and using a show of hands to indicate whether team members are for or against the decision. What would be the most legitimate reason to object to this decision-making approach?

    A. You are concerned some members will vote for the cheapest way to resolve the issue.

    B. You are concerned some members will vote for the fastest way to resolve the issue.

    C. You are concerned some members will not vote for the decision you want.

    D. You are concerned that there will be no ideas for a better alternative to the decision.

17. A decision needs to be made by the agile team. The team decides to go with the decision model of thumbs up/down/sideways. You can assume what the thumbs up and thumbs down indicate, but you've never seen the thumbs sideways vote. What does this mean?

    A. Team members with thumbs sideways don't care either way.

    B. Team members with thumbs sideways have a question that needs further discussion.

    C. Team members with thumbs sideways can't make up their minds.

    D. Team members with thumbs sideways don't have enough knowledge to vote.

18. Why is it important that all stakeholders are involved in decision-making?

    A. So they attend meetings

    B. So they can tell their management it was their decision

    C. So they are committed to the decision

    D. So they don't condemn a decision that wasn't theirs

19. Your agile leader has invited all stakeholders, including customers and sponsors, to scheduled planning meetings. All of the following choices are valid reasons for this invitation except for which one?

A. To hear all their concerns

B. To be sure all priorities are being addressed by all involved in the project

C. To uncover issues

D. To determine success or failure of a project member

20. How does your agile team leader ensure that stakeholders stay engaged?

A. Replace the first person who is not staying engaged in the team to set precedence

B. Report anyone who is not staying engaged to the person's manager

C. Report on benefits or issues regarding specific stakeholder involvement in status reports

D. Don't invite anyone who is not staying engaged to subsequent meetings

Questions and Answers

1. You are on an agile team that includes many stakeholders who have not worked with an agile project in the past. Several stakeholders have some valid concerns about some agile methods. How can you make them more comfortable with the process?

A. Explain that it has worked in the past

B. Tell the concerned stakeholders that this is how all future projects must be executed

C. Educate stakeholders, address their concerns, and keep them engaged

D. Manage their expectations

C. Once stakeholders show concern about the methods used on an agile project, the most effective way to put their fears to rest is to educate them and keep them involved in the project as it progresses. During an iteration, decisions are made with stakeholders' input, the team does some work, and when the iteration is coming to an end, the team gets back together with the stakeholders to show them the progress that was made.

A and B are incorrect because telling stakeholders that this process has worked in the past or this is the way of the future will not allow them to buy into the process. Most people need to see it to believe it. D is incorrect because, although always a good idea, managing expectations is not the best way to get people to be more comfortable with the agile approach.

2. Why is it so important to incorporate multiple touchpoints with stakeholders before, during, and after iterations?

    A. To hear about change requests and identify potential risks and issues

    B. To inform all stakeholders of the development team's direction

    C. To demonstrate the team's value with multiple meetings

    D. So the stakeholders understand everyone is working hard

> **A.** Meeting with the stakeholders often will ensure that the team hears their change requests and identifies potential risks and issues. Agile methods allow these multiple touchpoints in the methodology.
>
> B is incorrect because telling the stakeholders the direction the development team is going isn't part of an agile team's way of doing things. Incorporating stakeholders' ideas and values means making sure nothing is planned without the stakeholders' support. C is incorrect because scheduling multiple meetings doesn't demonstrate value. D is incorrect because telling the stakeholders that the project team is working hard isn't as valuable as the team creating results—that's what stakeholders want and value in the project.

3. A new stakeholder has joined your team. He is having a hard time focusing on really engaging with the team since his daily responsibilities are taking a lot of time. You've spoken with the team member's manager about this issue, but no solution has yet been proposed. What could the team do to help alleviate the problem?

    A. Pitch in to help the stakeholder get his daily job done

    B. Overload the stakeholder so he can't work on his daily responsibilities until the weekend

    C. Pay for a temp or contractor to take over his daily responsibilities to free him up to work on the project

    D. Go to his boss and explain how this is creating problems for the team

> **C.** Very often, the people selected to be on an agile project team are the busiest people in the organization because of their knowledge. But the team needs members who can most effectively help the team to understand the requirements and make the critical decisions. It might be beneficial for the project to pay to have someone take over the stakeholder's daily responsibilities to free up time to devote to the project.
>
> A is incorrect because the team cannot pitch in to help the stakeholder, which would compound the problem as then their work would slip behind schedule. B is incorrect because overloading the stakeholder would force him to decide where to place his time and is contrary to agile principles. D is incorrect because his manager is aware of the issues.

4. How do agile project charters differ from non-agile project charters?

   A. Agile charters set forth high-level goals, whereas non-agile charters are very detailed.

   B. Agile charters name team members, whereas non-agile charters define teams.

   C. Agile charters define the definitive outcome of the project, whereas non-agile charters define the desired outcome.

   D. Agile charters define a stable project plan, whereas non-agile charters outline a high-level project plan.

   A. An agile project and a non-agile project both have the same general goal, but the level of detail in an agile project is different. Since agile methods often involve technology or requirements that are uncertain and outcomes that cannot be definitively defined, the agile project charter has less detail than a non-agile project charter. The agile charter is a living document and subject to change as the project progresses.
   B, C, and D are incorrect because they are incorrect statements about agile project charters.

5. An essential discussion that should take place early in the project is the definition of "done." Why is this critical?

   A. This allows team members to negotiate the meaning of "done" early in the project.

   B. New tasks can be unveiled while discussing the meaning of "done."

   C. All stakeholders must understand fully what "done" means so there are no surprises at the last minute.

   D. To continue to define the meaning of "done."

   C. Defining "done" is critical for satisfying all stakeholders' expectations and to ensure everyone agrees as to what success is.
   A and B are incorrect because the definition of done is not meant to be used to negotiate new functionality or ideas, or to unveil new functionality at the last minute. D is incorrect because the definition of done isn't an evolving concept, but defines done for all elements of the project.

6. During an agile team meeting, there seems to be a misunderstanding of the requirements of a screen being developed. A team member begins to draw a wireframe of the screen on the whiteboard. What is the purpose of the wireframe?

   A. To test the design

   B. To determine what reports will be included in the output of the design

   C. To get a consensus regarding the content and flow of the design

   D. To understand how long the design will take to develop

C. Gaining consensus regarding the content and flow of a piece of software by developing a wireframe will confirm everyone has a complete understanding of what the output will entail.

A, B, and D are incorrect because wireframes are not detailed enough to test the design, determine what the output reports will be, or understand how long the build will take.

7. Agile teams very often create personas to help the team move forward in a project. Which of the following is the best description of a persona?

A. A persona is a high-level discussion of requirements.

B. A persona helps the team empathize with the users of the solution.

C. A persona is a new role developed to engage the stakeholders.

D. A persona is an image that helps communicate what the result of the project is.

B. Developing a persona for a project helps the team understand what the users of their solution need and how the solution will be used in real-life situations.

A, C, and D are incorrect because a persona is not a discussion of requirements, a role to engage stakeholders, or an image that helps communicate what the result of the project is; rather, it is a tool to help understand why a particular solution is required.

8. Which of the following is the preferred method of communication?

A. E-mail

B. Instant messaging

C. Face to face

D. Conference calls

C. Face-to-face communication provides the best opportunity to ask questions, get immediate feedback, and understand body language in order to acknowledge agreement or clarify misunderstandings.

A, B, and D are incorrect because, although these communication methods can be effective, they should be used only when a face-to-face discussion is not feasible.

9. Your agile team leader encourages knowledge sharing at which of the following points of a project?

A. When someone shows an interest in a task

B. At the end of an iteration

C. Throughout the entire project

D. At the end of the project

C. Knowledge sharing throughout the project ensures information is not in any one person's possession.

A, B, and D are incorrect because sharing information only when it is asked for or at the end of an iteration or the project is a certain setup for failure. At that point, it will be time consuming and costly to unravel mistakes.

10. You are a new project manager in your organization and your manager has asked you to read the Agile Manifesto. Since working collaboratively is highlighted in several parts of the Agile Manifesto, you find that your leader fosters the practice of engaging stakeholders much more frequently than you have seen in the past. How is this beneficial?

   A. The team receives better input and ideas, develops better problem-solving skills, and becomes more willing to take ownership.

   B. All stakeholders get to know each other better.

   C. The stakeholders stay in their swim lanes rather than being called out from overstepping.

   D. The frequent meetings are a good break from heads-down work.

   A. Many agile practices are based on a collaborative approach, which enables the team to share ideas, hear input and feedback from all stakeholders, and take ownership of successes and failures because they've participated in the decision. B is incorrect because stakeholders get to know each other's abilities and quirks by simply working together daily. Stakeholders in an agile project will learn that to have a successful project, there needs to be a highly collaborative team in place. D is incorrect because while some people will like meetings as a break from the work, that's not the best answer for this question.

11. Which of the following is the definition of a workshop?

   A. A gathering where delays are explained

   B. A meeting discussing why the last iteration was a success

   C. A meeting discussing what progress has been made

   D. A meeting defining activities and contributions

   D. Retrospectives, planning meetings, and estimating sessions are all examples of workshops. Workshops are designed for active participation by all stakeholders to uncover issues and make the process more understandable and simple.
   A, B, and C are incorrect because they are definitions of other types of meetings.

12. Why is it important for an agile leader to continuously improve their emotional intelligence?

   A. Emotional intelligence enables the agile leader to manage their own emotions and others' emotions.

   B. The leader's emotions have a direct impact on the deliverables.

C. Agile projects are often changing, so the leader should have the skills to gauge the productivity of the team.

D. The agile leader should continuously improve their emotional IQ.

A. An agile leader needs to be able to understand when team members are upset, angry, frustrated, or stuck in order to coach and assist them to a favorable outcome. When a leader walks into the team's area and starts to vent about something, the team will easily replicate the leader's emotion.
B is incorrect because emotional intelligence does not have an impact on the deliverables, but on the people creating the deliverables. C is incorrect because while agile projects do change often, the point of emotional intelligence isn't to gauge productivity. D is incorrect because the leader needs to continuously work on their emotional intelligence for the success of the team, which is different than just the leader's emotional IQ.

13. When your agile leader sends meeting invitations, the goals, rules, timing, and the meeting agenda are all clearly defined. Why is this practice highly beneficial?

A. You know you can schedule another meeting 15 minutes after this one ends.

B. There is no ambiguity about why the meeting was scheduled.

C. You know that at least for this timeframe you won't have any phone calls.

D. You can ask another team member a question that they have not yet responded to.

B. Stakeholders need to know that the leader is not calling a meeting just to waste their time. Including in the invitation the meeting's goals, ground rules (such as no cell phones or being late), timing, etc., assures stakeholders that it is a structured meeting that won't be a waste of time.
A, C, and D are incorrect because they are only incidental benefits of a detailed meeting invitation.

14. A disagreement about a project requirement has been brewing on your team. You've noticed that the agile leader is not taking any action to resolve this disagreement. What might be the agile leader's reason for keeping their distance for now?

A. The leader wants the people involved to try to resolve the difference themselves.

B. The leader doesn't know the answer or where to find the answer.

C. The leader's friend is on one side of the disagreement.

D. The leader is waiting for the point at which the team blows up to intervene.

A. A good agile leader evaluates the level of the disagreement and allows the team members to resolve the differences themselves if it is still at a manageable level. This will build the team members' support for the decision and respect for each other.

B is incorrect because an agile leader isn't expected to intervene if the team is attempting to be self-directed and resolve issues. C is incorrect because an agile leader doesn't takes sides based on friendship. The leader needs to take emotion out of their involvement and not take sides no matter who is on the team. D is incorrect because an agile leader steps in to diffuse a disagreement before it spirals out of control. The agile leader knows that conflict is often good and a self-directed team is empowered to make decisions in the project.

15. Since agile leaders are not project dictators, how are decisions made?

    A. The most senior member of management makes the decisions.

    B. The stakeholders collectively agree on and share decisions.

    C. The business partners make decisions.

    D. The development team typically makes decisions.

B. Agile methods foster team empowerment, which increases stakeholders' need for effective decision making. There are two methods by which this can be accomplished: collective agreement, where the team agrees with the decision or approach, and a shared decision, which means the team and the stakeholders arrive at decision together, rather than one party making the project decision. A, C, and D are incorrect because decisions are made by the whole project team, not just the most senior member of management, business partners, or the development team.

16. A decision needs to be made by the agile team. Someone on the team suggests saving time by skipping discussion and using a show of hands to indicate whether team members are for or against the decision. What would be the most legitimate reason to object to this decision-making approach?

    A. You are concerned some members will vote for the cheapest way to resolve the issue.

    B. You are concerned some members will vote for the fastest way to resolve the issue.

    C. You are concerned some members will not vote for the decision you want.

    D. You are concerned that there will be no ideas for a better alternative to the decision.

D. With just a "for" or "against" vote, there will be no discussion that might produce a better or alternative decision for the issue. Without a discussion, people won't know why a decision should be made for or against a particular solution.

A and B are incorrect because these answers don't address the primary issue of not allowing conversation regarding the decision (besides, voting for the cheapest or quickest way to resolve an issue is not in the best interest of the project or the stakeholders). C is incorrect because you want the team to make the best decision for the project, not the solution that you are in favor of.

17. A decision needs to be made by the agile team. The team decides to go with the decision model of thumbs up/down/sideways. You can assume what the thumbs up and thumbs down indicate, but you've never seen the thumbs sideways vote. What does this mean?

  A. Team members with thumbs sideways don't care either way.

  B. Team members with thumbs sideways have a question that needs further discussion.

  C. Team members with thumbs sideways can't make up their minds.

  D. Team members with thumbs sideways don't have enough knowledge to vote.

> **B.** Team members who have a thumb sideways vote have a concern or conflict with the decision and would like to discuss it further.
> A, C and D are incorrect because a sideways thumb doesn't mean that the person doesn't care, can't decide, or doesn't have enough knowledge to vote.

18. Why is it important that all stakeholders are involved in decision-making?

  A. So they attend meetings

  B. So they can tell their management it was their decision

  C. So they are committed to the decision

  D. So they don't condemn a decision that wasn't theirs

> **C.** If stakeholders are not involved in decision-making, they will not be committed to any decision made and subsequently will not be committed to the project.
> A, B, and D are incorrect because the reason for involving all stakeholders in decision-making isn't to get them to attend meetings, to enable them to take credit for decisions, or to prevent them from condemning decisions.

19. Your agile leader has invited all stakeholders, including customers and sponsors, to scheduled planning meetings. All of the following choices are valid reasons for this invitation except for which one?

  A. To hear all their concerns

  B. To be sure all priorities are being addressed by all involved in the project

  C. To uncover issues

  D. To determine success or failure of a project member

> **D.** The point of inviting the stakeholders to these meetings is not to determine the success or failure of a project team member.
> A, B, and C are incorrect because they are all valid reasons for the invitation. Agile methods emphasize bringing project priorities into alignment with stakeholders' priorities. Agile projects do not plan or initiate work that the stakeholders don't support or value.

20. How does your agile team leader ensure that stakeholders stay engaged?

   A. Replace the first person who is not staying engaged in the team to set precedence

   B. Report anyone who is not staying engaged to the person's manager

   C. Report on benefits or issues regarding specific stakeholder involvement in status reports

   D. Don't invite anyone who is not staying engaged to subsequent meetings

C. Reporting on stakeholders' contributions and giving credit where credit is due in a status report or steering committee report will keep their involvement visible and help maintain their interest and encourage further engagement. A, B, and D are incorrect because eliminating a person from the team or meetings or "tattling" on the stakeholder is not the right approach to take in this situation.

Leading Team Performance

In this chapter, you will

- Define the nine exam tasks of team performance
- Explore the concept of valuing people over processes
- Form the agile project team
- Lead the project team through the work
- Build a collaborative team space
- Monitor team performance
- Calculate team velocity per iterations

As an agile project manager, you know that projects are not completed by things and equipment, but by people. In software development projects, which are knowledge-based projects, the work that people do is invisible. It's tough to discern progress simply by looking at software development code. You can't just look at lines of code and determine if the project is progressing. The code can be spaghetti, full of defects, or it could be the best code in the world—but until the code is compiled, integrated, and presented as working software, there's no value. In agile projects, value is in working deliverables. Value, the whole point of doing any project, is in what's being created, not in the creation.

The development team members are the people developing the code, but the project team may include more than just developers. Your team might have testers, technical writers, and even trainers that'll contribute to the value your project creates. These people on your team are what we value as agile project managers. The people on the project team are generalizing specialists—they're able and willing to do more than one role on the project. One of the big goals of agile is for the project team to be cohesive, to be self-directed—and that means that people from all roles chip in wherever their help is needed to get things done. Your job, as a servant leader, is to help the people get their work done, to lead the team, and to promote interdependence among the individuals on the project team.

 For a more detailed explanation, watch the *Leading Agile Project Teams* video now.

This fourth exam domain, on team performance, is worth a chunky 16 percent of your exam score and you can expect about 19 questions on this topic. Exam questions on this topic will challenge you to create an environment of trust for the project team. An environment of trust means that people can explore, try new approaches, and will occasionally fail with their experiments. You'll also promote learning, collaboration, and building relationships with and among the project team members. Finally, as a servant leader, you'll need to recognize when you should step in to resolve conflicts and when you should step back and let the team to do their own conflict resolution.

Introducing the Team Performance Exam Domain

In this domain our focus will be all about the people involved in the project. So, we're going to talk about one of the primary principles of the Agile Manifesto: "We value individuals and interactions over processes and tools." We're going to look at defining the delivery team, the product owner, the team leader, and the project sponsor and what their roles and responsibilities on an agile project are.

For your exam you'll need to know the details about forming the agile team, developing the project team, leading the project team, and coaching team members. You'll also need insight into building a collaborative team space. For your exam you can also expect questions regarding team performance when it comes to colocated versus non-colocated team members. This domain is all about building high-performing teams. Keep your focus on valuing people and communications and putting others ahead of the goals of the project manager; it's all about team performance and getting the team what they need to create value.

Another topic we'll address is developing team roles and some processes to foster buy-in. I'm talking about interpersonal relationships, but also the skills the project team needs to do the project work. On an agile team we have the idea of generalizing specialists, team members who can do lots of activities. As generalizing specialists, they're not working in a silo, and can do more than one activity. We want to empower and encourage emergent leadership, so I'll talk about team motivators and demotivators.

One of the responsibilities as a servant leader is to shield the team from distractions. This requires a fine balance between allowing the business people to have access to work with the team and preventing the business people from distracting the team from getting work done. The project manager wants to align the team and the business people by sharing the project vision, something you will do over and over throughout an agile project.

Reviewing the Nine Tasks for Exam Domain IV

The team performance domain for the PMI-ACP exam has nine tasks divided into three subdomains. When you're faced with questions pertaining to this domain, look for opportunities to promote interdependence and team-led conflict resolution. You want the team to be self-led and self-directed, so that means you often stay out of the way when conflicts and team work decisions are made. Remember, the project manager in agile is not a command-and-control leader, so you'll defer project decisions to the team. Early in the project, you may be more involved in helping the team make decisions, but as the team gets moving forward, you let go of directing the team and allow emergent leadership to blossom and allow the project team to make decisions about getting the project work done.

Let's look at the three subdomains and tasks:

Team Formation

- Cooperate with the other team members to devise ground rules and internal processes in order to foster team coherence and strengthen team members' commitment to shared outcomes.

- Help create a team that has the interpersonal and technical skills needed to achieve all known project objectives in order to create business value with minimal delay.

Team Empowerment

- Encourage team members to become generalizing specialists in order to reduce team size and bottlenecks, and to create a high performing cross-functional team.

- Contribute to self-organizing the work by empowering others and encouraging emerging leadership in order to produce effective solutions and manage complexity.

- Continuously discover team and personal motivators and demotivators in order to ensure that team morale is high and team members are motivated and productive throughout the project.

Team Collaboration and Commitment

- Facilitate close communication within the team and with appropriate external stakeholders through co-location or the use of collaboration tools in order to reduce miscommunication and rework.

- Reduce distractions in order to establish a predictable outcome and optimize the value delivered.

- Participate in aligning project and team goals by sharing project vision in order to ensure the team understands how their objectives fit into the overall goals of the project.

- Encourage the team to measure its velocity by tracking and measuring actual performance in previous iterations or releases in order for members to gain a better understanding of their capacity and create more accurate forecasts.

Valuing People over Processes

One of the first concepts you'll need to master is that you value people over processes, which is one of the anchors in the Agile Manifesto. If we break that down, the idea is that people are doing the work. People need to have the permission to be empowered, to be innovative, to be creative, without fear of repercussions if something fails. In fact, we know that failure is going to happen and that not every innovation is going to work out, but people need permission to experiment and to try new things to be innovative.

Giving the project team space to be a self-organizing team is part of developing and supporting your team. Know this concept for your exam: the team is self-organizing, is self-empowered, and has permission to try new things and to make decisions as to who is going to do what in the sprint backlog or the integration backlog. Project team members are stakeholders. They are certainly affected by the project they are working on, and we know they can affect the project. In an agile project, we'll witness the concept of emergent leadership. Recall from Chapter 1 that emergent leadership occurs when an individual on the team takes on a leadership role. The individual emerges as a leader on the team. It doesn't have to be the project manager, and new leaders can emerge throughout the project based on what's happening in the project.

Anyone can be a leader on the team. ScrumMasters, or the project manager, have the idea of servant leadership; servant leaders remove impediments. Servant leaders are said to "carry food and water," meaning they provide to team members the resources they need to get the work done. Because agile covers many different approaches, you might see a project manager called a ScrumMaster in a Scrum project, or a coach in an XP, Lean, or hybrid environment. Coaches have the same role of servant leadership; they coach the team along and make sure team members have the resources that they need to do the work.

Throughout an agile project, you'll also be dealing with business representatives. You might know this as the product owner or the business people in your project. In previous chapters we talked a lot about the product owner and prioritizing the product backlog. The product owner, the customer, is just another name for a business rep, a person or group that is paying for the project or receiving the deliverables of the project.

You might also encounter the concept of a *proxy customer*, a representative for a large group of stakeholders. For example, you may be doing a project for a manufacturing department, and one individual may represent the entire manufacturing department. As a proxy customer, that person represents and speaks for the entire manufacturing department. Projects may also have a *value management team*, which looks for business value, for return on their investment, and for how the project and project requirements are going to make the organization more profitable and help grow the organization or reduce costs.

 EXAM COACH All projects come down to two real objectives: reduce costs or increase revenue. The project team should embrace this concept in their design and development of the product, as their work ultimately affects the value and the ability of the organization to realize these objectives.

Defining the Delivery Team

Your delivery team consists of the people doing the work and creating value. They are the people building the product. In an agile environment, we know it's an incremental delivery team because these are the people creating increments of the product through iterations. The delivery team works through sprints, iterations, or increments of what your project is creating, of what's going to be released.

The delivery team is self-organized and self-directed. To be self-organized means the team decides who's going to do what in the current iteration. Based on the product backlog, the project team selects the top requirements that they believe they can complete in an iteration. The project's selection of user stories from the product backlog becomes the sprint backlog or iteration backlog. From the iteration backlog, the team decides who's going to do what. The team chops up the work among the team members—they decide who'll take on what tasks.

The team is self-organized and self-directed to get things done, which means that the team also shares information. This transparency concept goes beyond the requirement of the project manager to be transparent and extends to the project team. So, the project team must also share information with one another freely. Team members don't hold back information if they're running into problems or running late on some of their deliveries. They share that information, good or bad.

While the team is self-organized and self-directed, there are still some responsibilities and expectations of your team. Consider the daily standup meeting. Team members must each report on what they did yesterday, what they are going to accomplish today, and whether there are any impediments to accomplishing their work. In the daily standup meeting, everyone speaks to the group, not just to the project manager, and everyone is accountable to one another, not just to the project manager.

The delivery team is also responsible for writing acceptance tests and embracing the test-driven development concept. Then they test their work, and they revise their work. They refactor their work; they clean it up. They're also responsible for the product demonstrations. Recall the sprint review in Scrum projects? This is a meeting to review and demonstrate what's been accomplished in the last sprint or iteration. The demo is not given by the project manager; the demo is led by the team, the people who did the work. After the sprint review, the team shifts into a retrospective. Retrospectives are also an opportunity for transparency as the team defines what worked well in the last iteration. The team also addresses areas they can improve upon for the next iteration. The project team and its transparency are involved in the whole project process.

Identifying the Role and Responsibilities of the Product Owner

Throughout this book, I've used the term *product owner* to describe the individual responsible for grooming or prioritizing the product backlog, and that's accurate, but you might encounter different names too. The product owner could be called the *customer*, referring to the people receiving the result of your product, the people using the software you're creating, or even a proxy customer representing a group of individuals, as in the manufacturing group example I previously discussed. The role of the product owner could also be called the (previously introduced) value management team, which is composed of business people who are interested in the ROI for the time and the monies invested in your project. The value management team also wants to know the release plan, the stability level of the software, and how soon the organization can begin earning back its investment in the project.

What do business reps do in an agile project? We already know the product owner prioritizes the product features and requirements in the product backlog. The product owner ensures that the project team and the people that they represent have a common understanding of what the project is accomplishing. I'm talking about the concept of the *shared project vision* of what the development team is creating, ensuring that everyone has a clear understanding of the definition of done. To meet the definition of done, we have to know both the requirements to satisfy quality expectations and the conditions of acceptance. Product owners provide acceptability criteria.

Product owners are also responsible for managing change requests. If a change comes in, it goes into the product backlog, and the product owner prioritizes the change. The product owner examines the change and determines where in the product backlog the change should fall based on its priority relative to the existing project requirements. The product owner is the person that officially makes and manages change requests. The product owner can change the product features and priorities—that's part of grooming the product backlog. The product owner facilitates the engagement of external project stakeholders, the people that they deal with, that they represent. Based on the needs of the organization, the product owner also gives a due date for the project. We've discussed already the fixed constraints of time and cost; the product owner determines the due date that will affect how much the team can create in the scope to fit the costs and timeline.

Throughout the project, the product owner will attend the planning meetings, reviews, and retrospectives. The product owner doesn't pop by the agile project, groom the backlog, and then go away; the product owner is involved throughout the project. Obviously, as project manager, you're going to deal with the product owner often throughout the project.

 EXAM COACH   Know that the project team, product owner, business reps, and business people all work in a partnership. It's not an us-against-them mentality, but rather a sense that we're all in this together. Agile success depends on keeping that sense of collaboration and sharing the project vision. There's no such thing in agile as sharing the project vision too much.

Defining the Team Leader Responsibilities

Let's discuss the responsibilities of the team leader. Let's start with you; as the project manager you are a team leader. You are the ScrumMaster, or coach, or team facilitator, or whatever term you use in your environment, and you will serve as a project team leader. For your exam, you can expect to see various terms used to describe this role, such as team facilitator, coach, ScrumMaster, or just project manager. Regardless of which term is used, it refers to the individual who helps the delivery team self-govern and self-organize and helps the project team make decisions.

The project manager is a facilitator, facilitating conversations, helping the team work through conflicts when needed, and helping to resolve issues. One of the big responsibilities of the team leader is to be an effective communicator. The leader ensures that people have the information they need and that the information is transparent and readily available. The leader coaches and mentors the delivery team and helps people overcome problems. Again, it's not command-and-control role in agile; it's more supportive.

 EXAM COACH Avoid the temptation to choose answers that indicate you, the project manager, are making team decisions.

The project manager is responsible for guiding the agile processes. This includes helping the product owner groom and prioritize the product backlog. It also includes helping to prioritize the requirements, and then helping the team size the product requirements (something we'll talk about in Chapter 5 in the context of adaptive planning).

The project manager also facilitates meetings. Think about your daily standup, your sprint reviews, and your retrospectives. Facilitating these meetings is part of your role as a project manager. Based on these meeting you'll need to also follow up on issues. You want to make certain that the team has answers to questions, information for the project work, and solutions. The project manager addresses issues that are impediments for the team. Consider missed deadlines, a resource the team needs, or if someone is not getting tasks done on time; those are all issues that the ScrumMaster helps resolve.

Recognizing the Project Sponsor

Now we need to talk about the project sponsor. The project sponsor is the champion for the project and delegates authority to the project manager. Ultimately, the project sponsor is the person who authorizes the project and signs the project charter. The project sponsor needs to be an individual who is high enough in the organization to have sufficient authority over the resources to be used in the project. For example, imagine that you and I are at the same level in the organization, and I write a charter for a group of people to use your resources without consulting you. Because we are at the same level, we're likely going to have a conflict. The sponsor needs to be someone who's above both of us in the hierarchy of the organization and thus able to say that my team can use your resources. The project sponsor must be a person with the right amount of authority.

In addition to signing the project charter and authorizing the project and the project manager, the project sponsor also needs to be the chief advocate for the project. This entails being a champion of the project, a defender of the project, and a positive stakeholder, sharing the project vision. The project sponsor gives direction to the product owner, the person who's going to prioritize the requirements, regarding what the requirements for the project should be. The sponsor is often the person who'll determine the project time and budget.

Sometimes the project sponsor may attend the iteration review meetings, but probably won't attend the retrospective. Attending the review meetings is important because it enables the project sponsor to see the demo of the project. Therefore, the project sponsor should always be invited.

You may not see many questions about the project sponsor on your exam, but remember that the project sponsor has a lot of authority, a lot of power in the organization. Obviously, the project sponsor is a significant stakeholder.

 EXAM COACH   Your project sponsor might be called something different in your organization, and that's fine. For your PMI-ACP exam, know that the person who authorizes the project and the project manager is the project sponsor.

Forming the Agile Project Team

Let's begin with a scenario. You're an agile project manager for your organization and your CEO has a hot idea for a new project that she wants you to manage. You are ready to recruit the team members and have some characteristics in mind. You don't want the team to be too big. Large teams get weighed down by all the processes and formalities, and it's a little tough to organize all those people. Ideally, we're talking about 12 people or fewer. On larger projects, subteams can be created to break up the work and manage it more efficiently.

You want to ensure that you have a team with sufficient skills and competency to do all the needed work, but you also want to make sure that it's not too big such that there's not enough work to go around for all the team all the time. If you have 25 people on your team, for example, and each person can offer only one skill set—one that isn't needed all the time in the project—you're going to have some bored people, wasted monies, and big, unwieldy meetings. You want your project team members to be able to shift from task to task, so you have to recruit people who have the skills to do so.

Team members need to have complementary skills. This is the previously mentioned concept of *generalizing specialists*, people who can offer more than one skill. You don't want everyone to be a developer and only a developer. Your project also needs testers, quality control folks, some people that can mentor newer team members, and so on, and they need to have a variety of skills. Your team needs complementary skills. Of course, all the team members must be committed to one purpose: to get things done, to reach that desired future state, which ultimately creates value.

Team members hold themselves mutually accountable as part of a self-led team. Recall that agile teams are self-organizing and self-directing. Agile team members are accountable to one another to do their assignments, to do their daily work. Team members have a shared outcome. The whole team is responsible for the success, or the failure, of the project, so they also have shared ownership. You want technical excellence on your team. You want people who know what they're doing.

A new term for you is *swarming*. Team swarming is when all the team members come together and work on one item at a time to finish that one item. The team can swarm when there's a challenging, labor-driven requirement. The team will focus all their energy on that one requirement, on that one product feature in the project. This approach helps everyone work together and work toward a common solution. We want the team to work as a group, not as a bunch of individuals, and swarming is a great way to accomplish that goal.

Working with Generalizing Specialists

I've mentioned this term several times already in this section and throughout the book. To reiterate, generalizing specialists are individuals on your team who can serve multiple roles and can quickly switch between different roles. This helps to resolve bottlenecks; for example, if we're stumped in an area, people can shift gears, can switch roles, and help where help is needed. Having a team of generalizing specialists also means that people are not waiting for assignments that fit their narrow qualifications or skillsets.

In practice, the idea of switching roles is that I'm a coder, but I'm going to help write a test, or I'm going to show you how to develop a piece of code or help you figure out why something's not working correctly. Or we'll switch, and I'll work on it for a while and you work on something else. Switching roles isn't the same thing as switching tasks. We know that task switching is one of the agile wastes; switching roles means that a person can go to the next feature in the iteration backlog rather than waiting for a specific type of work.

A generalizing specialist is a person who has more than just one technical specialty. For example, a generalizing specialist is not just a developer, but also someone who has at least a general knowledge of software development (probably more than general...we're talking about coders here). Generalizing specialists need an understanding of the business domain and how the organization operates. How the organization operates is linked to the project, as the organizational procedures, culture, and expectations will affect how the code is developed and what the software ultimately does.

 EXAM COACH   When it comes to generalizing specialists, we want people who are willing to gain skills and new expertise in other areas. We want the project team to be willing to learn, to take on challenges, and to go for opportunities to learn new things. For your exam, you will see the concept of generalizing specialists, so don't be alarmed. Know that term—know it means a person can do more than one activity—and you'll be fine.

Developing the Project Team

In agile projects, we allow the team to be self-organizing, meaning the team decides who does what in each iteration and throughout the project. The project manager allows the team to be in charge and make decisions. They use their knowledge and experience to organize the work and to decide who does what. The agile team structures their work based on the iteration goals and the iteration backlog. They'll decide from the list of tasks in the iteration backlog what is most critical. They'll attack that requirement first. The team will chop up the work among the team members and they'll own their decisions.

Self-organization may be a foreign concept for project team members, especially if they've not worked in an agile environment before. Early in the project, part of developing the team is to tell them, teach them, empower them on what it means for the team to be self-directed. You want to develop the project team and foster their growth so that in future iterations, as the team moves deeper and deeper into the project, they'll take on more and more responsibility of structuring the work and goals of each iteration. For the PMI-ACP exam, you need to know four things about self-directed teams:

- **Work collectively**   The team members work with one another. The team can do swarming if they feel they need to. They can do pair programming, as in XP. The project team is empowered to work collectively as a group.

- **Ownership of decisions**   The project team makes decisions about the work. The project team doesn't have to consult with the project manager about every decision. The team makes decisions for each iteration to reach the goals of that iteration.

- **Create estimates for the project work**   The project team estimates the project work. The terminology will make sense when we discuss adaptive planning in Chapter 5, but for now know that the team sizes the user stories to estimate the effort required to create the features of the product backlog. The project team also creates estimates on how much work they can achieve in an iteration, and the project manager tracks and predicts their achievements.

- **Fail safely**   No one wants to fail, but when the team is empowered to be innovative, not every innovation is going to be successful. Teams are going to make mistakes, but the team needs to operate in a safe environment where they don't fear repercussions for their failed experiments. The project team should experiment, they should try to be innovative, and when things don't work out, we want them to learn from the mistakes. Often great innovations are built on past failures.

To achieve these goals of self-directed teams in the first few iterations, the project manager will likely be involved in helping the team organize the work. As you get deeper and deeper into the project, as more and more iterations happen, the team should take on more of the work distribution responsibility. That's one of the goals of agile, so recognize that for your exam.

Building a High-Performing Team

Your goal as a project manager is to create, or at least to facilitate, a high-performing team. You want people to rely on one another, to work together, to be interdependent. Agile teams move through Tuckman's Model of Team Development, the five phases of which are shown in Figure 4-1 and described next. You should be familiar with this model and the characteristics of each phase as your team works toward the goal of being a high-performing team. Note that it's possible for the team to return to any stage of the model as circumstances change in the project.

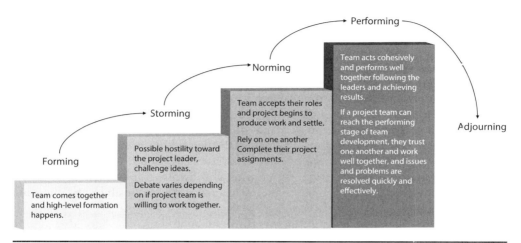

Figure 4-1   Tuckman's Model of Team Development moves the team through five stages.

- **Forming**   When teams first come together, there is initial pleasantness as introductions are made and people begin to learn about each other. You may not know everyone on the team, and team members may not know each other either, or even have worked together before. This first stage of team development is called forming.

- **Storming**   Over time, the team will shift into the storming stage, where people jockey for positions, claim ownership of what they want to work on, and even voice strong opinions on project objectives. Storming can appear to be combative and full of conflict, but it's a natural part of team development. Conflict isn't always bad; it helps teams find common ground, focus on what's important, and become more cohesive.

- **Norming**   Eventually (and thankfully) the combative storming phase calms down, and the team shifts into norming. Norming means things have normalized in the project and people are going about the business of doing the project. The team recognizes who's leading and who's following. People fall into their project roles and being to work together to achieve the project goals.

- **Performing**   As the team continues to work together, they begin to rely on one another, communicate more freely and transparently, and focus on creating value; they enjoy each other's company and are really firing on all cylinders. Now the project is fun and the team is a more cohesive unit. When our team is in a performing stage, we're getting things done, communication is easy, and the project is cruising along.

- **Adjourning**   The final stage of team development is adjourning. Once the project is done, the team disbands and the unit is no longer a team. It's sometimes sad as people move on to different teams and different assignments. In some organizations the team doesn't disband, but sticks together and goes on to the next project as a unit. This doesn't mean they won't go through some of the same stages and challenges in the ladder of team development.

Team members in the performing phase have interdependence when they create a collective shared vision for the project team. One of the responsibilities for the project manager is to help the team to understand and inherit the vision of the project. We want the project team to have a goal of creating the desired future state, of reaching the definition of done. The project team must have a clear vision of how the software they're creating will affect the organization. By creating and owning the shared vision of the project and how it will affect people's lives, the team can feel responsibility for the work they're completing.

There are eight characteristics of high-performing agile teams you should recognize for your exam:

- Agile teams are self-organizing; they'll decide who does what in the project.
- Agile teams are empowered to make decisions.
- Agile teams own their decisions.
- Agile teams have the mindset that they can solve any problem.
- Agile teams have a team identity to be committed to success.
- Agile team members trust one another.
- Agile teams communicate and aim for group consensus on decisions.
- Agile teams know that conflict is natural, but constructive feedback is needed.

Leading the Agile Project Team

When you think about leadership, you may think about aligning people, motivating people, directing people, and making people want to do the work. In agile, you do that as a ScrumMaster, the project manager, or the coach, but you also want the team members to have emergent leadership, as previously discussed. Different people can lead different initiatives. It doesn't always have to be one individual as the leader. High-performing teams allow multiple leaders; they recognize that people are going to shift from leaders to followers and followers to leaders, based on what's happening in the project. With this shift in leadership, we don't want power struggles when leaders change roles. This shift in leadership is part of agile and is part of high-performing teams. People willingly become leaders or followers based on the requirements the project team is focused on in any itera-tion. Other than the project manager, team leaders are self-selected, not assigned.

There is an expectation, of course, for the project manager to be a leader of the project team. For your exam, know the concepts of Tuckman's Model of Team Development as shown in Figure 4-2. First off, there is directing. Directing people happens when the team comes together in the forming stage of team development. When the team first gets

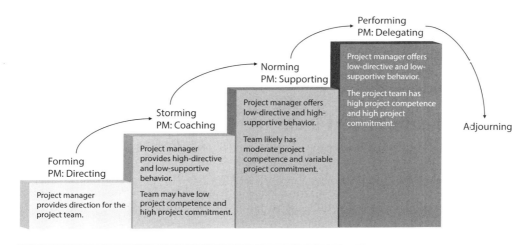

Figure 4-2   The project manager's role changes based on team development.

together, they don't have a lot of insight about the project, and they're likely not yet committed to the team. Leaders in this stage display a high-directive, low-supportive behavior. In other words, leaders are in command and control initially, introducing people and talking about the goals of the project. They're facilitating the initial steps during team forming.

Then, we go into storming, where people begin to jockey for position. Recall that phase involves struggle for who on the project is going to lead initially. So as the project manager, you'll take on more of a coaching role. Team members in the storming phase have more confidence in the project and its requirements for success. Some team members might still have a low commitment because there's some emotional intelligence happening here. Leaders in storming display a high-directive, high-supportive behavior. So now, as the project manager, you are supporting people, propping people up, and coaching people. From an agile project manager's perspective, storming is all about coaching and advising.

Once the team shifts into norming, where things begin to settle down, and starts to make progress in the project, the project manager takes more of a supportive role. Team members have a moderate to high competency but variable commitment to the project. Some people might be committed, but some are still uncertain. Leaders now have a low-directive, high-supportive behavior. They're supporting the decisions of the project team.

Once the team shifts into performing, then you'll see more delegating happening. In the performing phase, team members have a high competency and a high commitment. As a project manager, you become even more of the servant leader. You're no longer in command and control at all, but rather assume a low-directive, low-supportive behavior. You're hands-off and allow the team to take charge.

Directing, coaching, supporting, and delegating are the characteristics of agile team leadership. Recognize those as a project manager. It's what you're going to do with your team. You will likely see that concept on your exam, so recognize the characteristics, attributes, and role of the project manager in each phase of team development. By recognizing the scenario of each phase of team development, you'll be able to identify whether the project manager is expected to direct, coach, support, or delegate to the project team.

Motivating the Project Team

Motivating the project team means keeping people excited about and invested in the project. It builds synergy among the team. Motivating the team includes empowering the team; you allow and encourage the team to experiment, to try new approaches, to innovate, and to fail safely. Make no mistake: agile teams should experiment. The project team should try new methods. It's okay to fail. Not every innovation is going to work out, as we know.

I'll tell you about a hobby that I have: I'm a bit of a rock hound. A pretty exciting hobby, right? I look for an unusual rock called a Petoskey Stone. This rock has a unique pattern on it that you can really only see when the stone is wet. Once you find one of these treasures, you have to sand it over and over, then polish it, and add a special coating to get the pattern to really shine. It's a long, tedious process to get one beautiful stone.

So, I asked myself, what if I sanded a rock with a belt sander? Not a good idea, as it turns out. I put the stone on the belt sander and in a few moments the rock shot across the garage. With persistence, I made the sander work, but soon burned up the cheap sander. After several trials and errors, and plenty of research, I found a better way, and now I have a better sander, a better approach, and I can sand these stones quickly.

I failed and learned and failed and learned and I'm still learning. So, it's okay to fail. In agile project management we embrace the mindset that it's okay to fail as long as we learn from the failure.

In our agile projects, we want to create an *engagement culture*, which means that we reward people for solving problems. So, we want to encourage people to collaborate, share ideas, and share what they've discovered. You don't discover a great innovation and then hide it only for yourself while everyone else is still struggling. You share it. It's open. We want people to experiment, to learn, and then to share what they've learned.

Another aspect of team motivation is introduced in Herzberg's Theory of Motivation, which tells us that we have two types of agents, hygiene agents and motivating agents, as depicted in Figure 4-3. *Hygiene agents* are things like job security, a paycheck, an acceptable working environment, and your relationship with your boss and colleagues. Hygiene factors must exist first to motivate even a low level of performance. If you don't get your paycheck, you don't want to come into work for free. These are called "hygiene" agents because they are necessary just to maintain the employer–employee relationship.

Motivating agents are things that motivate people to excel. These factors promote performance. Motivating agents are factors like a bonus, opportunity for advancement, appreciation, recognition, additional responsibility, and education. They're motivating

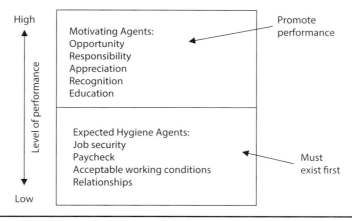

Figure 4-3 Herzberg's Theory of Motivation identifies hygiene agents and motivating agents.

agents only if the individual is genuinely motivated by what's being offered as the reward, the motivator. If your team member Bob is not motivated by more responsibility, more responsibility is not going to excite him to do more work. The reward must be something that the individual is motivated and excited about receiving.

 EXAM COACH   If hygiene agents don't exist, motivating agents don't really matter.

Training the Project Team

Another aspect of developing the project team is training, coaching, and mentoring. Training the project team is about making sure that the team members have the skills and competency they need to do their jobs. Pretty straightforward. Coaching is about facilitation, so you're facilitating to help individuals develop and improve performance. Mentoring is more of a professional relationship. It's more free-flowing. It's more conversational and one-on-one. For example, a project team member could mentor a new hire on how to code, or the project manager could mentor someone on how to be a project manager.

For your PMI-ACP exam, you'll want to know the Dreyfus Model of Adult Skill Acquisition, as depicted in Figure 4-4, which has five stages. First off, we have a novice, a person who is brand new to a skill. Novices typically just follow the rules and make analytical decisions. As a novice, an individual is not going to stray too far from the norm or be too innovative, because they're in rookie mode.

Once a novice has gained experience, they shift into the role of an advanced beginner in the competent stage of skill acquisition. This person is still following the rules, but based on experience they can better understand the context of the rules. After gaining more experience, an individual is competent, meaning they can determine which rules are best for each situation.

Figure 4-4 The Dreyfus Model of Adult Skill Acquisition identifies five stages of learning a new skill.

As a person gains more experience, they become proficient. This means they can actively choose the best strategy rather than just rely on the rules. The next level is expert mode, where decision-making becomes intuitive. An expert understands the rules and knows when it's okay to bend—and sometimes break—the rules. Finally, an expert matures into a master. In the master phase the person can rely on intuition, can achieve goals and objectives quickly, can break and bend the rules based on circumstances, and can see the whole picture and effect of situations.

In the context of software development, a novice is an individual who is brand new to developing code. As that persons goes through each of the stages of the Dreyfus Model, they become increasingly more competent and then more proficient, gradually building their confidence in the results they produce to the point at which they are considered an expert or master. That's what we want to happen within our team as well.

Another agile concept you'll need to know for your exam is the Shu-Ha-Ri Model of Skill Mastery. In the first stage, Shu, you learn the skill by following the guidelines. In the Ha stage, you no longer rely on the guidelines and are able to work more intuitively. Ri is the stage at which you have fully mastered the skill and can innovate beyond the guidelines. Know Shu-Ha-Ri for your exam.

Coaching Project Team Members

When you coach team members, you are helping them to become better in their careers. A coach is not exercising command and control, but rather is advising, leading, and helping individual team members. As a coach, you're leading someone to a decision, leading them to a result, and you're not deciding for them. There are four things you want to know about coaching:

- **Half a step ahead** The first rule or factor of coaching is that when you coach someone, you meet them a half a step ahead. Consider an individual who has an issue, or doesn't understand how to do a task, or feels overwhelmed. As a coach, you don't tell them what to do. You talk through the problem. You meet them half a step ahead and lead them along to the solution. You ask questions like "How can we work this out?" or "What's the real problem? Can we break that problem down?" You talk with the person and help them make a decision that is going to be suitable for the situation.

- **Guarantee safety** The next factor to keep in mind as a coach is that when an individual comes to you with a problem, or needs some coaching, you don't blab about it to anyone else. You take them aside, talk one-on-one, and give some confidential coaching. It's a little bit of hand-holding and assurance that they're in a safe environment and can have trust in you. You confirm that the coaching relationship is a trust relationship.

- **Partnership** Coaching also means the individual can partner with a manager for insight and expertise to help make the project decisions. The agile project manager also communicates to other managers what the project team has accomplished, and gives credit where credit is due.

- **Respect** A coach respects the relationship. You treat all project team members and stakeholders with respect, trust, openness, and honesty. As the agile project manager, you embody the characteristics you want your team members to have. Respect also means keeping the terms and conversation of the coaching relationship private.

As an agile project manager, you also encourage constructive disagreement. Disagreement is a good thing. If everyone says yes to every project decision, then we aren't getting any innovation. Debate and conflict are natural and healthy. Constructive conflict is going to lead to better decisions and buy-in. The goal is convergence, not divergence. Divergence means the team is going to argue and debate without resolution. Convergence means the team comes together, through debate, conversations, and experimentation, to utilize confrontation problem solving.

For your PMI-ACP exam, know the five dysfunctions of a team:

- **Absence of trust** If we don't trust one another, we're going to have a tough time completing this project.

- **Fear of conflict** If people never want to have a conflict, we aren't going to have innovation.

- **Lack of commitment** When people are not interested in the project, don't see the value, or don't know why they're doing the agile approach, they won't be excited about the project and probably won't be committed to the project work.

- **Avoidance of accountability** When people place blame and avoid being accountable for their decisions and contribution, there's no teamwork or interdependence. Accountability means that we're each responsible for our own actions, but also responsible as a group.

- **Inattention to results**   If the team is not paying attention to the work that's being created, that results in defects and sloppy work. We want quality. We want deliverables to conform to requirements, and we want the final product to be fit for use.

Building a Team Space

For your PMI-ACP exam you'll need to recognize the characteristics of a collaborative team space. This is the idea that we *colocate* the team; that is, bring members together in one environment for the duration of the project. Certainly, that's not very realistic when people work all over the globe, or even on a big campus where your team may work in different buildings or on different floors. But for your exam, know that colocation is a desirable thing. It's desirable in the real world too: whenever it is practical to do so, bring people close together.

In a collaborative team space, we first want an open floor plan. This provides a line of sight for everyone and contributes to easy and fast communication. Ideally, everyone is within 33 feet (10 meters) of each other. If possible, the space should have no physical barriers, no doorways or walls. We don't want people tucked away in confined offices. Again, I know it's not always realistic out in the real world, but in agile two or more people working together is ideally better than each person hidden away in a single office or cubicle where they can't see each other.

Caves and commons are two terms that describe a collaborative team space. A collaborative team space includes one or more caves and commons. *Caves* are designated areas for quiet thinking, private conversations, or working without interruption. *Commons* is the term for the big common area in an open floor plan, an open space for team members to interact and collaborate.

A collaborative team space also supports the attitude of openness and trustworthiness. You want the team members to try new things, to be innovative, and to be empowered to fail. You already know that failure's going to happen. It's okay. We don't hand out punishments for failure. We want the project team to feel safe, and we know that the team can learn from failure and move forward.

Working with Different Agile Team Locales

As just discussed, a colocated team is preferred in an agile environment, and certainly is the preferred choice for an exam question asking you to identify the ideal team space. However, what if you have team members distributed around the world or around a campus? Well, you can attempt to emulate a shared space with collaborative software. Although using collaborative software is not as effective as the colocated team because it can't provide face-to-face, quick communication, if your team has no other option, there are several web collaboration software solutions available, such as Skype, Google Hangouts, and other video-conferencing products.

 EXAM COACH   There are many different web-based software solutions to emulate a colocated team, but virtual teams have communication challenges. On your exam, the preferred option is always to bring people together physically.

Identifying Osmotic Communications

Sometimes communication is like osmosis: you absorb information that you overhear. Imagine a project team in an open team space. Steve and Mark are having a conversation near a third person, Pat, who is busy working. Later, if Steve and Mark are out of the office and someone has a question for them related to the earlier conversation, Pat, who overheard their conversation, might be able to answer in their place. Pat is learning by overhearing a conversation. This is osmotic communication, and it is one of the benefits of a colocated team.

There are some considerations for osmotic communication. Physical proximity is a must, obviously, for osmotic communication. A great example of this proximity is in XP where the team participates in pair programming. The two people working together are physically seated together and are learning from each other. Their proximity allows them to absorb information from each other.

A caution, however, is that you can absorb incorrect information or misconstrued information from those around you. For your exam, recognize that osmotic communication can be beneficial, but also recognize that the information you absorb passively isn't necessarily correct. Also recognize that osmotic communication can be negatively impacted by disruptive behavior, gossip, rumors, and so forth. In a chaotic environment, you're more likely to tune out altogether than to keep your antennae up for snippets of useful conversation.

Defining the Project Team Space

Let's talk a little bit more about creating a team space. When we go about defining a team space, it's a location for all our team members. You might know this as a war room or a project office. The name project office, though, could lead to confusion in an organization that has a project management office (PMO), so the team space is often called the war room or the project headquarters. In this space you will have visible information, such as an information radiator or a big signboard of what's happening in the project. You might post project metrics, a burndown or a burnup chart, a Kanban board, and other project information. The project team space also has lots of whiteboards and task boards, providing lots of transparent communication.

Your team space should have caves and a commons. Recall that caves are private spaces for alone time or one-on-one conversations. The commons is the primary work area where people come together. When people work physically close together, they can communicate quickly and accurately about the project work, where things are located, and details about the project work, and many people can hear and participate in the conversation—that's an example of tacit knowledge sharing.

Tacit knowledge describes knowledge that you have acquired just by doing particular work in a particular place over a period of time. In your line of work, whatever industry you're in, there are certain activities that you do that an outsider wouldn't know how to do without instruction. Examples of tacit knowledge include how to restart a company e-mail server, where to turn on the lights in your environment, or what drive you save your work to. Larger groups, however, have more difficulty with tacit knowledge because different people complete the common tasks each day.

Managing Team Diversity

As emphasized in the Agile Manifesto, we value people over processes. Part of valuing people is valuing the cultures, beliefs, values, and backgrounds they bring to the project. As the agile project manager, you must consider the culture of the team members. Team members must respect each other and their varied and diverse backgrounds and belief systems. Teams need to understand work ethics and culture and how that can affect the project.

If you have a non-colocated team, such as a diverse team located in various places around the world, you might have to deal with issues such as different time zones, communication preferences, cultural characteristics, languages, and holidays that are going to affect your project and how your team communicates and works with one another. A challenge for a distributed team is that they may feel like they are not one team, but six or seven teams, because team members tend to only talk with people in their own location. As agile project managers, we want to encourage collaboration regardless of the locations of our team members.

A term that you might see on your exam is *ethnocentrism*, which means that an individual judges other cultures based on their own culture. If I were to go to a foreign country, or even to a different region within the United States (consider the contrast, for instance, between the U.S. West Coast and Appalachia), I might experience culture shock initially, but I might also judge their culture based on my own culture. Ethnocentrism usually characterizes individuals who believe that their own culture is superior, but it could also be the inverse. If I go to Paris and interact with Parisians, and Paris seems sophisticated, a big beautiful city, I might think, "Oh, they're so much smarter and more advanced than my culture." Maybe they are. But ethnocentrism is where I judge other people's culture by my own, and that affects my collaboration and relationship with others.

 EXAM COACH   Use frequent communication when dealing with virtual teams. You need intensified facilitation, meaning you need to take more of an active role when it comes to getting people to communicate in a distributed team.

Monitoring Agile Team Performance

One of your responsibilities as an agile project manager is to monitor the team performance. You want to know how quickly the team is moving through the requirements and how efficiently and effectively the team is performing. Because we're dealing with knowledge work, sometimes it's tough to measure performance or to see who's working hard and who's not, who's working efficiently or inefficiently, or who's working effectively or ineffectively. We know that our goal is success for the whole project, not just individuals on the project, but we do want some insight into how each team member is performing. That's one of the reasons why you should do a daily standup—it's a great mechanism for checking what each project team member accomplished yesterday and what they plan to accomplish today.

Measuring performance in an agile project is different than measuring performance in a predictive project, because in agile we're dealing with knowledge work. Because agile projects deliver chunks of work on a regular basis, we can routinely gather data on how quickly and efficiently the project team is delivering value. You'll have good insight at the end of each iteration as to how much work has been completed and how much work is remaining. That stat alone provides insight into how well the project team is performing, and that allows you to do some forecasting for the project.

Agile teams do measure results, but our results are based on what the team delivers, not based on what we predict it will deliver, so it's proven information versus our best guess. With an agile team, you want to limit estimation to the current iteration. You don't want to make long-term predictions for the project. The smaller the chunks of work, the more likely the people are to deliver. And with smaller chunks of work, it is easier is to forecast what the team can complete. One of the goals of agile project management is to limit the number of items in the work in progress (WIP) category. The fewer the items in WIP, the easier is to get those items done. Of course, you need to maintain a good balance, as you don't want the workload to be too light, and you don't want the team to be overwhelmed with the amount of work they promise to complete per iteration. Over a series of iterations, you and the project team will become more proficient at estimating how much work can be feasibly done per iteration.

 EXAM COACH *Velocity* just means how quickly the team is completing requirements per iteration. The first few iterations of the project may have some wild swings in velocity as the project team is getting used to the work, maybe trying innovations, and learning to work with one another.

Building Burn Charts

Now that you know agile team members are going to be measured as a group on how efficiently and how effectively they perform, let's discuss burnup and burndown charts. Let's look first at a burnup chart. A burnup chart, as shown in Figure 4-5, displays the amount of work accomplished in each iteration. This number sums up to the total number of story points the team has accomplished this far in the project. Rather than looking at the backlog and saying how many items are left, a burnup chart looks at how much the team has accomplished. A burnup chart looks at the accumulation of what's done versus the sum of what's left to do.

In this example, our ideal velocity is represented by the goal line and the reality of what the team has accomplished is represented by the completed line. The whole chart shows us how many points the team has knocked out for each iteration and for the whole project. You can also create a burnup chart for the number of story points the team is aiming to accomplish in the current iteration, rather than looking at the whole project. You can create a burnup chart for each day of the project, where the number of story points for the iteration is accumulated each day and compared to the days prior.

As part of being open and transparent, you'll need a visual display of project progress. One chart you'll want to know for your PMI-ACP exam is the burndown chart, an example of which is shown in Figure 4-6. Each bar represents 10 points. We'll discuss story points

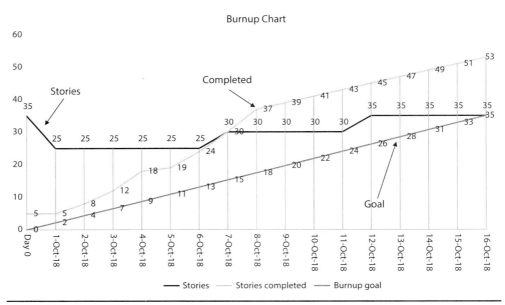

Figure 4-5 Burnup charts show each iteration's amount of work accomplished.

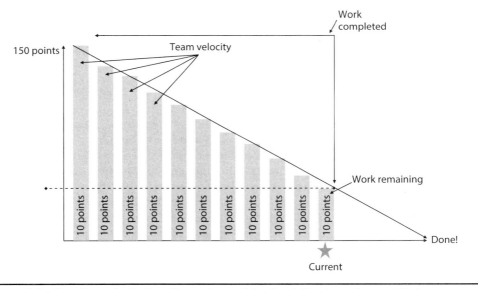

Figure 4-6 Burndown charts show the work remaining in relation to work completed.

in Chapter 5, but the idea is that our requirements in the product backlog have points assigned to them. Each one of those bars, even though they're different sizes, represents one iteration or 10 points. So, we do a four-week sprint, and we knock out 10 points against the product backlog, and then we go to the next iteration, and we knock out 10 points. As we continue to knock out iterations, the number of remaining requirements burns down.

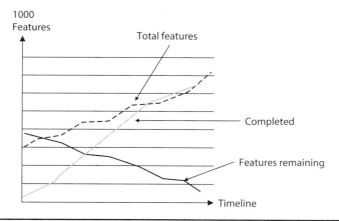

Figure 4-7 Features charts show the requirements remaining, features completed, and added features.

The left side of the burndown chart indicates the total number of points for the project requirements. That represents the total product backlog. In this example, there are 150 points in the product backlog. If your team consistently completes 10 points per iteration, that is your team velocity. The bars are going down in size because each represents how much total work is remaining in the product backlog.

Based on the velocity of the team and the number of items remaining in the product backlog, you can forecast when all the requirements will be completed. This is an ideal scenario, but in the real world, team velocity is going to fluctuate. Sometimes you aren't going to get all 10 points done, or sometimes you aren't able to take on 10 points in an iteration. What's left to do is still a prediction.

Figure 4-7 shows an example of a features chart, which is just a combination of a burnup chart and a burndown chart. This chart shows the number of requirements remaining and the number of features that have been completed, and it could also show if features have been added to the product backlog. In this example, the solid line that's trending down is the burndown portion of the chart and it shows the number of features remaining. The solid line that's curving up, starting in the lower left at zero, shows the total number of features the team has completed. Finally, in Figure 4-7 the dashed line shows the total number of features, gradually increasing as features were added to the backlog.

Calculating Project Team Velocity

I want to address team velocity in more detail as it's an important concept for your exam. Recall that team velocity is the capacity of work the team can complete per iteration. It's how many story points, how much work, the team can get done in one sprint, for one iteration. Velocity is measured in the same unit that the team uses to estimate the work. We've talked a little about story points; story points are tied directly to velocity. Early in the project, as the team completes the first iterations, velocity is going to fluctuate because we're figuring out how we operate as a team, how we're going to work together, how everyone can work efficiently and effectively, and how much work we can feasibly take on per iteration.

Velocity is unstable early and then stabilizes over time. At some point, your team's velocity is going to plateau, it's going to normalize, based on the team's effectiveness. Velocity is the measure of the team's capacity for work per iteration, and it's used as a prediction for how long the project is going to last and how much work can be done in future iterations.

If in the first two or three iterations the team can do six to eight story points in each iteration, then you can reasonably expect the team to begin to consistently knock out ten story points in each iteration. That's a good sign that the project team has stabilized; the team has determined how many user points are realistic. You also have to consider, however, the product backlog and how the team estimates the effort to create the items in the backlog. There's a correlation between requirements sizing and the velocity in each iteration. You can create a velocity chart to show the team's capacity per work iteration. This chart tracks each iteration to show the team's stability in velocity.

Chapter Summary

You're making great progress in your pursuit of earning the PMI-ACP. You've completed an important chapter on the team performance exam domain. In this chapter we talked about managing agile teams and engaging agile teams. Again, this exam domain is worth 16 percent of your PMI-ACP exam score and there are nine tasks you'll need to master. You can expect about 19 questions on your exam from the information in this chapter.

One of the key elements of this chapter ties back to the Agile Manifesto: we value people over processes. As an agile project manager, you'll work to make the agile team self-led and empowered to make decisions and take actions in a safe environment. Your goal is for the team to be a high-performing team, capable of working out issues, dividing up the project work, and then working together to reach the definition of done for all requirements in the project and in the iteration backlog. Of course, that goal of making your group of people a high-performing team takes time, as the team members must learn to trust one another, work through the phases of team development, and experience emergent leadership throughout the project.

Recall that emergent leadership is the idea that anyone can become a leader on the project team based on what's happening in the project. The development team will become self-organized and self-directed. The team, not the project manager, decides who is going to tackle what tasks in the current iteration. From the iteration backlog, the team decides who's going to do what. The team chops up the work among the team members—they decide who'll take on what tasks. That's the idea of being self-directed, but in the early iterations of the project the team may look to the project manager to help with assignments and responsibilities.

In this chapter we also talked about the responsibilities of the product owner and the project sponsor. Recall that the project sponsor is the person with the authority to launch the project, give the project manager control over the project resources, and sign the project charter. The product owner is the person that works with the project team in the iteration planning to prioritize the requirements of the product backlog. The product owner is also the person that manages change requests and prioritizes those changes in the product backlog.

You'll also want to know the concept of generalizing specialists for your exam. A generalizing specialist is a person that has more than just one skill. A generalizing specialist can switch from role to role as needed in the project. This doesn't mean they'll switch from task to task, but that they're able and willing to do whatever is needed in the project next to get things done. Generalizing specialists need an understanding of the business domain and how the organization is linked to the project.

We explored team development and the five stages of team development: forming, storming, norming, performing, and adjourning. Team development happens naturally, but the project manager can, to an extent, facilitate some of the developmental stages. Team development also means training the project team to do their work, if needed. This part of the chapter introduced the Dreyfus Model of Adult Skill Acquisition. This model illustrates how we all move from novice, to competent, to proficient, and finally, over time and with experience, we become an expert. You'll also need to recognize the Shu-Ha-Ri Model of Skill Mastery. Shu means you start by following the rules. Ha is when the team or the individual has mastered the guidelines and can move away from those guidelines a little bit and work more intuitively. Ri is when the team reaches full mastery and can transcend the rules.

It's ideal for agile project teams to work in a collaborative, open space. We talked about caves and the commons. The commons is the large open work area of the open office concept. Caves are the hideaways for thinking, private conversations, and working without interruption. Collaborative spaces also promote osmotic communication, enabling you to learn about things just by being within hearing distance of nearby conversations—you absorb the information that's around you.

In this chapter you also learned about burndown and burnup charts. A burndown chart shows the number of requirements remaining in the product or iteration backlog. As the team creates requirements, the number of requirements diminishes until the team has completed them all or run out of project time. A burnup chart shows the total number of requirements that the team has completed so far. The number of requirements that a team can complete in each iteration is the team velocity. Velocity shows performance of the project team and helps you to create some forecasts.

There's lots of information to learn in this chapter, but you did it! Keep going—you can do this.

Key Terms

Adjourning   Adjourning is the final stage of Tuckman's Model of Team Development. Once the project is done, the team disbands, and the unit is no longer a team.

Burndown chart   A burndown chart shows the total number of requirements remaining in the product backlog as each iteration completes a portion of the requirements. The chart shows that the team is burning down the total amount of work to do through their velocity in each iteration. The more consistent the velocity, the better the prediction of project completion for all requirements.

Burnup chart   A burnup chart illustrates each iteration's amount of work accomplished. It shows the cumulative total of requirements the team has completed for the whole project and in each iteration.

Caves   In a collaborative team space, caves are private areas for conversations, concentration, and to avoid interruptions.

Collaborative team space   An open floor plan that provides line of sight for everyone and provides easy and fast communication.

Commons   In a collaborative team space, the commons is the big common area in an open floor plan, an open space for team members to interact and collaborate.

Dreyfus Model of Adult Skill Acquisition   In the Dreyfus Model of Adult Skill Acquisition, learners move through five stages to acquire skills: novice, competent, proficient, expert, and master.

Emergent leadership   Emergent leadership occurs when an individual on the team takes a leadership role. It doesn't have to be the project manager, and new leaders can emerge at different times based on what's happening in the project.

Engagement culture   An engagement culture encourages people to collaborate, share ideas, and share what they've discovered, and rewards people for solving problems.

Ethnocentrism   Ethnocentrism refers to judging other cultures based on one's own culture. It is based on assumptions and prejudices that the individual's culture is superior or inferior rather than the understanding that cultures are just different, not necessarily better or worse.

Features chart   A features chart is a combination of a burnup chart and a burndown chart. This chart shows the number of requirements remaining and the number of features that have been completed, and can also show whether features have been added to the product backlog.

Forming   Forming is the first stage of Tuckman's Model of Team Development, in which a team first comes together. This stage is marked by initial pleasantness as introductions are made and people begin to learn about each other.

Generalizing specialist   A generalizing specialist is an individual on your team who can serve multiple roles, so team members can quickly switch between different roles on your team.

Herzberg's Theory of Motivation   Herzberg's Theory of Motivation describes two types of agents: hygiene agents and motivating agents. Hygiene agents include job security, a paycheck, an acceptable working environment, and your work relationship. These are called "hygiene" agent because they are necessary just to maintain the employer-employee relationship. Motivating agents motivate people to excel in performance and include factors like bonuses, opportunity for advancement, appreciation, recognition, and education.

Norming   Norming is the third stage of Tuckman's Model of Team Development, when things have normalized in the project and people are going about the business of doing the project.

Osmotic communication   Learning by overhearing others' conversations in a collaborative team space is osmotic communication.

Performing   Performing is the fourth stage of Tuckman's Model of Team Development. As the team continues to work together, they begin to rely on one another, communicate more freely and transparently, and focus on creating value; they enjoy each other's company and are really firing on all cylinders.

Project sponsor   The project sponsor is the champion for the project with organizational authority to delegate authority to the project manager and launch the project. The project sponsor signs the project charter.

Proxy customer   A proxy customer is a representative for a large group of project stakeholders.

Self-organized   A team that is self-organized decides who's going to do what in the current iteration and doesn't always rely on the project manager for instructions.

Shu-Ha-Ri Model of Skill Mastery   The Shu-Ha-Ri Model of Skill Mastery describes three stages. In the first stage, Shu, you learn the skill by following the guidelines. In the Ha stage, you no longer rely on the guidelines and are able to work more intuitively. Ri is the stage at which you have fully mastered the skill and can innovate beyond the guidelines.

Storming   Storming is the second stage of Tuckman's Model of Team Development in which people jockey for positions, claim ownership of what they want to work on, or even voice strong opinions on project objectives. Storming can appear to be combative and full of conflict, but it's a natural part of team development.

Tacit knowledge   Knowledge a person has gained through their experience and doing work is tacit knowledge. Teams have tacit knowledge about the project work and how things operate in their colocated environment.

Tuckman's Model of Team Development   Tuckman's Model of Team Development is a model that shows project team members moving from forming through storming, norming, and performing. Teams may shift back to earlier stages based on project conditions. Adjourning is a fifth stage that the team goes through when it disbands.

Value management team   The value management team is composed of business people looking for return on investment for the project work. They look for opportunities to increase value, predict breakeven points, and forecast how the project will contribute to cutting costs in the organization and/or increasing revenue.

Velocity   Velocity is the capacity of work the team can complete per iteration. Velocity is defined by how many story points the team can complete in one iteration.

Questions

1. You have been identified as a stakeholder on an agile software development team. As you join your first meeting, you are surprised that there are only ten people on the team; you thought it would be a much bigger team since it is a large implementation. Why do you think the team is so small?

   A. The agile methodology is so new, no one wanted to be on the team.

   B. One person was selected from each department.

   C. Agile methods recommend the delivery team to be 12 or fewer members.

   D. Agile methods call for very specialized roles.

2. Your agile team consists of generalizing specialists. What is a generalizing specialist?

   A. A person that knows just one skill

   B. A person that is skilled in more than one discipline

   C. A person that knows what each role is responsible for

   D. A person that know their job duties well

3. Your agile team leader has described the iteration goals at a high level and is allowing the team to decide how to complete the iteration. What does this action prove to the team?

   A. That the leader doesn't know how to accomplish the iteration

   B. That the leader trusts the self-organizing team and their expertise to complete the goal

   C. That the team leader is busy working on his normal job

   D. That the team leader is not a micro-manager

4. You are on a self-directing agile team and would like to take the lead on a task that you are very familiar with and feel very strongly about. What is the process to take the lead?

   A. Explain and show to your team that this task falls within your expertise and you know you can lead it to success

   B. Ask the project leader if it would be okay to lead this process

   C. In a meeting with stakeholders, explain that you've done this task before and it would be a good idea for you to take the lead

   D. Subtly overpower the leader and take charge of the task

5. Your team leader has built a safe environment for disagreement. How has this empowered the team to move forward without obstacles?

    A. There is a method to create a list of reasons why tasks cannot be completed and brought to management.

    B. The team decided to avoid conflict.

    C. The team leader takes responsibility for all decisions made.

    D. The team is encouraged to join in constructive conflict to make better decisions.

6. You are on a new agile team and your leader keeps emphasizing that for the first iteration, everyone needs to follow the rules that have been described by previous agile teams in the organization. Why do you think this is so important to your leader?

    A. It is best to start a project by following a method that has been tested, proven, and refined by others.

    B. The leader wants to be able to explain the rules and then go back to her normal job and let the team work on its own.

    C. The leader wants the team members to prove they can follow rules.

    D. The team leader doesn't want the team to try to move the project off course early in the process.

7. As a member of an agile team, at what level of mastering a skill do you think you can make the best decision rather than relying on the rules?

    A. Competent

    B. Competent

    C. Proficient

    D. Expert

8. The formation and development of teams normally follow the Tuckman Model of forming, storming, norming, and performing. Your team leader is obviously aware of this model, but he is new to the organization and is having trouble understanding why the forming stage has gone so quickly. Which of the following might be the reason?

    A. The team was handpicked by management, so they know they must get along.

    B. Most of the team members have worked together on previous projects.

    C. They team members really don't care if they get along or not.

    D. Most of the team members are from the same department.

9. You are the project manager of a new agile project for your organization and you're explaining to the business team how agile works. You explain that at which of the following stages of adaptive leadership the leader may ask many questions?

   A. Directing

   B. Coaching

   C. Supporting

   D. Delegating

10. You are an agile team leader and you've come to realize that there is very little interest in the project coming from team members. What is a good method to motivate team members for the duration of the project?

    A. Offer them a raise if they become engaged

    B. Offer a bonus if the project is a success

    C. Align the project goals to the corporate goals

    D. Align the project goals to team members' personal goals

11. In the middle of an iteration, the team leader noticed that one member was having an issue with a decision the entire team made. The leader asked the team member for a one-on-one discussion. What type of session do you think this was?

    A. Training

    B. Coaching

    C. Mentoring

    D. Directing

12. Beth is the project manager for an agile project in her organization. She's explaining to the team how the team should communicate effectively in the project. What is the preferred method of communication for an agile team?

    A. Secured and saved e-mail so there is a paper trail

    B. Conference calls where attendance is mandatory

    C. Face-to-face discussions

    D. One-on-one phone calls

13. You are the project manager of an agile project for your organization and you'd like the team to be colocated. When is an agile team considered to be colocated?

    A. When all team members are within 33 feet of each other with no barriers

    B. When all team members are located on the same floor of a building

    C. When all team members are in the same city

    D. When all team members are on the same campus

14. You are on a colocated agile team and sometimes the team area gets so noisy that it is hard to concentrate. On these days, you are very glad to have access to which of the following?

    A. Cafeteria

    B. Your boss's office

    C. A small private office, sometimes known as a cave

    D. Another floor

15. You are on an agile team and in a meeting one of your co-workers said she learned how to correct a piece of code by osmotic communication. What does this mean?

    A. She dreamed what the correction should be

    B. She did a search on Google

    C. She read about the solution in a book

    D. She overheard a conversation in the agile team's commons that discussed the solution

16. You are leading an agile team whose members are located in several areas of the world. You've arranged conference calls and insisted that everyone have their computer cameras on so that team members can associate names and faces with participants. It is impossible to have the team members meet face to face because of the cost. What is an alternate method of enabling team members to get to know each other?

    A. Have them send each other pictures

    B. Have each member write a short biography and share it with team members

    C. Pair up team members to work on tasks, and rotate the pairs

    D. Have team members get to know each other's primary language

17. You have been selected to lead a team with members located all over the world. You pushed to use the agile method of running a team and upper management thought that was an excellent suggestion. Why is running a distributed team with an agile methodology feasible?

    A. Being agile allows you to select two or three people in each location to work together with the project's goals in mind.

    B. Agile teams use short iterations to complete tasks and receive feedback to ensure the project is on the right track.

    C. Almost everyone has Internet access, which allows for immediate communication.

    D. Agile teams are used to running themselves, so your involvement as the leader will be minimal.

18. You are looking at a burndown chart located in the agile team area. What is this chart telling you?

    A. How many members are rolling off the project

    B. How much work needs to be completed on the project

    C. How many test scripts have been run

    D. When you can schedule your vacation

19. You are looking at a burnup chart located in the agile team's area. What is this chart telling you?

    A. When to add additional members to the project

    B. How many test scripts are left to execute

    C. How much work has been completed

    D. When the project will end

20. You are the project manager for your organization and you're sharing a velocity chart with the product owner. What is measured in a velocity chart?

    A. The team's capacity

    B. How many members are on the team at any given time

    C. How quickly the project is progressing

    D. How many hours have been burned on the project

Questions and Answers

1. You have been identified as a stakeholder on an agile software development team. As you join your first meeting, you are surprised that there are only ten people on the team; you thought it would be a much bigger team since it is a large implementation. Why do you think the team is so small?

    A. The agile methodology is so new, no one wanted to be on the team.

    B. One person was selected from each department.

    C. Agile methods recommend the delivery team to be 12 or fewer members.

    D. Agile methods call for very specialized roles.

    C. Agile methods recommend that a team of 12 or fewer be assembled to allow the members to form relationships and be able to communicate more directly. If more team members are needed, teams will be broken into subteams and their work will be coordinated. Agile team members are selected based on the ability to commit to a common purpose, agree on how goals are measured, and take shared ownership of the project.
    A is incorrect because the newness of the agile approach in an organization isn't the best choice for the team size limit. B is incorrect because agile teams are formed by skills, not by representatives from each department. D is incorrect because agile calls for generalizing specialists on the project team.

2. Your agile team consists of generalizing specialists. What is a generalizing specialist?

    A. A person that knows just one skill

    B. A person that is skilled in more than one discipline

    C. A person that knows what each role is responsible for

    D. A person that know their job duties well

    B. A generalizing specialist is a person that is skilled in multiple disciplines. A team composed of generalizing specialists can share the workload and avoid bottlenecks that many project encounters. If a coder that also has the skills to interview an end user of the product a handoff can be avoided from the interviewer to the coder which will avoid a misinterpretation and save time and money.

    A is incorrect because a generalizing specialist is not a person with just one skill, but a person who has more than one skill related to the project discipline.

    C and D are incorrect because the term generalizing specialist doesn't refer to a person that understands each role and responsibility or to a person that knows their job duties well.

3. Your agile team leader has described the iteration goals at a high level and is allowing the team to decide how to complete the iteration. What does this action prove to the team?

    A. That the leader doesn't know how to accomplish the iteration

    B. That the leader trusts the self-organizing team and their expertise to complete the goal

    C. That the team leader is busy working on his normal job

    D. That the team leader is not a micro-manager

    B. The team leader recognizes that the team members are in the best position to organize the work, which in turn alleviates the roadblocks when a list of tasks is pushed to the team. Agile leaders are there to serve the people doing the work by blocking any interruptions, removing roadblocks, communicating, and providing support.

    A, C, and D are incorrect because encouraging the project team to be self-organizing is the agile leader's role, and attributing any other reason to this decision would be mere speculation.

4. You are on a self-directing agile team and would like to take the lead on a task that you are very familiar with and feel very strongly about. What is the process to take the lead?

    A. Explain and show to your team that this task falls within your expertise and you know you can lead it to success

    B. Ask the project leader if it would be okay to lead this process

    C. In a meeting with stakeholders, explain that you've done this task before and it would be a good idea for you to take the lead

    D. Subtly overpower the leader and take charge of the task

A. A feature of a high-performing agile team is that leadership can be switched seamlessly without a power struggle. If the team understands that you can have a successful outcome, either in a small task or a complete iteration, the likely reaction will be, "Go for it!"
B is incorrect because members of a self-organizing team should not have to ask for permission or nudge someone out of the way to take the lead. C is incorrect because the team member wouldn't ask permission from the stakeholders, but would address the project team. D is incorrect because leading a portion of the project isn't a political game, but is an example of emergent leadership from the project team.

5. Your team leader has built a safe environment for disagreement. How has this empowered the team to move forward without obstacles?

   A. There is a method to create a list of reasons why tasks cannot be completed and brought to management.

   B. The team decided to avoid conflict.

   C. The team leader takes responsibility for all decisions made.

   D. The team is encouraged to join in constructive conflict to make better decisions.

   D. Constructive conflict is encouraged because better decisions are made, and team members can stand behind their agreement.
   A is incorrect because this answer doesn't describe the safe environment or the agile approach to getting things done. B is incorrect because avoiding conflict guarantees the wrong decision or a single person making decisions. C is incorrect because the agile team leader is not there to take responsibility for good or bad decisions, but to remove roadblocks, communicate, deflect interruptions, and provide what the team requires.

6. You are on a new agile team and your leader keeps emphasizing that for the first iteration, everyone needs to follow the rules that have been described by previous agile teams in the organization. Why do you think this is so important to your leader?

   A. It is best to start a project by following a method that has been tested, proven, and refined by others.

   B. The leader wants to be able to explain the rules and then go back to her normal job and let the team work on its own.

   C. The leader wants the team members to prove they can follow rules.

   D. The team leader doesn't want the team to try to move the project off course early in the process.

   A. Original agile teams have tried and tested many theories to learn how to begin a project. They found that before you can understand how and why all pieces work together, you need to develop a high-level understanding of the process. So, following the rules that have been tested, proven, and refined will get you to the basics of the project.

B is incorrect because an agile leader should be fully committed to their project, so there is no conflict between jobs. C is incorrect because following rules in the beginning will keep a project on course, rather than introducing scope creep, and isn't intended to prove anything. D is incorrect because changing the rules of agile is acceptable, but only after the team has mastered the rules and has good reasons to change.

7. As a member of an agile team, at what level of mastering a skill do you think you can make the best decision rather than relying on the rules?

   A. Competent

   B. Competent

   C. Proficient

   D. Expert

   C. At the proficient level of mastering a skill, your decision making is still analytical, but you are becoming more comfortable relying on a gut feel rather than a rule.

   A is incorrect because at the advanced beginner stage, you are beginning to understand the context of the rules, which isn't the best stage to begin tailoring the processes or changing the agile rules. B is incorrect because during the competent stage, you are deciding which rules are best for the situation. D is incorrect because becoming an expert means decisions are intuitive and spontaneous.

8. The formation and development of teams normally follow the Tuckman Model of forming, storming, norming, and performing. Your team leader is obviously aware of this model, but he is new to the organization and is having trouble understanding why the forming stage has gone so quickly. Which of the following might be the reason?

   A. The team was handpicked by management, so they know they must get along.

   B. Most of the team members have worked together on previous projects.

   C. They team members really don't care if they get along or not.

   D. Most of the team members are from the same department.

   B. Not all teams will follow this model completely, and the team lead needs to look for signs of which phase the team is in and plan accordingly. Most of this team has worked together previously, so the initial phase, forming, is not as necessary as it would be for a completely new team.

   A is incorrect because even teams that are selected by management may still go through forming. C is incorrect because teams do need to care if they get along. D is incorrect because even teams from the same department may still need to move through forming if they've not worked together in the past and as they learn about the project.

9. You are the project manager of a new agile project for your organization and you're explaining to the business team how agile works. You explain that at which of the following stages of adaptive leadership the leader may ask many questions?

A. Directing

B. Coaching

C. Supporting

D. Delegating

A. Early in a team's formation, the leader directly helps with project activities and lays out a picture of what needs to be accomplished. The leader may also ask a lot of questions to ensure the team understands the team's direction. B is incorrect because in the coaching phase, the leader mainly resolves conflicts so that relationships are not damaged. C is incorrect because during the supporting phase, the leader is still needed for conflict resolution in addition to challenging the team with high-level goals. D is incorrect because the delegating stage is rarely achieved because teams are empowered.

10. You are an agile team leader and you've come to realize that there is very little interest in the project coming from team members. What is a good method to motivate team members for the duration of the project?

A. Offer them a raise if they become engaged

B. Offer a bonus if the project is a success

C. Align the project goals to the corporate goals

D. Align the project goals to team members' personal goals

D. A good method of motivating the team is to understand the individual goals of the project team members and show the correlation between the project goals and the individual goals.
A and B are incorrect because offering a raise or bonus might engage team members for a short time, but probably not for the long run. C is incorrect because aligning the project goals to the corporate goals still does not answer "What's in it for me?" for the team members, but aligning the project goals to the individual's personal goals (for example, a promotion to a management position) will give them the motivation to be successful.

11. In the middle of an iteration, the team leader noticed that one member was having an issue with a decision the entire team made. The leader asked the team member for a one-on-one discussion. What type of session do you think this was?

A. Training

B. Coaching

C. Mentoring

D. Directing

B. Coaching is defined as helping a team member to stay on track, improve skills, and overcome issues. During an iteration is the right time to address individual team members, whereas between iterations it is more practical to coach the entire team.

A is incorrect because training is teaching a skill by instruction and is very structured. This is not the right situation for a training session. C is incorrect because mentoring involves having a relationship with someone you can bounce ideas off and ask for advice. D is incorrect because directing is when the project manager gives direct instructions for how to do a task, something that is not generally encouraged in agile projects.

12. Beth is the project manager for an agile project in her organization. She's explaining to the team how the team should communicate effectively in the project. What is the preferred method of communication for an agile team?

   A. Secured and saved e-mail so there is a paper trail

   B. Conference calls where attendance is mandatory

   C. Face-to-face discussions

   D. One-on-one phone calls

   C. Face-to-face discussions are the recommended method of communication on agile teams.

   A, B, and D are incorrect choices as e-mail, conference calls, and one-on-one phone calls are considered alternative methods if people can't meet in person, but agile recommends face-to-face communication to avoid misinterpretation or confusion.

13. You are the project manager of an agile project for your organization and you'd like the team to be colocated. When is an agile team considered to be colocated?

   A. When all team members are within 33 feet of each other with no barriers

   B. When all team members are located on the same floor of a building

   C. When all team members are in the same city

   D. When all team members are on the same campus

   A. An agile team is only considered to be colocated when all team members are within 33 feet of each other with no barriers.

   B, C, and D are incorrect because the team members are not sufficiently proximate to be considered colocated in agile. When team members are dispersed and use technology to communicate, they are considered virtually colocated even if the team members are on the same floor, city, or campus. Within 33 feet of one another is the best choice to describe colocation.

14. You are on a colocated agile team and sometimes the team area gets so noisy that it is hard to concentrate. On these days, you are very glad to have access to which of the following?

   A. Cafeteria

   B. Your boss's office

   C. A small private office, sometimes known as a cave

   D. Another floor

   C. Common areas ("commons") sometimes can be very distracting. Agile teams often include private offices, or "caves," in their team space so that private conversations, calls, or just quiet time for a team member can take place.
   A, B, and D are incorrect because going to a different area can be time consuming and, in some cases, even more distracting.

15. You are on an agile team and in a meeting one of your co-workers said she learned how to correct a piece of code by osmotic communication. What does this mean?

   A. She dreamed what the correction should be

   B. She did a search on Google

   C. She read about the solution in a book

   D. She overheard a conversation in the agile team's commons that discussed the solution

   D. Osmotic communication is described as useful information that is overheard when working in a common area.
   A is incorrect because osmotic communications doesn't describe finding answers by dreaming solutions. B is incorrect because searching Google is an example of research, not osmotic communications. C is incorrect because reading a book may be a good source of information, but it's not osmotic communication.

16. You are leading an agile team whose members are located in several areas of the world. You've arranged conference calls and insisted that everyone have their computer cameras on so that team members can associate names and faces with participants. It is impossible to have the team members meet face to face because of the cost. What is an alternate method of enabling team members to get to know each other?

   A. Have them send each other pictures

   B. Have each member write a short biography and share it with team members

   C. Pair up team members to work on tasks, and rotate the pairs

   D. Have team members get to know each other's primary language

C. Pairing up team members on a task or iteration gives them the opportunity to talk one-on-one more often and learn how to react and deal with each other. A and B are incorrect as pictures and a biography will not help team members get to know each other's work ethics and goals. D is incorrect because learning each other's primary language is an admirable goal, but not realistic for most projects.

17. You have been selected to lead a team with members located all over the world. You pushed to use the agile method of running a team and upper management thought that was an excellent suggestion. Why is running a distributed team with an agile methodology feasible?

    A. Being agile allows you to select two or three people in each location to work together with the project's goals in mind.

    B. Agile teams use short iterations to complete tasks and receive feedback to ensure the project is on the right track.

    C. Almost everyone has Internet access, which allows for immediate communication.

    D. Agile teams are used to running themselves, so your involvement as the leader will be minimal.

    B. The short iterations during an agile project require continuous collaboration and coordination. Each iteration is similar to a mini-project, meaning it is complete when delivered, making chunks of work easier to manage than an entire project at the end of the project's life cycle.
    A is incorrect because virtual teams don't have to work in groups of two or three people. C is incorrect because, while virtual teams do use Internet connectivity for communications, it's not the best answer presented. D is incorrect because teams may eventually be self-led and self-organized, but the project manager will still be involved in facilitating and coaching the team.

18. You are looking at a burndown chart located in the agile team area. What is this chart telling you?

    A. How many members are rolling off the project

    B. How much work needs to be completed on the project

    C. How many test scripts have been run

    D. When you can schedule your vacation

    B. A burndown chart indicates how much work is left to complete the project. A burndown chart can also show the remaining tasks in the current iteration. It is the team's decision on what will be measured on a burndown chart, such as hours, stories, iterations, etc.

A is incorrect because a burndown chart doesn't show the number of people leaving the project team. C is incorrect because a burndown chart doesn't show the number of test scripts completed. D is incorrect because a burndown chart can allude to a project's likely completion, based on the number of tasks completed, but its primary goal is to show the amount of work left to complete in the project. Other matrices exist that show team members' status, how many test scripts have been run, or a calendar for the team to schedule time off.

19. You are looking at a burnup chart located in the agile team's area. What is this chart telling you?

   A. When to add additional members to the project

   B. How many test scripts are left to execute

   C. How much work has been completed

   D. When the project will end

   C. A burnup chart indicates how much work has been completed. The advantage to a burnup chart is that it can also track the project scope, items not started, or what is in progress.
   A, B, and D are incorrect because a burnup chart doesn't show these items. There are other matrices that will track members, what work is left to complete, and when the project will end.

20. You are the project manager for your organization and you're sharing a velocity chart with the product owner. What is measured in a velocity chart?

   A. The team's capacity

   B. How many members are on the team at any given time

   C. How quickly the project is progressing

   D. How many hours have been burned on the project

   A. A velocity chart measures the team's capacity for work per iteration. After tracking several iterations, the velocity chart will become a powerful tool for planning and estimating by using the team's average velocity of the previous iterations. Another benefit of the velocity chart is that it takes into consideration interruptions and scope creep.
   B, C, and D are incorrect because a velocity chart doesn't show these items. Other matrices can be used to track members, time, and how many hours have been used to date.

CHAPTER 5

Planning for Agile Projects

In this chapter, you will

- Define the ten exam tasks of adaptive planning
- Explore the principles of adaptive planning
- Timebox meetings and events
- Create and size user stories
- Estimate the project size
- Visualize the project product
- Create release and iteration plans for your project

This chapter is probably the most important chapter of the entire book when preparing for your PMI-ACP exam because it touches all areas of an agile project. Adaptive planning covers the agile planning concepts you'll need to know for your exam and it complements so much of what we've already discussed thus far. In this chapter we are going to get into user stories, how to write some user stories, and what you can expect for your exam. We'll talk about grooming the backlog a bit more and how the product owner plays a big part in adaptive planning.

Another topic you'll need to understand for your exam is how to estimate the size of the requirements, the user stories. In this chapter I'll discuss affinity estimating, a technique for estimating items in the backlog, and we're going to play some poker. Well, not really, we're going to do some "planning poker" and we're going to create a product roadmap. I'll talk about creating release and iteration plans and how we do that with the team and the product owner and how that effects our schedule and the project. In this chapter I'll nail down the concept of spikes and how that helps us create some framework for our project. I've already discussed the idea of visioning the project, and in this chapter I'll discuss visioning the releases.

I'll also talk about transparent planning, a theme that we've seen throughout this book and when dealing with stakeholders. We're going to manage expectations by refining plans. Of course, we'll do that throughout the project. You know change is going to happen in agile, we welcome change, and we'll manage the changes based on priorities to incorporate those into the product backlog.

 For a more detailed explanation, watch the *Planning Adaptive Projects* video now.

A big topic for this chapter is sizing the items in our backlog. The sizing of the items in our backlog will affect the team velocity (discussed in Chapter 4), but we'll size the items independently of the team velocity. We'll also adjust our work to accommodate maintenance, operations, and the known unknowns that are going to interrupt our work and constrict our velocity. We'll carry on the idea that planning is ongoing, and that agile planning is different than predictive planning.

Introducing the Adaptive Planning Domain

Adaptive planning is different than predictive planning. In a predictive project, like building a house, we can plan exactly what's needed, plan how long each task will take, and be very specific in our pricing. Adaptive planning takes a higher-level view, adapts to changes, and plans the project work in iterations. Agile planning utilizes special terms, ceremonies, and approaches that you'll need to know for your exam—and I'll explain them in this chapter.

One term that you probably already know is *rolling wave planning*, an approach that uses waves of planning and then executing. That's something we do in agile by design: we plan the iteration's work, then we complete the work in the iteration. The project team does this over and over throughout the project through iteration planning and then executing the work of the iteration. This is also the idea of *progressive elaboration*, where we start with a broad idea of the project, then break it down into smaller and smaller items and components. Rolling wave planning is an example of progressive elaboration.

In adaptive planning, as project manager, you'll also continue to be transparent with the project stakeholders and the project team. There's a direct message that the initial estimates may very well be flawed, especially if you've not done this type of work before—you don't know what you don't know. Estimates of velocity in the first few iterations of the project may be wildly incorrect, but with experience the velocity will stabilize and the team will move into performing and getting things done. You and the team will adjust your plans based on what's happening in the project and the product owner's prioritization of the product backlog.

Another theme of adaptive planning is to not adjust the size of the requirements, the user stories, based on the velocity of the project team. We don't shift our approach to fit our velocity, but we do adjust the number of requirements we believe we can accomplish in an iteration based on experience. If our velocity is falling consistently below the number of requirements we believe we can complete per iteration, the project team will need to take on fewer items to fit their stabilized velocity. As the project progresses, and the team gets more experienced and competent in the project work, the velocity may increase so more features can be tackled in an iteration.

Planning is an ongoing activity. You and the team will plan the project at a high level, then you'll plan the iterations at a specific level. The actual rate of work, the velocity, is what you'll use to predict duration and scoping for the project, not wild guesses or assumptions. You'll also incorporate risk into planning. Risk is an uncertain event that can negatively affect your project, so you should take on risk-laden items early in the project, and overcome them, to improve your odds of project success.

Reviewing the Ten Tasks for Exam Domain V

The adaptive planning exam domain has lots of tasks to know but is only worth 12 percent of the PMI-ACP exam; that's roughly 14 questions. There are ten tasks in three exam subdomains you'll need to know for your exam. The primary goal of these tasks is to create and maintain a plan that can evolve throughout the project based on the conditions within the project. As changes enter the project and with each iteration, the project team will plan on how best to complete the work. Much of this work is done with the product owner, not as a separate activity by the project team.

In agile, plans are lightweight and we strive to ensure that plans and all other documentation are barely sufficient. We don't get bogged down in long, thick plans like you might in a predictive project. Our planning does address how the project team will create value, take on and manage project risks, deal with constraints, and communicate with project stakeholders. For your PMI-ACP exam, know that planning is essential, but it has a cadence and timeboxed approach, rather than long, intense planning sessions. As declared in the Agile Manifesto, value is in working software, not in documentation.

Let's look at the three subdomains and tasks:

Levels of Planning

- Plan at multiple levels (strategic, release, iteration, daily) creating appropriate detail by using rolling wave planning and progressive elaboration to balance predictability of outcomes with ability to exploit opportunities.

- Make planning activities visible and transparent by encouraging participation of key stakeholders and publishing planning results in order to increase commitment level and reduce uncertainty.

- As the project unfolds, set and manage stakeholder expectations by making increasingly specific levels of commitments in order to ensure common understanding of the expected deliverables.

Adaptation

- Adapt the cadence and the planning process based on results of periodic retrospectives about characteristics and/or the size/complexity/criticality of the project deliverables in order to maximize the value.

- Inspect and adapt the project plan to reflect changes in requirements, schedule, budget, and shifting priorities based on team learning, delivery experience, stakeholder feedback, and defects in order to maximize business value delivered.

Agile Sizing and Estimation

- Size items by using progressive elaboration techniques in order to determine likely project size independent of team velocity and external variables.

- Adjust capacity by incorporating maintenance and operations demands and other factors in order to create or update the range estimate.

- Create initial scope, schedule, and cost range estimates that reflect current high level understanding of the effort necessary to deliver the project in order to develop a starting point for managing the project.

- Refine scope, schedule, and cost range estimates that reflect the latest understanding of the effort necessary to deliver the project in order to manage the project.

- Continuously use data from changes in resource capacity, project size, and velocity metrics in order to evaluate the estimate to complete.

Building a Strong Adaptive Planning Foundation

Because adaptive planning is significantly different in its approach than predictive planning, many project managers struggle with the adaptive planning concepts. The secret, for your PMI-ACP exam, is to focus on just the next most important thing. It's all about setting priorities for the product backlog and the work you'll do in the current iteration's backlog. You don't worry over features and requirements that aren't top priority. The opportunities for planning are sometimes called *ceremonies*. We've already talked about the daily standup, backlog prioritization, and the sprint retrospective where we discuss what worked well and what didn't work so well. In this chapter our focus will be on these planning opportunities and the strategies to plan to make the project better, smoother, and more precise without getting bogged down in long, drawn-out planning sessions.

One of the fundamental parts of adaptive planning is to create a strong product vision. Recall that the product vision is a summary we use to communicate our project's end goal. In the product vision, we define how the project's product differentiates us from our competitors, how the product supports the overall strategy of the organization, how it gives the boundaries of what the project will deliver, and what the project will not create. This vision statement is kind of an elevator pitch to communicate our end goal.

Tied to the vision statement is the product roadmap. A product roadmap is just a big picture of the functionality of our deliverables and how that functionality satisfies the product vision. The product roadmap is a way of keeping our team and our stakeholders involved and keeping us focused on what we are creating as a result of the project. Some people say it's the initial cut at the product backlog, but it's really a high-level description of what the project team aims to accomplish.

The next term you'll want to know for your exam is *release planning*, which determines when are we going to have releases available. The project manager, the product owner, and the project team determine the next set of functionalities that can be released as part of an incremental approach. The product owner decides what's valuable for release. As the project manager, you must be synced up with what set of requirements the project owner will create, and those requirements have to equate to the release that could go into production. It doesn't mean, to be clear, that at the end of each iteration we have a release.

A release plan defines when a set of requirements are done, then that set of completed requirements can equate to a release. We provide a boundary over what functionality is needed to have a minimal viable product (MVP). The set of requirements, the set of stories that are done, when we complete these, then we can have a release. That's what's in our release plan.

Recall that once we have a set of selected user stories from the product backlog, that becomes our sprint or iteration backlog. Those user stories move into our next iteration, which is where the team becomes self-organizing and decides who is going to do what. Our sprint or iteration backlog defines what tasks the team will do in this iteration to create a potentially shippable functionality.

Once we have an iteration backlog, we can create a burndown chart for the iteration. We can do a burndown chart that's just for this iteration, or we'll call it a sprint burndown chart if you're working in a Scrum project. It helps us have a vision of our goal for this iteration, and it also creates a boundary that says these are the items we must do to reach our iteration goals. We do no more and no less in this iteration. This is our focus in this iteration, or this sprint if you're in a Scrum project.

An increment is a portion of the final product. It's a component of the fully developed, working, potentially shippable product. This doesn't mean that at the end of each sprint or iteration we're going to have an increment to add, but a combination of increments could equate to a release. The product owner doesn't have to release every increment to the customer. The product owner could say, "When we have all of these items, the accumulation of several increments, then the product could be released."

So, when to release an increment? Each increment is ready to be released once there is enough aggregated value. The collection of all these items that your team creates, all of these increments together, equals value that should be released into production.

 EXAM COACH   Increments, iterations, and sprints all have some similar characteristics. They are all chunks of work that contribute to the overall project. Increments are like train cars: each car is a completed component of the train, ready for delivery, and linking all the cars together with the engine forms the complete train. An iteration also appends to the existing work, but there's typically a final release of the product, rather than several releases. In a Scrum project, sprints are iterations of work that could, if the product owner requires, have several releases as well.

Reviewing the Key Tasks of Adaptive Planning

Adaptive planning is all about how we are going to get to the definition of done. Adaptive planning defines how we'll get there through iterations of planning and doing. Let's revisit the product backlog, our large set of prioritized requirements. If we're using MoSCoW for prioritization, we have requirements sorted by must have, should have, could have, and would like to have but not at this time. The definition of done would look at the prioritized set of requirements and define what absolutely needs to be completed to create value. In most projects there's going to be a line of demarcation below which the items don't fit into the amount of time or the amount of funds we have available. The completion of requirements above that line equates to the definition of done and represents the value for the organization.

Along with the definition of done we have the definition of quality. Quality addresses the product the project team creates. The product must conform to requirements and must be fit for use. By achieving quality in our work, we'll reach acceptance. Quality and acceptance apply to the increment and the aggregation of increments that will allow the product to be released and go into production and create value.

Adaptive planning is all about how we achieve quality and acceptability. With adaptive planning we continue to ask how we manage a selection of prioritized requirements, without being too verbose and without being too restrictive on what our project team members are allowed to do. Of course, as project managers we want the project team to be self-organizing and self-directed, so that we can focus on guiding and coaching, but we don't want to make decisions for the project team as we get deeper and deeper into the project.

As you might guess, a lot of fluctuation can happen with adaptive planning. The first key here, with adaptive planning, is to keep in mind that it's all about value. Agile projects are value driven. As a project manager, or as any member of an adaptive team, we want to minimize anything that is not adding value. By minimizing non-value work, we're promoting and creating things that are of value. The entire project team needs to have the mindset that we're going to be re-planning, that there are opportunities, iterations of planning, that are going to happen throughout this project. We don't need to plan everything at once, just the first chunk of prioritized requirements.

If you have a new team coming from a predictive background, they might not be used to this approach of iterative planning throughout the project. They might wonder, "Why don't we just plan the whole thing?" Well, we know there are too many variables and that approach doesn't work well with adaptive projects. We only focus on little chunks of prioritized work at a time; this approach allows changes to enter the project and prevents us from wasting time planning for requirements that may never happen.

Of course, early plans are necessary, like the product road map and the vision, but truthfully, these early plans are likely flawed because we don't have all the information yet. Plans are necessary, but they aren't going to be perfect. And that's okay, that's expected in agile projects. We don't get upset when changes happen—changes happen as part of the perfection of the project, not just the project plan. There's no value in a plan; the value is in the result of the project work.

Defining Agile and Non-Agile Planning Activities

Let's compare agile and non-agile planning activities. First, in agile, trial and demonstration help to uncover true requirements. We often must experiment, test, and go back and forth to really understand what's needed in the project. In agile, of course, we have less up-front planning than in a predictive project. Agile projects utilize iterative planning. Before every sprint, we have sprint planning. Then, we have midcourse adjustments, so as we're moving along on one path, changes to the product backlog will likely prompt us to adjust our approach. It's part of trial and demonstration, which is part of change in agile. We need to have the mindset and expectation that changes aren't just to the product backlog, but also in how we do our work. You, the project manager, need to communicate that expectation to stakeholders and the project team early and often.

Trial and error happens as part of an adaptive project by doing prototyping. Remember those wireframes and use case diagrams in Chapter 3? Using those is a form of trial and error. We'll also leverage our demonstrations to show the product owner what we've created, and then the product owner will offer feedback. Demonstration in the sprint or iteration review will help to avoid the gulf of evaluation. Recall that the gulf of evaluation is the difference between what the stakeholder wants and what the project team understands. It helps everyone involved to be on the same page and to have the same vision. It also helps communicate our agile planning practices, communicate our approach. Iterative planning is distributed throughout the project life cycle through sprint planning, sprint reviews, and retrospectives.

We want to consider planning efforts over the project life cycle, so we know that there's going to be planning opportunities throughout the whole project life cycle. It's not all up front. There are planned opportunities to plan the next chunk of work.

 EXAM COACH   More planning typically occurs in an agile project than in a predictive project. Changes to plans are normal in agile. Change is expected. Knowledge work, such as software development, does not follow a predictive plan.

Defining the Principles of Agile Planning

One of the most important concepts of agile planning is that we plan at multiple levels. This means that the project manager, the product owner, and the project team are working together to plan at a high level for the project, at the product level, at the user story level, and at the level of individual tasks, as depicted in Figure 5-1. As the project manager, you want to engage the team and the customer in planning. It's not an us-against-them mentality, but rather a mentality that we're all on the same team.

Scrum provides a good example of the agile planning concepts, as shown in Figure 5-2. Starting on the left, our product backlog is prioritized, as represented by the chunks. Based on the amount of work that our team believes they can do in an iteration, those chunks feed into our sprint backlog. The sprint backlog, all those cubes in Figure 5-2,

Figure 5-1   Agile planning happens at several different levels in the project.

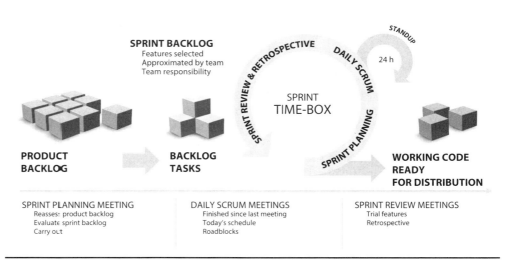

SPRINT BACKLOG
Features selected
Approximated by team
Team responsibility

SPRINT REVIEW & RETROSPECTIVE

DAILY SCRUM

STANDUP

24 h

SPRINT
TIME-BOX

SPRINT PLANNING

PRODUCT
BACKLOG

BACKLOG
TASKS

WORKING CODE
READY
FOR DISTRIBUTION

SPRINT PLANNING MEETING
Reasses: product backlog
Evaluate sprint backlog
Carry out

DAILY SCRUM MEETINGS
Finished since last meeting
Today's schedule
Roadblocks

SPRINT REVIEW MEETINGS
Trial features
Retrospective

Figure 5-2 The Scrum project life cycle uses several instances of project planning.

represents the features, the requirements, the user stories that our team believes they can get done in one sprint. Then we move into our sprint timebox. Now we have our sprint planning where the team decides who'll do what task in the sprint. At the start of the sprint the project manager and team have the sprint planning meeting. In this planning meeting, the team determines what they are going to accomplish. The team is asking what can be delivered in this sprint.

Throughout the sprint, we'll have our Daily Scrum, during which each person, after stating what they accomplished the day before, states what they plan to accomplish that day and whether any impediments exist to accomplishing it. The Daily Scrum is a quick planning and communications meeting. It helps the team understand what's happening in the project and gives the project manager an opportunity to understand any impediments she needs to address.

At the end of the sprint, the team has a product increment, the sum of all the work that they've completed during a sprint. The product the team creates must be usable, reliable, and provide evidence of value. If the team hasn't completed all their sprint backlog items, the remaining items go back into the product backlog to be reprioritized and the process starts over. The product owner decides when an increment is available for release. Just because the team has completed an iteration doesn't mean the work will immediately go into production.

At the end of the sprint we have our sprint review. This is where the team meets with the key stakeholders and the team provides a demo of what they've created. Based on the demo, the stakeholders provide feedback on whether the product is acceptable. The sprint review is about collaborating with the product owner and other key stakeholders. This meeting is also about accountability for the team's work, their ownership of the project, and the value they are creating for the organization.

Next is the sprint retrospective where the team can discuss how well they've worked as a team and what has or has not worked regarding the people, processes, tools, and relationships. The retrospective is a private meeting just for the project team and the project manager, giving them an opportunity to learn from the last sprint and then to decide how to improve.

After the retrospective the team returns to working with the product backlog and the product owner. Once again, the product owner and the team address the prioritization of the requirements, determine what can go into the next sprint, and then move on to sprint planning.

Working with Emergent Plans

Agile teams work with emergent plans rather than traditional design or predictive plans. Working with emergent plans requires *agile discovery*, which means that that the project team discovers through experiments and innovation the best approach to accomplish their work. Often the preplanning activities are for consensus, like the backlog refinement, but we don't often know the details and approach until the team gets into the work and creates a path.

In agile, we estimate uncertain work with a range of variance, such as plus or minus 50 percent or even 100 percent. If we've never done the work before or we're uncertain about it, it's nearly impossible to say with certainty how long or how much effort it will take to reach the definition of done. This is a classic example of succumbing to the first-time, first-use penalty. You've never done the work before, so it's the first time or first use. It's like trying to predict how long it'll take an artist to paint a masterpiece—it's impossible to predict due to all the factors and unknowns of the creative process.

Certain work describes work that the team has done before. With certain work we have a good sense of how long it will take to complete and how much effort will be required, so our confidence level is higher than when estimating uncertain work. For example, think about new product development versus a repeatable project that you've done ten times before. Or consider the type of project that a team likely has done several times before, such as designing a website, versus the type of project that may be entirely new to a team, such as developing a whole new technology.

With agile discovery, our goal is to narrow the cone of uncertainty, as represented in Figure 5-3. The cone of uncertainty describes how a large range of uncertainty exists at the beginning of the project, and over time and with experience the cone becomes smaller and smaller. It's like eating an ice cream cone: the closer you get to the end, the smaller and smaller the cone gets. In the project, as our team gets more and more experience, and we repeat our planning opportunities, the cone of uncertainty narrows and gets smaller. This is because our confidence level goes up based on what we've already created and experienced in the project.

 EXAM COACH *Agile discovery* simply means that the project team discovers through experiments and innovation the best approach to accomplish their work. Plans emerge from the work, not through thinking about the work. Not every innovation will succeed, and many failed innovations might be needed to allow the plan to emerge on how best to do the project work.

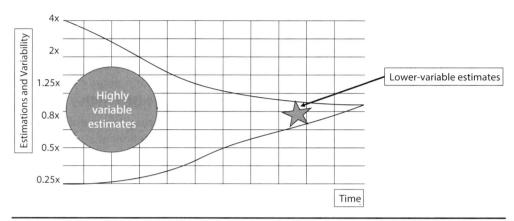

Figure 5-3   Estimates early in the project are highly variable, while estimates late in the project are lower-variable estimates.

Leading Progressive Elaboration

If I want you to build a new mobile app for me, you'd interview me for all the details of the app. As I talk about the details, you'd ask more questions for more information. Then you and your team might tinker with a prototype, and you'd gather more information from me. The more information that you have, the more questions and precision you'll have to develop the app. This is progressive elaboration. Progressive elaboration just means that I am progressively elaborating on the product, on the project scope, on the requirements, on any facet of the project, as more and more information becomes available.

Progressive elaboration is getting a sense of what the product will have and then continuing to elaborate and elaborate and get very specific. You're doing a type of requirements elicitation where you continue to gather information, steadily, in small increments. You're elaborating on your plans, on your estimates on risk, on requirements, on software designs and even test scenarios.

In progressive elaboration, you're getting people to talk more and more about the product. You are gathering requirements and information as more information becomes available. You might also know this as *rolling wave planning*. Progressive elaboration doesn't have to happen in waves like rolling wave planning does, but it often does. In adaptive planning, we consider the broad scope of the requirements backlog, then we select the prioritized user stories. For the selected user stories, we plan the work, we do the work, then we repeat the process.

Performing Value-Based Analysis

For your PMI-ACP exam, always consider the creation of value to be a top priority. To create value, we must first understand what constitutes value for the customer, and this requires value-based analysis. Value-based analysis is looking at the business value and assessing the worth of what the project will create. Value-based analysis is the business benefit minus the cost of the project. It's answering the question "What is the worth

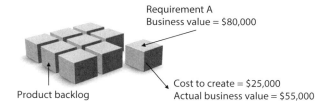

Requirement A
Business value = $80,000

Product backlog

Cost to create = $25,000
Actual business value = $55,000

Figure 5-4 Value-based analysis considers the cost of creating the requirement.

of the project deliverable and how much did it cost to create?" In Figure 5-4 we have a business benefit that is worth $80,000. The cost to create it, though, was $25,000, so the real value is $55,000. That's value-based analysis.

When utilizing value-based analysis we want to know if the project's product is a one-time value or if the product will have residual value for each given time. You'll think through the business value on each return of that investment for each period and a cumulative business value for the entire product life cycle.

Business value typically addresses the entire project's product—the value is in the working software and result of the project. However, you can also consider the business value of each individual requirement to pare down the product, to get the project to completion faster, and to help prioritize the product backlog. A high-business-value item, though, might be dependent on a low-business-value item. Consider the product backlog and your most high-priority items, then consider if there are constituent components that are required that might be lower in value but needed to make the higher-value items a reality in the final product.

Value-based decomposition is a visual decomposition of the project scope, requirements, features, or even risk. Value-based decomposition is another way to examine the requirements and determine the value of each requirement for prioritization and relationships among the components. You'll consider if you and the team can take requirements and identify affinity. By breaking down features into smaller elements, you can identify the relationships of the elements, estimate how they contribute to value, and determine which elements truly contribute to value and which elements could be possibly lowered in priority to realize value sooner.

One approach for value-based analysis is to create a product box, as in Figure 5-5. A product box shows the value of what we're creating. It's a way of visualizing what the top features of the product are. You and the team can identify, for example, what the top three functional elements are, the prioritization of features, and really encapsulate the value. A product box is all about visualizing value and it's a way of telling a story and capturing attention to see the value of what's being created for the customer.

For your PMI-ACP exam, consider coarse-grained requirements and fine-grained requirements. *Coarse-grained requirements* are high-level, chunky descriptions of the project requirements. For example, it's an app to find restaurants in your neighborhood. *Fine-grained requirements* are much more detailed and very specific on acceptability. Coarse-grained requirements and fine-grained requirements are both about the depth of granularity. Granularity describes how small and precise the requirements are captured. The more specific you are in the requirements, the more granularity you have captured.

Figure 5-5 A product box helps to visualize the top benefits of the project for the customer.

Keeping requirements initially coarse-grained delays commitments on implementation details until your last responsible moment. Coarse-grained requirements are a way of keeping requirements and decisions at a high level and unrefined. In other words, we're not spending a lot of time in the product backlog polishing, refining, and progressively elaborating. Instead, we're waiting until the last responsible moment to really nail down the details for requirements and commitments in the design and architecture of the solution. This helps our approach too, because requirements are probably going to change as the project moves forward. The goal of coarse-grained requirements is to focus on value and to minimize waste. If you're spending a lot of time refining requirements that are going to change, that's wasted time, a non-value-add activity.

EXAM COACH Your exam is all about recognizing value. Always consider how the outcome of a scenario in your test question affects value. Value is in working software, in meeting quality, and being efficient and effective in decisions.

Creating Estimate Ranges

A mistake I see project managers make often is to give a precise estimate for the duration of work. For example, a project manager and the team might say the project will take 12 weeks. An estimate of 12 weeks is really precise, and that precision introduces risk and pressure for the project work. What's needed instead is an *estimate range*, where you give a range of commitment—for example, 12 weeks plus or minus 25 percent, or 12 weeks plus or minus 3 weeks. An estimate range is not as precise as predictive planning. In predictive planning, we have a very broad range, called the *rough order of magnitude (ROM)*, with a range of variance of plus 75 percent to minus 25 percent. And with a detailed set of requirements, you'd use a definitive estimate that offers a tight range of variance, such as plus or minus 5 percent or even 3 percent.

In agile projects you have much more uncertainty than in predictive projects, so a range of variance can be wild based on the set of requirements, the experience the team has with the work, and customer expectations. You always want to include a range of variance in agile for time and cost. Not that you are hedging your bets or building in artificial buffers, but you must have some acknowledgment of project uncertainty and the uncertainty in knowledge work.

A convergence graph, like the cone of uncertainty, shows how initial estimates are really flawed and, over time, with progressive elaboration, the range of variance gets smaller and smaller. Across the bottom of this convergence graph, the initial cone represents a large swatch of uncertainty. We don't know exact costs and size. With approved product definition, prioritized requirements, and product specs, detailed design specs, and into completing the product, the range of uncertainty can diminish. Once the project is done you're very certain how long the work takes—you've evidence of duration.

Timeboxing Meetings and Events

A timebox is a predetermined, fixed duration for a project event. You define a set of activities and then allot an amount of time for the activities to be completed; for example, four weeks for an iteration or 15-minutes for the daily standup meeting. For timeboxed iterations you match the amount of work to the amount of time allotted, ideally, about 12 work items, depending on how big your team is. If the team completes 8 items of the 12, then the remaining 4 items return to the product backlog for prioritization and selection again.

When timeboxing an iteration and determining how much work the team can complete, you consider the team size. You also consider the requirements that come into your sprint backlog and how the team will divide the work and get things done. The size of the team and their efficiency will affect velocity. You don't want your team to be too big—about 8 to 12 people; 12 people is ideal. A team beyond that size becomes cumbersome and has difficulty being self-led and making decisions as to who's going to do what. A misconception is that the more people a team has the faster the team can get through the work. Not true. When you have too many team members, they begin to get in each other's way and the effectiveness of the team decreases. When a project manager adds more people to get the work done faster, it's called *crashing*. Crashing is great for labor-driven activities, like construction projects, but can be counterproductive for knowledge work projects where you're dealing with invisible work.

Another term that you want to be familiar with is *Parkinson's law*, which states that work expands to fill the time allotted to it. If a team gives itself four weeks to complete eight requirements that realistically could be completed in three weeks, it'll take four weeks. The idea is that sometimes teams bloat or pad their estimates to account for anomalies in the project. The problem is that the activities eat into the bloated estimate and the team will take the allotted time even if there were no issues with the work.

Working with Ideal Time

Ideal time describes the ideal amount of time it will take to create the items in the product backlog. An ideal time estimate does not consider interruptions or delays in the project work. An ideal day might be eight hours, but as you know, in the real world, that's probably not realistic. Ideal time, however, is when we assume that all the time in the estimate is just for the project work.

Ideal time is just an assumption for the project task duration. There are also other assumptions to consider when it comes to sizing and estimating. You know that details emerge as the project moves through progressive elaboration. In a project, as more information becomes available, you can more accurately predict how long activities, or user stories, are going to take to create. The assumption here is that the initial estimate is going to be flawed; you don't know what you don't know. Project plans are adjusted based on feedback and on the reality of the project work duration. As the project team completes iterations and velocity begins to normalize, then you and the team can be more accurate with your duration estimating.

Managing Time Constraints

All of us have the same 24 hours in a day, but how efficiently we work determines how productive we are in that allotted amount of time. Project teams must consider how efficient, how competent, they are with the technology, the requirements, and their approach to manage their time effectively. Competency, like time, is a constraint that affects the project. In the early iterations of the project, the project team likely has low competency on the project work as they're forming, storming, and working out their approach to the project work. After two or three iterations, their velocity will normalize and their competency and confidence in the work they are doing will increase. As their competency increases, so too does their effectiveness to deliver on their estimates.

Recall from Chapter 1 that in agile we work with an inverted pyramid, as depicted in Figure 5-6, compared to the predictive approach. Time and costs are fixed, so the scope must meet the amount of time and the amount of funds available. To manage scope, items are prioritized and lower-priority items are shifted out of the project to meet the amount of time and funds available. If the project team is having difficulties delivering the work—that is, their velocity is too low to meet the needed set of requirements—then

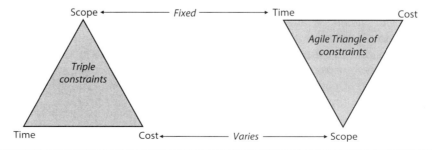

Figure 5-6 Time and costs are fixed constraints in agile projects.

the time constraint becomes a risk in the project. The project manager, the project team, and the product owner need to discuss the feasibility of meeting the target deadline. Bear in mind, the initial iterations will be unpredictable, but with more iterations and experience, the velocity will normalize and then the project manager can decide the likelihood of hitting the time constraint for the project team.

Working with User Stories

A user story is a small chunk of business functionality. User stories are written from the customer's perspective and describe a feature of the product you're creating. For the project team to do the work to make a user story a reality usually takes one to three days, though some user stories may take up to 40 hours to complete. User stories are written on index cards or sticky notes and are the items that make up the product backlog. I prefer using index cards on a bulletin board with tacks, as sticky notes might get less sticky as you, the project team, and product owner move them around to prioritize the product backlog.

There are three Cs of user stories you should know:

- **Card**   An index card or sticky note with just enough text to identify the story
- **Conversation**   The details that are communicated between the customer and the development team
- **Confirmation**   The customer confirmation that the story has been implemented correctly in the product

These three Cs help the creation of the user stories through communication and understanding. When the team completes the user story, the result is part of the product for confirmation in the product demo and final output of the project.

Another approach you can use with user stories, and one you want to know for your exam, is to use the acronym of INVEST. This means user stories are

- **Independent**   The story can stand alone from the other user stories. Independent stories can be prioritized in any order.
- **Negotiable**   There might be some tradeoffs and negotiation. Negotiation can be based on the priority of the user story, risks involved, value to the organization, and how the user story can affect other features of the product.
- **Valuable**   The result creates business value. User stories must create business value when the team creates the feature in the product.
- **Estimable**   You can create an estimate of effort based on the user story. The team will examine the user stories and determine an estimate of effort to create the feature.
- **Small**   The stories aren't too big and don't need further decomposition. User stories are usually between one and three days of work.
- **Testable**   The team can write tests for the product to confirm the successful inclusion of the user story. Test-driven development is based on user stories.

Writing User Stories

When you go about creating user stories, you'll begin with potential user stories that are called candidate stories or candidate user stories. User stories define the role of the story, usually the end user of the feature, and why the role wants the feature and outcome. User stories are written from the perspective of the user or the customer of the product and are written with three components according to a formula:

- **Role**   As a role…
- **Functionality**   I want this functionality…
- **Benefit**   So I can have this business benefit.

User stories can appear to be quick and easy to write, but when you apply a story against the INVEST acronym, you might find that you need to be more granular in your functionality and benefit portions of the user story formula. Here are a few samples of user stories:

- As a user, I want mobile access to my accounts, so I don't have to carry frequent shopper cards.
- As a photographer, I want to build a library of photos for quick access and sharing.
- As a salesperson, I want my client info accessible everywhere, so I can make more sales.

User stories define the role's given scenario, the conditions of the action, and the business value result. So again, consider this user story: As a salesperson, I want my client info accessible, so I can make more sales. The scenario is that a salesperson wants his client information available everywhere and increased sales is the value result. The condition is that the client information must be accessible. The business value result is more sales.

Really large user stories that are difficult to break down into smaller user stories are called *epics*. Epics are usually too large for just one iteration. They can span multiple iterations of work and, in some extreme cases, even span different projects. Most of the time, epics are placeholders for a collection of related user stories. If you have five or more related user stories, that's an epic.

Here are a few examples of epics:

- As a customer, I want my personal data secure, so I don't have to worry about fraud.
- As a salesperson, I want to access customer information from my phone, so I can make more sales.
- As a manager, I want to pull sales reports, so I can make informed decisions.
- As a database administrator, I want to track my database activity, so I can maintain the servers remotely.

- As a security manager, I want to control who can access the data, so I can ensure privacy for customers and sales people.
- As a business owner, I want to see sales reports, customer reports, and trends, so I can do cashflow forecasting.

Epics are large user stories. Epics hold lots of value, have related components, and are difficult to break down into independent user stories. Epics are large user stories that can span multiple iterations. Epics need to be broken down as much as possible to clearly identify the business value and the team will need to test all parts of the epic for acceptability.

Creating the User Story Backlog

The end result of creating the user stories goes into the user story backlog, which I've talked about as the product backlog. Typically, all user stories are listed in one backlog and then the project manager, the project team, and the product owner work to prioritize the user stories. The prioritization of the user stories is the responsibility of the product owner, but the project manager and the project team can help in the planning meetings.

There is only one backlog for the project. You put all user stories into the product backlog. Prioritizing the backlog is based on business value—you might see such prioritization called *grooming* the backlog. When changes enter the project, they are added to the product backlog, not to the current iteration. Changes are welcome, but they are entered in the backlog and the product owner doesn't interrupt the current iteration. The new features go into the backlog, and then the backlog is prioritized, so it's possible that new features may bubble to the top if they're more important than what's left in the product backlog. Changes can even cause older stories to be shifted down in priority or removed altogether.

The project team, based on the prioritized backlog, determines how many of the user stories they can take into the next iteration. The selected stories become the iteration, or sprint, backlog. Within the iteration planning meeting, the team may need to break down a user story even more for task assignment. This process of breaking down user stories to a more granular level is called *slicing* or *disaggregation*.

Sizing and Estimating User Stories

Now that you have a prioritized backlog, the project team and the product owner will meet to begin sizing the story stories. The goal of sizing the user stories is to create an analogy between the different stories. So, for example, we might say, "Well, that's a really large story, and this is a small story. Based on those two stories, this third story must be a medium." The team determines the size of the story and its relationship compared to the other story sizes. For example, a medium story could be considered to be twice as big as a small story, or an extra-large story could be considered to be twice as big as a large story. Again, sizing stories is just a way of creating an analogy between the sizes of the user stories.

When sizing the user stories, you don't want to base sizes on time. Instead, think about effort. With knowledge work, it's difficult, if not impossible, to create an absolute estimate, especially if you've never done that work before. If a team bases their sizing on hours, then they're creating a duration estimate and not considering ideal time, innovation time, and the learning curve that inevitably happens in knowledge-work projects.

Next, in the planning meeting, the team will assign story points to story size. A *story point* is a scale that maps to the sizing, such as a large story is worth five points, a medium story is worth three points, and a small story is worth one point. Story points use a common scale to size user stories relative to one another. Once the stories have been sized and the story points have been assigned, then the team will determine how many points they believe they can accomplish in a current iteration.

There are some techniques you can apply to size your stories. One approach that I use with my project team is based on the Fibonacci sequence, which is a pattern of numbers where each number is the sum of the two preceding numbers. For example, zero plus one equals one. One plus one equals two. Two plus one equals three. Three plus five equals eight, five plus eight is thirteen, thirteen plus eight is twenty-one, and so on. Each user story is assigned a value from the Fibonacci sequence when we size the stories.

If you convert the sequence to measurements they will form the little curl that you see in Figure 5-7, and this is found all through nature, photography, and art. For example, the way a seashell curls out is a Fibonacci sequence. You can continue expanding this sequence beyond 21 as a hobby, but for agile, you'll usually only go up to 21, and some environments limit it to 13 or 8; it depends on how tight you want to make your story sizing. In my projects, I keep things simple and only use 1, 2, 3, 5, and 8.

You might be dealing with a large user story that needs to be broken down more in the product backlog. As mentioned previously, this is called disaggregation or slicing. When you break down the story into two new stories, for example, the two new stories don't have to total the original user story points. For example, if you have a story with eight story points and the team breaks the story into two new stories, the team could determine that one user story is now worth four points and the second user story is now only worth three points. The two new stories don't have to equal eight story points.

Figure 5-7 In the Fibonacci sequence, each number is the sum of the prior two numbers.

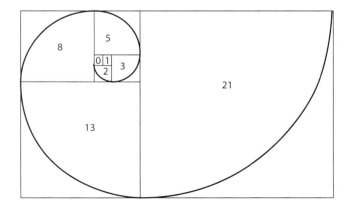

Breaking Down the Project for Releases

After your team breaks down the scope of the project into user stories, the team takes a chunk of the user stories into their iteration backlog and slices them into tasks and assignments for that iteration. At the end of an iteration, your team may have created an increment. The aggregate of increments will take us to a product release. That's breaking down the project—from a large scope, to specific features, to the work, and ultimately to a product release.

Before the product is released to production or to your customers, you want to do release planning. Working with the product owner, you and the project team will decide what increments or set of features equate to a valuable release. The product owner will decide what completed user stories will equate to a release. Within the product backlog, the product owner may identify the groups of user stories and features that will equate to a release. And then they'll identify the next batch of user stories for the next release, and so on. Changes to the product backlog can change the release plan. In some projects, the product owner may say that all of the features have to be included before the product is ready for release.

There are several questions you and the product owner need to answer during release planning for the product:

- Who will need to attend the release planning in addition to the product owner, the project manager, and the project team?

- What user stories will equate to a specific release?

- What are the logistics of the release?

- How will the released product be supported?

- What's the operational transfer and ownership of the released product?

- How will you, the project manager, coordinate multiple teams or distributed teams for the release?

Assuming you have previous releases, you'll look at the results of previous releases for lessons learned. You'll review stakeholder feedback on the product, market situations, and deadlines. Before a product may be released, you'll have to confirm that your team has reached the definition of done for the planned release. You can't release the product if there are tasks that need to be finished or defects that need resolution. Your team will also need to confirm that the development and architecture information is stable and has passed testing. As the team is working toward a release date, you'll have to consider the velocity from previous iterations and how that affects your release plan. Working with the product owner, and perhaps the value management team, you'll need to confirm that the release doesn't interfere with business cycles and organizational and personal calendars.

As part of your preparation for the release planning meeting, you should be aware of some tools and techniques. The first is facilitating the release planning meeting. Based on an agenda, you will walk through the agenda and the purpose of the meeting. You or the product owner will discuss the product vision and roadmap. Your goal is to keep the larger picture in the forefront of the conversation. Then you'll discuss the development status and how the identified increments will lead the project to release. In this meeting you'll welcome participants to identify new information, considerations, and risks or issues that may affect the value of the release. To help identify each release, you'll ideally have a release name and theme.

In the release planning meeting, you'll also discuss the team velocity and what you estimate the velocity will be for the remainder of the project. Present the velocity being used for the release and consider the velocity the team must obtain to hit a target date. Based on the velocity, you'll discover the release schedule and the number of iterations to get to a release. You'll also review key milestones, identify collaborative decisions to be made, and open the floor to discuss any issues or concerns about the release.

In release planning, the product owner, project team, and any subject matter experts should be available to answer questions, do elaboration for acceptance, and map stories to iterations in the release plan. As part of mapping stories, the team will need to consider if there are any dependencies among the stories or assumptions that have been made about work. Dependencies and assumptions can make the planning complex and may ultimately affect what stories will go into the release. Once you have reached some consensus, you'll get into making a commitment for the next target release date. If there is some contention, you might have to do some voting, such as the Fist of Five method, to make certain everyone can address concerns and work toward consensus on the release plan.

Toward the end of release planning you'll address communication and the logistics for the release. Some organizations require a formal operational transfer plan that addresses who'll support the release and the coordination between the project team and the support personnel. Everyone will leave the meeting with their identified action items and a plan of attack to hit the release date. Post-meeting, you can offer a release planning retrospective to identify what worked well, or didn't.

 EXAM COACH   Release planning can happen multiple times in an agile project. For each release planning session, your goal is to understand what's needed to create a quality product that's fit to be released to the customer.

Grooming the Backlog

The product backlog is probably the most important artifact in the agile project. As you know, the product backlog is a prioritized list of all the requirements. It's prioritized first by business value, but also by risk. The product backlog offers much more detail than the product road map as it includes the specific user stories and specific features and technically defines the scope of the project.

Items near the top are of higher priority than those near the bottom. The product owner is the role responsible for prioritizing the backlog, though the project team may help. As previously mentioned, prioritizing the backlog is also called *grooming* the backlog and it's one of the first steps in the agile process. Once the product owner has updated and prioritized the product backlog, the project team may select the user stories and get to work slicing the stories, making assignments, and creating the product.

The product owner can prioritize the backlog before each sprint but can't change the priorities of what's already in the current sprint or iteration. The product backlog is your single source of requirements and it's *dynamic*, meaning that the backlog is never complete until the team reaches the definition of done. Changes can enter the backlog, be prioritized again, and then, in the next sprint planning, be selected by the team in the next chunk of work for that iteration.

Using Affinity Estimating

When we discuss release planning, sizing the user stories, and the product backlog, we must also discuss affinity estimating. Affinity estimating is a way of grouping user stories into similar categories or collections, then you'll size the user stories. For example, in IT, we often will group things by hardware, software, data, and network. As requirements come in or they're identified, they fall into one of these categories. Now in your projects, you could group items by function, features, or characteristics, but it's just a way of grabbing user stories and chunking them out into like collections. You can also group items based on story points, so you'll group items by large, medium, and small, for example. Affinity estimation is really like triangulation, meaning that you can see the related stories based on their size, based on their risk, and based on their priority. Affinity estimating is a way of triangulating and getting a sense of whether you have a good distribution and whether your estimating is correct.

This approach also allows everyone to see all our user stories by the points that we've assigned. If everything is designated as four points, that's a problem. We want to have a distribution of user stories. It's very unlikely you're going to have everything bunch up as a four. Affinity estimating also involves the product owner, the project team, and the project manager.

To start the affinity estimating process, we take the user stories on the note cards or sticky notes and often we compare a story to something that's been proven in the past to start the sizing activity. As we get deeper in the project, we can look at our estimates and say that a selected story is similar to an activity the team has completed earlier in the project. The participants can examine the previous story and its story points, change their mind on its original scoring, and then properly size the current story based on their experience. For example, a completed story could have been scored as a six, but based on experience, the team now knows that original story should've been scored as an eight. Now, with this current similar story, the team can use triangulation and score the current story as an eight. This approach uses analogous estimating and utilizes the affinity to what the project team has accomplished.

For affinity estimating to be successful, you match stories with comparable features. The selected story must have a similar type of work and similar requirements to determine whether the original estimate was accurate based on the work the team has completed and then to properly size the current story.

Sizing T-Shirts for User Stories

A long, long time ago in my life when I was in college, I worked in the men's department for a large retail store at the mall. It was not an exciting job. One of my responsibilities was to stack all of the jeans so that customers could see the different sizes. I used to really hate this job. It was tedious and boring because the jeans would come in big box and weren't in any logical order. I'd have to pull them out and sort them based on the size from biggest at the bottom to smallest at the top.

In agile there is a similar approach, except instead of jeans we use the idea of T-shirts. Imagine a big stack of T-shirts and you and the project team have to put the T-shirts in the order small, medium, large, and extra-large. The shirts have no tag, so you just have to look at the size and make a determination of what size the shirt is supposed to be. You could see that a small is relative to a medium, and a medium is relative to a large, and so on. Instead of actual T-shirts, I'm really talking about user stories. With our product backlog, we're defining the relationship between small and large user stories.

Sizing T-shirts is a way of checking the true sizes of our stories when we compare them to each other. We'd ask if this story is really a medium or should it be a large based on our relationship to an extra-large or small story. The idea is that we want to be consistent as we assign points to user stories. With this approach, user stories are assigned T-shirt sizes, so small, medium, large, or extra-large. That's it. That's the idea of T-shirt sizing.

Sizing Stories with the Wideband Delphi Technique

Let's say that you and I and our manager are invited to a meeting to talk about risk, or to talk about estimates, or to talk about what the requirements are for a project. We both really like our manager, don't want to make her look bad, and respect her opinion. So, whatever the manager says in the meeting we tend to agree with. We won't say anything that might conflict with what our manager says, even though the potential conflict could be important for the project. That is called following the HiPPO—Highest Paid Person's Opinion—something we don't want in a project.

What a project can use instead is called the Wideband Delphi Technique, or simply the Delphi Technique. The Delphi Technique has rounds of anonymous surveys to create estimates, gather risks, or gather requirements. It helps to build consensus without everyone jumping on the bandwagon, following one person's point of view, or following the HiPPO. The Delphi Technique helps to get rid of groupthink. The results of the first survey are tabulated and then a new survey is distributed to the participants so that everyone can respond to what's been collected. The participants can respond to the answers, and the process repeats until there is some consensus.

The Delphi Technique was started by the Rand Corporation in the 1950s to study technology and as a forecasting tool. It's named Delphi because of the Oracle at Delphi. Not that you need to know the Greek mythology part for your exam, but maybe that'll help you remember it because the Greeks loved logic and reason and that's what the Delphi Technique attempts to incorporate.

Sizing with Planning Poker

Let's talk about poker. One of my favorite hobbies is to play poker. I love to play poker. It's something that over the last 20 years I've fallen in love with. I'm not saying I'm very good at it, but I like to play poker. It's fun to hang out with my friends, tell jokes and stories, and have a great time. And there's some strategy, some bluffing, some tells—all the good stuff that comes with the game. Well, in agile projects, this is not quite the same.

I'm talking about "planning poker" for estimating user stories. Planning poker can still be kind of fun and it's a great way to predict the sizes of your user stories.

Planning poker begins with the poker cards. Instead of including the different face cards like in a regular deck of cards, you use only the cards that have numbers on them. In my projects we again use the Fibonacci sequence of 1, 2, 3, 5, and 8. Then you (the PM) and the team look at each user story and everyone privately chooses whichever poker card they think correctly sizes the story, and everyone places their card face down on the table. In unison, everyone turns over their card to get a consensus of the size of the story. If everyone agrees on the story size, which rarely happens, that's the number of story points assigned to the story. If there are wild differences in the estimate, then there's a discussion to arrive at the best score for the user story.

This approach combats group think and keeps everyone involved and really pondering what the story size should be. It's a great facilitation technique to get people involved and understanding the story sizes.

There are some software apps your team can add to their phones to do this approach, but I do prefer the low-tech, high-touch approach. That's it! That's planning poker. You deal with some cards like you're playing poker and then you flash your cards all at the same time. Like all user story sizing, this is based on the size of the story, not the estimated hours to do the tasks. You'll also consider the risk and the types of features your team is voting on.

Creating Release and Iteration Plans

Let's talk a little bit more about defining our releases and our different iterations. Iterations are short, timeboxed periods of time during which your team creates the product. Each iteration usually lasts from two to four weeks. Releases are the aggregate of increments that get the project from being built to actually being released into production.

There are some iteration terms you'll need to know for your PMI-ACP exam. The first term is Iteration Zero. Iteration Zero is the first iteration or sprint, where your team sets up the development environment. The team builds out the test servers, perhaps databases, and preparing for JUnit or NUnit testing. Iteration Zero is also where your team establishes continuous integration architecture, designs the team rules, and, if colocated, sets up a war room. Iteration Zero really provides no deliverables for the customer, but it's that important first chunk of time to get ready to do the project. That's why it's called Iteration Zero.

Another term to know is Iteration H. Iteration H is called thus because it's the iteration that involves hardening, or a hardening sprint, to clean up and stabilize the code. It helps wrap up the product for release and it's all about stabilizing the code and refactoring everything for a good, clean release. In Iteration H you might have to document the product; though documentation usually is not considered of value in agile, sometimes you're required to provide some documentation. Iteration H is your final assembly where you compile everything and complete any final testing.

 EXAM COACH Iteration Zero and Iteration H will likely make an appearance on your exam. Remember that *H* is for hardening, making the code hard and solid. Zero represents the preparation phase in which you do zero work on the actual product.

Spiking the Project

As I mentioned in Chapter 2, I have four brothers, and we were always wrestling and beating up on each other, and all the stuff that boys tend to do (my poor mother!). One of my brothers used to sneak up on me, yell "Spike!," and then punch me right in the back. Such brotherly love, right? That was a "spike" and it hurts me now to think about it.

So why am I talking about that in a book on agile project management? You have spikes in agile projects too. That punch in my back will help you remember these terms—and they too can be painful. First, an *architectural spike* is experimentation that the team performs (ideally) early in the project to prove that what they're trying to accomplish in the project is feasible; it's a proof-of-concept exercise. An architectural spike is a time-boxed effort to test your approach, to make sure that you have the right architecture and approach to build the software.

 EXAM COACH Architectural spikes allow for fast failures for the project. Fast failures are the determination of the proof-of-concept for the project's unlikelihood of being successful.

Then you have a *risk-based spike*, a brief investigation the team performs early in the project to identify and test risks within the project. If your project includes new technology, there's risk in the new technology. The goal is to determine the probability that the risk may occur and the effect the risk may have on the project goal and value. You want to determine if the risk is going to mushroom and wreck your project.

Those are the two spikes you want to know for your exam. It's a punch right in the back of your project. An architectural spike is about proof of concept and proving your environment and team can build the solution. A risk-based spike is about investigating project risks, especially when dealing with new technology. Now you won't forget those for your exam.

Visioning Project Releases

We've talked about release planning already, but let's go back to the idea of visioning and sharing the vision. Remember that you have a product vision, the vision of what you're trying to create, the definition of done. If you think about it, high-level planning is really visioning. High-level planning occurs prior to planning for that first release. During high-level planning, you, the team, and the product owner are mapping out your overall approach to the project and setting goals. High-level planning must include the product owner because it's their vision, include the project team because they need to inherit the vision, and include you, the project manager, because you need to share the vision clearly and consistently throughout the project.

When you break down the product vision, you're really defining a vision for the releases. You're envisioning the value of each release. Your goal is to make sure that you're mapping out the work correctly, and that the product owner and team both have the right priorities for each release and how to realize the most value from each release. You're creating a vision for the releases to define how the project is going to get from the current state to the desired future state with each release.

The product owner consistently prioritizes the backlog, and each prioritization must support the overall vision for the project. The releases, in turn, support the realization of value for the project. The coarse-grained estimates for user stories help to create the goals of each release and to target a release date. With a goal for the release dates, with an acceptable range of variance, you'll still consider convergence and the cone of uncertainty. You'll need to discuss the range of variance and how feasible it may, or may not, be to hit a release date early in the project. As more information becomes available, as you do more progressive elaboration, you'll be able to give a more precise date for releases and vision realization.

 EXAM COACH   Visioning, like most things in agile projects, looks to realize value. Release visioning is making the connection between the value for the whole product and the value for the parts, the releases, of the project.

Planning for Releases

Now that you have a clear vision of the project's definition of done and you're working with release visioning, let's talk about planning for project iterations, and really planning for project increments, and ultimately planning for each release. You know that as the team completes an iteration, they'll do sprint planning in a self-organizing manner. The team will determine who's going to do what in each iteration.

The team's decisions affect the release, and their decisions may not always work out, but their safe environment and your encouragement to be innovative motivate the team try new things, to discover, and to formulate a plan on how they'll reach the end of the iteration and contribute to the release. The increment is an intermediate result, as it's a portion of the product. Each increment appends to what's been created and each increment should contribute to value. The accumulation of increments will lead the project team to the final release and the minimum viable product for the customers, the stakeholders, and end users.

You do need a release planning meeting to prep for each release and for the final release of the project. All key stakeholders should be represented in release planning. This doesn't mean that all project stakeholders are present in the meeting, but that every stakeholder group is represented in the meeting by a representative or ambassador. The goal of release planning is to determine which stories from the prioritized product backlog are going to be completed in which iterations. The release planning meeting also identifies which increments will go into what release. Remember, several increments can contribute to one release rather than each increment being appended and released over and over in production.

In release planning you examine the prioritized backlog and the story sizing to confirm that the product owner has sorted the stories by each release, by priority, and that each increment increases overall value for the customer. Release planning helps to define an initial roadmap for the product. Of course, with changes you will update the release plan as you move through the project.

Another consideration for release planning is that you might have to slice (split) user stories to fit the release plan and target dates. Sometimes you might have compound stories where an individual story has other independent stories that need to be completed first. These dependent relationships need to be identified so the team can plan, create the correct architecture, and design their work to meet the release vision. You'll also need to consider if there are epics that can't fit in one iteration, or even one project, and how epics affect release planning.

Performing Iteration Planning

At the beginning of each iteration, the project team plans what it will accomplish in the iteration. The goal of iteration planning is to discuss all the stories in the iteration backlog. The team selects the user stories, refines them, and defines who will do what. Also, iteration planning is where the project team defines the acceptance criteria for each user story. The acceptance criteria are based on an acceptance test. The team breaks down the user stories into tasks, estimates the tasks, and decides who does what. The completion of tasks contributes to the completion of user stories, and through user story completion you will find the velocity. Remember, velocity is our throughput as we complete stories. It defines how quickly stories done are per iteration. This is where the burnup chart or the burndown chart comes back into play.

Usually, with iterations, you'll use a burndown chart. The vertical bars represent how much work is remaining. So as the team get closer to the end of the iteration, you want the bars to go down in size because the team has completed more and more work. In the first few iterations the velocity is likely going to vary, because estimates may not be precise and the team's project competency is low at the start but increases over time.

Velocity is the only measurement that's calculated after the fact. The aggregate velocity of the team, not individuals, is what matters. There's no real value in comparing velocity between teams because each team has a different project. In addition, the user stories should be estimated in a consistent manner. If you aren't consistent, it wrecks your velocity. You do estimate the entire set of user stories before the project work starts, and then use relative estimating, like affinity estimating.

A general rule of velocity is that one-third of available time is what we should expect in the first iteration. For example, suppose you have nine programmers and 28 days, as shown in Figure 5-8; that's $9 \times 28 = 252$ days of effort. So, a third of that time would be

Figure 5-8 Initial iterations are planned with limited velocity.

9 Programmers

X

28 days

=

252 days of effort

252 days /3 =

84 days of iteration work

84 days of iteration work. You include project overhead, which allows the team to learn the ropes and to get things going. Then, once things normalize, you can estimate with ideal days.

Hosting Daily Standup Meetings

Let's really nail down this idea of the daily standup meeting, or Daily Scrum. I realize I've discussed the daily standup/Daily Scrum several times in this book, but I guarantee you're going see questions about this meeting on your PMI-ACP exam. First off, if you have a task, you have to attend the meeting. Only people who have tasks should talk in this meeting. Usually that means all the development team members, not stakeholders or the product owner.

The individuals in the meeting address the whole team, not just the project manager. That's an important rule as it keeps everybody focused and transparent and provides good communication for the entire project team. You do not allow side conversation. Everyone focuses on the one person who's speaking. If new tasks are discovered, you put those on sticky notes and add the tasks to your Kanban board or iteration's backlog of tasks.

You'll want to discuss issues after the standup meeting. So, if there's an issue that's going to take away from the point of the meeting, document it and then table the issue to be discussed after the meeting, because you don't want to hold up everyone who's not involved in that issue. Always solve problems offline and outside of the standup meeting.

Remember that the whole point of the daily standup is transparent communication. The team answers three questions:

- What did I do yesterday?
- What am I going to accomplish today?
- Are there any roadblocks, or impediments, that are going to get in the way of the individuals moving toward its goal?

Those are the rules and guidelines for the daily standup. Be familiar with these rules as you go in to pass your PMI-ACP exam.

Chapter Summary

In this chapter we talked all about agile planning. We looked at agile discovery and value-based analysis. Value in an agile project is your business value, the return on investment. Value, as we know from the Agile Manifesto, is in working software. We covered the concept of timeboxing meetings and events. You also read about creating estimate ranges, providing a range of variance, and working with the cone of uncertainty and how that decreases as you get closer to the end of the project.

In this chapter we also discussed the details of user stories. You learned how to write effective user stories and how to use the INVEST model for user stories. Recall that INVEST means that stories are independent, negotiable, valuable, estimable, small, and testable. Know that for your exam. We also discussed how user stories follow a formula of role, functionality, and benefit. For example, as a customer (role) I want to find a car dealership in my ZIP code (functionality) so that I can browse for cars on my mobile phone (benefit).

We also looked at grooming the backlog. The product owner is responsible for prioritizing the backlog, keeping it updated with changes, and determining the priority of user stories before each iteration begins. The project manager and the project team may also help with prioritizing the backlog, identifying risk-laden stories, and then selecting the top user stories the team believes they can complete in an iteration. One method of sizing user stories is to utilize affinity estimating, which involves comparing user stories for size and characteristics of features and functions. We discussed T-shirt sizing and using triangulation based on user stories that have been completed in prior iterations to better size current stories for selection.

I also introduced you to the concept of planning poker, in which each player votes on the size of stories in an effort to gain consensus and to facilitate conversation about the story sizing. We then discussed creating release and iteration plans. We looked at the product road map as a high-level vision of what we are creating. The product roadmap helps the project team and the product owner do planning for product releases. Tied to product releases is the product vision; you create a vision for releases.

Remember spikes? We discussed architectural spikes and risk spikes (and getting "spiked" by my brother!). Architectural spikes are opportunities to confirm feasibility, and risk spikes are time allotments to tackle the probability and effect of risk events. We also discussed two important iterations to know for your exam: Iteration Zero and Iteration H. Iteration Zero is for setting up the development environment. Iteration H is for hardening the release, cleaning up the code, and taking care of any bugs before the product is released.

Let's talk a little bit about your determination to pass the PMI-ACP exam. You've made it this far in the book, so I'm assuming you're determined to finish. You need to be determined in the mindset I've discussed: you're not preparing to take the exam, you're preparing to pass the exam. As you prepare to pass the exam, keep that mindset. Keep reviewing your key terms. Keep a positive mindset—you can do this! Great job! Keep after this—you're making great progress toward passing your PMI-ACP exam.

Key Terms

Affinity estimating   Affinity estimating is a way of grouping user stories into similar categories or collections. For example, in IT, we often group things by hardware, software, data, and network. Affinity estimating groups similar stories and then uses relative estimating for the stories.

Agile discovery   Agile discovery means that the project team discovers through experiments and innovation the best approach to accomplish their work.

Architectural spike   An architectural spike is experimentation that the team performs early in the project to prove that what they're trying to accomplish in the project is feasible; it's a proof-of-concept exercise. An architectural spike is a timeboxed effort to test your approach, to make sure that you have the right architecture and approach to build the software.

Ceremonies   Ceremonies are the meetings and events in an agile project. Ceremonies include sprint planning meetings, daily standup meetings, iteration reviews, and iteration retrospectives.

Coarse-grained requirements   Coarse-grained requirements are high-level, chunky descriptions of the project requirements.

Cone of uncertainty   The cone of uncertainty describes how a large range of uncertainty exists at the beginning of the project, and over time and with experience the cone becomes smaller and smaller because certainty increases.

Convergence graphs   Convergence graphs shows how initial estimates are flawed and, over time, with progressive elaboration, that the range of variance gets smaller and smaller and the certainty of estimate increases.

Epics   Epics are large user stories that are too large for just one iteration. Epics can even span different projects in some cases. Most of the time, epics are placeholders for a collection of five or more related user stories.

Fibonacci sequence   The Fibonacci sequence is a pattern of numbers where each number is the sum of the two preceding numbers. For example, zero plus one equals one. One plus one equals two. Two plus one equals three. Three plus five equals eight, five plus eight is thirteen, and thirteen plus eight is twenty-one, and so on.

Fine-grained requirements   Fine-grained requirements are much more detailed and granular and are specific on acceptability requirements.

First-time, first-use penalty   First-time, first-use penalty describes a condition where the project team has never done this type of work before. The penalty is that the work may take longer and/or cost more than anticipated.

Ideal time   Ideal time describes the ideal amount of time it will take to create the items in the product backlog. An ideal time estimate does not consider interruptions or delays in the project work.

INVEST   INVEST is a user story acronym to confirm that user stories are independent of each other, negotiable, valuable, estimable, small, and testable.

Iteration backlog   The iteration backlog is the backlog of user stories the team has selected to accomplish in the current iteration.

Iteration H   Iteration H is called thus because it's the iteration that involves hardening, or a hardening sprint, to clean up and stabilize the code. It helps wrap up the product for release and it's all about stabilizing the code and refactoring everything for a good, clean release.

Iteration Zero   Iteration Zero is the first iteration or sprint, where your team establishes the development environment. The team builds out the test servers, databases, and preparing for JUnit or NUnit testing. Iteration Zero is also where your team will establish continuous integration architecture, they'll design the team rules, and if you're colocated you'll set up your war room.

Parkinson's law   Parkinson's law states that work expands to fill the time allotted to it. This law describes the danger of padding estimate sizes, as the work will expand to fill the size of the duration estimate.

Planning poker   Planning poker uses cards that have the Fibonacci sequence of 1, 2, 3, 5, and 8. The project manager and the team look at each user story and everyone privately chooses whichever poker card they think correctly sizes the story, and then everyone places their card face down on the table. Cards are revealed in unison and discussion follows each round of voting with the poker cards.

Product boxes   A product box is a mockup of your project solution as if it were for sale and contained in a product box on a store shelf. The product box show the value of what the project is creating. It's a way of visualizing what the top features of the product are.

Product roadmap   A product roadmap is a big picture of the functionality the team's deliverables and how that functionality satisfies the product vision. The product roadmap is a way of keeping our team and our stakeholders involved and keeping focus on the project result.

Product vision   The product vision is a summary to communicate the project's end goal. The product vision statement describes how the project's product will differ from competitors' products and support the overall strategy of the organization. It also sets the expectations of what the project will deliver and what it won't deliver.

Progressive elaboration   Progressive elaboration is an adaptive planning technique that starts with a broad idea of the project and then breaks it down into smaller and smaller items and components as the project progresses.

Release plan   A release plan defines a set of requirements that when completed may be released. Release planning determines when we are going to have releases available. The project manager, the product owner, and the project team determine the next set of functionalities that can be released as part of an incremental approach.

Risk-based spike   A risk-based spike is a brief investigation the team performs early in the project to identify and test risks within the project.

Rolling wave planning   Rolling wave planning uses waves of planning and then executing and is a characteristic of adaptive projects.

Sizing T-shirts   Sizing T-shirts is a way of determining and sorting the true sizes of user stories by comparing them. For example, comparing a user story previously labeled as medium to a small or large user story may reveal that the medium story is more likely a large or small. It's a type of affinity estimating.

Slicing   Slicing is the process of breaking down a large user story into smaller stories or tasks.

Sprint retrospective   A sprint retrospective is a meeting in which the team discusses how well they've worked as a team and what has or has not worked regarding the people, processes, tools, and relationships. The retrospective is just for the project team and the project manager. While this is typically used in Scrum projects, you can utilize a retrospective in an agile approach.

Sprint review   A sprint review is a meeting between the team and the key stakeholders during which the team provides a demo of what has been created. The team can offer the demonstration and the stakeholders provide feedback or approval. While this is typically used in Scrum projects, you can utilize a retrospective in an agile approach.

Story points   Story points are points assigned to user stories for purposes of sizing them relative to each and estimating how long each will take to complete. Using story points provides a scale with which to size user stories relative to each other, such as a large story is worth five points, a medium story is worth three points, and a small story is worth one point.

Three Cs of user stories   The three Cs of user stories are the card, conversation, and confirmation. A card is an index card or sticky note with just enough text to identify the story. A conversation is the details that are communicated between the customer and the development team. A confirmation is the customer confirmation that the story has been implemented correctly in the product.

Timeboxing   A timebox is a predetermined, fixed duration for a project event.

User story   A user story is a small chunk of business functionality. User stories are written from the customer's perspective and describe a feature of the product you're creating.

User story backlog   The user story backlog, also known as the product backlog, contains all the requirements in a user story format.

User story formula   The user story formula includes role, functionality, and benefit and is seen as: As a <role> I want this <functionality> so that I'll receive this <benefit>.

Value-based analysis   Value-based analysis examines the business value and assesses the worth of what the project will create. Value-based analysis is the business benefit minus the cost of the project.

Value-based decomposition   Value-based decomposition is a visual decomposition of the project scope, requirements, features, or risk. Value-based decomposition is a way to examine the requirements and determine the value of each requirement for prioritization and relationships among the components.

Wideband Delphi Technique   The Wideband Delphi Technique, sometimes called just the Delphi Technique, has rounds of anonymous surveys to create estimates, gather risks, or gather requirements. It helps to build consensus without everyone following one person's point of view.

Questions

1. You are an agile project manager and your team, which is new to agile project management, is concerned about planning the project. You advise the team that adaptive planning is the most effective and efficient way to plan the course of an agile project and offer which of the following reasons?

   A. Adaptive planning allows team members to become adjusted to the plan.

   B. Adaptive planning is based on the concept that the plan is in motion.

   C. Adaptive planning allows the business partners to share the plan with their teams.

   D. Adaptive planning is stable after the prototype is complete.

2. You are new to an agile team. You have been hearing the term "agile discovery" and are not quite sure what that means. You asked your team leader and she explained it as which of the following?

   A. The project plan developed in the beginning of the project is being followed and tracked.

   B. The plans and requirements developed in the beginning of the project are ever-changing, so broad estimates are used to reflect the uncertainty.

   C. The team is learning how to develop a solid project plan.

   D. The team is anticipating roadblocks and trying to avoid them.

3. You are an agile project manager and your agile team is approaching their next iteration. There seems to be a disagreement about how the work items are prioritized since new functionality has been introduced. How can you assist the project team and the product owner when analyzing the priorities?

   A. By analyzing the value of each task and delivering the highest-value items first

   B. By determining how long it will take to complete each task and do the quick ones first

   C. By analyzing the impact of testing and leaving the longer durations to the end of the iteration

   D. By determining what functionality the users determined to be most critical and delivering that first

4. Beth is leading a new agile project and her team is uncertain of some of the concepts. The team doesn't understand the idea of timeboxing a portion of the project. In an agile team's environment, what is a timebox?

   A. An alarm that sounds when a task needs to end

   B. A time period during which designated work is completed

   C. The agile term for a month

   D. The minimum amount of time a task should take to complete

5. While on an agile project team, you've already gone through the value-based analysis of prioritization for the first few iterations along with all stakeholders. Now you need to estimate how long each iteration will take to complete. What process does agile prefer for making such estimates?

    A. Decompose, or break down, requirements into chunks of work, estimate how long each task will take to complete, and plan the task

    B. Understand how many people are available, determine how many tasks need to be completed, and split the tasks between the team

    C. Determine how many tasks are in the entire project, chunk the tasks into specific iterations, and determine how long each iteration will take

    D. Allowing the team leader to determine the time frame of each iteration

6. You have been on several agile teams, so you are very familiar with user stories. There are several new people on your team and you've been asked to describe what a "user story" is. How do you explain this in just a few words?

    A. A user story is a small chunk of functionality that should take one to three days to finish.

    B. A user story is a narrative of requirements.

    C. A user story is the background of the user community.

    D. A user story is how the user community plans to use the product.

7. Once all user stories are written, they are compiled to create a backlog, or master list, of all work that needs to be completed, sorted by priority. As a story is completed and delivered, it is removed from the backlog. How is this process beneficial?

    A. Having all work to be done listed in a single document is a key agile practice, which shows the progress of scope and the status of the project.

    B. Having all work on one list makes it easier to bypass a story that didn't pass testing successfully.

    C. It provides a visual display of how long the project is going to take.

    D. It provides a visual display of how much the project is going to cost.

8. The business partner continuously refines, or grooms, the backlog. This includes adding new stories, reprioritizing stories, and removing stories. What is the development team responsible for in this process?

    A. Adding new story functionality

    B. Deleting stories that don't work

    C. Estimating the work so the customer can prioritize effectively

    D. Changing the business needs

9. Making absolute estimates on how long it will take to complete a task is very difficult, so agile teams use which of the following methods to estimate more accurately?

   A. Estimate how many user stories can be done in a day

   B. Base absolute estimates on hour rather than day

   C. Use comparative estimates or relative sizing

   D. Use value-based priority

10. Who should own the process of story point sizing?

    A. The PMO

    B. The agile team

    C. The agile team leader

    D. The business partner

11. When your agile team is estimating story points, it is important to include which of the following?

    A. Vacations and sick days

    B. Testing and refactoring

    C. Server backup time

    D. Meeting times

12. When your agile team is nearing the end of creating story point estimates, you go through a reality check by which of the following processes?

    A. Affinity estimating

    B. T-shirt sizing

    C. Story maps

    D. Relative sizing

13. Your agile team has decided to display a product roadmap. What is this roadmap used for?

    A. To display where the team is in the project life cycle

    B. To display how many user stories have been completed

    C. To display product releases and what will be included

    D. To display the total number of story points in the project

14. Your agile team has decided to use planning poker to determine point estimates for their user stories. What happens when several members estimate a user story at three points or under and several members estimate the same story at ten points?

    A. The points assigned to the story are averaged.

    B. The high and low are discarded and then the points remaining are averaged.

    C. The user story is changed so everyone can agree upon the point value.

    D. The story is discussed again to come to a consensus.

15. There is a tool that agile teams use that is usually timeboxed and explores an approach, investigates an issue, or reduces a project risk. What is this tool called?

    A. Iteration

    B. Spike

    C. User story

    D. Relative unit

16. One of the iterations your agile team was going to work on was deemed a "fast failure." What does this mean?

    A. The iteration was too large.

    B. All the work for the iteration was developed, tested, and failed.

    C. The proof-of-concept of the iteration wasn't successful.

    D. There were not enough user stories in the iteration to succeed.

17. Your agile team is in the release planning phase for the next iteration. What is the most accurate tool to use to determine how much work can be done in the next release?

    A. User stories

    B. Velocity

    C. Story points

    D. Affinity estimating

18. Why is the velocity of completed iterations used to estimate the project's progress and duration estimates for the remainder of the project?

    A. Previous iterations include all variables of development.

    B. The same number of user stories are completed in each iteration.

    C. The same team members should be on each iteration.

    D. The team is more capable of completing tasks after several iterations.

19. Your agile team is planning for the next iteration. How should this process begin?

    A. By breaking down user stories into tasks

    B. By defining the acceptance criteria

    C. By selecting what user stories should be in the iteration

    D. By analyzing the user stories in the backlog

20. Once an iteration is in progress, a daily standup meeting occurs. This is a very quick meeting that is timeboxed at 15 minutes or less, and the team members stand so the meeting stays focused and on track. There are only three questions that should be answered by every team member that has an active task. Which one of the following is not a question included in the daily standup meeting?

    A. What have I worked on since the last meeting?

    B. What do I plan to finish today?

    C. How far behind am I?

    D. Are there any impediments to my progress?

Questions and Answers

1. You are an agile project manager and your team, which is new to agile project management, is concerned about planning the project. You advise the team that adaptive planning is the most effective and efficient way to plan the course of an agile project and offer which of the following reasons?

    A. Adaptive planning allows team members to become adjusted to the plan.

    B. Adaptive planning is based on the concept that the plan is in motion.

    C. Adaptive planning allows the business partners to share the plan with their teams.

    D. Adaptive planning is stable after the prototype is complete.

    B. Recognizing that the plan devised in the beginning of the project is most likely flawed, agile embraces adaptive planning, based on the concept that the plan is in motion. An effective way to be successful on an agile project is to plan to replan. Distributing planning throughout the life cycle of the project allows the team to better adjust to new information.
    A is incorrect because adaptive planning is not allowing the project team to become adjusted to the plan. C is incorrect because adaptive planning isn't the project team share plans with partners. D is incorrect because the project plan isn't stable after the prototype.

2. You are new to an agile team. You have been hearing the term "agile discovery" and are not quite sure what that means. You asked your team leader and she explained it as which of the following?

    A. The project plan developed in the beginning of the project is being followed and tracked.

    B. The plans and requirements developed in the beginning of the project are ever-changing, so broad estimates are used to reflect the uncertainty.

    C. The team is learning how to develop a solid project plan.

    D. The team is anticipating roadblocks and trying to avoid them.

    B. Agile discovery is a term used to describe the evolution and fluidity of agile project plans in contrast with designing a plan in the beginning of the project. A, C, and D are incorrect as agile discovery isn't reliant on the project plan being defined and followed at the beginning of the project. Agile discovery is not focused on the team removing roadblocks, but does acknowledge that roadblocks may take time and resources to address to keep the project moving forward.

3. You are an agile project manager and your agile team is approaching their next iteration. There seems to be a disagreement about how the work items are prioritized since new functionality has been introduced. How can you assist the project team and the product owner when analyzing the priorities?

    A. By analyzing the value of each task and delivering the highest-value items first

    B. By determining how long it will take to complete each task and do the quick ones first

C. By analyzing the impact of testing and leaving the longer durations to the end of the iteration

D. By determining what functionality the users determined to be most critical and delivering that first

A. Agile planning is based on value-based analysis, meaning the business value of deliverables is analyzed and delivered first. Agile teams can assist the business partners by factoring in likely development costs to make informed decisions. The time it takes to complete a task needs to have a cost associated with it before the priority is determined. The users typically don't contribute to this process, but the value management team and the product owner will determine business value.

B is incorrect because the team doesn't do the quick tasks first, but does the tasks by prioritization. C is incorrect because the team also doesn't do the longer durations at the end of an iteration. D is incorrect because the prioritization is based on the overall business value.

4. Beth is leading a new agile project and her team is uncertain of some of the concepts. The team doesn't understand the idea of timeboxing a portion of the project. In an agile team's environment, what is a timebox?

A. An alarm that sounds when a task needs to end

B. A time period during which designated work is completed

C. The agile term for a month

D. The minimum amount of time a task should take to complete

B. An agile timebox is typically a short period of time in which designated work is completed. The team can use an iteration timebox that represents how many tasks can be completed during that timeframe. If a task is not completed during the given amount of time, it is moved to the next timebox and reprioritized. Choices A, C, and D are incorrect as these answers are incorrect definitions of a timeboxed duration.

5. While on an agile project team, you've already gone through the value-based analysis of prioritization for the first few iterations along with all stakeholders. Now you need to estimate how long each iteration will take to complete. What process does agile prefer for making such estimates?

A. Decompose, or break down, requirements into chunks of work, estimate how long each task will take to complete, and plan the task

B. Understand how many people are available, determine how many tasks need to be completed, and split the tasks between the team

C. Determine how many tasks are in the entire project, chunk the tasks into specific iterations, and determine how long each iteration will take

D. Allowing the team leader to determine the time frame of each iteration

A. Breaking down the requirements into small, refined chunks of work will enable your group to better estimate how long each task will take and plan a reasonable iteration.

B is incorrect because while knowing how many team members are available to complete the tasks is also critical, agile first considers the decomposition of the work and then the team assigns the work accordingly. C is incorrect because this approach is not based first on value and doesn't consider the likelihood of change. Agile address the known requirements for each iteration during iteration planning. D is incorrect because iterations are pre-determined at the start of the project.

6. You have been on several agile teams, so you are very familiar with user stories. There are several new people on your team and you've been asked to describe what a "user story" is. How do you explain this in just a few words?

   A. A user story is a small chunk of functionality that should take one to three days to finish.

   B. A user story is a narrative of requirements.

   C. A user story is the background of the user community.

   D. A user story is how the user community plans to use the product.

   A. A user story is a small chunk of functionality that typically takes one to three days to complete. The user story should answer the questions that the team needs answered to define the task in more detail. There is no set of right or wrong questions to ask or answers; the team should come up with what best fits their needs.

   B, C, and D are incorrect as these definitions are inaccurate descriptions of user stories.

7. Once all user stories are written, they are compiled to create a backlog, or master list, of all work that needs to be completed, sorted by priority. As a story is completed and delivered, it is removed from the backlog. How is this process beneficial?

   A. Having all work to be done listed in a single document is a key agile practice, which shows the progress of scope and the status of the project.

   B. Having all work on one list makes it easier to bypass a story that didn't pass testing successfully.

   C. It provides a visual display of how long the project is going to take.

   D. It provides a visual display of how much the project is going to cost.

   A. Managing the project requirements in a single document is a fundamental agile practice. A single source of information about the work being done lends itself to effective communication and provides a visual of scope and status.

   B, C, and D are incorrect because the backlog process isn't meant to bypass a story or determine how long the project will last or the cost of the project.

8. The business partner continuously refines, or grooms, the backlog. This includes adding new stories, reprioritizing stories, and removing stories. What is the development team responsible for in this process?

    A. Adding new story functionality

    B. Deleting stories that don't work

    C. Estimating the work so the customer can prioritize effectively

    D. Changing the business needs

    C. The only task the development team is responsible for in the grooming process is estimating the work so that the customer can prioritize it to ensure it is value-based.
    A, B, and D are incorrect. The development team doesn't add new story functionality, delete stories, or change the business needs.

9. Making absolute estimates on how long it will take to complete a task is very difficult, so agile teams use which of the following methods to estimate more accurately?

    A. Estimate how many user stories can be done in a day

    B. Base absolute estimates on hour rather than day

    C. Use comparative estimates or relative sizing

    D. Use value-based priority

    C. Agile teams rely on relative sizing, which uses a relative unit called story points. Estimating in terms of relative size rather than absolute allows the making of more useful estimates rather than trying to predict an absolute time period. The team can only complete so many user stories per iteration.
    A is incorrect because user stories are not mapped to days of an iteration. B is incorrect because estimates are not made by hours, but rather by relative sizing of the user stories. D is incorrect because value-based prioritization is how the product backlog is organized, not how user stories are estimated.

10. Who should own the process of story point sizing?

    A. The PMO

    B. The agile team

    C. The agile team leader

    D. The business partner

    B. The story point sizing process is created and owned by the agile team. The team is the most qualified to determine the amount of effort required to complete each story.
    A and D are incorrect because the PMO and business partner are not involved with that level of detail of the project. C is incorrect because the agile team leader supports the team in creating the story point sizing, but is not responsible for the task.

11. When your agile team is estimating story points, it is important to include which of the following?

   A. Vacations and sick days

   B. Testing and refactoring

   C. Server backup time

   D. Meeting times

> **B.** Story point estimates should include all known activities required to complete the story, which should include testing and refactoring, level of complexity, level of risk, etc. Including all activities proves to be more accurate, in contrast to adding a certain fudge factor.
> A, C, and D are incorrect. Vacations and sick days should not be a factor in the estimate, only the known activities should be considered. Server backup times are not included as part of the story point estimating. Meeting times are also not included in estimating the stories.

12. When your agile team is nearing the end of creating story point estimates, you go through a reality check by which of the following processes?

   A. Affinity estimating

   B. T-shirt sizing

   C. Story maps

   D. Relative sizing

> **A.** Affinity estimating is a comparative view of the estimates. You want to compare the sizes of story points to each other. Confirm that all story points with an estimate of three story points are all about the same size, effort, level of risk, etc.
> B is incorrect because T-shirt sizing refers to an actual process of estimating the story sizes. C is incorrect because a story map is a tool to determine the project priorities. D is incorrect because relative sizing is the agile method used to assign the story points.

13. Your agile team has decided to display a product roadmap. What is this roadmap used for?

   A. To display where the team is in the project life cycle

   B. To display how many user stories have been completed

   C. To display product releases and what will be included

   D. To display the total number of story points in the project

> **C.** A product roadmap is a visual display of the product releases and what will be included in each release. This is a high-level planning tool that should be revised as necessary.
> A, B, and D are incorrect because the team's status, completed user stories, and total story points are not reflected in the product roadmap, which reflects the project at a much higher level.

14. Your agile team has decided to use planning poker to determine point estimates for their user stories. What happens when several members estimate a user story at three points or under and several members estimate the same story at ten points?

    A. The points assigned to the story are averaged.

    B. The high and low are discarded and then the points remaining are averaged.

    C. The user story is changed so everyone can agree upon the point value.

    D. The story is discussed again to come to a consensus.

    D. When there is a difference in the estimated points of this extent, there is most likely a misunderstanding or not all user story information has been shared. The user story needs to be discussed further and the team needs to come to a consensus of the point value of the story.
    A, B, and C are incorrect because they are not rules of planning poker.

15. There is a tool that agile teams use that is usually timeboxed and explores an approach, investigates an issue, or reduces a project risk. What is this tool called?

    A. Iteration

    B. Spike

    C. User story

    D. Relative unit

    B. A spike is a key tool used by agile teams to resolve problems as early as possible. A spike is a short effort that can be done at any time during a project. It is not unusual for spikes to be scheduled at the beginning of a project before any development efforts begin.
    A, C, and D are incorrect choices. Iterations, user stories, and relative units do not investigate issues or project risks.

16. One of the iterations your agile team was going to work on was deemed a "fast failure." What does this mean?

    A. The iteration was too large.

    B. All the work for the iteration was developed, tested, and failed.

    C. The proof-of-concept of the iteration wasn't successful.

    D. There were not enough user stories in the iteration to succeed.

    C. Fast failure means the proof-of-concept effort was not successful and therefore the iteration was eliminated. The term fast failure is primarily used for entire projects to allow a company to reduce the cost invested, allowing those funds to be placed on viable projects.
    A, B, and D are incorrect because fast failure does not apply to the size of the iteration, development, or how many user stories are in an iteration; the failure of the iteration is decided prior to the iteration starting.

17. Your agile team is in the release planning phase for the next iteration. What is the most accurate tool to use to determine how much work can be done in the next release?

    A. User stories

    B. Velocity

    C. Story points

    D. Affinity estimating

    B. Agile generally uses the velocity trend over the last several iterations to plan how much work can be completed in the next release. Gathering groups of user stories or summing story points factor into the velocity in which iterations are completed.

    A, C, and D are incorrect choices as user stories, story points, and affinity estimating are not used to determine how much work can be done in the next release of the project.

18. Why is the velocity of completed iterations used to estimate the project's progress and duration estimates for the remainder of the project?

    A. Previous iterations include all variables of development.

    B. The same number of user stories are completed in each iteration.

    C. The same team members should be on each iteration.

    D. The team is more capable of completing tasks after several iterations.

    A. Previous iterations typically include all tasks and pitfalls of an iteration. B is incorrect because the same number of user stories can't be used to predict future progress since not all stories are equal in complexity. C is incorrect because although consistent team membership is a plus, changes in members should not change the velocity of an iteration. D is incorrect because the tasks of each iteration will be different.

19. Your agile team is planning for the next iteration. How should this process begin?

    A. By breaking down user stories into tasks

    B. By defining the acceptance criteria

    C. By selecting what user stories should be in the iteration

    D. By analyzing the user stories in the backlog

    D. The process of planning for the next iteration should begin by analyzing the high-value user stories in the backlog and having the business partners prioritize or reprioritize the stories.

    A, B, and C are incorrect because, although they are included in the planning meeting, analyzing the user stories in the backlog is performed first.

20. Once an iteration is in progress, a daily standup meeting occurs. This is a very quick meeting that is timeboxed at 15 minutes or less, and the team members stand so the meeting stays focused and on track. There are only three questions that should be answered by every team member that has an active task. Which one of the following is not a question included in the daily standup meeting?

A. What have I worked on since the last meeting?

B. What do I plan to finish today?

C. How far behind am I?

D. Are there any impediments to my progress?

C. "How far behind am I?" is not a question that participants answer in the daily standup.

A, B, and D are incorrect because they are the only questions that should be answered by each member with an active task. If there needs to be any further questioning or discussion, it should occur after the meeting.

Detecting and Resolving Problems

In this chapter, you will

- Define the five exam tasks of problem detection and resolution
- Anticipate and control project problems
- Create a safe and open project environment
- Actively detect project problems
- Identify trends in agile projects
- Create a risk-adjusted backlog
- Resolve problems in an adaptive project

While the agile approach has many benefits, it's not a magic potion for project management. There will still be problems in agile projects. Issues will come up, and risks will threaten the project goals. The project team will experience some road bumps as they strive to adapt the agile mindset and become a self-organized team. You'll likely also experience communication problems and stakeholders who aren't in favor of your project, the agile approach, or the way your team is getting the work done.

In this chapter, we'll look at controlling project problems, evaluating the cost of change, resolving technical debt, and identifying failure and success modes in agile projects. A really important topic that we'll cover in this chapter is lead time and cycle time, and what the differences are between them and some things concerning them to look for on your PMI-ACP exam. While this is a short chapter, it covers important topics to know that can affect your entire project.

When you and your team have a plan of what you can complete in a project iteration and you come up short on your goals, you'll have a variance. This chapter introduces variance analysis and includes coverage of cost variance, schedule variance, and identifying trends for future performance. In agile projects you'll also need to set control limits and deal with risk, create a risk-adjusted backlog, and create a risk burndown chart.

 For a more detailed explanation, watch the *Problem Detection and Resolution* video now.

While this domain is worth 10 percent of your exam, roughly 12 questions, there are plenty of terms you'll need to recognize and understand for your PMI-ACP exam. You'll want to hone in on prevention, identification, and resolution of threats and issues in this domain. Our primary objective for problem detection and resolution is to create a safe and open environment in which to bring up problems. You want to engage your project team in resolving threats and issues. And then you'll resolve issues and reset expectations based on your resolution. Throughout the project you will maintain a visible list of threats and issues and what their status is in the project. Part of this threat list includes threat remediation efforts that need to be added to the iteration backlog.

Introducing the Problem Detection and Resolution Domain

Agile projects will encounter problems, so your goal as an agile project manager is to anticipate problems and then work with the team to manage the problems to keep the project moving forward. You'll work to continuously identify problems and risks in the project. Your PMI-ACP exam will test your ability to identify and monitor problems and communicate the resolution status of each in an efficient manner to the correct stakeholders. As part of this domain you'll also want to take actions to prevent similar problems from occurring again in the project.

A theme you've seen already throughout this book and in your preparation to pass the PMI-ACP exam is that you need to create and maintain an open and safe environment for the project team. An open and safe environment is one in which the team feels secure not only to innovate and experiment with the project work but also to surface problems without fear of backlash. As a project manager, you don't want the team to feel embarrassed or scared to admit to finding a problem. Ignoring a problem is never a good thing in an agile project, as future development may be adversely affected by a current problem if it's ignored.

Reviewing the Five Tasks for Exam Domain VI

The problem detection and resolution domain has just five tasks, which will equate to 12 exam questions, so it's not a large domain for your exam, but still important. These tasks are about transparency and visibility of the detected problems you will encounter in a project. The project team members are the people closest to the work, so they likely will identify project problems, but as the project manager, you need to consider operational and resource management issues related to problem identification, resolution, and reporting. When a problem arises, you'll add the problem to a list of threats to for resolution; the list is visible for accountability, transparency, and tracking of the problems.

Ninety percent of project management is communication—and that's no different in an agile project. In previous chapters, we've discussed that agile promotes communication by colocating the team in an open office environment and maintaining highly visible information radiators. When dealing with problems and issues, you'll continue to embrace communications and transparency of the issues through a threat list. You don't hide problems from the product owner or key stakeholders, and you don't want the project team members to hide problems from you and the rest of the team either.

Let's look at the five tasks for the problem detection and resolution exam domain:

Problem Detection and Resolution

- Create an open and safe environment by encouraging conversation and experimentation, in order to surface problems and impediments that are slowing the team down or preventing its ability to deliver value.

- Identify threats and issues by educating and engaging the team at various points in the project in order to resolve them at the appropriate time and improve processes that caused issues.

- Ensure issues are resolved by appropriate team members and/or reset expectations in light of issues that cannot be resolved in order to maximize the value delivered.

- Maintain a visible, monitored, and prioritized list of threats and issues in order to elevate accountability, encourage action, and track ownership and resolution status.

- Communicate status of threats and issues by maintaining threat list and incorporating activities into backlog of work in order to provide transparency.

Controlling Project Problems

In an ideal world, problems would not happen in any project. The reality is, problems, issues, threats, risks, and mild concerns are going to bubble up in your project regardless of what type of approach you take, agile or predictive. To be clear, *risks* are uncertain events that threaten the project goals and *issues* are risks that have come into existence in the project.

First off, you need to understand the problem, and you do that through root cause analysis (RCA). Root cause analysis is the examination of the problem and the causes that are contributing to the effect you are experiencing. RCA identifies the causal factors, not just the symptoms of the problems. You must understand the problem, not just the symptoms of the problem. Project managers need the ability to detect problems, investigate and understand what the real problems are, and estimate the severity level of those problems and what their impact may be on the project. When performing root cause analysis, you can use a fishbone diagram, as shown in Figure 6-1, sometimes called an Ishikawa diagram. The fishbone diagram helps to identify the contributing causes of the effect, and facilitates a conversation to resolve the effect the project is experiencing. As problems are identified, you'll manage the threats and issues. Your goal is to solve the problems so that the project can move forward without any delays, and to prevent the problems from happening again.

Figure 6-1 A fishbone diagram helps facilitate cause-and-effect analysis.

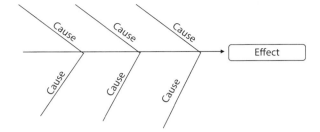

Think of negative risks and how they threaten the project objectives: delays in the work, underestimating the size of user stories, and the potential for key project team members to leave the organization. With each risk you'll examine the probability and impact. Specifically, you're trying to determine the likelihood of a risk happening, and if it does happen, what's the true effect on the project time, cost, scope, quality, and other risks. To do this effectively, you and the team will do risk identification in an iterative nature. As risks are identified, you'll track them with a risk log, or some way of visualizing the risks and monitoring them.

As I've mentioned, issues and risks are related. Risks are uncertain events that have not yet happened. Issues are risk events that have occurred. Examples of issues are someone quits the project, you have defective code, or you have escaped defects. You must deal with issues and resolve the problem. The goal is to understand the real problem that needs to be resolved. What may appear as a small risk or a small issue can mushroom. Even a small risk or issue can cause ripple effects in the project if left unchecked.

I know that sometimes there are little risks that don't seem like a big deal. I've been guilty of taking the attitude that a risk is tiny and we can just live with it or ignore it. And then that tiny risk begins to fester and creates new risks that are more significant, and they begin to cause more and more risks. Teams often look for a quick fix that can address the symptom rather than the problem, and this introduces the idea of a secondary risk. A *secondary risk* happens when you solve one risk but the solution inadvertently creates one or more new risks.

One area of your project affects all other areas of your project. If you do a poor job in planning your sprint backlog, then that can influence risk, communications, scope, time, cost, quality, resource management, and even procurement and stakeholder management. That's part of project integration management, which is the focus of Chapter 4 in the *PMBOK Guide, Sixth Edition*. While you don't need to know every detail of project integration management, know the concept that what you do in one area of the project has a direct effect on the remainder of the project.

EXAM COACH Risk analysis utilizes qualitative and quantitative analysis. Qualitative analysis is fast and subjective and isn't totally reliable. The goal of qualitative analysis is to decide which risks should go into quantitative analysis. Quantitative analysis quantifies the probability and impact of a risk event. Quantitative analysis takes more time to do, but it's much more reliable than qualitative analysis.

Considering the Cost of Change

Agile projects, by design, welcome change. Change can happen to the product backlog at any time throughout the project, and it's no surprise to anyone with the agile mindset that change is going to happen. When you think of change in an agile project, the product backlog probably comes to mind first. However, change can come about in the project strategy, how you manage issues and risks, and even the team's approach. Faulty work is change—it's a change from what was expected for the project to be acceptable.

As a project manager, you want the team to be self-organized, but when you see a defect or problem, if you totally ignore it, the more expensive the defect or problem will cost as the project moves forward. It's like going to the dentist. You have a toothache and you don't want to go to the dentist, but that toothache is there and the longer you wait, the worse it's going to get.

In project management, the longer you or the project team waits to address an issue or risk, the more expensive it will become. The incorrect mindset is that pausing to address an issue or risk is too costly or too time-consuming right now. But waiting for the perfect time to address risks and issues can affect more areas of the project. There are financial impacts of the problems, the risk, and the issues that are in our project. We can't ignore the issue or risk, so we need a way to track problems and a strategy to effectively address them.

Examine Figure 6-2. This is a timeline of costs in relation to schedule. The curve represents the costs and the schedule as the team completes the work. If you identify an issue halfway through your schedule, the issue may affect completed work. If you ignore the issue and continue to build code, that issue can affect future work, and now there are two different problems. You first have the work that was pre-issue, and the work that was after the issue. You must address the problem to unravel completed work, and you may have problems that affect future work. When you address an issue, you must consider if the resolution will break work that's already done and how your resolution will affect the balance of work to come.

Figure 6-2   Issues found later in the project can greatly affect time and costs.

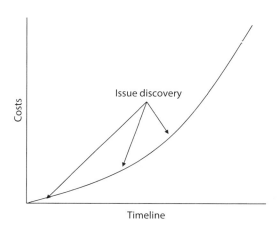

Issues are going to arise in every project. It's impossible to say that you can have a project with no issues or zero risk. That's not realistic. The longer you wait to address issues and risks, the more expensive they're going to be in both time and cost. When you or your team identifies an issue, you go to the problem, analyze the root cause, and look for a solution that has minimal impact but truly solves the problem to create a good, quality deliverable.

Reviewing Technical Debt

Technical debt is the backlog of work that's caused by the team failing to do regular clean-up of the project code. It's the maintenance, standardization, and refactoring of the code. Project teams need to resolve technical debt, and one primary approach is to use the red-green-refactor strategy, also known as red-green-clean. This calls for the developer to first create a test. Then the developer creates code against that test. Once the code passes the test, the person should clean up the code. Know that refactoring standardizes code and makes it easier to support. Refactoring time should be included in your estimates and sizing.

Technical debt is like borrowed money. If the team doesn't consistently refactor, then the debt accumulates interest to be paid back later. It's going to take additional time to fix those little problems if the team doesn't clean up code as the project progresses. The primary issue with technical debt are the little shortcuts developers often take to get their code to pass the test—that's just sloppy code.

Poorly defined requirements or poorly written user stories can also contribute to technical debt. In addition, if there is pressure for quick value delivery, that can create technical debt. In addition, it's dangerous to the project success to have a "clean it all up at the end" attitude. That approach is going to take a lot more time, because what is cleaned up at the end of an iteration or before a release will likely affect other code.

Another aspect of technical debt is lack of documentation. While you want documentation to be light and barely sufficient, your project may require some level of good documentation. It's true that in agile projects documentation does not add value, but you'll likely need some documentation, even if it's simply comments in the code. Ignoring that requirement means the team has to go back to the code and add documentation, which might be faulty because memory isn't often the best source for documentation.

You might be working with parallel development, such as pair programming in an XP project or multiple people working on one user story in agile. That duplication of effort, while beneficial, may cause technical debt as developers can develop atop one another and create messy "spaghetti code" that's difficult to unravel and support. Consider the contiguous nature needed in code; if it's not contiguous, if it's not refactored, problems will occur when we compile all the code. The team needs a good set of rules and standards for the development approach to keep the code clean, simple, and recognizable by any developer.

Creating a Safe and Open Environment

When you consider issues, risk, and threats to your project success, you also must consider the physical environment where your developers are working and their culture and attitude toward your project team. The PMI-ACP exam is going to favor a safe and open environment, so embrace this idea throughout the exam. Remember, you want people to experiment and to be innovative, so this means you must create a safe and open environment where your project team can operate without fear. People should feel comfortable, and they need to know they're empowered, that they have permission, as part of a self-organizing team. When people get stuck in a task, they need to feel comfortable in sharing that they're stuck and asking for help without risk of feeling foolish or being chided by the project manager or other project team members.

Safe environments are also conducive to coaching opportunities. Coaching means you'll help people find solutions and lead them to discover. Remember, you are supporting the team by getting people to work together. Some examples of how to create a safe and open environment include

- **Brainstorming** Bring people together to brainstorm a problem. The team can do this on their own, but the project manager may need to call for the sessions and facilitate the approach.
- **Retrospectives** Ask what worked well and how the can team improve in the next iteration. Get people involved in the conversation.
- **Experiment** Software development is a creative activity, so the team is encouraged to experiment and be innovative. Agile projects are not a manufacturing environment.

You need a culture that promotes this safe and open environment. The culture in which you operate can influence the agile project. You first need to have the agile mindset, and then you need to encourage your team and stakeholders to embrace the mindset, with the ultimate goal the entire organization adopting the agile mindset too.

Identifying Failure and Success Modes

As individuals, we make mistakes, all of us. No one's perfect. Mistakes are going to happen. In an agile project, we prefer to fail conservatively. That's why agile projects have small, timeboxed iterations; if failure happens, everyone can learn from the failure and improve. The team fails forward. An agile principle is that the project team should prefer to invent rather than research; experiment, try ideas, be inventive, be creative.

All people are creatures of habit. You probably have a particular way that you load the dishwasher, start your day, or host your standup meeting. If you're a developer, you probably have a particular way that you develop. That habit can unintentionally lead to failure, so it's good to periodically look at your work habits and determine if the habit is contributing to failure. Then you acknowledge, as an individual, that you are inconsistent, that it's just part of human nature; you must also understand that inconsistency is going to cause threats and issues in a project. Failure mode consists of all the actions that don't contribute to project success: sloppy, rushed work, lack of skills, refusing to ask for help. These are behaviors we don't want in an agile project—or in our lives.

Success mode describes our habits that contribute to success. First, people are good at looking around. People can find the information they need. When the project team encounters problems, the team can look around for a solution, contribute to the solution, and keep moving forward.

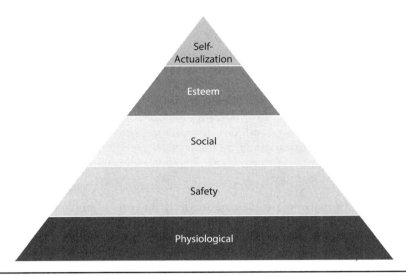

Figure 6-3   Maslow's Hierarchy of Needs identifies five needs for humans.

Another part of the success mode is that you want to learn from mistakes. If things don't work out, you learn and move forward. You are malleable, can adapt and overcome, and you can deal with problems. In success mode, people take pride in their work. Motivating people to take pride in their work involves helping them to become self-actualized, the top of five levels in Maslow's Hierarchy of Needs, depicted in Figure 6-3, which describes what motivates humans. People won't be motivated to become self-actualized unless they have satisfied their needs at the lower four levels. This means they have met their physiological needs first (water, food, etc.), then their safety needs, social needs, and esteem needs. To be self-actualized means you have a sense of purpose in your work, which also means you're taking pride in your work and wanting to do it properly.

Exploring Success Strategies

As a project manager, you want your project to be successful. For your project to be successful, the project team has to be successful. As previously described, this means you'll need to create a safe and open environment where people can work to achieve success. You also want to create some success strategies. This means that we balance discipline with tolerance to innovate and be creative. Discipline meaning that we are logical, methodical, following a proven approach to getting the work done. We balance that discipline with taking chances, being innovative, and trying other methods to reach project goals. For example, you start with something concrete and tangible—for example, the product backlog. That's concrete, and completing these requirements is the overall goal of the project.

Based on that goal, your team does intangible work to create tangible value. As part of their knowledge work, the team will copy, adapt, and alter. The team, in their success strategy, doesn't have to start their code from scratch every time. It's just like in project management: if you have a form or project plan, you don't need to start from scratch; you can use it like a template. The team can do the same thing with development.

As a project manager, you need to trust the team in their intangible knowledge work. We stay out of the way of the production and allow the team to copy and alter, to watch and listen and to be observant. The team members can do trial and error, experiment, and determine why results are happening. Developers create, then observe to see what's happening. The project manager provides support for their concentration. Part of that support includes ensuring the team's physical environment has caves and commons where team members can work as needed. Often team members need quiet, time to think, and an environment in which to concentrate.

Early in the project, you want to match work assignments with the appropriate people as the team becomes more self-organizing. You need to know, and trust, people's skills and desire to learn, to take on challenges. You'll work to retain the best talent, as you do want good, talented people on your team. If you're like me, you want the highest possible skillset on your team. You want to retain the best talent and support the team.

If you can, use rewards that preserve joy and think about what's valuable to the team. Give praise and recognition to your project team when they do good work. If you can't give monetary rewards, consider other items you can give team members, such as company shirts, coffee mugs, or some other token acknowledging their effort. Avoid zero-sum rewards, though. A *zero-sum reward* is one that only one person can win, such as employee of the month. That can create envy and make the non-winners feel poorly about their work and their contributions. You also want to avoid combining rewards. As a project manager, you don't want to combine rewards. You want to say this is a reward for zero defects, for example, and this is a reward for hitting the deadline.

And then get feedback from your team. You'll get some feedback in the retrospective, but you should also get feedback through daily standups. Make certain you are listening to what people are saying; don't fall into a routine of being present but not listening to the conversation. Respect your team; give them the freedom to innovate, to be creative, and to experiment to get results.

Detecting Problems and Defects

According to the Agile Manifesto, the highest priority is to satisfy the customer through early and continuous delivery of valuable software. Delivering working software frequently is another stated principle. Upholding these principles means your team is going to be making frequent changes to the code and refactoring it before delivery. This requires you to consider how refactoring or changing the code may introduce new defects and cause problems. When defects happen, you want to capture the defects. For the PMI-ACP exam, there are five things you want to know about detecting problems and defects:

- **Escaped defects**   These are defects that slip through testing and into production. Escaped defects are the most expensive type of defect because they get out to the end users. The project team must fix defects upon discovery in each iteration. You don't want to release an increment that is defective.

- **Regression testing**   Regression testing should happen on all functionality throughout the project. As the team compiles code, they do regression testing to ensure that what they've added to existing software doesn't break anything.

- **Demonstrations** Demonstrations are good because they show the user stories in action and how the team has created the user story and value.

- **Consistent testing** Software development projects require user acceptability testing and end-to-end testing. Your goal is to discover and fix defects before the software is released.

- **Daily standup meetings** You consistently ask in the daily standup if there are any impediments or roadblocks to address. This prompt is often the first step to detecting problems. It fits right in with ensuring that the team feels safe.

 EXAM COACH Agile projects are typically for software development, but the PMI-ACP exam won't test you on developing code. You don't have to be a programmer to pass the PMI-ACP exam.

Identifying Lead Time and Cycle Time

Two terms that you need to know for your PMI-ACP exam are lead time and cycle time. *Lead time* is how long something takes to go through the entire process. For example, you begin with a concept, as in Figure 6-4, and it moves all the way to a finished increment that is a shippable product. The time to move from concept to finished increment is lead time. Lead time is simply how long it takes an item to move through the whole project process.

Cycle time is really a subset of lead time, as depicted at the bottom of Figure 6-4. *Cycle time* is how long something takes to go through a part of the process, such as how long it takes a feature to go from coding to testing. That's your cycle time.

 EXAM COACH Lead time is how long something takes to move through the whole project process. Cycle time is how long it takes to move through just a portion of the process.

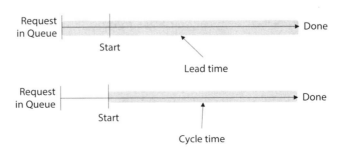

Figure 6-4 Lead time and cycle time describe the duration of activities in a process.

Tracking cycle time may give you clues about potential bottlenecks because it shows how long individual units of work take to complete. Based on this information you can examine where the bottleneck exists, why the delay is occurring, and then work with the team to resolve the bottleneck. As a project manager, consider a task and how long it takes to go through development to release. Now consider changes to the product that disrupt work already completed. Changes to work that's already been completed mean the team is working on items they considered done but now have to be touched and managed again. This is customer-driven, and while we welcome changes, many changes to the backlog could affect cycle time.

A goal with tracking lead time is to improve the efficiency of the system. One way you can do this is to increase the capacity of the project team. You could put more than one or two developers on a feature. By adding labor, you might be able to bring down the duration. Of course, this solution won't work with every user story, but for large user stories, you can improve lead time by slicing the story and getting more people involved in completing the feature. When multiple people attack a single problem, user story, or task, this is called *swarming*.

 EXAM COACH Another way you can improve lead time is to stop taking requirements. At some point you're not adding new requirements to the project—you must get to the definition of done. That's not always feasible, I know, but that is one option to improve your lead time.

Recall that WIP is the work in progress and it helps you track velocity. Remember velocity is a measure of how many user stories, or story points, the team can complete in an iteration. Each item in your WIP can be tracked for its lead time and cycle time. If velocity is below target, the number of story points the team believes they can do is a clue. The problem could be the team has unrealistic story point sizing. The average amount of work the team can get done in the duration of the project is the rate of efficiency. Productivity is how much work gets done. Efficiency is how quickly the the work is completed without defects. Just because a team has the capacity to be more productive doesn't mean that the team will be more productive. The stories they assigned a seven, for example, might be more realistically assigned as a ten, and what's a three should be a seven.

The *project cycle time* is the duration of the entire project. However long the project lasts is the cycle time for the whole project. It's the duration of the entire project management process, not just a portion of the process; the endeavor it takes to move from the launch to the closure. This brings us back to Parkinson's law: Work expands to fill the time allotted to it. With cycle time you set goals for efficiency and you set goals for productivity. You want the team to develop a system to get the work done quickly and accurately.

Defect cycle time is the amount of time between when a defect is discovered and when it's resolved. The longer the defect cycle time, typically the more expensive that defect will be in the project. If the defect hangs around, it will affect other things. *Escaped defects* describes the defects that slip all the way through testing and out to production. These are the most expensive defects to fix because the code is already published. The *defect rate* measures the frequency of how many defects are found. An increase in escaped defects indicates you have a problem with some process, which could be testing, poorly written tests, poor requirement definitions, or even bad code. You'll need root cause analysis to determine why defects are escaping the process.

Completing Variance Analysis

Whenever you are dealing with a variance, you're subtracting something from something. A *variance* is the difference between what was planned and what was experienced. For example, consider a team that believed they could accomplish ten story points in this iteration, but they actually only completed eight story points. That's an easy-to-see variance of two story points. But consider if the team is consistently off by two story points—that can be a whole iteration of story points over time. Variance analysis is the identification of the variance and the examination of why the variance exists.

You can also examine cost variance and schedule variance. Recall from our discussion of earned value management (EVM) in Chapter 2 that cost variance is earned value minus our actual cost (EV – AC). How much the work is worth minus what you spent to do the work equates to the cost variance. Cost variances affect value as the total cost of the project increases. Schedule variance, in earned value management, is earned value minus planned value (EV – PV). Schedule variance is the value of project work today minus the value of what the project should be worth. I've not personally met many agile project managers utilizing EVM, but it is a consideration for your PMI-ACP exam.

More realistically, there are lots of reasons why you might have a variance. Common cause variation is the average day-to-day differences. Your team is going to have great days where everything works and they accomplish much. And they'll have bad days where experiments and innovations just don't work out. There are going to be ups and downs in productivity and efficiency. If you're having a continuous variance, that's a reason for root cause analysis. It might be your user stories and your story points are too aggressive and the project team hasn't sized the user stories properly.

You might also have special cause variation. Special causes of variance are unusual occurrences that influence project progress. For example, maybe the power went out for two days, or three team members caught the flu, or there was an emergency in the business, or a hurricane in your locale interrupted the project work. Those are all special causes of variance that you don't have a lot of control over. Be able to recognize special causes of variances for your exam—I suspect you'll see a question or two about them.

Identifying Project Trends

As I just mentioned, if you're having the same types of variances over and over in your iterations, then you likely have a trend. A trend is something that is happening on a regular, almost forecastable basis. Trends are time series data—over time you can see the same occurrences and possibly predict when the occurrence will happen again. You're comparing the same data in each time period, like velocity in each iteration. The goal is to identify relationships between two or more factors that are causing the trend.

Trend analysis allows you to predict future performance based on what's happened already in the project. When you rely on trend analysis, you are relying on past experiences.

Past experiences are called *lagging metrics*. Lagging metrics are based on performance to this point of the project. Lagging metrics allow you to look for trends and then, based on what you find, predict the future with some degree of confidence. Predictions don't always come true—just look for trends in the stock market.

Leading metrics provide a view into the future. Leading metrics are trends that you predict will happen. With trend analysis you're aiming to predict performance, problems, and repeatable results so that you can anticipate problems and opportunities to combat the problems, and exploit the opportunities.

Setting Control Limits

Do you ever feel like your project is out of control? By "out of control," I mean it's more than just wildly unpredictable or a big mess.

You must have a method to set control limits to look at the team's maximum productivity and lowest allowed productivity. Those are your upper and lower control limits. You'll see those limits as upper specifications and lower specifications when talking about productivity in a project. These control limits are boundaries to operate within. These boundaries offer a window of performance and provide a level of expectation for productivity.

You already have dealt with control limits: your WIP. You limit the amount of work in progress, so that's a control limit. If you use a Kanban board, you likely limit the number of items in each phase of your project to keep the queue for productivity at a manageable level. That too is a control limit. Basically, a control limit is both a way to restrict how much work is currently happening and a way to establish and measure expectations for productivity.

A control chart, as in Figure 6-5, is a way of visualizing project performance. A control chart shows how the team performed within the control limits for each increment of a project. The solid black bars are our upper and lower specifications; that's the best and the worst we expect to do. The dashed lines are the upper and lower control limits, our goals of productivity within our specifications. And then we have a mean, our expected level of productivity.

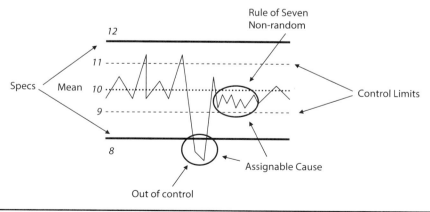

Figure 6-5   Control charts show performance over time and help identify trends.

Here's how it works. You define both the maximum number of story points your team could feasibly do in an increment and the minimum number of story points that the team must complete. For this example, let's say 12 is the maximum and 8 is the minimum; 12 and 8 story points are your best-case scenario and worst-case scenario. Our upper and lower specifications tighten up those requirements to a more realistic maximum of 11 story points and a minimum of 9 story points. That's our control limits, where we expect our performance to happen. The mean is 10, right in the middle. (You could do normal distribution using the formula of pessimistic minus optimistic divided by six, and find the mean, but I just made it easy for us and said it was 10.) Ten user story points completed per iteration is our expectation in this example.

The peaks and valleys represent the result of each iteration, the team's actual productivity for the number of story points completed in each iteration. Each point in the graph represents an increment in a project. If you look about halfway through, we have one dip that is below our specifications and even below our control limits. That is out of control. When a measurement is out of control, it's also called an *assignable cause*. An assignable cause means there's some reason why this variance happened.

You'll next notice the circle that's also identified as an assignable cause. Whenever you have the results of seven consecutive measurements all on one side of the mean, that represents a trend and is an assignable cause. That's called the *rule of seven* and it's a non-random event. There's some reason why the performance is consistently, in this example, below the mean. I wouldn't get too bogged down on control charts. You might have one question on that for your exam.

Creating a Risk-Adjusted Backlog

I've discussed in detail the product backlog and how the product owner prioritizes the items based on the expected value. The project manager, the project team, and the product owner should also consider a *risk-adjusted backlog*, which adjusts the priority of user stories with a consideration of risks. You don't want a user story with a huge risk lurking in the backlog if that risk can wreck the project. You want to look at that item early in the project, because if you can't get by the big risk, or the risk proves to be too expensive or ruins the feasibility of the project, identifying it early in the project saves time and money. In other words, an organization doesn't want to invest thousands of dollars and weeks of work only to have it go to waste as a result of a risk that wasn't addressed early in the project.

Risk, as an uncertain event or condition, is considered anti-value. A risk-adjusted backlog is the idea that you adjust the backlog to attack the high-risk items earlier rather than later in the project. A risk-adjusted backlog is a way of looking at the items with the greatest value and the items with the greatest risk and then moving these items to the top of the backlog. You don't allow risk to just percolate and lurk in the backlog. You want to attack those risk items as soon as possible. To be clear, a risk-adjusted backlog isn't a separate document or product backlog. It means that you, the product owner, and the project team have worked together to adjust the backlog in consideration of the risk-laden requirements to take those on sooner rather than later.

Risk event	Probability	Impact	Ex$V
A	.30	−$45,000	−$13,500
B	.20	−$75,000	−$15,000
C	.10	−$25,000	−$2,500
D	.40	−$85,000	−$34,000

Contingency reserve = $65,000

Figure 6-6   Risk probability and risk impact help discover the expected monetary value.

The return on investment for the project can be broken down for each story so you can see how risk affects the project's ROI. The value management team or product owner can assign ROI to each item in the backlog to see how a risk, or what risks, may potentially affect the value of each story and the entire project. Understanding how risk can affect value helps to better prioritize the user stories for risks and value.

One approach you and the product owner can use is to find the *expected monetary value (EMV)*, which is the financial exposure of the risk. Expected monetary value is found by examining a risk, its probability, and its effect on the project. In the example given in Figure 6-6, Risk A has a 30 percent probability of occurring and would have an impact of −$45,000 if it were to occur. Thus, the expected monetary value of Risk A is −$45,000 × 30 percent = −$13,500. This calculation of EMV is done for each risk in your backlog. You do this in a risk probability-impact matrix. The sum of all the expected monetary values, the last column in Figure 6-6, is the risk exposure for the project. In this case, it's negative $65,000. The contingency reserve is shown as the inverse of that amount, positive $65,000. A *contingency reserve* is money set aside to offset potential risk events in your project.

Determining Risk Severity

Instead of risk probability and using dollar amounts, you can use a simple scale, an ordinal scale. Rather than dollar amounts, you'll use low, medium, high. Some organizations use a scale that also includes very low and very high to provide a few more factors to judge risk severity. It's the same formula with this model: risk probability times risk impact. For example, you could decide that very low times high is going to equal a medium. Or low times medium equals low. In this model you'll have a risk score, rather than an expected monetary value for each risk event. The project manager and team define the scales of probability and impact rules for each project with this approach.

If you use dollar amounts and create a contingency reserve, you're really hedging your bets on which risks will or won't happen. For example, that $65,000 contingency reserve in the previous scenario is all the money we have for all the risks in the project. Some of those risks could eat up a big chunk of that contingency reserve. If that happens, we're hedging our bets that other risks are not going to happen. To rely on this approach describes the organization's risk appetite and your confidence in the identified probability and impact.

You'll then need to look at the distribution of risk. If some of those big risks are early in the project, based on a risk-prioritized product backlog, and you can get beyond those risks, the overall risk exposure for the project goes down because you didn't have to spend the money. Your project didn't have to experience the impact of that large risk event.

Notice in Figure 6-6 that you have $65,000 set aside, but Risk B is estimated to cost $75,000 if it happens. That's more than your contingency reserve in this example. But there's only a 20 percent chance of Risk B occurring. That unease that you feel with that risk is your utility function, your risk tolerance. You know $75,000 is going to wreck your contingency reserve, so are you willing to take that 80 percent chance that Risk B won't happen? Is your risk appetite strong enough that you're willing to take it on? Or are you not happy about Risk B? A high project priority may mean you have a lower tolerance risk.

If you're willing to take on Risk B because there's a high likelihood it won't happen, you'll be factoring risk and reward. By taking on the risk, you don't have to spend the money to avoid that risk, or to mitigate it. If you get over that risk hump, then you can deal with Risk C and Risk D. The farther along you get in the project the greater your odds of success for the project.

Creating a Risk Burndown Chart

While you do want to take on risks as soon as you can in the project, there are likely to be risks distributed throughout the project. The further we get in the project without risk rearing its head, the greater the odds of success. A risk burndown chart is used to represent this concept of risk exposure.

A risk burndown chart, as depicted in Figure 6-7, is a stacked graph similar to a user story burndown chart. A risk burndown chart is a graph of cumulative project risk severity. In other words, it shows how severe the risk exposure is at the beginning of the project through the end of the project. As the project team gets by more and more risk, exposure diminishes all the way down to zero. This chart is a way to visualize risk events for each iteration in the project. The severity of each risk is plotted in the chart to illustrate the accumulation of all the project risk is represented in the risk burndown chart. You're burning down the risk. Your exposure diminishes once you get past those key risk events in your project.

Figure 6-7 Risk burndown charts show that risks diminish as the project progresses.

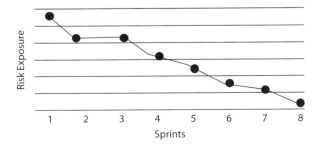

Solving Problems in Agile Projects

One of your key goals in this domain is to solve problems. By solving problems, you're really doing continuous improvement. One approach you can take is to use problem-solving games. These are games that are intended to get team members to work through problems, to think critically, and to be creative and innovative to combat problems. While the games themselves do not solve problems, they are icebreakers and tools to help facilitate problem solving. You won't need to recognize any specific game for your exam—and there are hundreds of games online—but you should know that problem-solving games help the team talk through problems and discover solutions.

Your goal is for team engagement. In the problem-solving games, you want to involve the whole team where it's appropriate and how the project team can be most helpful to solve problems. You only want to solve real-world problems, not hypotheticals and what-ifs. You know risk is uncertain, but you don't want to create problems just for the sake of solving problems.

You need team cohesion, but you might encounter situations in which team members form different camps on how to resolve a problem. You must talk through the two sides, or facilitate the team conversation, to get people on the same team to solve the problems. You should also check in with people after project changes and make certain that their commitment is still high for the project. You want to know how a change may affect iterations and the overall project product. Team members will likely feel frustrated when changes affect the work they've already done.

You also need to acknowledge that some problems just can't be solved, even with team engagement; that's the nature of the work that you're doing. For example, you may be required to use a resource that's not congruent with your project. Or you may be tasked with to develop software in a specific coding language. Or you must deal with a certain vendor. There will be some constraints that you just have to deal with. You must work around those types of problems, which means you avoid them altogether. You still track and monitor the problems, but you make sure they aren't continuing to haunt your project and causing more problems.

Some risks you'll have to create a response for. There are four risk responses you want to know for your exam:

- **Mitigation**   Mitigation is anything that you do to reduce the probability or impact of a risk event.

- **Transference**   Transference is anything that you do that transfers the risk to someone else, usually with a contractual relationship. You hire someone to manage that part of the risk.

- **Avoidance**   You just avoid the risk. You might take the requirements out of scope because it's too risky.

- **Acceptance**   A risk is small or there's nothing you can do about it, so you accept the risk.

Chapter Summary

You, the project manager, have to manage problems in your projects. Specifically, you have to manage issues and risks. Recall that a *risk* is an uncertain event or condition that can have a negative effect on your agile project. An *issue* is a risk event that has occurred. You, the project team, and the product owner work together to identify risk and prioritize them in the product backlog. A risk-adjusted backlog addresses risks quickly in the project timeline. Your team also has to deal with issues, manage the issues, and determine how issues may affect the project.

Changes to the project requirements are welcome and expected in an agile project, but changes in your project can also mean changes to the project strategy and approach. A change to the project requirements can affect work that's already been completed, introduce new risks, and, in some cases, cause frustration and diminished support of the project by the project team. Change, when dealing with an issue, needs to be addressed quickly—the longer an issue goes unchecked, the larger the effect the issue can have on the project.

In this chapter we also discussed the idea of paying down your technical debt. Technical debt accumulates through shortcuts, sloppy code, poor requirements documentation, and quick fixes, all of which are common when a team attempts to speed up value delivery by not refactoring and not consistently cleaning up the code. Technical debt can also accrue from parallel development. Technical debt, when ignored, can make a larger mess in the project because it can affect other portions of the project that are built atop the poor code.

Failure modes and success modes are two important concepts also discussed in this chapter. Failure mode is the acknowledgement that people make mistakes, our preference to fail conservatively, our desire to invent rather than research, our bad habits and inconsistencies. Success mode includes the project team's ability to look around, learn, change, and adapt, as well as the pride the team takes in their work. These two types of modes will both happen in a project, but the important thing is to ensure that the team learns from either mode. Retrospectives and iteration planning are opportunities to recall what's worked in the past and to plan how better to prepare for the future.

Lead time is how long something takes to go through the entire process, such as from concept to the shippable product. Cycle time is a subset of lead time and describes how long something takes to go through a part of the process, such as coding through testing. However long the project lasts is the cycle time for the entire project. Defect cycle time is the amount of time between when a defect is discovered in the project and when the defect is resolved. The longer the defect time the costlier the defect usually is for the project.

In this chapter we also discussed variance analysis with a quick overview of earned value management. While I don't expect you to see many, if any, questions on earned value analysis on the PMI-ACP exam, it's possible you might see one or two questions on that topic. Variance is the difference between what was planned and what was experienced. Variance in a project is typically caused by average day-to-day differences, where the team has good days and bad days. Special causes of variances are unusual, unexpected events that create problems in the project. For example, you lose power, hardware fails, personnel get sick, or a business emergency interrupts your project.

At the start of your project the odds of success are at the lowest; there is risk in just doing the project. As your project team progresses, the odds of project success increase. As your team does more and more work, the odds of success go higher and higher. As the odds of project success increase, the odds of project failure decrease. A risk burndown chart can be used to show the total project risk exposure and how the risk exposure goes down with each iteration that you're able to successfully manage the project and the project risk. As the project nears its completion and stakeholder acceptability, the risk is very low and the odds of project success are very high.

Great job finishing this chapter! You're so close to the end of this project that your odds of success are very high. Keep going—you can do this!

Key Terms

Acceptance   Acceptance is the typical response to risks that are small or can't be mitigated, transferred, or avoided.

Assignable cause   In a control chart measurements that are out of control are deemed an assignable cause. Assignable causes are measurements of performance that are out of control; an assignable cause means there's some reason why a variance happened.

Avoidance   You just avoid the risk. You might take the requirement out of scope because it's too risky.

Control chart   A control chart shows how the team performed within the control limits for each increment of a project. The control chart defines the expected performance within control limits, trends, and assignable causes.

Control limits   Control limits are boundaries to operate within. These boundaries offer a window of performance and provide a level of expectation for productivity.

Cycle time   Cycle time is how long something takes to go through a part of the process. Cycle time is a subset of lead time, which is how long something takes to go through the entire process.

Defect cycle time   Defect cycle time is the amount of time between when a defect is discovered and when it's resolved. The longer the defect cycle time, typically the more expensive that defect will be in the project.

Escaped defects   Escaped defects are defects that slip through testing and into production. Escaped defects are the most expensive type of defect because they get out to the end users.

Expected monetary value   The expected monetary value is the financial exposure of the risk. Expected monetary value is found by multiplying the risk probability times the risk impact.

Fishbone diagram   A fishbone diagram, also called a cause-and-effect diagram and an Ishikawa diagram, is used in root cause analysis to identify the contributing causes of the effect. The diagram can be used to facilitate a conversation to resolve the effect the project is experiencing.

Issues   Issues are risks that have been realized in the project, and their effect must be managed.

Lagging metrics   Lagging metrics are based on performance to this point of the project. Lagging metrics allow you to look for trends and then, based on what you find, predict the future with some degree of confidence. Lagging trends are proven.

Lead time   Lead time is how long a requirement takes to go through an entire process within the project.

Leading metrics   Leading metrics provide a view into the future. Leading metrics are trends that you predict will happen. Leading trends have uncertainty and are not yet proven.

Maslow's Hierarchy of Needs   Maslow's Hierarchy of Needs describes the five levels of human needs: physiological, safety, social, esteem, and self-actualization. To be self-actualized means you have a sense of purpose in your work, which also means you're taking pride in your work and want to do it properly.

Mitigation   Mitigation is anything that we do to reduce the probability or impact of a risk event.

Project cycle time   Project cycle time is the duration of the entire project. However long the project lasts is the cycle time for the whole project.

Qualitative analysis   Qualitative analysis is fast and subjective and isn't totally reliable. The goal of qualitative analysis is to decide which risks should go into quantitative analysis.

Quantitative analysis   Quantitative analysis quantifies the probability and impact of a risk event. Quantitative analysis takes more time to do, but it's much more reliable than qualitative analysis.

Regression testing   Regression testing confirms that what's been developed in the past still works once new code has been compiled into the software. Regression testing should happen on all functionality throughout the project. As the team compiles code, they do regression testing to ensure that what they've added to existing software doesn't break anything.

Risk-adjusted backlog   A risk-adjusted backlog adjusts the priority of user stories with a consideration of risks. This approach addresses risks earlier in the project, rather than later in the project. The risk-adjusted backlog takes on risks quickly to avoid significant damage or increased costs later in the project. Taking on risk project work earlier in the project helps determine if the project is feasible and if the project team can overcome the defined risks without investing too much time and costs into the project.

Risk burndown chart   A risk burndown chart is a stacked graph, similar to a user story burndown chart, that shows cumulative project risk severity. It charts the risk exposure from the beginning of the project through the end of the project.

Risk probability-impact matrix   A risk probability-impact matrix is a table of risk events that shows each risk's probability and impact, and a risk score or the expected monetary value of the risk event. The risk score is found by multiplying the risk probability times the risk impact.

Risk tolerance   Risk tolerance describes a person's or organization's willingness to take on risks in a project. High-priority projects generally have a lower risk tolerance than low-priority projects.

Risks   Risks are uncertain events or conditions that can have a negative effect on an agile project.

Root cause analysis (RCA)   Root cause analysis (RCA) is the analysis of the problem, the causal factors, and the determination of how the problem may be resolved. RCA defines the root problem, not symptoms that are causing those problems.

Rule of seven   Whenever you have the results of seven consecutive measurements all on one side of the mean in a control chart, that represents a trend and is an assignable cause. That's called the rule of seven and it's a non-random event.

Secondary risk   Secondary risk occurs when one risk is solved but the risk solution inadvertently creates one or more new risks.

Special causes of variance   Special causes of variance are unusual occurrences that influence project progress. For example, the power went out for two days, or three team members caught the flu, or there was an emergency in the business.

Swarming   Swarming happens when multiple people, often the entire project team, attack a single problem, user story, or task.

Technical debt   Technical debt is the backlog of work that's caused if the team fails to do regular clean-up on the project code. It's the maintenance, standardization, and refactoring of the code.

Transference   Transference is anything that you do that transfers the risk to someone else, usually with a contractual relationship. You hire someone to manage that part of the risk.

Trend analysis   Trend analysis allows you to predict future performance based on what's happened already in the project.

Zero-sum reward   A zero-sum reward means that only one person can win, such as employee of the month. That can create envy and make the non-winners feel poorly about their work and contributions.

Questions

1. Beth is the project manager of a new agile project in her organization. Her team has identified a significant problem, though the problem may not happen until late in the project timeline. What is the best way to minimize the impact of a problem during a project even if may not occur to late in the project?

   A. Ignore the problem

   B. Don't waste time trying to fix the problem until later in the project

   C. Identify it early, diagnose it, and fix it as soon as possible

   D. Make the fix a task in the next iteration

2. As the agile team leader, you have visibility to the project's budget and you realize that as the team progresses through iterations, the cost of the project continues to increase. What might be the cause?

   A. Scope creep

   B. Technical debt

   C. Unexplained increase of hours worked

   D. Adding testers to the team

3. Your agile team leader has asked the entire team to submit the cycle time for the next three iterations. What does the leader mean by cycle time?

   A. The time it takes to complete each iteration from start to finish

   B. The time it takes to determine what is in the iteration

   C. The time it will take to complete all three iterations

   D. The time that is between each iteration for review and feedback

4. When the agile team leader notices that the throughput of the team has gone up, the team leader can attribute the increase to which of the following?

   A. The productivity of one team member has increased.

   B. The testing went well.

   C. The iteration was estimated more accurately.

   D. The development was more efficient.

5. Your agile team leader has decided to track defect cycle time. Which of the following best describes what is being tracked?

   A. How many defects were discovered during a cycle time

   B. How long it took to fix a defect from introduction to completion of the fix

   C. Which developer was creating the defects during a cycle time

   D. How inaccurate the estimate was of the cycle time

6. Your agile team leader posts the team's defect rates found by month and found by release. The team keeps a very close eye on these charts and does their best to keep these rates as low as possible. Occasionally, a defect will make it all the way through testing and quality assurance. What are these types of defects called?

   A. Run-away defects

   B. Technical debt

   C. Escaped defects

   D. Failure mode

7. Your agile team's defect rates seem to vary quite a bit from iteration to iteration. Your team leader understands that not every iteration will be the same, but feels the variation is significant enough to investigate. What type of variation can your leader label this?

   A. Common cause variation

   B. Special cause variation

   C. Severe variation

   D. Mild variation

8. Your agile team leader has been tracking the iteration velocity and has compared that to the time left on the project. The leader has determined that the fewest number of iterations that can be done per month is seven and the most possible is ten iterations. What is this measurement called?

   A. Trend analysis

   B. Control limits

   C. Variance analysis

   D. Cycle time

9. An agile team begins with a list of business features, broken out into logical groups of work. This list is then prioritized by business value by attributing a dollar value to each iteration. Once the agile development team analyzes the list and adds the risks and threats, along with the risk impact in dollars, the list is then reprioritized. What is the result of this activity called?

   A. Risk-adjusted backlog

   B. Expected monetary value

   C. Risk probability

   D. Risk impact

10. An agile team analyzes the risks of the requirements to assign a risk probability and an impact score to each risk. Those scores are used to calculate risk severity. How are the high-risk items handled by the agile team?

   A. They change the requirement so it isn't a risk.

   B. The team schedules the high-risk items in early iterations to be handled before they become compounded.

   C. The team asks the business partner to create a new requirement.

   D. The team leaves the high-risk items all in one iteration toward the end of the project.

11. There are lots of opportunities for problem solving and transparency throughout the project. What agile tasks are used to minimize the need for ad hoc problem solving?

   A. Writing user stories

   B. Using trend analysis

   C. Iteration reviews and retrospectives

   D. Determining the special cause variation

12. Your agile team leader has scheduled a problem-solving session because development has stopped due to a roadblock. The agile method is to involve not only the business partner and project lead but also the entire team. Why is this method beneficial?

   A. The developers have the best theoretical solutions.

   B. Having the entire team involved will keep the meeting shorter.

   C. The team will introduce multiple fixes to select from.

   D. The team together can identify, diagnose, and solve the issue, which facilitates buy-in.

13. When your agile team leader involves the entire team in problem solving, what message does that send to the team?

   A. The team lead doesn't trust one person's recommendation.

   B. The team lead believes team members can be supportive beyond their roles.

   C. The team lead doesn't think the business partners have the resolution.

   D. The team lead doesn't know the resolution.

14. The new agile team leader learned early in the project what types of problems should be vetted through the entire team for consensus. What types of problems require team involvement?

   A. When a task cannot move forward

   B. To make decisions on training standards

   C. When developers can't agree on successful code

   D. To determine how to reduce project costs

15. Why is it important for the agile team leader to ensure there is a safe and open environment for the team?

  A. So there is no turnover in the team

  B. So the team feels free to admit to problems and failures and ask for help

  C. To protect the budget

  D. So the entire team becomes friends

16. In addition to providing caves for agile team members to retreat to for some quiet time, what else can the team leader suggest to allow team members time to concentrate?

  A. Allowing colocated team members to work remotely

  B. Scheduling team members to go to caves

  C. Designating a certain period as a quiet work time in colocated areas

  D. Banning cell phones in the work area

17. Consider the importance of project communications among the project team stakeholders. With what method does your agile leader encourage feedback from stakeholders?

  A. Having a weekly conference call with stakeholders

  B. Sending out status reports to stakeholders and asking for feedback

  C. Conducting iteration reviews that include all stakeholders

  D. Enlisting stakeholder feedback only when there is a roadblock

18. When analyzing variances and it is determined that the difference is a common cause variance, what is the next step the agile leader should take?

  A. Accept the variance and move forward

  B. Get all stakeholders' approval to accept the variance

  C. Have the agile team determine how to close the variance

  D. Evaluate the variance again to see if the difference can be closed

19. Your project's business partner is pushing to add more features to each iteration. Your agile team has already projected what the next few iterations will include based on the business partner's priorities and the team's risk analysis. What do you think the business partner is missing by pushing for additional features?

  A. The time it takes to perform housekeeping of code

  B. Team members get sick or schedule vacation days during iterations

  C. The time it takes to write user stories

  D. The time it takes to test code

20. Your team leader uses several agile tools to uncover potential problems before they occur. Which of the following is one of those tools?

A. Affinity estimating

B. User story

C. Iteration planning

D. Daily standup meetings

Questions and Answers

1. Beth is the project manager of a new agile project in her organization. Her team has identified a significant problem, though the problem may not happen until late in the project timeline. What is the best way to minimize the impact of a problem during a project even if may not occur to late in the project?

A. Ignore the problem

B. Don't waste time trying to fix the problem until later in the project

C. Identify it early, diagnose it, and fix it as soon as possible

D. Make the fix a task in the next iteration

C. Beth should identify the issue early so it can be diagnosed and fixed before it begins to affect the rest of the project.
A is incorrect because Beth shouldn't ignore the problem—that won't resolve the problem. B is incorrect because waiting until later in the project to address the problem may allow the problem to grow larger and it doesn't prepare the team for tackling the problem. D is incorrect because this too is a delay tactic. Beth should address the problem as soon as possible with the project team.

2. As the agile team leader, you have visibility to the project's budget and you realize that as the team progresses through iterations, the cost of the project continues to increase. What might be the cause?

A. Scope creep

B. Technical debt

C. Unexplained increase of hours worked

D. Adding testers to the team

B. Of all the choices, the best answer for the cost increase is technical debt. Technical debt is the backlog of things that should be done, but aren't, because of a push to deliver features, such as regular cleanup, maintenance, and refactoring. This increases the cost of development in future iterations because these tasks need to be done at some point. It is much easier and efficient to factor the time it takes to complete this maintenance during the iteration opposed to doing it at some other time.

A is incorrect because scope creep refers to the small, undocumented changes that enter the project. C is incorrect because the hours worked are mapped against each user story. D is incorrect because there is no evidence in the question that additional testers have been added to the project team.

3. Your agile team leader has asked the entire team to submit the cycle time for the next three iterations. What does the leader mean by cycle time?

   A. The time it takes to complete each iteration from start to finish

   B. The time it takes to determine what is in the iteration

   C. The time it will take to complete all three iterations

   D. The time that is between each iteration for review and feedback

   A. Cycle time is the time it takes to complete an iteration from start to finish. Cycle time is a subset of lead time, which measures the time it will take to complete the entire project.
   B, C, and D are incorrect because cycle time doesn't address the time required to determine what's in the iteration, the duration of the iterations, or the timeboxed ceremonies between iterations.

4. When the agile team leader notices that the throughput of the team has gone up, the team leader can attribute the increase to which of the following?

   A. The productivity of one team member has increased.

   B. The testing went well.

   C. The iteration was estimated more accurately.

   D. The development was more efficient.

   A. The best answer is that throughput is increasing because the productivity of one team member has increased, which could be a cause of the other choices in this question. There could be many reasons for the increase in throughput; adding more team members or outsourcing a piece of the project are more examples.
   B is incorrect because testing could still go well without velocity being affected. C is incorrect because iterations can be estimated accurately, but productivity meets the estimate. D is incorrect because development could still be efficient, but productivity could not increase.

5. Your agile team leader has decided to track defect cycle time. Which of the following best describes what is being tracked?

   A. How many defects were discovered during a cycle time

   B. How long it took to fix a defect from introduction to completion of the fix

   C. Which developer was creating the defects during a cycle time

   D. How inaccurate the estimate was of the cycle time

B. Defect cycle time is the measurement of how long it took to fix a defect once it was discovered. The defect cycle time length directly affects the cost and time frame of an iteration, or cycle time.
A is incorrect because it's not how many defects were discovered, but how long it takes to fix a defect. C is incorrect because who is creating the defects isn't part of the defect cycle time. D is incorrect because accuracy of the estimate of a cycle time is tracked, but it's not part of the defect cycle time amount.

6. Your agile team leader posts the team's defect rates found by month and found by release. The team keeps a very close eye on these charts and does their best to keep these rates as low as possible. Occasionally, a defect will make it all the way through testing and quality assurance. What are these types of defects called?

   A. Run-away defects

   B. Technical debt

   C. Escaped defects

   D. Failure mode

   C. Defects that make it through all checkpoints to production are called escaped defects. This is the costliest type of defect since its remediation will require a significant amount of rework, testing, retesting, and discovering any dependent code and then repeating the testing process.
   A is incorrect because run-away defects isn't a valid term. B is incorrect because technical debt describes the code and solution that needs to be refactored or cleaned before releasing the product. D is incorrect because failure mode describes the team's attitude and habits in the project.

7. Your agile team's defect rates seem to vary quite a bit from iteration to iteration. Your team leader understands that not every iteration will be the same, but feels the variation is significant enough to investigate. What type of variation can your leader label this?

   A. Common cause variation

   B. Special cause variation

   C. Severe variation

   D. Mild variation

   A. A common cause variation is one that refers to day-to-day differences of doing work.
   B is incorrect because special cause variation is variance caused by special or new factors. C and D are incorrect because severe variation and mild variation aren't valid agile terms.

8. Your agile team leader has been tracking the iteration velocity and has compared that to the time left on the project. The leader has determined that the fewest number of iterations that can be done per month is seven and the most possible is ten iterations. What is this measurement called?

A. Trend analysis

B. Control limits

C. Variance analysis

D. Cycle time

> **B.** This tool, or measurement, is called control limits. Setting a minimum and maximum of a certain entity, whether it be velocity, budget, time off, etc., lets the agile stakeholder know exactly what can be done, spent, or utilized in a given period.
> A is incorrect because trend analysis is a forward-looking analysis estimating what might happen in the future. C is incorrect because variance analysis is the difference between estimates. D is incorrect because cycle time is the duration of time it will take to complete a task.

9. An agile team begins with a list of business features, broken out into logical groups of work. This list is then prioritized by business value by attributing a dollar value to each iteration. Once the agile development team analyzes the list and adds the risks and threats, along with the risk impact in dollars, the list is then reprioritized. What is the result of this activity called?

A. Risk-adjusted backlog

B. Expected monetary value

C. Risk probability

D. Risk impact

> **A.** A risk-adjusted backlog does not really produce a precise dollar value for either the list of work to be done or the risks or threats involved in the development. Instead, the exercise is used to facilitate discussions between the business team and the agile team about how to sequence the work items.
> B is incorrect because expected monetary value (EVM) is the probability of a risk times the impact of the risk event. C is incorrect because risk probability is the odds of a risk happening. D is incorrect because risk impact represents the effect the risk will have on the project objectives.

10. An agile team analyzes the risks of the requirements to assign a risk probability and an impact score to each risk. Those scores are used to calculate risk severity. How are the high-risk items handled by the agile team?

A. They change the requirement so it isn't a risk.

B. The team schedules the high-risk items in early iterations to be handled before they become compounded.

C. The team asks the business partner to create a new requirement.

D. The team leaves the high-risk items all in one iteration toward the end of the project.

> **B.** High-risk requirements are scheduled in early iterations, if possible, to be dealt with and even avoided in the project because the risks were identified and scheduled earlier in the project timeline rather than later.
> A is incorrect because changing the requirement will not make the project a success. C is incorrect because creating a new requirement doesn't address the risk event. D is incorrect because leaving high-risks requirements to be done at the end of a project is not a viable option as the risk can have a greater impact later in the project than earlier in the project because it can affect work that's already been completed.

11. There are lots of opportunities for problem solving and transparency throughout the project. What agile tasks are used to minimize the need for ad hoc problem solving?

A. Writing user stories

B. Using trend analysis

C. Iteration reviews and retrospectives

D. Determining the special cause variation

> **C.** Efforts to identify issues during an iteration's review and retrospective are included in the estimate of the iteration. Agile methods consider the team's lessons learned to be too critical to be saved for the post-mortem of a project, so they are presented at the end of each iteration.
> A is incorrect because user stories don't address problems in the project. B is incorrect because trend analysis uses lagging metrics to see what's already happened in the project. D is incorrect because determining the special cause variation isn't an agile task that's part of the agile project management approach.

12. Your agile team leader has scheduled a problem-solving session because development has stopped due to a roadblock. The agile method is to involve not only the business partner and project lead but also the entire team. Why is this method beneficial?

A. The developers have the best theoretical solutions.

B. Having the entire team involved will keep the meeting shorter.

C. The team will introduce multiple fixes to select from.

D. The team together can identify, diagnose, and solve the issue, which facilitates buy-in.

> **D.** One of the most important benefits of an all-inclusive problem-solving session is that the team will buy into a fix that they have discussed and solved, whereas they might not buy into a fix coming from someone that has not seen the entire picture of the issue.

A is incorrect because there's no evidence that developers have the best theoretical solutions. B is incorrect because the duration of the meeting won't necessarily affect the benefits of the meeting. C is incorrect because while the team may introduce multiple solutions, this isn't the best answer presented.

13. When your agile team leader involves the entire team in problem solving, what message does that send to the team?

   A. The team lead doesn't trust one person's recommendation.

   B. The team lead believes team members can be supportive beyond their roles.

   C. The team lead doesn't think the business partners have the resolution.

   D. The team lead doesn't know the resolution.

   B. When the entire team is involved in problem solving, that sends them the message that they are not pigeonholed to be only a developer, tester, coder, etc. Since agile teams work so closely, they are more apt to bounce ideas off each other. A and C are incorrect because an agile team leader wouldn't go to one person or a business partner to solve a problem or even try themselves but should instead involve the whole team. D is incorrect;just because the agile leader asks for input does not indicate they don't know what to do, rather, it demonstrates the leader values the input of others. The agile methodology is to engage the entire team.

14. The new agile team leader learned early in the project what types of problems should be vetted through the entire team for consensus. What types of problems require team involvement?

   A. When a task cannot move forward

   B. To make decisions on training standards

   C. When developers can't agree on successful code

   D. To determine how to reduce project costs

   A. The agile team leader should not bring the team together to problem solve when the issue is focused to specific roles.
   B and C are incorrect because, for example, developers may not have an opinion on how trainers should standardize their documentation, and a technical writer probably cannot help solve a coding issue. The team should be brought together when every team member potentially has valuable input on the issue. D is incorrect because reducing the project costs isn't a team problem-solving challenge and usually happens prior to the project, with the product owner and value management team.

15. Why is it important for the agile team leader to ensure there is a safe and open environment for the team?

   A. So there is no turnover in the team

   B. So the team feels free to admit to problems and failures and ask for help

C. To protect the budget

D. So the entire team becomes friends

B. Having a safe and open environment is critical to reassuring team members that they will not be criticized for admitting to a problem or failure. Asking for help allows the team to meet deadlines, avoid cost overruns, and try different approaches.
A is incorrect because while no or little staff turnover is an admirable goal, it's not the best choice presented. C is incorrect because the safe and open environment is not created to protect the budget. D is incorrect because, while agile projects do promote some social aspects, friendships among the project team isn't the best choice or goal of the open and safe environment.

16. In addition to providing caves for agile team members to retreat to for some quiet time, what else can the team leader suggest to allow team members time to concentrate?

A. Allowing colocated team members to work remotely

B. Scheduling team members to go to caves

C. Designating a certain period as a quiet work time in colocated areas

D. Banning cell phones in the work area

C. Designating a certain amount of time daily to allow team members to focus on their task without interruption is a good idea.
A is incorrect because working remotely is not always a typical option, although sometimes it cannot be avoided. B is incorrect because scheduled cave time may be counterproductive by removing members at a time that may not be convenient. D is incorrect because cell phones are common tools for organizational communication. A rule may be created, however, to take phone calls out of the common area.

17. Consider the importance of project communications among the project team stakeholders. With what method does your agile leader encourage feedback from stakeholders?

A. Having a weekly conference call with stakeholders

B. Sending out status reports to stakeholders and asking for feedback

C. Conducting iteration reviews that include all stakeholders

D. Enlisting stakeholder feedback only when there is a roadblock

C. Confirming and soliciting feedback from stakeholders at the end of each iteration not only saves time by ensuring the team is on the right path, but also saves cost due to unnecessary rework.

A and B are incorrect because conference calls and status reports may spark feedback, but having an iteration review ensures all stakeholders are working from the same requirements. D is incorrect because the project manager and the project team want stakeholder feedback for positive and negative scenarios, not only when there are roadblocks to the project.

18. When analyzing variances and it is determined that the difference is a common cause variance, what is the next step the agile leader should take?

    A. Accept the variance and move forward

    B. Get all stakeholders' approval to accept the variance

    C. Have the agile team determine how to close the variance

    D. Evaluate the variance again to see if the difference can be closed

    A. When the agile team has determined the difference is a common cause variance, the team leader should accept that there will be small differences and move on to the next task. Trying to rectify a common cause variance is a form of micromanaging the project instead of focusing on true roadblocks.
    B is incorrect because common causes of variances are implicitly accepted. C and D are incorrect because common causes of variances are part of the agile framework and don't need to be closed.

19. Your project's business partner is pushing to add more features to each iteration. Your agile team has already projected what the next few iterations will include based on the business partner's priorities and the team's risk analysis. What do you think the business partner is missing by pushing for additional features?

    A. The time it takes to perform housekeeping of code

    B. Team members get sick or schedule vacation days during iterations

    C. The time it takes to write user stories

    D. The time it takes to test code

    A. Since business partners are focused on their requirements and the value that is added to the business, they may overlook the time it takes to perform housekeeping on the code being written. This cleanup and simplification, called refactoring, is essential to having solid code that works now and is easy to maintain in the future.
    B is incorrect because team members getting sick or vacation days isn't a consideration in ideal days of agile projects. C is incorrect because writing user stories doesn't happen during the iteration. D is incorrect because testing code is part of the iteration timeline.

20. Your team leader uses several agile tools to uncover potential problems before they occur. Which of the following is one of those tools?

A. Affinity estimating

B. User story

C. Iteration planning

D. Daily standup meetings

D. Daily standup meetings are an important tool used to identify potential problems by answering the question if there are any roadblocks that need to be removed.

A is incorrect because affinity estimating is an approach to sizing stories, not addressing potential problems. B and C are incorrect because while user stories and iteration planning are valuable tools to use to identify issues, the best approach that's part of the agile framework is to utilize the daily standup meeting.

Leading Continuous Improvement

In this chapter, you will

- Define the six exam tasks of continuous improvement
- Lead continuous improvement as an agile process
- Complete systems thinking
- Participate in process analysis
- Facilitate project meetings for improvements
- Review the project feedback methods
- Complete team assessments

Continuous improvement aims for the organization, the project manager, the project team, and the processes of an agile project to improve. This exam domain has some lofty goals for the project manager and the organization as it focuses on continuous improvement. Continuous improvement is an agile process, not a tool or technique. Every project is different, so the approach you'll take to improve the product, processes, and people will vary by the project and by the presented scenario. The goal is always the same, however, and that's to increase value.

In this chapter we'll examine several new concepts for your PMI-ACP exam: systems thinking, participating in process analysis, and process mapping. By creating some value stream maps, we'll examine our processes and look for bottlenecks and threats to value. Our goal as project managers is to protect value, but also to increase the value of the project. By reducing errors and increasing productivity, the value of the deliverable increases because the cost of creating the deliverable decreases.

In this chapter we'll also discuss another opportunity for increasing value: hosting a project pre-mortem. Other agile ceremonies we'll cover include product review sessions, examining a product feedback loop, reviewing our feedback methods, understanding approved iterations, and leading a retrospective.

For a more detailed explanation, watch the *Continuous Improvement for Agile Projects* video now.

The continuous improvement exam domain is worth just 9 percent of your exam score, and that equates to about 11 questions. The essential task in this domain is to periodically review and tailor the processes for your environment, keeping in mind that each environment is different. The PMI-ACP exam is likely to present scenarios and questions that ask you to consider an organization's environment and the best practices of continuous improvement and then choose the best answer for that scenario.

In an agile project, you work with the product owner and key stakeholders to receive feedback in sprint reviews with demonstrations. The project team is also involved, so be sure to defer to the team to provide the demonstration of what they've created. You want the team to take the credit, good or bad, for what they've created in an iteration. The team leads the demonstration, not the project manager. This is part of your goal to create an environment for continued learning, both structured learning and creative or exploratory learning.

In this chapter we'll also discuss values analysis, influencing improvements to other groups in the organization, quality assurance, quality control, and how you first work to prevent defects and then you'll inspect the work for evidence of quality. That's an important exam topic. Let's keep moving forward; you're almost done, but there's just a bit more to knock out for your exam prep.

Introducing the Continuous Improvement Exam Domain

When you think about continuous improvement, it's natural to think about quality. Quality can be an esoteric concept: what's "good" to you may not be "good" to a stakeholder. Quality is a conformance to the product requirements, but it's also creating something that's fit for use. I'm sure you'll agree that a project team could create software that meets all the requirements but still isn't fit for use. Just imagine a team that creates software that hits all the user stories but is consistently buggy, has poor user interface design, or only works on a Linux box. That'd result in some disappointed customers.

What's really happening in that scenario, however, is that the requirements were probably too loose, too generic, and the team made decisions without consulting the product owner, the value management team, or the business analyst to really understand what the result of the project should be. While that's a wild example, it provides a fundamental point for all projects: projects fail at the beginning, not the end. Poor requirements will only contribute to poor deliverables. Quality begins first with a definition of what equates to quality, and that brings us back to the definition of done. Recall that the definition of done is all about understanding what constitutes acceptability by the product owner and key customers. We must first understand what the customer really wants for the project team to create it.

Next in this domain is to continuously improve our agile practices and our development of the product. We can have an excellent set of requirements, but if the team is sloppy, untrained, or not interested in the work, they'll likely have poor quality in their execution. Sloppy work increases the costs of the project and can have damaging effects on the organization and the customers of the product the team is creating. The project manager is responsible for continuous improvement of the project, for keeping the team on track, and for building some excitement about what the team is creating.

Reviewing the Six Tasks for Exam Domain VII

The overarching theme of the continuous improvement exam domain is to look for and act upon opportunities to improve the people, processes, and the product of the project. This exam domain is where you'll consider tailoring processes in your agile environment. This means you'll have to understand how your organization works, how the project team is performing, their depth of experience with agile, and how what's being tailored directly affects the value of the project.

This exam domain requires lots of communication from the project manager. You're expected to communicate with the project team, the product owner, and stakeholders; facilitate meetings to improve upon the project and the organization; and communicate across projects and organizational boundaries. You'll be leading product review sessions, hosting retrospectives, and completing team assessments. Communication is vital for this chapter—open, transparent communication, but also controlled communication and having some emotional intelligence with your team and customers. Emotional intelligence means that you're able to control your emotions, influence the emotions of others, and understand people's emotions and reactions to different situations.

Let's look at the six tasks for the continuous improvement exam domain:

Continuous Improvement Exam Domain Tasks

- Tailor and adapt the project process by periodically reviewing and integrating team practices, organizational culture, and delivery goals in order to ensure team effectiveness within established organizational guidelines and norms.

- Improve team processes by conducting frequent retrospectives and improvement experiments in order to continually enhance the effectiveness of the team, project, and organization.

- Seek feedback on the product by incremental delivery and frequent demonstrations in order to improve the value of the product.

- Create an environment of continued learning by providing opportunities for people to develop their skills in order to develop a more productive team of generalizing specialists.

- Challenge existing process elements by performing a value stream analysis and removing waste in order to increase individual efficiency and team effectiveness.

- Create systemic improvements by disseminating knowledge and practices across projects and organizational boundaries in order to avoid re-occurrence of identified problems and improve the effectiveness of the organization as a whole.

Leading Continuous Improvement as a Process

A *process* is a set of actions that we follow to reach a predefined result. For example, risk identification is a process. To identify risk in our project, we use tools and techniques to identify and document risk. Consider all the different processes in project management that bring about a predefined result. If we think about leading continuous improvement as a process, we're talking about improving our processes that we use in the project but also improving the processes of leading a project and how we get work done.

It's an ongoing effort to improve processes. We're looking at the effectiveness or the efficiency or both to meet objectives. We also examine our WIP and our velocity. Once the team's velocity has stabilized, we can tailor and tweak processes to improve velocity. When we tailor projects, we need to make certain that we have realistic goals. Your team will focus on regularly improving the quality of the product they deliver, the process they use to deliver that product, and their performance as a team.

Throughout the project we'll do lessons learned. Lessons learned or happened in each iteration. So, in our sprint review and to some extent in our retrospective, this allows us to learn from what's happened in the past and apply that knowledge to subsequent iterations of the project. A phrase that I like in this context is, "Lessons are repeated until they are learned." Lessons are repeated until they are learned. If your team is making the same mistakes over and over, they've not yet learned the lesson and you need to repeat it.

An approach that we can use with continuous improvement as a process is Kaizen. Kaizen is a Japanese word meaning "change for the better." The Kaizen approach is to do small incremental steps for improvement. The idea is that taking small steps for improvement makes it easier to absorb those steps and incorporate them into the way that we do our work, an opportunity that is lost when making one big sweeping change in the project.

At the heart of any work on continuous improvement is the PDCA (plan-do-check-act) cycle (see Figure 7-1), based on Japanese quality initiatives and popularized by Edward W. Deming. Deming later redefined this as the plan-do-study-act (PDSA) cycle. Your team first plans the delivery of their prioritized work and predicts the results of a cycle. Your team then works to complete the planned iteration. After that, with your support throughout the cycle, your team assesses the result of the work they've delivered, their processes, their relationship, and their overall team function. Based on their findings, the team will act: make corrections or move on in the project.

Figure 7-1 PDCA requires the actions of plan-do-check-act for continuous improvement.

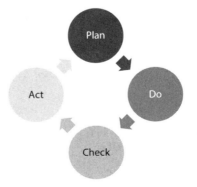

Tailoring Processes

To *tailor* a process means you make some adjustments and you change the depth of how detailed and how rigid you are in the process. There's always some risk, though, when you introduce tailoring, because the project may be a little wonky due to the tailored process. Things may not work exactly as hoped. When you start tailoring processes, you're moving away from what's been proven in the past, so you and the team will need to monitor the process change and how it affects velocity and the comfort level of the team, and then you'll adjust and adapt to continue to try and improve.

Risk is uncertain, you know, so when you tailor a proven process to an unknown process, you're introducing risk. I don't mean to imply that you should not tailor because of risk, but rather that you should tailor for reward. The tailoring of a process may save time and be more efficient. You want a balance of risk and reward when it comes to process tailoring.

The team should be mature and comfortable in implementing the standard principles of agile before considering changes. Some methodologies, like Scrum, tend to focus more on common practices and guidelines, where tailoring the process is not often recommended. A Scrum mentor is likely to suggest that your team not deviate from the typical execution of events and rules without suffering a loss in the benefits of an agile approach. With other philosophies, like Kanban, the approach expects customization to suit the needs of the team. If you and the team are new to agile project management, it's best to stick to proven agile processes before you consider changing or tailoring the processes.

It's possible that a hybrid model is appropriate for your environment or your team. So, you could use elements from different agile models, like XP, Scrum, Lean, and Kanban, and pick and choose what works best in your environment. There's no right or wrong hybrid model or right or wrong agile approach, as long as we get to value in the results. Your PMI-ACP exam, however, will expect you to know the rules of the common agile approaches and know that tailoring processes involves risk.

Completing Systems Thinking

Agile is rooted in the principle of adaptability, and an agile team embraces the concept of change to provide the highest level of value to the customer. Agile projects are complex systems with many different influences on the project, people, processes, and product. *Systems thinking* is a structured approach to doing the work and includes analysis of the system's processes to reach the defined result. The system, in this case, is the agile project management environment. This introduces the idea of *methodology success patterns*. There are four things you need to know when it comes to methodology success patterns:

- **Interactive face-to-face communication** It's the cheapest and the fastest channel for exchanging information.

- **Balance of methodology** The agile methodology shouldn't be too light or too heavy, but just right. If your methodology is bloated or too heavy and restrictive, then that's costly. Heavy agile methodologies rob efficiency and productivity. Methodology that is too light won't be effective and provide enough structure.

- **Team size affects structure**   Larger teams need a heavier methodology because larger teams require more structure. You simply cannot be as loose with a large team as you could with a team of eight to ten people.

- **Project criticality requires ceremony**   Projects that are of higher priority generally require greater ceremony. They require more framework, more governance, than a lower priority project.

The development team's goal is to make the most valuable product possible. Their knowledge work is complicated, and each software product is unique. Your agile team will adapt to any issue, the processes that the team follows, and the work they produce. The issues may be positive or negative, predicted or not. Regardless, while responding to the combined impact of all the moving parts, your team's primary focus remains on achieving maximum value for all stakeholders involved.

Ideally, your team works together toward a shared vision of providing the greatest value possible to the users of your software. The more players, processes, and work products involved, the more complicated your project becomes. When projects become more and more complex, there's an increased need for transparency, clear communications, and constant focus on the real purpose of the project.

 EXAM COACH   The Five Whys is a an exercise often used in retrospectives as a root cause analysis approach. The Five Whys asks why five times for each problem. It's tedious, but it can help prompt the team to dig into issues and find causal factors for effects you're trying to solve.

Participating in Process Analysis

Process analysis means studying the processes of how your project operates and how the project team gets work done. Process analysis takes the process flow, breaks it down, and identifies the things needed for a process to work properly. You consider the inputs, the actions needed to complete the process, and the tools and techniques. You also consider the outcome of the process. If you've looked through the *PMBOK Guide*, you've seen this already: inputs, tools and techniques, and outputs. This helps you better understand how a process works, and it allows you to identify opportunities for improvement, to be more efficient and effective.

A term that you need to know for the exam is *Failure Modes and Effects Analysis (FMEA)*. FMEA is one of the primary tools for process analysis because it allows you to address all failures, starting from the largest and working toward the smallest. With FMEA, you first identify all the steps in the process. You're likely going to map these out in a workflow. And then you look at failure mode. You identify everything that could go wrong at each point in this process. And then you identify the failure causes. You're aiming to identify what could cause the failure to happen. Once you've identified the failure points and possible causes, your next step is to identify the failure effects. Your goal is to identify the consequence of each failure should it happen.

Flowcharts are another thing that you want to understand for your PMI-ACP exam. Flowcharts allow you to see how a process operates. Sometimes this is called *process configuration mapping*. Mistake-proofing the process is a balance of being defect-free and efficient. While you could invest time, money, and energy to make a process totally defect-free, you would likely have to slow down the process so much that it wouldn't be cost effective to do so. You need a balance between perfection and good.

Techniques for Process Analysis

There are many ways to complete process analysis in an agile project. The *project premortem* is an event that happens before any delivery occurs on your project. It's the earliest opportunity for your team to consider improvements to their software process. This event produces a detailed look from your team of all potential causes of failure on the project ahead, ranked by priority.

The other regularly scheduled event that digs deeper into analyzing and improving processes is the *retrospective meeting*. This event is held at the end of each iteration and is a time for the team to assess their team improvement for the past iteration, including the processes the team used. The retrospective is the primary time that your team will spend digging into the results of your process analysis work. The team will be able to determine whether any process changes have increased process efficiency and the team can also look for additional solutions or tailoring.

The last event that can help your team to improve processes is the *introspective*. The term is not frequently used, but these ad hoc team meetings are focused on resolving a roadblock or other issue and frequently occur on agile teams. Depending on the nature of the discussion, your team may be focused on analyzing a process that needs improvement or on deciphering the root causes of a process failure. Introspectives are an opportunity to have a series of process analysis techniques ready and waiting for any time your team needs them.

Another method, derived from manufacturing, is called *control limits*, introduced in Chapter 6. A team calculates an upper and lower limit as acceptable variations in their process. When a team utilizes a Kanban board to limit the number of items in progress, they're applying control limits to their work. This analysis can be used to reveal bottlenecks in a process, which can often be attributed to the need for more team members to become generalized specialists or for their level of generalization to go further.

Value stream mapping is a great approach for an objective, quantitative look at how efficient your team's delivery process is. If you use this method a second time after your team has made a process adjustment, you'll be able to calculate the amount of efficiency your team's delivery process has gained or lost. Next, we'll dig further into the details of the creation of the technique used to create value stream maps.

Creating Value Stream Maps

It can be tough to help a group agree on what process they are following now as opposed to the process or tailored process they should be following. It can be even more difficult to encourage the group to take an objective look at the process and agree on ways to change it, especially when that process is a regular part of their work life. To help your team to step outside of their delivery processes and to look at them more objectively, consider using the value stream analysis technique to create a map of the processes in question and eliminate any steps that don't provide sufficient value. This technique works best for teams that know their current process well. It's not ideal to consider if your team is not relatively mature and well-versed in their delivery processes.

Value stream analysis is a Lean manufacturing technique that studies the current state of a process and then designs the future state for the process with a goal of efficiency and improvement. The first step is to identify the product or service to analyze. This step should be straightforward, as your team will focus on the product you're planning to deliver. The next step is to gather data across at least one iteration on what your process includes. It's best to gather information for each backlog item completed over the course of an iteration, as the times can vary widely and may be dependent on whether an item falls into a specialized area. Value stream analysis isn't something that's best done in a meeting in which you discuss the process, but more an exercise completed over the course of an iteration.

Before starting the exercise, make sure to teach your team two definitions that are critical to your analysis:

- **Value-added time**   This is the time that is spent actually working on the item, adding value to the process. This is the time your delivery team can successfully work on the assignment, which can include designing, developing, and testing the item. This will vary depending on your team's definition of done.

- **Non-value-added time**   This is all the other time spent on everything else but the work on the assignment. Any delays, wasted time, and roadblocks are included here.

For each item started within the iteration, put a sheet of paper on the wall of your information radiator with a timeline divided across the length of your iteration, as shown in Figure 7-2. When your team is adding value, draw the time above the timeline and label the type of work being done. For the time when your team is not adding value, draw the time below the timeline and label the type of waste. Repeat this process for all items started in your iteration. Average the amount of non-value-added time and provide this information to the team.

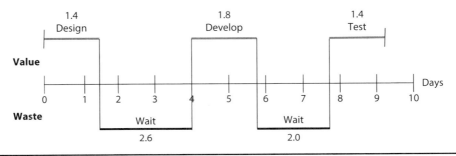

Figure 7-2   Value stream maps illustrate value-added and non-value-added activities.

There are two important metrics you'll want to calculate from this data. The first is total cycle time, which is simply all the value-added time and non-value-added time combined. In Figure 7-2, the total cycle time is 9.2 days. The second metric you'll calculate is process cycle efficiency. This is the amount of value-added time divided by the total cycle time. In Figure 7-2, the value-added time is 4.6 days, yielding a process cycle efficiency of 50 percent.

EXAM COACH   I don't expect you to encounter lots of questions on value stream maps, but I would be familiar with the formula for calculating process cycle efficiency. It's a simple formula that shows overall efficiency for your project.

Facilitating Project Meetings

What I dread the most in project management are meetings. Meetings, especially regularly held meetings, are usually a big waste of time. I do everything I can to prepare for meeting success—especially if I'm the one hosting the meeting. Far too often in my experience meetings are scheduled with a simple goal, but then fall short of reaching that goal due to poor preparations, lack of an agenda, or a sense of obligation to use the entire scheduled time. Meetings should be concise, to the point, and respectful of everyone's time in the room. Just think, ten people in an hour-long meeting is really ten hours of work.

I'm not saying that all meetings are a waste of time, as there are several agile meetings you'll hold with the purpose of continuous improvement. As the project manager, there are a few key concerns you'll want to keep in mind for your meetings. Remember that many people don't enjoy offering criticism, and especially dislike being critical in a public forum. It can be stressful and awkward for the team to be forced to discuss negative thoughts or to feel like they're under the microscope. It can be difficult at times to get your team to participate, but if you help make it happen, it can also yield amazing benefits.

First, meetings must be a place where the team feels safe and open to admit failure or to offer constructive criticism. The work on creating this space starts before the meeting begins. Encourage the team to share any mistakes or problems as early as they can from the start of the project. Second, make sure the team knows that fast failure is considered a good outcome and is part of the agile mindset. During the meetings, ensure that comments are focused on the team, not on placing blame or being critical of stakeholders. Meet any admissions of failure with encouragement and help the team focus on how to make it better.

EXAM COACH   As an agile project manager you're also a facilitator, so in meetings you'll facilitate the conversation. Aim for the team to be collaborative and seek input from the full team. It's important not to allow any one person to overtake the conversation, and to seek input from those people who like to hide in the background and never share their concerns. Get people involved and working toward the meeting goal.

Hosting a Project Pre-Mortem

Think of a project pre-mortem meeting as a post-mortem meeting in reverse. The benefit of a pre-mortem meeting is that it can make a difference on the current project, rather than only benefiting future projects. Ask your team to think through what might go wrong in the future and prepare their work in the current project accordingly. Rather than creating and then ignoring lessons-learned documentation, your team will be putting what they've learned into action immediately. The pre-mortem prompts the team to be realistic about problems and to vocalize solutions. Your team may feel liberated when they're asked to speak up about something they may not have felt comfortable addressing.

Set aside up to a couple of hours for the project pre-mortem. And at a minimum, invite your delivery team and product owner. If you feel that the team can speak freely with other stakeholders on the project present, you can invite others as well to get their buy-in on solutions. You don't want to invite too many people outside of the team though, as project team members may feel awkward sharing what can be perceived as failures or may fear looking foolish in front of stakeholders.

To make this meeting effective, you have a bit of prep work as project manager. Before you bring the team together in the same room, make sure everyone knows the basics of what the project is about and have each team member think through risks they've identified. To generate a comprehensive list, you might offer questions for the project. Consider:

- What concerns do you have about this project?
- What could slow us down from achieving a viable product in the shortest time possible?
- What could cause this project to cost more than it should?
- What might cause the project to be cancelled?
- What concerns were ignored on past projects?

Once it's time to facilitate the meeting, have each person gather in a room, face to face if possible. To use the round-robin style of presenting risks, participants have prepared responses to the preceding list of questions, ask each person in turn to offer one item from their list of concerns about the project, and continue rounds until all the items have been mentioned. Then ask each person in turn what could slow down the team from achieving a viable product in the shortest time possible, again going around as many times as necessary to exhaust everyone's list. Follow this pattern for each question. During this round-robin, the team only listens to the concerns and doesn't try to solve problems. You'll create a list of the items on a whiteboard as each person offers a risk.

Next, the team votes on which concerns are most important. Ask the team to determine how many votes per person to dole out. Then, each person adds dots or checkmarks to their biggest concerns on the list. They can choose to spend all their votes on one item or spread them out to several different items. After your team has completed their voting process, take the items with the greatest number of dots or checkmarks and write a new prioritized list of potential failures for the items with votes. There are likely to be some issues that have no votes, which can be set aside for now.

With your prioritized list for all to see, lead your team to think through how to avoid each of the problems entirely. Listen and document potential plans for those risks. Guide your team to set rules as needed to eliminate or mitigate the risks. If the team feels that any top issue can't be avoided, discuss their ideas on how to reduce the negative impact and document these ideas. For the rest of the items that didn't make the top priority list, you can choose to address some or all of them if you have extra time or address them in another meeting.

Don't treat this meeting as a one-time event. Every few iterations, work with your team to review what's on the list and reconsider potential failures. It may be that some of the risks have increased in likelihood or already happened. The reminder of your risk avoidance and mitigation plans can help your team better prepare for the issues or actively handle risks should they be realized.

Leading Product Review Sessions

After your team completes the first iteration, you and the product owner jointly facilitate a review to get the product in front of stakeholders. This demonstrates whether the value your team is providing is in sync with the vision for the product. Keep in mind that review sessions are typically held after each iteration of a product, but this is not the only type of review. You can consider any product feedback or retrospective as a type of product review session as well.

First, make sure that these sessions are highly informal. There should be minimal time involved in the team preparing for the session outside of their daily work, usually under two hours. There's no prepared presentation, as you want to keep this meeting light, quick, and to the point: show the value of what's been done by the project team. The review meeting is less focused on demonstration of functionality than it is on ensuring that stakeholders are regularly participating by inspecting the product. The session itself should not be long either—for example, a maximum of four hours if sprints are a month long.

Next, you'll guide the delivery team to discuss what went well during the iteration. The team will discuss any issues or roadblocks they encountered and how they resolved those problems. Next, the team, not the project manager, will demonstrate each of the items that were done, which should be identical to the features selected for completion in the iteration. As the project team demonstrates the new features of the product, they'll answer stakeholder questions about the product.

The full team then works together to decide on the focus for the upcoming iteration. Does the team like what was built or is it not what was in mind? Is what the product owner and stakeholders asked for what they still want? Did the delivery team do a good job of providing the value? The full group will collectively provide the input needed for the upcoming planning session in which the team discusses the vision for the next iteration.

Finally, the product owner should lead a discussion on any changes in the product roadmap, including changes in the competitive environment or the use of the product. The project manager or the product owner can wrap up the conversation with a quick review of the release timeline, project costs, and upcoming functionality. The final deliverable from this session is an updated product backlog with candidate items for the upcoming iteration.

Reviewing the Feedback Methods

In communications, feedback is when the sender of a message receives a message in response to what they've said. It's not so different in agile projects. You, the project manager, and the project team want feedback from stakeholders and one another in the project. Along with iteration review sessions, there are several methods for gathering feedback. The idea of frequently collecting product feedback is a key part of the agile mindset.

You want to receive feedback from stakeholders quickly, as the longer you wait to receive feedback, the riskier the lack of feedback is to the project. If you learn late that there was a disconnect between what the customer wants now and what your team has produced, it can be a painful, costly, and lengthy process to get back on track.

To gather feedback as early as possible, it's important to provide visual messaging to the customer. Product review sessions are your primary avenue for providing this information, but there are a couple of other methods to consider. A *product prototype* is a model used to test out a product idea and learn what customers think before the team invests hours implementing the concept into the product. Prototypes are a great method for gathering feedback from stakeholders that can't envision how something might work in the product, and a quicker method for the team than creating full functionality. Another method of feedback is the creation of a *simulation*, which is also a type of model that re-creates a specific scenario and mimics some of the functionality that could be placed into your product.

Examining a Product Feedback Loop

The more tools and techniques you and the project team use to gather feedback from the customer, the greater the likelihood of producing a quality product that fulfills the project goal. The timing of when feedback occurs is the primary driver of the value of the feedback loop. The end goal of any of the loops is expressed well by Deming's PDCA cycle introduced earlier and shown in Figure 7-1. Feedback loops incorporate the check and act stages of the cycle.

Consider the product feedback loop created when your team uses the pair programming approach. One developer creates software and another developer provides feedback very quickly about errors, alternatives, and quality. This feedback is quicker and cheaper than to collect bugs found in unit testing. That's even quicker feedback than what another person provides during acceptance testing of the work, in which the tester provides feedback about anything that is not functioning as desired. And that method of gathering information is far cheaper than what a customer might find when software delivered to the end user is not working as intended. Those problems could be of an emergency nature and corrections are far more costly than others, not to mention the damage those issues can do to the reputation of a product and company.

Considering Reviews and Retrospectives

Reviews and retrospectives are the capstone events of each iteration, typically held on the last day of the cycle. While the review meeting focuses on what was done by the team, the retrospective focuses on how it was done. The product review helps minimize problems with the gulf of evaluation, which causes a disconnect between the stakeholders' vision and your delivery team's vision of the product. Retrospectives don't involve the stakeholders and are the regularly scheduled time for the team to devote to themselves. As you offer insight into agile standards, the team focuses on their own performance and what they can do to improve their project performance.

The bulk of your team coaching activities will be on the borderline of each iteration, when product reviews and retrospectives are held. This is the primary time for you to shepherd your team away from practices that are straying from the agile mindset and to provide support for any new continuous improvement solutions they'd like to try. At the end of both of these events, you can expect the team to have a renewed focus on increasing the efficiency of the team, spreading specialized knowledge throughout the group, improving delivery quality, and the ability to take on more work due to increasing efficiencies.

If you think with your delivery team in mind, you can imagine that demonstrating something built recently can be a nerve-wracking experience. When you consider the product owner inviting additional stakeholders to the product reviews, it can be an even more stressful experience for your team to demonstrate their work. This is one of the occasions in which your effort to create a safe and open environment is critical to holding an effective meeting. Stakeholders should know beforehand that any criticism they provide should be offered in a constructive way. Your team should know that stakeholder input is as valuable as the input of others in the review. You must ensure that respect is practiced consistently throughout the project.

One of the other key pieces of the agile mindset that is critical to successful reviews and retrospectives is your team's attentiveness to refactoring. Encourage your team to regularly inspect and adapt their work to maintain an organized, streamlined, and standardized product as a good foundation for the next cycle. Refactoring should be built into agile estimates. As new approaches and standards are discovered, the delivery team should take the time to bring past efforts in line with their new, more efficient work. Remember the relevant guiding principles in the Agile Manifesto: your "agile processes promote sustainable development" and your team's "continuous attention to technical excellence and good design enhances agility."

To help your overall organization become more agile, it's also a great idea to guide your team to share their successes with other product teams. If properly shared, good design on your project can enhance the agility of your entire company. In addition to sharing successes, it's also a benefit to share failures across your organization. If your team was able to nimbly fail fast, you may save another team from attempting that approach at all.

Leading a Retrospective

Think back to your last lessons-learned meeting. Was it helpful? Did most of the team speak up openly and honestly about their true feelings? If the meeting was like many I've attended, it either didn't happen at all or the team didn't openly discuss any significant issues. Why? Because they weren't compelled to talk, or they didn't feel safe enough to speak freely. Admittedly, it can be awkward to be open and honest in a reflection on your own team. Facilitating this session can be a tough job for agile leaders, and the meeting, like many meetings, can turn into a waste of time.

The retrospective is an opportunity for the team to complete self-inspection and to adapt accordingly for areas needing improvement prior to the next iteration. This meeting is hosted prior to the planning session for the next iteration and maxes out at three hours for projects with four-week-long iterations. Your role in the meeting is to ensure the team feels safe and speaks constructively and honestly about what they can do better.

The scope of the questions asked includes the people, relationships, processes, and tools used for the last cycle. The team takes an approach similar to your daily standups and they self-organize to answer:

- What did we do well?
- What areas can we improve?
- What should we do differently?

The role of the project manager in this session is as a peer who watches over the agile process, product, and company standards as the team self-evaluates. It's important to encourage each member of the delivery team to provide their own feedback, just as everyone does in daily meetings. The team should collaboratively come up with ideas for the next cycle without any member of the team dominating the conversation or insisting on a solution.

The result of this session is a list of planned improvements for the next iteration. Examples of typical improvements may be a change to a process or a change in the team's definition of done. Your role, relevant to these improvements, is to enable and guide the team to implement the plan. Your help can be especially important for the improvement of relationships or people-focused areas like skill improvement.

Understanding Approved Iterations

An iteration (or sprint) is the two to four weeks of work where the team creates a product increment that will eventually become part of the released product. During the review at the end of each iteration, your team will show what they've done. It's an opportunity for stakeholders and the product owner to give feedback and approve of the work. Stakeholders will look at the demonstration of the product increment and they'll expect that what your team created is in alignment with the selected features from the product backlog.

Each increment reduces risk to the project as the product value increases. The closer the project is to completion, the lower the risk of project failure. When the project team demonstrates each increment, this also allows the stakeholders to ensure that what they asked for is still what they want. Stakeholders will confirm that what your team produced agrees with what they requested. Your team will continue to provide additional increments that lead up to the next, and ultimately, the final release. Recall that releases are defined in the product roadmap, so a series of increments may contribute to just one release.

If the demo uncovers bugs or crashes and burns, it should be no surprise that the product owner isn't going to approve the increment. If the product has defects, those issues are added to the product backlog. Once those are combined and prioritized with the rest of the backlog, your team is ready to plan the next iteration. Regardless of defects, if the product owner finds the team has provided sufficient value during the cycle, the product owner will approve the iteration. Once you've received approval that you've completed your committed items, the next iteration can begin. The addition of defects and the reprioritization of the backlog is another example of the concept of adaptive planning I discussed in Chapter 5.

For internal teams, this notion of approval may not hold significant value. If the project is not approved, the team will likely continue to the next iteration, perhaps with different items in the iteration due to the priority of the product owner shifting to the unapproved work. However, if you're part of a vendor team, if the product owner disapproves the iteration, you may not receive full payment for your services. Depending on your contract, your team may need to produce a quality demonstration of the increment to get paid.

Completing Team Assessments

One of the more onerous responsibilities of a project manager in traditional project management is to write reviews of project team members. The good news is that as an agile project manager, you don't have that responsibility. You'll need to regularly observe and mentor your team toward continuous improvement, but the agile focus on improving delivery performance is the job of the team. In agile, it's important that you reinforce a continuous culture of safety in which your team feels comfortable to evaluate their performance as a collective group. The focus is never on blaming or singling out individuals, but rather assessing benefits for the whole team and, as a result, benefits for the project.

Aside from simply discussing improvements, there are also formal scoring models that can assist with team self-assessment, including models from both Shore and Tabaka. In Shore's version, the team plots scores across the areas of planning, developing, thinking, collaborating, and releasing along a radar diagram, as shown in Figure 7-3. In Tabaka's model, teams score themselves on questions in several areas, including self-organization, empowerment, and participatory decision making. With data in hand, teams can then focus on the areas with the lowest scores for improvement.

Improving Team Performance

Once the team agrees on focus areas for improvement, it's time for the team to come up with solutions on how to make it happen. Performance improvements tend toward two different paths. On one path, the team is focused on increasing knowledge to increase the

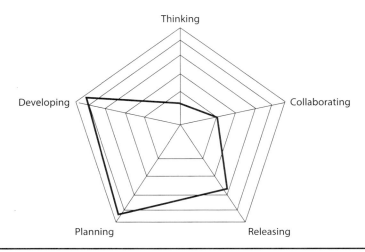

Figure 7-3 Radar diagrams allow teams to complete a self-assessment of several performance factors.

skillset of some or all the team members. On the other path, the team focuses on problem resolution beyond skillsets. Through the resolution of specific issues, the team can then improve overall performance by removing the roadblock.

At some point, your team will encounter a need to increase their overall team knowledge of a skill. Individuals on the team may be skilled in an area, but if that ability is not spread adequately throughout the team, queues will be created while the team waits for the person with the needed skillset to complete their work. If the team notices roadblocks when it comes to a certain method of delivery or a certain function, then knowledge of that area should be shared throughout the team. You'll want to encourage your team members to set aside time for training in those areas and enable them to spend adequate time learning. As the coach of your team, if you've delegated training and learning activities to be something that happens only during off-hours, then you're not effectively serving your agile project. Generalizing team knowledge throughout the project is a key area of focus in developing your people and serving your project.

As you notice the growth of abilities across your team, make sure to allow team members to fulfill leadership opportunities when they are well-suited to their skills. Agile teams encourage leaders to emerge by allowing them the opportunity to showcase strengths and teach other team members. In my experience, project team members are happy to share what they know with others. By allowing emerging leaders to share what they know, demand for a resource can be reduced and the project can operate more efficiently. Granted, for complex skills, it'll take time for a team member to become as efficient as the teacher.

During the team's self-evaluation of potential areas for improvement, they may notice deficiencies in the project. Retrospectives are a primary supply for the types of ideas your team may implement to correct their course. Once a potential solution is identified, it's your job to assist the team in enacting the solution, especially if it involves others outside of the project team. Keep in mind that some of the more complicated problems may require a workshop in which a bigger problem is resolved through team collaboration.

Your project team's ability to consistently reach a high level of performance is a byproduct of the agile mindset. Empower your team to direct their work and organize. Encourage your team to grow their leadership skills through experience and modeling your approach to servant leadership. Ensure that the space in which your team performs is an emotionally safe place to be. Your team should be encouraged to experiment and to speak appropriately in an honest and transparent way. Finally, your team should know how to engage in constructive conflict regarding problems and solutions. Self-reflection and continuous improvement are hard work.

Sharing Knowledge Among the Project Team

There are several key areas of knowledge that the project team should regularly share to reach top levels of performance. Team members should share information on general practices and procedures, relevant to the company and to the project team. As anyone on the team learns about a new process, they should share the information and spend as little time on documenting the change as the situation requires. Remember, documentation should be sufficient and not overbearing.

Whenever a team faces problems, it's important to share knowledge about the problem and its solution to limit the likelihood that a given issue will reoccur. One of the easiest ways to do this is through team collocation, which stimulates knowledge sharing through osmotic knowledge. Team members learn of a problem impacting the group by listening within their space. It spreads quickly, with little time required to type up e-mails or hold meetings. If the information may affect other project teams, it's also important to pass that information along outside of the project.

Although sharing knowledge through colocation is ideal, most organizations don't keep their agile teams in the same physical space. Most project managers don't have the luxury of a full team onsite, which makes the ability to disseminate knowledge and regularly monitor team improvement much more complicated. For virtual teams, you'll have to get creative with collaboration tools for information sharing and work to ensure your team is able to adequately self-assess without the benefit of frequent face-to-face communication. You can expect that any team members who live in other countries will have behaviors or cultural norms that are different that your culture and behaviors. This isn't to say one is better or worse, but only different. As the project manager, you need to expect this difference and continue to treat others with respect.

Chapter Summary

Continuous improvement is an exam domain that spans all parts of a project. Your overarching goal, as a project manager, is to work with the product owner, the project team, and stakeholders to continuously improve the people, product, and processes of agile project management and your organization. I know, I know, that's a lofty goal! The improvement of people, product, and processes, however, supports an increase in value for the organization, so it makes sense that continuous process improvement is key in agile project management. This exam domain represents just 9 percent of the PMI-ACP exam, so just 11 exam questions, but you shouldn't skimp on the time you spend getting to know the concepts and terms from this chapter.

One of the first topics we tackled in this chapter was tailoring processes. As a general rule, we don't start tailoring processes until we first fully understand the processes and have a good sense of how the processes should work. If you're working with a new agile team, it's best to stick to a proven framework for awhile in the project before you start tailoring processes or dropping the formality of agile project management. It's always better to understand the rules and why they exist before you start changing rules.

In this chapter we also discussed creating value stream mapping and value stream analysis. Recall that this technique examines the value-added time and the non-value-added time in each iteration. Based on the total cycle time and the value-added time, you can find your process cycle efficiency. Basically, the less non-value-added time you have in your iteration, the higher your process cycle efficiency. When you have a low process cycle efficiency, there are bottlenecks or roadblocks you need to address to improve your overall cycle time and value for the project.

We also talked about my least favorite project component: meetings. Meetings need to be facilitated, have an agenda, and be timeboxed so that they don't waste anyone's time. One beneficial meeting that you can conduct early in the project (before any delivery) is the project pre-mortem, the goal of which is to identify opportunities to improve the current project, rather than waiting until the end of the project to do a lessons-learned meeting (and then ignore the lessons-learned document for all future projects). A pre-mortem allows the team to implement improvements in the current project. We also discussed the review meetings and retrospectives—something you've seen plenty of in this book. Recall that the review is for demonstrations and the retrospective is for improving the team cohesion, performance, and processes for the next iteration.

Once again, great job on completing the final chapter in your quest to earn the PMI-ACP certification. You can do this! Continue studying, know your key terms, and get this done. You can do it!

Key Terms

Continuous improvement   Continuous improvement is a process in which actions are taken to identify deficiencies in performance, goals are set for improvement, and continued actions are undertaken to meet those goals. Continuous improvement aims for the organization, the project manager, the project team, and the processes of an agile project to improve.

Failure Modes and Effects Analysis (FMEA)   FMEA is one of the primary tools for process analysis and begins with the largest failures and works toward the smallest. FMEA requires identification of all steps in a process and then examines everything that could go wrong at each point in the process. Next, FMEA identifies the failure causes and effects.

Feedback loops   Feedback loops describe the phenomenon of an entity, system, or person that gives an output which will cause an input to the same entity. For example, the project team gives an update to the product owner, which causes the product owner to speak to the project manager, which causes the project manager to coach the project team on their next iteration of work.

Introspectives Introspectives are ad hoc team meetings focused on resolving a road-block or other issue. Introspectives are an opportunity to have a series of process analysis techniques ready and waiting for any time your team needs them.

Kaizen Kaizen (a Japanese word meaning "change for the better") is a continuous improvement approach that requires small, incremental steps that accumulate to broad changes over time.

PDCA (plan-do-check-act) cycle The PDCA (plan-do-check-act) cycle based on Japanese quality initiatives is also known as the Deming cycle. It's widely associated with quality assurance and quality control. PDCA prompts the project manager and the team to complete the actions of plan, do, check, and act to improve and control quality within the work.

Process A process is a set of actions that we follow to reach a predefined result.

Process analysis Process analysis involves studying the processes of your project and how the project team gets work done. Process analysis takes the process flow, breaks it down, and identifies what items are needed for a process to work properly.

Process cycle efficiency Process cycle efficiency is a metric in value stream analysis that is calculated by dividing the amount of value-added time by the total cycle time. The higher the process cycle efficiency value, the more successful the project is. Lower values indicate a high amount of non-value-added activity and waste in the project.

Project pre-mortem The project pre-mortem is an event that happens before any delivery occurs on your project. It's the earliest opportunity for your team to consider improvements to their software process. This event produces a detailed look from your team at all potential causes of failure on the project ahead, ranked by priority.

Shore's Self-Assessment Chart Shore's Self-Assessment Chart calls for the team to plot scores across the areas of planning, developing, thinking, collaborating, and releasing along a radar diagram.

Systems thinking Systems thinking is a structured approach to do the work and includes analysis of the system's processes to reach the defined result.

Tabaka's Assessment Model Tabaka's Assessment Model allows teams to score themselves on questions on self-organization, empowerment, and participatory decision making. With data in hand, teams can then focus on the areas with the lowest scores for improvement.

Value stream analysis Value stream analysis is a Lean manufacturing technique that begins with identifying the product or service to analyze. Value stream analysis studies the current state of a process and then designs the future state for the process with a goal of efficiency and improvement. Value stream analysis gathers data across at least one iteration on what your process includes and determines overall efficiency for each iteration.

Questions

1. Your team leader has created a high-level outline for the first few iterations. You are new to agile project management and asked why lessons learned are in each iteration rather than at the end of the project. Your team leader gave which of the following explanations?

   A. To add time to the iteration in case any roadblocks are encountered

   B. To enable the team to apply the benefits of lessons learned to the next iteration, and so on

   C. To show the business partners that we are sharing information

   D. To show the business partners that we understand the project goals

2. You are on a new agile team and the stakeholders are using the agile methodology without trying to tailor the processes at all. Why is this a good idea?

   A. With any change, the team is at risk of losing the benefit for which the methodology was designed

   B. To make the project move faster

   C. So a project manager or team lead can be eliminated

   D. So all the predesigned organizational templates can be used

3. Your agile team leader is discussing whether to tailor the agile methodologies because of what he refers to as systems thinking. Which of the following best describes systems thinking?

   A. When the software is being analyzed for defects

   B. Analyzing a project that is far off course

   C. Classifying projects in terms of their complexity

   D. When the stakeholders cannot agree on requirements

4. Your agile project manager has asked for a proof of understanding from the team describing the customer's requirements. What would you deliver?

   A. A written document describing, in the team's terms, the customer's requirements

   B. A high-level prototype of the requirements

   C. A project plan listing requirements and sequence of events

   D. A feedback meeting where the team describes their understanding to the business partners

5. While your agile team is going through a value stream mapping exercise, you have been asked for total cycle time. What two factors should be considered when calculating total cycle time?

    A. Value-added time and non-value added time

    B. Systems thinking and process analysis

    C. Building and testing

    D. Testing and documenting

6. Your agile team leader recognizes that the team is disagreeing and seems to be overthinking a requirement. The team feels that a value stream mapping session would help identify the discrepancy. Once the scenario is defined, what is the next step?

    A. Define the starting point and ending point

    B. Review the requirements

    C. Write user stories

    D. Write test scripts

7. As you look at your agile team's high-level project plan, you notice there are three pre-mortems scheduled. You ask your leader to define a pre-mortem. Which of the following is the explanation given?

    A. It is a session that identifies the business requirements.

    B. It is a session that identifies why the project will be a huge success.

    C. It is a session that envisions failures and how to mitigate them.

    D. It is a session that identifies which team members need to be added to the team.

8. The agile method of developing in small increments, delivering a product, and receiving stakeholders' feedback lends itself to which of the following?

    A. Value stream mapping

    B. Systems thinking

    C. Process analysis

    D. Continuous improvement

9. Methods used in agile projects to elicit feedback include prototypes, simulations, and demonstrations. Why is it essential to deliver one of these methods to users of the product for feedback, sooner rather than later?

    A. It allows users to begin training on the new functionality.

    B. To learn if there are differences between requirements and what is wanted.

    C. It allows users to create new forms that will be required for the new system.

    D. It allows users to eliminate certain roles in their group.

10. Your agile team leader has scheduled retrospectives for the team after each iteration. The purpose of this meeting is best described by which of the following?

   A. It's an opportunity for the team to inspect and improve their methods and teamwork.

   B. It allows the team to voice their grievances.

   C. It allows the team to prioritize new requirements.

   D. It allows team members to switch roles.

11. Your agile team leader feels strongly about the benefits of retrospectives being held after each iteration. Why do you think it is so important to her?

   A. Non-productive team members can be eliminated.

   B. It proves to the stakeholders that the team leader is taking charge of the project.

   C. It allows the team leader to know all the details of each iteration.

   D. The results of a retrospective can offer immediate improvements.

12. In an agile environment, the steps set the stage, gather data, generate insights, decide what to do, and close represent which process?

   A. Value stream mapping

   B. Feedback

   C. Pre-mortems

   D. Retrospectives

13. During a retrospective, your team leader may single out an issue that was faced during an iteration and ask the team to go through the exercise of the five whys. What is this meant to accomplish?

   A. It typically gets to the root of the cause.

   B. It prevents the team from shifting blame.

   C. It gathers five reasons for the issue.

   D. It allows five team members to offer their opinion.

14. Your agile leader occasionally asks the team to do a self-assessment, meaning a team self-assessment, not an individual self-assessment. The questions that the team addresses for this assessment revolve around which of the following?

   A. How the team gets along

   B. How the team performs and delivers together

   C. How the team reacts to business partners

   D. How the team makes decisions

15. When your agile team is going through a pre-mortem, each member is asked to write down possible reasons they think some task or action might fail. The best method to reveal everyone's list and consolidate it is to go around the room round-robin. What is the top benefit of this approach?

    A. No one is reading an entire list of problems.

    B. When common issues are identified, other team members can cross it off their list.

    C. Each issue can be discussed when presented.

    D. It forces everyone to attend and stay for the entire meeting.

16. After conducting a retrospective for your last iteration, what type of improvement could you expect to see on your agile team?

    A. Productivity

    B. Attendance

    C. Remote access

    D. Fewer meetings

17. When the result of a retrospective has identified issues and root causes, the next step is to decide how to avoid the same types of issues going forward. What is one agile method to accomplish this process?

    A. Fishbone analysis

    B. Prioritize with dots

    C. Triple nickels

    D. SMART goals

18. When starting a new agile project, you are told you will be using a hybrid model. What does this mean?

    A. The first half of the project will be done in a traditional project method.

    B. The team member selection will be done traditionally.

    C. An agile model is used in combination with a traditional method.

    D. There will be no user acceptance until the end of the project.

19. Setting the stage for a retrospective includes which of the following?

    A. Inviting all stakeholders

    B. Distributing a clear and concise agenda

    C. Asking for anonymous input

    D. Defining a specific start and stop time

20. Which of the following is a method utilized to close a retrospective and reinforce its value?

A. Have a stakeholder dinner

B. Have the team hold a separate meeting to discuss wins

C. Give out awards to the best performer

D. Go through a plus/delta exercise

Questions and Answers

1. Your team leader has created a high-level outline for the first few iterations. You are new to agile project management and asked why lessons learned are in each iteration rather than at the end of the project. Your team leader gave which of the following explanations?

A. To add time to the iteration in case any roadblocks are encountered

B. To enable the team to apply the benefits of lessons learned to the next iteration, and so on

C. To show the business partners that we are sharing information

D. To show the business partners that we understand the project goals

B. Taking immediate action from lessons learned is critical for agile projects where the environment changes quickly or a high degree of risk exists, because not making any adjustments in the projects trajectory could result in project failure.

A is incorrect because adding lessons learned to each iteration may add time to the process but it is not intended to be used as a buffer. C is incorrect because the value of lessons learned is not to show business partners that you're sharing information. D is incorrect because lessons learned are opportunities for improvement, not to show the understanding of project goals.

2. You are on a new agile team and the stakeholders are using the agile methodology without trying to tailor the processes at all. Why is this a good idea?

A. With any change, the team is at risk of losing the benefit for which the methodology was designed

B. To make the project move faster

C. So a project manager or team lead can be eliminated

D. So all the predesigned organizational templates can be used

A. Making changes to the agile methodology prior to learning the benefits can be risky. Agile methods have been developed and refined based on many projects and by experienced team leaders and members. Most agile tasks are related and dependent on other tasks, so dropping or adding tasks may throw the agile project out of balance.

B is incorrect because tailoring can, once the approach of agile project management is mastered, make the project move faster. C is incorrect because tailoring doesn't remove the project manager or team lead. D is incorrect because the goal of tailoring is to customize the approach for a specific environment and to add value to the project, not to fit the project to organizational templates.

3. Your agile team leader is discussing whether to tailor the agile methodologies because of what he refers to as systems thinking. Which of the following best describes systems thinking?

   A. When the software is being analyzed for defects

   B. Analyzing a project that is far off course

   C. Classifying projects in terms of their complexity

   D. When the stakeholders cannot agree on requirements

   C. One part of systems thinking includes classifying projects in term of their complexity in two areas: project requirements and the technological approach. Complex projects have some uncertainty with requirements and technology, so they are well suited for the out-of-the-box agile methodology. Projects that have a low or simple complexity can tailor some of the agile methods to suit the project.
   A is incorrect because looking for defects in the software is part of software testing. B is incorrect because systems thinking doesn't address projects that are performing poorly. D is incorrect because systems thinking is not part of conflict resolution for project requirements.

4. Your agile project manager has asked for a proof of understanding from the team describing the customer's requirements. What would you deliver?

   A. A written document describing, in the team's terms, the customer's requirements

   B. A high-level prototype of the requirements

   C. A project plan listing requirements and sequence of events

   D. A feedback meeting where the team describes their understanding to the business partners

   B. Building a prototype that describes the team's understanding of requirements is the most efficient way to show proof of understanding. This prototype can be used going forward as part of the building of the product.
   A is incorrect because writing a document that could be set aside could be a waste of time and is not considered of value in agile. C is incorrect because building a project plan is not an agile project management approach. D is incorrect because there's not a specific feedback meeting or ceremony for giving evidence of a team's understanding on the business requirements.

5. While your agile team is going through a value stream mapping exercise, you have been asked for total cycle time. What two factors should be considered when calculating total cycle time?

   A. Value-added time and non-value added time

   B. Systems thinking and process analysis

   C. Building and testing

   D. Testing and documenting

   > A. When going through a value stream mapping exercise, both value-added and non-value-added time must be accounted for to get an accurate total cycle time metric. Throughout the process, the non-value-added time should be closely evaluated to identify delays and roadblocks that should be removed. There is more time that needs to be calculated into building, testing, and documenting than what those tactical tasks entail, which is the non-value-added time.
   > B, C, and D are incorrect because value stream mapping does not consider systems thinking, process analysis, building, testing, or documenting as part of the total cycle to the same depth as identification of value- and non-value-added activities.

6. Your agile team leader recognizes that the team is disagreeing and seems to be overthinking a requirement. The team feels that a value stream mapping session would help identify the discrepancy. Once the scenario is defined, what is the next step?

   A. Define the starting point and ending point

   B. Review the requirements

   C. Write user stories

   D. Write test scripts

   > A. Begin mapping the value stream by identifying the starting point and ending point. Next, identify the steps in the process, any supporting groups, and alternative flows. Once all time estimates are calculated, examine the value-added and non-value-added times to determine what can be eliminated.
   > B is incorrect because reviewing the requirements is not as robust as identifying both the starting point, which could include the requirements, and the ending point of the project. C and D are incorrect because neither writing user stories nor writing test scripts is best next step as part of the value stream mapping activity.

7. As you look at your agile team's high-level project plan, you notice there are three pre-mortems scheduled. You ask your leader to define a pre-mortem. Which of the following is the explanation given?

   A. It is a session that identifies the business requirements.

   B. It is a session that identifies why the project will be a huge success.

   C. It is a session that envisions failures and how to mitigate them.

   D. It is a session that identifies which team members need to be added to the team.

C. A pre-mortem is a session where all stakeholders will meet to generate a list of potential failure points and determine how to mitigate the possibility of the failure. The business owner's participation is required since the team will offer resolutions to avoid a failure that the business owner will need to agree with. A is incorrect because business requirements are identified prior to a pre-mortem, since they are the source for the discussion. B is incorrect because at the point of conducting a pre-mortem, it would be improbable that the team envisions everything working as planned. D is incorrect because All team members are identified by the time of a pre-mortem.

8. The agile method of developing in small increments, delivering a product, and receiving stakeholders' feedback lends itself to which of the following?

   A. Value stream mapping

   B. Systems thinking

   C. Process analysis

   D. Continuous improvement

   D. The agile method of developing in small increments, delivering a product to stakeholders at each iteration, and receiving feedback often lends itself to continuous improvement. This method may uncover the true business requirements by making improvements and enhancements, which results in an improvement to the requirements. Each iteration may add another layer of improvement as the project moves closer to the final business purpose solution. A, B, and C are incorrect because value stream mapping, systems thinking, and process analysis are all methods used to achieve continuous improvement.

9. Methods used in agile projects to elicit feedback include prototypes, simulations, and demonstrations. Why is it essential to deliver one of these methods to users of the product for feedback, sooner rather than later?

   A. It allows users to begin training on the new functionality.

   B. To learn if there are differences between requirements and what is wanted.

   C. It allows users to create new forms that will be required for the new system.

   D. It allows users to eliminate certain roles in their group.

   B. Delivering this type of feedback is used to learn if there are any differences between what the requirements indicate compare to what the users find valuable. There may have been fields or even complete functions that were overlooked and can be uncovered prior to the development getting too far down the road. The user groups should take no action other than providing feedback when offered one of these methods.

A is incorrect because these are feedback elicitation techniques, not truly opportunities for providing functionality for the customers. C is incorrect because the goal isn't to introduce new forms, but to ensure requirements. D is incorrect because these approaches do not eliminate roles, but help to confirm requirements.

10. Your agile team leader has scheduled retrospectives for the team after each iteration. The purpose of this meeting is best described by which of the following?

   A. It's an opportunity for the team to inspect and improve their methods and teamwork.

   B. It allows the team to voice their grievances.

   C. It allows the team to prioritize new requirements.

   D. It allows team members to switch roles.

   A. Retrospectives are meant to allow a team to inspect and improve their methods and teamwork. During a retrospective, three questions should be addressed: What is going well? What areas could use improvement? What could we be doing differently? When solutions are identified, they are validated. If they work well, they can be adopted as part of the ongoing process. If they fail, the team can consider trying something else or going back to the earlier process. B is incorrect because the point of a retrospective is not to air grievances, but to improve upon the approach. C is incorrect because the product owner will prioritize the product backlog before each iteration begins, not in the retrospective. D is incorrect because the team doesn't switch roles in the retrospective.

11. Your agile team leader feels strongly about the benefits of retrospectives being held after each iteration. Why do you think it is so important to her?

   A. Non-productive team members can be eliminated.

   B. It proves to the stakeholders that the team leader is taking charge of the project.

   C. It allows the team leader to know all the details of each iteration.

   D. The results of a retrospective can offer immediate improvements.

   D. In a traditional project, retrospectives, or lessons learned, typically are held at the end of the project, offering lessons learned to the next project manager, who may or may not read the findings. The agile method of conducting a retrospective after almost every iteration offers immediate improvements to be made while the project is still in motion, benefiting the current project. A is incorrect because retrospectives are not an opportunity to remove project team members. B is incorrect because retrospectives aren't to prove to stakeholders the role of the project team. C is incorrect because the team leader will already know the status of the iteration.

12. In an agile environment, the steps set the stage, gather data, generate insights, decide what to do, and close represent which process?

  A. Value stream mapping

  B. Feedback

  C. Pre-mortems

  D. Retrospectives

  D. Retrospectives follow these five steps to provide valuable lessons learned to each subsequent iteration. The team can take the roadblocks and problems encountered during an iteration, along with their resolutions, and act upon them to improve the process in the next iteration.
  A, B, and C are incorrect as these steps are not applicable to value stream mapping, feedback, or retrospectives.

13. During a retrospective, your team leader may single out an issue that was faced during an iteration and ask the team to go through the exercise of the five whys. What is this meant to accomplish?

  A. It typically gets to the root of the cause.

  B. It prevents the team from shifting blame.

  C. It gathers five reasons for the issue.

  D. It allows five team members to offer their opinion.

  A. Typically, when the first question regarding an issue is asked, an automatic response is offered, usually giving an excuse of why something became an issue. When the question of "why" is asked multiple times, the participants normally get to the root cause of the issue as they peel away excuses.
  B is incorrect because this exercise is for root cause analysis, not to hide issues or shift blame. C is incorrect because the approach isn't looking for five reasons, but root cause analysis. D is incorrect because the approach isn't looking for five opinions from project team members, but is looking for root cause analysis.

14. Your agile leader occasionally asks the team to do a self-assessment, meaning a team self-assessment, not an individual self-assessment. The questions that the team addresses for this assessment revolve around which of the following?

  A. How the team gets along

  B. How the team performs and delivers together

  C. How the team reacts to business partners

  D. How the team makes decisions

B. The team self-assessment is meant to gauge the team members performance together. The results of this assessment will identify what is working well and where improvements can be made. The team then meets to determine how to implement improvements and how to celebrate what is working well.
A is incorrect because the assessment isn't intended to determine how the team is getting along, but is more performance-driven. C is incorrect because assessments don't address reactions to business partners. D is incorrect because the assessment isn't about how the team makes project decisions.

15. When your agile team is going through a pre-mortem, each member is asked to write down possible reasons they think some task or action might fail. The best method to reveal everyone's list and consolidate it is to go around the room round-robin. What is the top benefit of this approach?

   A. No one is reading an entire list of problems.

   B. When common issues are identified, other team members can cross it off their list.

   C. Each issue can be discussed when presented.

   D. It forces everyone to attend and stay for the entire meeting.

   C. Presenting issues one at a time allows for discussion in the moment in addition to keeping the entire team engaged. When the list of failure points is complete and agreed upon, the team can prioritize the list and incorporate the fixes in the upcoming iterations.
   A is incorrect because while this statement is true, it's not the best reason why the round-robin approach works well. B is incorrect because while this statement is also true, the goal is to discuss the issues, not simply cross them off team members' lists. D is incorrect because the goal isn't to force attendance, but participation and problem solving.

16. After conducting a retrospective for your last iteration, what type of improvement could you expect to see on your agile team?

   A. Productivity

   B. Attendance

   C. Remote access

   D. Fewer meetings

   A. Several benefits can be uncovered, but productivity of the team might increase by applying lessons learned and reducing rework. In addition, capabilities might be improved because of better knowledge sharing, and quality may improve by removing potential causes of defects.

B is incorrect because attendance isn't usually something that needs to be improved as part of a retrospective. C is incorrect because many teams don't work in a collocated environment, so remote access is somewhat typical in agile project teams. D is incorrect because fewer meetings isn't usually an outcome of retrospectives.

17. When the result of a retrospective has identified issues and root causes, the next step is to decide how to avoid the same types of issues going forward. What is one agile method to accomplish this process?

   A. Fishbone analysis

   B. Prioritize with dots

   C. Triple nickels

   D. SMART goals

   D. Team members can turn their action items into goals that are SMART, meaning: specific, measurable, attainable, relevant, and timely. Once there is a clear understanding of the goals, each issue is discussed and correlated into a SMART goal. Adjustments are made if necessary, then the fix is executed where appropriate. A is incorrect because fishbone analysis is referring to the fishbone chart, which is used during the root cause analysis approach. B is incorrect because prioritize with dots is a user story or feature prioritization scheme, not an outcome of a retrospective. C is incorrect because triple nickels is a brainstorming technique used in retrospectives based on five minutes of brainstorming and discussion.

18. When starting a new agile project, you are told you will be using a hybrid model. What does this mean?

   A. The first half of the project will be done in a traditional project method.

   B. The team member selection will be done traditionally.

   C. An agile model is used in combination with a traditional method.

   D. There will be no user acceptance until the end of the project.

   C. In some cases, using a combination of agile methodology and traditional project methods can make sense, depending on the project. Finding the lowest-risk option to bring a project to success is, by far, the best route to go. Being rigid in your perception of the correct methodology may not always be the best methodology, and agile is meant to accommodate change.
   A is incorrect because the hybrid approach doesn't follow a set formula of a portion being predictive and another portion being agile. B is incorrect because the hybrid approach doesn't really address team member selection. D is incorrect because there's always some formality to user acceptance of the project outcomes.

19. Setting the stage for a retrospective includes which of the following?

    A. Inviting all stakeholders

    B. Distributing a clear and concise agenda

    C. Asking for anonymous input

    D. Defining a specific start and stop time

    B. Defining a clear purpose and agenda for the meeting sets the expectation that this is not just another get-together to discuss the project. There is a need to establish team values and working agreements laying out what behavior is acceptable and what is not.

    A is incorrect because not all stakeholders are invited to the retrospective. C is incorrect because anonymous input isn't part of the retrospective. D is incorrect because while a specific start and stop time is a good idea, it's not the best answer presented. Meetings should always have an agenda and rules.

20. Which of the following is a method utilized to close a retrospective and reinforce its value?

    A. Have a stakeholder dinner

    B. Have the team hold a separate meeting to discuss wins

    C. Give out awards to the best performer

    D. Go through a plus/delta exercise

    D. While all answers might be acceptable, the method most likely would be going through a plus/delta exercise listing on the plus side—what the team would like to do more of and on the delta side—what types of things that didn't go well.

    A, B, and C are incorrect choices. While hosting a dinner, having meetings to discuss wins, and giving out awards can be fun for the project team, the team also needs to address the negative aspects that need improvement in the project.

Critical Exam Information

Exam candidates want to pass their PMI-ACP exam on the first attempt. Why bother sitting for an exam if you know you're not prepared? In this appendix, you'll find the details that you must know to pass the exam. These facts won't be everything you need to know to pass the PMI-ACP exam—but you can bet you won't pass if you do not know the critical information in this appendix.

Exam Test-Passing Tips

For starters, don't think of this process as preparing to *take* an exam; think of it as preparing to *pass* an exam. Anyone can prepare to take an exam: just show up. Preparing to pass the PMI-ACP exam requires agile project management experience, diligence, and a commitment to study.

Days Before the Exam

In the days leading up to your scheduled exam, here are some basics you should do to prepare yourself for success:

- **Get some moderate exercise**   Find time to go for a jog, lift weights, take a swim, or do whatever workout routine works best for you.
- **Eat and drink smart and healthy**   If you eat healthy food, you'll feel good—and feel better about yourself. Be certain to drink plenty of water, and don't overdo the caffeine.
- **Get your sleep**   A well-rested brain is a sharp brain. You don't want to sit for your exam feeling tired, sluggish, and worn out.
- **Time your study sessions**   Don't overdo your study sessions—long cram study sessions aren't that profitable. In addition, try to study at the same time every day at the time your exam is scheduled.

Practice the Testing Process

If you could take one page of notes into the exam, what information would you like on this one-page document? Of course, you absolutely cannot take any notes or reference materials into the exam area. However, if you can create and memorize one sheet of notes, you absolutely may re-create this once you're seated in the exam area.

Practice creating a reference sheet so you can immediately, and legally, re-create this document once your exam has begun. You'll be supplied with several sheets of blank paper and a couple of pencils. Once your exam process begins, re-create your reference sheet. You cannot begin creating your reference sheet until you've started the exam.

Testing Tips

The questions on the PMI-ACP exam are direct and not too verbose, but they may offer a few red herrings. For example, you may face questions that state, "All of the following are correct options except for which one?" The question wants you to find the incorrect option, or the option that would not be appropriate for the scenario described. Be sure to understand what the question is asking for. It's easy to focus on the scenario presented in a question and then see a suitable option for that scenario in the answer. The trouble is that if the question is asking you to identify an option that is *not* suitable, you just missed the question. Carefully read the question to understand what is expected for an answer.

For some answer choices, it may seem like two of the four options are both possible correct answers. However, because you may only choose one answer, you must discern which answer is the best choice. Within the question, there will usually be some hint describing the progress of the project, the requirements of the stakeholders, or some other clue that can help you determine which answer is the best for the question.

Answer Every Question—Once

The PMI-ACP exam has 120 questions—of which 100 are "real questions." You don't have to answer every question correctly; just answer enough correctly to pass. In other words, don't waste two of your three exam hours laboring over one question—the hard questions are worth just as much as the easy ones. And you know, I'm sure, that you never leave any question blank—even if you don't know the answer. A blank question is the same as a wrong answer. As you move through the exam and you find questions that stump you, use the "mark question" option in the exam software, choose an answer you suspect may be correct, and then move on. When you have answered all the questions, you are given the option to review your marked answers.

Some questions in the exam may prompt your memory to come up with answers to questions you have marked for review. However, resist the temptation to review those questions you've already answered with confidence and haven't marked. Often, your first instinct is the correct choice. When you completed the exams at the end of each chapter, did you change correct answers to wrong answers? If you did it in practice, you'll do it on the actual exam.

Use the Process of Elimination

When you're stumped on a question, use the process of elimination. For each question, there'll be four choices. On your scratch paper, write down "ABCD." If you can safely rule out "A," cross it out of the ABCD you've written on your paper. Now focus on which of the other answers won't work. If you determine that "C" won't work, cross it off your list. Now you've got a 50-50 chance of finding the correct choice. If you prefer, the exam testing software also includes the ability to "mark out" answers from the selection choices, but I prefer to do this process on the scratch paper to add any notes and references to the specific question should I need to come back to it later in the exam.

If you cannot determine which answer is best, "B" or "D" in this instance, here's the best approach:

1. Choose an answer in the exam (no blank answers, remember?).

2. Mark the question in the exam software for later review.

3. Circle the "ABCD" on your scratch paper, jot any relevant notes, and then record the question number next to the notes.

4. During the review, or from a later question, you may realize which choice is the better of the two answers. Return to the question and confirm that the best answer is selected.

Everything You Must Know

As promised, this section covers all of the information you must know going into the exam. It's highly recommended that you create a method to recall this information. First, study according to exam value—spend the bulk of your study time on the exam objectives that carry the most weight:

- Domain I: Agile Principles and Mindset – 16 percent
- Domain II: Value-Driven Delivery – 20 percent
- Domain III: Stakeholder Engagement – 17 percent
- Domain IV: Team Performance – 16 percent
- Domain V: Adaptive Planning – 12 percent
- Domain VI: Problem Detection and Resolution – 10 percent
- Domain VII: Continuous Improvement (Product, Process, and People) – 9 percent

From the exam domains, you can see that your order of study and concern should be in this order:

- Domain II: Value-Driven Delivery – 20 percent
- Domain III: Stakeholder Engagement – 17 percent
- Domain I: Agile Principles and Mindset – 16 percent
- Domain IV: Team Performance – 16 percent

- Domain V: Adaptive Planning – 12 percent
- Domain VI: Problem Detection and Resolution – 10 percent
- Domain VII: Continuous Improvement (Product, Process, and People) – 9 percent

Granted, three of these exam domains are about the same percentage, but you get the idea. Don't spend the bulk of your time on exam domains that aren't heavily represented on the exam. I'm not saying to ignore the lesser domains, just make your studying efforts to be in alignment with the domains that'll affect your exam score the most.

Embracing the Agile Principles and Mindset

You need to *be* agile, not just *know* agile, for the PMI-ACP exam. This means that you should always compare your answers against the idea of the agile mindset. So, how do you do that? Know backward and forward the Agile Manifesto. When you're faced with a tough question, compare the answers against the Agile Manifesto and the Declaration of Interdependence for the answer that is most in alignment with these documents.

Recall the Agile Manifesto key points:

- Individuals and interactions over processes and tools
- Working software over comprehensive documentation
- Customer collaboration over contract negotiation
- Responding to change over following a plan

And here's the Agile Declaration of Interdependence:

- We increase return on investment by making continuous flow of value our focus.
- We deliver reliable results by engaging customers in frequent interactions and shared ownership.
- We expect uncertainty and manage for it through iterations, anticipation, and adaptation.
- We unleash creativity and innovation by recognizing that individuals are the ultimate source of value, and creating an environment where they can make a difference.
- We boost performance through group accountability for results and shared responsibility for team effectiveness.
- We improve effectiveness and reliability through situationally specific strategies, processes and practices.

The two documents are quick to learn and should be a strong foundation for answering many of the PMI-ACP exam questions. Certainly not every question will be answerable with these two agile mindset elements, but many of them will be.

Recognizing the Different Agile Flavors

The PMI-ACP exam expects you to understand the different flavors of agile. While you don't need to be a master of all of these approaches, you should have a general understanding of each of them for your exam.

Scrum

Scrum is probably the most common agile methodology you'll encounter on your exam. Scrum begins with the product owner's prioritized backlog. The development team selects a chunk of work they can accomplish in a two-to-four-week iteration called a sprint. The chunk of selected work is the sprint backlog. Sprint reviews are opportunities to demo the project work for the product owner. Sprint retrospectives are opportunities for the project team and the ScrumMaster to review what did, and did not, work in the previous sprint to make adjustments in the project for the next sprint.

XP

XP is short for eXtreme Programming. XP uses two-week iterations of development. The requirements are called user stories, and the development team sizes the user stories to see how much work they can accomplish in the next iteration. *Spikes* is an XP term you should know. An architectural spike is an iteration to set up the development environment, ensure the design is not overly complicated, and provide some feasibility of the project goals. A risk spike aims to mitigate or eliminate risks that have been identified in the project and threaten the project success.

Kanban

Kanban, which means signboard in Japanese, is an agile approach that helps to visualize the flow of the work through a system. Kanban shows work in queue, work in progress, and completed items on a signboard. This use of a low-tech, high-touch tool to help manage the project work is an agile concept. Kanban is a pull system, pulling work from the queue into the work in progress (WIP) and workflow. When a team member completes an item, it triggers the next item to be brought into the system. When there are additional steps, such as testing, the item pulled into the next task column can also trigger other team members to address or pull that item into their queue of work. Kanban doesn't use iterations like Scrum and XP, but just continues to pull to-do items into the WIP and through the established workflow.

Lean Product Development

Lean uses a visualization of what needs to be done, creates requirements based on the customer's definition of value, and includes opportunity for learning and process improvement throughout the project. There are seven principles within Lean that you should recognize for your exam:

- Eliminate waste
- Quality is built in
- Create knowledge

- Defer commitments
- Deliver fast
- Respect people
- Optimize the whole

Dynamic Systems Development Method (DSDM)

DSDM is a predecessor of today's agile project management and relied on a business case to show value and a feasibility study to determine if the development team could actually create the architecture and requirements the customer identified. While you likely won't see many questions about DSDM on the PMI-ACP exam, you should recognize these eight principles:

- Business need is the primary goal.
- Deliver working software on time.
- Collaborate with the development team and the business people.
- Quality cannot be comprised.
- Build incrementally based on firm foundations.
- Develop iteratively.
- Provide clear and consistent communications.
- Demonstrate control.

Feature-Driven Development (FDD)

FDD is an iterative approach to software development that bases its progress on the client's values of features the software will provide. FDD utilizes a backlog of features that are prioritized based on customer values then created through iterations of project work. There are five stages to the FDD process:

- Develop an overall model
- Build the feature list
- Plan by feature
- Design by feature
- Build by feature

Crystal

Crystal utilizes methodology, techniques, and policies to manage the project. Crystal focuses on people, interaction, community, development team skills, talents, and communication as its core principles. From lightest criticality to most serious project criticality, here are the eight levels of Crystal:

- Crystal Clear—small, easy projects
- Crystal Yellow

- Crystal Orange
- Crystal Orange Web
- Crystal Red
- Crystal Maroon
- Crystal Diamond
- Crystal Sapphire—top priority projects

Delivering Value ASAP

One of the goals of an agile project is to deliver value as quickly as possible for stakeholders. Value describes the benefits for the customer. Anti-value is anything that detracts from the customer benefits, so you'll have to combat waste in projects too. The items at the top of a prioritized backlog are the top priorities for the team—and they represent the most value for the customer. To combat waste, and improve value, you'll need to use strategies to combat Poppendieck's Seven Wastes:

- Partially done work
- Extra features
- Relearning
- Handoffs
- Delays
- Task switching
- Defects

These items rob the project of creating value. Time and energy spent on these items is time and energy lost from working on value. Know these seven wastes for your PMI-ACP exam.

Measuring Project Performance

To measure your understanding of project performance, you might see a few earned value management questions on your PMI-ACP exam. Table A-1 shows the EVM formulas you should know for the exam.

Filtering Project Requirements

You'll likely have a few exam questions on prioritizing requirements. Though sorting and refining the product backlog (grooming) is the responsibility of the product owner, the project team and the project manager can help with the process. Know these approaches to requirements prioritization:

- **MoSCoW approach** Each requirement is marked and sorted as must have, should have, could have, or would like to have but not at this time.

Name	Formula
Planned value	PV = % complete where the project should be × BAC (budget at completion)
Earned value	EV = % complete × BAC (budget at completion)
Cost variance	CV = EV – AC (actual cost)
Schedule variance	SV = EV – PV
Cost performance index	CPI = EV / AC
Schedule performance index	SPI = EV / PV
Estimate at completion, standard formula	EAC = BAC / CPI
Estimate at completion, future work at planned costs	EAC = AC + BAC – EV
Estimate at completion, initial cost estimates flawed	EAC = AC + Estimate for remainder of project
Estimate at completion, SPI and CPI affect remainder of work	EAC = AC + [BAC – EV/(CPI × SPI)]
Estimate to complete	ETC = EAC – AC
To-complete performance index (BAC)	TCPI = (BAC – EV) / (BAC – AC)
To-complete performance index (EAC)	TCPI = (BAC – EV) / (EAC – AC)
Variance at completion	VAC = BAC – EAC

Table A-1   Project Management Earned Value Management Formulas

- **Kano analysis**   Requirements are sorted into the five categories of must-be quality, one-dimensional quality, attractive quality, indifferent quality, and reverse quality.
- **Voting with dots**   Participants vote on the requirements priority with dots, check marks, or even sticky notes. Voters have a predetermined amount of dots, or votes, to use when voting on requirements, often fewer than the total number of requirements presented.
- **Monopoly money**   Participants are given an amount of pretend money to "spend" on requirements. Each stakeholder has an equal amount of pretend cash to spend on the different items in the requirements backlog. Participants spend their money on the requirements based on how valuable they perceive the items to be in the project.
- **Voting with 100 points**   Each stakeholder in the requirements prioritization meeting has 100 points to vote on requirements as they see fit.
- **Requirements prioritization model**   Four factors — benefit, penalty, cost, and risk — are voted on from a value of one to nine.

Identifying Project Stakeholder Engagement

The project manager has the responsibility of identifying stakeholders. The project team and other stakeholders can help with the process, but it's the project manager's responsibility. Typical stakeholders in a project include

- Customers
- Project sponsor
- Project leaders
- Development team
- Vendors
- End users

All stakeholders need representation in the project. For a large group of stakeholders, a representative of the group will work with the project manager and the development team in the project. The representative can be the product owner, a proxy, or ambassador for the group of stakeholders. This person will make decisions on behalf of the group they represent, and they must be involved throughout the project.

Creating a Project Charter

An agile project charter embraces change and the value of the project in the shared project vision. The agile project charter summarizes the key success factors and should be displayed for everyone to see. The project charter defines boundaries and agreements between the project team and stakeholders. The project charter, at a minimum, should define

- Who are the engaged stakeholders?
- What is the central goal of the project?
- Where will the project work take place?
- What are the project start and end dates?
- Why are we doing this project?
- What's the project methodology?

The project charter shouldn't be very long. Some project charters include an elevator statement, which is a way to define the project goals, purpose, and characteristics in the amount of time of an elevator ride, about a minute or less. Other trends include creating a project tweet—like something you'd post on Twitter. A project tweet defines the project in 280 characters or less.

Communicating with Stakeholders

Communication is important for the project manager and project team. Hearing and listening are not the same things. Hearing means you hear the noise, the words, without really considering the message. Listening is the reception and understanding of what's being said. Listening is really understanding what someone is trying to say. There are three levels of listening you want to recognize for your exam:

- **Level one, internal listening** The listener is hearing words but is not very attentive.

- **Level two, focused listening** The listener is attentive and listening to the speaker's perspective. The listener is listening and picking up on the non-verbal language.

- **Level three, global listening** This level is built on top of level two and is a higher level of awareness. The listener is looking for subtle clues about the message meaning. This level helps the listener develop a fuller context of the message.

Recognizing Self-Directed Teams

For your PMI-ACP exam, you'll need to know four attributes of self-directed teams:

- **Work collectively** The team works with one another. The team can do swarming, can do pair programming (as in XP), and is empowered to work collectively as a group.

- **Ownership of decisions** The project team makes decisions about the work. The project team doesn't have to consult the project manager about every decision.

- **Create estimates for the project work** The project team estimates the project work. The sizing of the user stories, done by the project team, creates estimates on the effort required to create the features of the product backlog. The project team also creates estimates on how much work they can achieve in an iteration.

- **Fail safely** No one wants to fail, but when the team is empowered to be innovative, not every innovation is going to be successful. Every team is going to make mistakes, but the team needs to operate in a safe environment where they don't feel repercussions for their failed experiments.

Investing in User Stories

You might encounter a question or two on user story attributes. Know how to use the acronym of INVEST. This means user stories are

- **Independent** The story can stand alone from the other user stories. Independent stories can be prioritized in any order.

- **Negotiable** There might be some tradeoffs and negotiation. Negotiation can be based on the priority of the user story, risks involved, value to the organization, and how the user story can affect other features of the product.

- **Valuable** The result creates business value. User stories must create business value when the team creates the feature in the product.

- **Estimable** You can create an estimate of effort based on the user story. The team will examine the user stories and determine an estimate of effort to create the feature.

- **Small** The stories aren't too big and don't need further decomposition. User stories are usually between one and three days of work.

- **Testable** The team can write tests for the product to confirm the successful inclusion of the user story. Test-driven development is based on user stories.

Managing Technical Debt

Technical debt is the backlog of work that's caused by a lack of regular clean-up of code. It's the maintenance, standardization, and refactoring of the code. Project teams need to resolve technical debt, and one primary approach is to use the red-green-refactor, also known as red-green success or red-green-clean. This strategy calls for the developer to first create a test. Then the developer creates code against that test. Once the code passes the test, the person should clean up the code. Know that refactoring standardizes code and makes it easier to support. Refactoring time should be included in your estimates and sizing.

Managing Problems and Defects

As part of the problem detection and resolution exam domain (Domain VI), you'll likely have to answer questions dealing with project problems and defects. There are five things you want to know about detecting problems and defects:

- **Escaped defects** These are defects that slip through testing and into production. Escaped defects are the most expensive type of defect because they get out to the end users.

- **Regression testing** Regression testing should happen on functionality throughout the project. As the team compiles code, they do regression testing to ensure that what they've added to existing software doesn't break anything.

- **Demonstrations** Demonstrations are good because they show the user stories in action and how the team has created the user story and value.

- **Consistent testing** Software development projects require user acceptability testing and end-to-end testing.

- **Daily standup meetings** The project manager consistently asks in the daily standup if there are any impediments or roadblocks to address. This prompt is often the first step to detecting problems.

Managing Project Risks

Risks are uncertain events that can negatively affect an agile project. The product backlog can be prioritized to address significant risk events earlier in the project to determine project feasibility based on a significant risk. For your exam, know risk burndown charts,

Figure A-1 Risk burndown charts show that risks diminish as the project progresses.

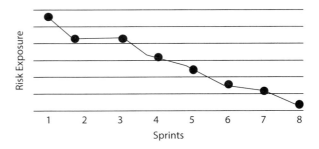

an example of which is shown in Figure A-1. The risk burndown chart is a stacked graph and is similar to a user story burndown chart. A risk burndown chart is a graph of cumulative project risk severity.

The chart shows how severe the risk exposure is at the beginning of the project through the end of the project. As the project team gets by more and more risk, exposure diminishes all the way down to zero. This chart is a way to visualize risk events for each iteration in the project. The severity of each risk accumulates to show all of the project risk is represented in the risk burndown chart.

There are four risk responses you want to know for your exam:

- **Mitigation** Mitigation is anything that you do to reduce the probability or impact of a risk event.

- **Transference** Transference is anything that you do that transfers the risk to someone else, usually with a contractual relationship. You hire someone to manage that part of the risk.

- **Avoidance** You just avoid the risk. You might take the risk event out of scope because the event may be deemed too risky.

- **Acceptance** A risk is small or there's nothing you can do about it, so you accept the risk.

Completing Systems Thinking

Agile projects are complex systems with many different influences on the project, people, processes, and product. Systems thinking is a structured approach to do the work and includes analysis of the system's processes to reach the defined result. The system, in this case, is the agile project management environment. This introduces the idea of methodology success patterns. There are four things you need to know when it comes to methodology success patterns:

- **Interactive face-to-face communication** It's the cheapest and the fastest channel for exchanging information.

- **Balance of methodology** The agile methodology shouldn't be too light or too heavy, but just right. Heavy agile methodologies rob efficiency and productivity. Light approaches to agile don't accomplish the goals of agile and may be too loose to be effective.

- **Team size affects structure**   Larger teams need a heavier methodology because larger teams require more formality and ceremony.
- **Project criticality requires ceremony**   Projects of higher priority require greater ceremony. They require more framework and governance than a lower-priority project.

Leading a Retrospective

The retrospective is an opportunity for the team to complete self-inspection and to adapt accordingly for areas needing improvement prior to the next iteration. This meeting is hosted prior to the planning session for the next iteration and lasts a maximum of three hours for projects with four-week-long iterations. The scope of the questions asked includes the people, relationships, processes, and tools used for the last cycle. The team takes an approach similar to daily standups to define what went well and what can be improved.

About the Digital Content

The CD-ROM included with this book comes complete with

- Total Tester customizable practice exam software with hundreds of practice exam questions for PMI-ACP
- Video training from the author
- A secured PDF copy of the book for studying on the go

NOTE: If you do not have a CD-ROM drive, you may download Total Tester by simply going to this URL:

www.totalsem.com/1260115976d/

To access the secured book PDF and videos, visit McGraw-Hill Professional's Media Center by going to this URL:

https://www.mhprofessionalresources.com/mediacenter/

Enter your e-mail address and this 13-digit ISBN: 978-1-26-011597-0. You will then receive an e-mail message with a download link for the book PDF and videos.

System Requirements

The software requires Windows Vista or later and 30MB of hard disk space for full installation, in addition to a current or prior major release of Chrome, Firefox, Internet Explorer, or Safari. To run, the screen resolution must be set to 1024×768 or higher. The PDF files require Adobe Acrobat, Adobe Reader, or Adobe Digital Editions to view.

Total Tester Premium Practice Exam Software

Total Tester provides you with a simulation of the live exam. You can also create custom exams from selected certification objectives or chapters. You can further customize the number of questions and time allowed.

The exams can be taken in either Practice Mode or Exam Mode. Practice Mode provides an assistance window with hints, references to the book, explanations of the correct and incorrect answers, and the option to check your answer as you take the test. Exam Mode provides a simulation of the actual exam. The number of questions, types of questions, and time allowed are intended to be an accurate representation of the exam environment. Both Practice Mode and Exam Mode provide an overall grade and a grade broken down by certification objectives.

To take a test, launch the program and select the exam suite from the Installed Question Packs list. You can then select Practice Mode, Exam Mode, or Custom Mode. After making your selection, click Start Exam to begin.

Installing and Running Total Tester Premium Practice Exam Software

From the main screen, you may install Total Tester by clicking the Total Tester Practice Exams button. This will begin the installation process and place an icon on your desktop and in your Start menu. To run Total Tester, navigate to Start | (All) Programs | Total Seminars, or double-click the icon on your desktop.

To uninstall the Total Tester software (Windows Vista/7), go to Start | Settings | Control Panel | Programs And Features and then select the Total Tester program. Select Remove, and Windows will completely uninstall the software. To uninstall the Total Tester software (Windows 8/10), go to Start | Settings | Apps and then select the Total Tester program. Select Remove, and Windows will completely uninstall the software.

Video Training from the Author

Video MP4 clips provide detailed examples of key certification topics in video format direct from the author of the book. You can access the videos directly from the Video table of contents by clicking the Videos link on the main page.

Secure PDF Copy of the Book

The entire contents of the print book are provided as a PDF on the CD-ROM. This file is viewable on your computer and many portable devices.

- **To view the PDF on a computer,** Adobe Acrobat, Adobe Reader, or Adobe Digital Editions is required. A link to Adobe's website, where you can download and install Adobe Reader, has been included on the CD-ROM.

 NOTE: For more information on Adobe Reader and to check for the most recent version of the software, visit Adobe's website at www.adobe.com. Search for the free Adobe Reader or look for Adobe Reader on the product page. Adobe Digital Editions can also be downloaded from the Adobe website.

- **To view the PDF on a portable device,** copy the PDF file to your computer from the CD-ROM, and then copy the file to your portable device using a USB or other connection. Adobe offers a mobile version of Adobe Reader, the Adobe Reader mobile app, which currently supports iOS and Android. For customers using Adobe Digital Editions and an iPad, you may have to download and install a separate reader program on your device. The Adobe website has a list of recommended applications, and McGraw-Hill Education recommends the Bluefire Reader.

Technical Support

Technical Support information is provided as follows, by feature.

Total Seminars Technical Support

For questions regarding the Total Tester software or operation of the CD-ROM, visit **www.totalsem.com** or e-mail **support@totalsem.com**.

McGraw-Hill Education Content Support

For questions regarding the video or PDF content, e-mail **techsolutions@mhedu.com** or visit **http://mhp.softwareassist.com**.

For questions regarding book content, e-mail **hep_customer-service@mheducation .com**. For customers outside the United States, e-mail **international_cs@mheducation .com**.

100-point voting Each stakeholder in the requirements prioritization meeting has 100 points to vote on requirements as they see fit. A stakeholder can distribute their points equally among the requirements, in big 25-point chunks, or even spend all 100 points on one single requirement.

Acceptance Acceptance is the typical response to risks that are small or can't be mitigated, transferred, or avoided.

Acceptance test–driven development (ATDD) This approach has the entire team writing tests before developing the code. ATDD addresses three perspectives and their respective questions:

Customer perspective: What problem are we trying to solve?
Development team perspective: How will we solve this problem?
Testing staff perspective: What about this hypothetical scenario?

Active listening Active listening is conversational. The message receiver is paying attention to the sender and is involved in the conversation. Active listening means it's a dialogue and the sender and receiver are listening to each other and confirming the understanding of the message being offered. Active listening is to really hear what's being said.

Actual cost (AC) Actual cost is the actual amount of monies the project has spent so far.

Adjourning Adjourning is the final stage of Tuckman's Model of Team Development. Once the project is done, the team disbands, and the unit is no longer a team.

Affinity estimating Affinity estimating is a way of grouping user stories into similar categories or collections. For example, in IT, we often group things by hardware, software, data, and network. Affinity estimating groups similar stories and then uses relative estimating for the stories.

Agile discovery Agile discovery means that the project team discovers through experiments and innovation the best approach to accomplish their work.

Agile life cycle The agile life cycle works with dynamic requirements for the development team to deliver working software frequently through small releases.

Agile Manifesto The Agile Manifesto is a broad document that establishes the values of agile project management. The four values are individuals and interactions over processes and tools; working software over comprehensive documentation; customer collaboration over contract negotiation; responding to change over following a plan.

Agile mindset   The agile mindset is a way of thinking about and doing agile projects. Having the agile mindset means you exemplify the values and principles of agile in how you work, how you lead a project, and how you share a passion for agile with others.

Agile modeling   Agile modeling is way to illustrate solutions and ideas. There are five principles of agile modeling: *communicate* ideas and solutions; *simplify* a complex idea and make it easier to understand; give *feedback* to the sender of a message as part of the conversation; foster *courage* to state ideas, be involved, and to try new ideas and let go of old ideas; and express *humility*, as even the best developers need to acknowledge that they don't know everything and respect one another's opinions.

Agile project accounting   This methodology ties financial accountability to the deliverables the team creates. It tracks the cost and ROI of the project and the iterations of the project.

Agile project charter   An agile project charter allows more flexibility than a charter in a traditional project because an agile project is more ambiguous and subject to change as requirements are developed and prioritized.

Architectural spike   An architectural spike is experimentation that the team performs early in the project to prove that what they're trying to accomplish in the project is feasible; it's a proof-of-concept exercise. An architectural spike is a timeboxed effort to test your approach, to make sure that you have the right architecture and approach to build the software.

Assignable cause   In a control chart measurements that are out of control are deemed an assignable cause. Assignable causes are measurements of performance that are out of control; an assignable cause means there's some reason why a variance happened.

Avoidance   You just avoid the risk. You might take the requirement out of scope because it's too risky.

Backlog refinement meeting   A backlog refinement meeting is a Scrum event where the product owner, the ScrumMaster, and the development team work together to discuss the backlog items and prioritize the items.

Barrier   A barrier is anything that prevents communication from occurring, such as speaking different languages or an error with the technology used in the communication.

Burndown chart   A burndown chart shows the total number of requirements remaining in the product backlog as each iteration completes a portion of the requirements. The chart shows that the team is burning down the total amount of work to do through their velocity in each iteration. The more consistent the velocity, the better the prediction of project completion for all requirements.

Burnup chart   A burnup chart illustrates each iteration's amount of work accomplished. It shows the cumulative total of requirements the team has completed for the whole project and in each iteration.

Caves   In a collaborative team space, caves are private areas for conversations, concentration, and to avoid interruptions.

Ceremonies   Ceremonies are the meetings and events in an agile project. Ceremonies include sprint planning meetings, daily standup meetings, iteration reviews, and iteration retrospectives.

Coach   This is an XP role that is like a project manager but is more of a mentor and facilitator. The coach mentors people on the project team, helps get things done, and serves as the hub of communications for the project stakeholders.

Coarse-grained requirements   Coarse-grained requirements are high-level, chunky descriptions of the project requirements.

Code standards   An XP concept is that all programmers on the development team follow defined and communicated standards for developing the code.

Collaboration   Collaborate means two people or groups can be in disagreement, but it's not heated and they work together for a good, viable project solution.

Collaborative team space   An open floor plan that provides line of sight for everyone and provides easy and fast communication.

Collective code ownership   Collective code ownership means that any developer can edit any code at any time; an XP concept.

Commons   In a collaborative team space, the commons is the big common area in an open floor plan, an open space for team members to interact and collaborate.

Communication model   The communication model describes how information is transferred between people in any communication modality.

Compromise   Compromising means that both parties have to give up something as part of the conflict resolution. Compromising is lose-lose.

Cone of uncertainty   The cone of uncertainty describes how a large range of uncertainty exists at the beginning of the project, and over time and with experience the cone becomes smaller and smaller because certainty increases.

Continuous improvement   Continuous improvement is a process in which actions are taken to identify deficiencies in performance, goals are set for improvement, and continued actions are undertaken to meet those goals. Continuous improvement aims for the organization, the project manager, the project team, and the processes of an agile project to improve.

Continuous integration (CI)   Continuous integration is a way to merge all the code from different developers to confirm that the compiled code is still working successfully. CI aims to build and test the code several times a day from a shared repository.

Control chart   A control chart shows how the team performed within the control limits for each increment of a project. The control chart defines the expected performance within control limits, trends, and assignable causes.

Control limits   Control limits are boundaries to operate within. These boundaries offer a window of performance and provide a level of expectation for productivity.

Convergence graphs   Convergence graphs show how initial estimates are flawed and, over time, with progressive elaboration, that the range of variance gets smaller and smaller and the certainty of estimate increases.

Cost performance index (CPI)   CPI measures the project based on its financial performance. The formula is earned value divided by actual cost (EV / AC). The closer to 1, the better the project is performing financially.

Cost variance   The earned value of the project minus the actual cost spent reveals the cost variance. The formula is EV – AC.

Crystal   Crystal is an agile approach that uses eight different schemes of agile project management based on several factors, such as the complexity of the project, the number of project team members, and the criticality of the project.

Cumulative flow diagram (CFD)   A CFD can help identify and track bottlenecks in an agile project. A CFD shows how many work items are in the different stages of the project, how long each item stays in a stage or queue, when items move into the next queue of the project, and when items leave any stage of the project.

Customer   A project customer is anyone who will pay for and/or use the results of the project.

Cycle time   Cycle time is how long something takes to go through a part of the process. Cycle time is a subset of lead time, which is how long something takes to go through the entire process.

Daily Scrum   This is a daily 15-minute meeting during which the team members share progress updates; it is sometimes called a standup meeting because everyone stands for the duration. The Daily Scrum happens every day at the same time, in the same place.

Data model   A data model is a structure with which to organize your data. The data model designers must think about user interaction in the software.

Decoder   A decoder, part of the communication model, is a device, such as the receiver's e-mail system, that decodes a coded message back into useable information.

Defect cycle time   Defect cycle time is the amount of time between when a defect is discovered and when it's resolved. The longer the defect cycle time, typically the more expensive that defect will be in the project.

Definition of done   The definition of done describes what constitutes done for any element of the project and for the project as a whole. The project manager and team consider planning, design, development, testing, continuous integration, builds, releases, resolution of bugs, limited support, and stakeholder acceptance when defining done.

Development team   The development team is responsible for sizing the requirements of the product backlog and getting work done in each sprint. The development team is self-organizing and self-led, and its members are called generalizing specialists because they can often do more than one function on the team. An ideal Scrum team has no less than five people and no more than eleven people.

Dreyfus Model of Adult Skill Acquisition   In the Dreyfus Model of Adult Skill Acquisition, learners move through five stages to acquire skills: novice, competent, proficient, expert, and master.

Dynamic Systems Development Method (DSDM)   DSDM is one of the predecessors of today's agile project management and relied on a business case to show value and a feasibility study to determine if the development team could create the architecture and requirements the customer identified.

Earned value (EV)   This formula measures the amount of work completed to date and the authorized budget for that work. Earned value is the percent complete times the project's budget.

Elevator statement   An elevator statement is a quick definition of the project goals, purpose, and characteristics that can be expressed in the amount of time of an elevator ride, about a minute or less.

Emergent leadership   Emergent leadership occurs when an individual on the team takes a leadership role. It doesn't have to be the project manager, and new leaders can emerge at different times based on what's happening in the project.

Empirical processes   Empirical processes are based on observation, trial and error, and the experience of the person doing the work. Agile projects rely on the knowledge worker to be creative, innovative, and to figure out the work to reach the desired results.

Encoder   An encoder, part of the communication model, is a device, such as an e-mail system, that encodes the message to be sent.

End users   End users are similar to the project customers but are ultimately the people who'll use the product your project is creating.

Engagement culture   An engagement culture encourages people to collaborate, share ideas, and share what they've discovered, and rewards people for solving problems.

Epics   Epics are large user stories that are too large for just one iteration. Epics can even span different projects in some cases. Most of the time, epics are placeholders for a collection of five or more related user stories.

Escaped defects   Escaped defects are defects that slip through testing and into production. Escaped defects are the most expensive type of defect because they get out to the end users.

Estimate at completion (EAC)   This formula predicts where the project is likely to end up financially based on current performance. The formula is

EAC = budget at completion (BAC) / cost performance index (CPI)

Estimate to complete (ETC)   ETC shows how much more money will be needed to complete the project. The most common formula is

ETC = budget at completion (BAC) – earned value (EV)

Estimate to Complete based on Atypical Variances   This formula is used when the project has experienced some unusual fluctuation in costs, and the project manager doesn't believe the variances will continue within the project. The formula is

ETC = BAC – EV

Estimate to Complete based on Typical Variances   This formula is used when the project has experienced some fluctuation in costs, and the project manager believes the variances will continue within the project. The formula is

ETC = (BAC – EV) / CPI.

Ethnocentrism   Ethnocentrism refers to judging other cultures based on one's own culture. It is based on assumptions and prejudices that the individual's culture is superior or inferior rather than the understanding that cultures are just different, not necessarily better or worse.

Expected monetary value   The expected monetary value is the financial exposure of the risk. Expected monetary value is found by multiplying the risk probability times the risk impact.

Exploratory testing   Combined with scripted tested, exploratory testing is based on the tester trying different things in the software, exploring the different parts of the application, and playing "what if" with combinations of commands. The exploratory tester is free to try anything and everything in the software to see what conforms, or does not conform, to requirements. Exploratory testing is more freewill, ad hoc, and spontaneous than scripted testing.

Face-to-face communication   Face-to-face communication provides the highest "bandwidth" of all communication types, meaning it's the easiest and the most acceptable way to communicate ideas and messages.

Failure Modes and Effects Analysis (FMEA)   FMEA is one of the primary tools for process analysis and begins with the largest failures and works toward the smallest. FMEA requires identification of all steps in a process and then examines everything that could go wrong at each point in the process. Next, FMEA identifies the failure causes and effects.

Feature-Driven Development (FDD)   FDD is an iterative approach to software development that bases its progress on the client's values of features the software will provide.

Features chart   A features chart is a combination of a burnup chart and a burndown chart. This chart shows the number of requirements remaining and the number of features that have been completed, and can also show whether features have been added to the product backlog.

Feedback loops   Feedback loops describe the phenomenon of an entity, system, or person that gives an output which will cause an input to the same entity. For example, the project team gives an update to the product owner, which causes the product owner to speak to the project manager, which causes the project manager to coach the project team on their next iteration of work.

Fibonacci sequence   The Fibonacci sequence is a pattern of numbers where each number is the sum of the two preceding numbers. For example, zero plus one equals one. One plus one equals two. Two plus one equals three. Three plus five equals eight, five plus eight is thirteen, thirteen plus eight is twenty-one, and so on.

Fine-grained requirements   Fine-grained requirements are much more detailed and granular and are specific on acceptability requirements.

First-time, first-use penalty   First-time, first-use penalty describes a condition where the project team has never done this type of work before. The penalty is that the work may take longer and/or cost more than anticipated.

Fishbone diagram   A fishbone diagram, also called a cause-and-effect diagram and an Ishikawa diagram, is used in root cause analysis to identify the contributing causes of the effect. The diagram can be used to facilitate a conversation to resolve the effect the project is experiencing.

Fist of Five voting   Fist of Five voting is a participatory decision-making technique where participants show their degree of support for a decision by displaying the corresponding number of fingers. Showing all five fingers means total support, while showing just one finger means low support. A variation of this approach allows participants to show a closed fist if they are strongly opposed to the decision.

Fixed-price work package   This agile approach to contracting enables the vendor to examine each work package and estimate their costs and time to deliver the item. As more information becomes available, such as detailed requirements, risks, and shifting priorities, the vendor can modify their estimate based on the new information. This approach allows the vendor to take on a portion of the project and manage that portion as they see fit—as long as they deliver value on time and as promised.

Focused listening   Focused listening, which is level two of the three levels of listening, is where you're paying attention and listening to the speaker's perspective. You can empathize with the speaker. You are listening and picking up on not only the words but also the nonverbal language like facial expressions and gestures. You're paying attention to paralingual aspects such as the speaker's pitch and tone, the emotional indicators.

Forcing   Forcing the resolution of a conflict occurs when a person with authority forces their opinion on a subordinate. Sometimes a project manager has to resort to this authoritarian style of conflict resolution if it is the only way to fulfill a project requirement, such as compliance with a safety regulation that is burdensome to the team.

Forming   Forming is the first stage of Tuckman's Model of Team Development, in which a team first comes together. This stage is marked by initial pleasantness as introductions are made and people begin to learn about each other.

Free-for-all approach   A free-for-all approach is a brainstorming technique where everyone comes to the meeting and throws out as many ideas as possible.

Future value (FV)   Future value is what a present amount of funds will be worth in the future. The formula for future value is $FV = PV(1 + i)^n$, where i is the given interest rate and n is the number of time periods (years, quarters, etc.).

Generalizing specialist   A generalizing specialist is an individual on your team who can serve multiple roles, so team members can quickly switch between different roles on your team.

Global listening   Global listening, which is level three of the three levels of listening, involves an even higher level of awareness than focused listening (level two). You're looking for the subtle clues about the meaning, such as the speaker's posture and energy.

Graduated fixed-price contract   A graduated fixed-price contract allows the buyer and the seller to share some risks in an agile project. With this model the hourly rate of the contracted work varies based on performance within the project. For example, the vendor's hourly rate for software development could be $120 if they finish the project on time and as planned. If the vendor is late, however, the hourly rate decreases to $110. If the vendor completes the project ahead of schedule, the hourly rate increases to $130.

Green zone   Individuals in a green zone take responsibility for their actions, work collaboratively, and respond non-defensively.

Herzberg's Theory of Motivation   Herzberg's Theory of Motivation describes two types of agents: hygiene agents and motivating agents. Hygiene agents include job security, a paycheck, an acceptable working environment, and your work relationship. These are called "hygiene" agent because they are necessary just to maintain the employer-employee relationship. Motivating agents motivate people to excel in performance and include factors like bonuses, opportunity for advancement, appreciation, recognition, and education.

Highsmith Decision Spectrum   The Highsmith Decision Spectrum is a group decision-making technique that presents the group with a spectrum of possible choices from in favor to opposed. Participants then put a check mark on the spectrum to indicate how they feel about an idea. People can vote in private so that they are not influenced by the group; then the project manager tallies the votes.

Ideal time   Ideal time describes the ideal amount of time it will take to create the items in the product backlog. An ideal time estimate does not consider interruptions or delays in the project work.

Identify stakeholders   The first of the four processes in stakeholder management is to identify stakeholders. This is an initiation process and aims to identify and document stakeholders in a stakeholder register.

Incremental development   By working in increments the development team addresses the most valuable requirements first, incorporates risk management into the project approach, and offers reviews and continued prioritization of the requirements.

Incremental life cycle   The incremental life cycle works with dynamic requirements for the development team to quickly deliver working software through increments of product releases.

Incremental project   An incremental project delivers value in increments—short pieces of functional deliverables that the business can take advantage of while the project is still in motion.

Industrial-work projects   Industrial-work projects utilize defined approaches to complete processes and tasks; the project team members know exactly what to do and what to expect in the project and in the project management approach. Construction is an example of an industrial-work project.

Information radiator   An information radiator is a highly visible display of all the information regarding your project. A project's information radiator could be composed of graphs, bar charts, burndown charts, or your Kanban board. An information radiator is out in the open, and everyone can see it; it's easily accessible. An information radiator might also be known as visual controls.

Intangible business value   Intangible business value is derived from the invisible elements that a project creates, such as goodwill, reputation, brand recognition, public benefit, trademarks, and strategic alignment for your organization.

Internal listening   Internal listening is level one of the three levels of listening and means you're hearing words but you're not very attentive.

Introspectives   Introspectives are ad hoc team meetings focused on resolving a roadblock or other issue. Introspectives are an opportunity to have a series of process analysis techniques ready and waiting for any time your team needs them.

Inverted triple constraint   Agile projects invert the traditional triple constraints (or iron triangle) so that time and cost are fixed, but the scope is now flexible.

INVEST   INVEST is a user story acronym to confirm that user stories are independent of each other, negotiable, valuable, estimable, small, and testable.

Issues   Issues are risks that have been realized in the project, and their effect must be managed.

Iteration backlog   The iteration backlog is the backlog of user stories the team has selected to accomplish in the current iteration.

Iteration H   Iteration H is called thus because it's the iteration that involves hardening, or a hardening sprint, to clean up and stabilize the code. It helps wrap up the product for release and it's all about stabilizing the code and refactoring everything for a good, clean release.

Iteration Zero   Iteration Zero is the first iteration or sprint, where your team establishes the development environment. The team builds out the test servers, databases, and preparing for JUnit or NUnit testing. Iteration Zero is also where your team will establish continuous integration architecture, they'll design the team rules, and if you're colocated you'll set up your war room.

Iterative life cycle   The iterative life cycle works with dynamic requirements for the development team to create a single delivery of the software solution at the end of the project.

Iterative project   An iterative project repeats iterations until the project is done. Each iteration builds on the iteration before all the way through the entire project life cycle.

Kaizen   Kaizen (a Japanese word meaning "change for the better") is a continuous improvement approach that requires small, incremental steps that accumulate to broad changes over time.

Kanban   Kanban is a Japanese word that means signboard. This approach started at Toyota and it helps to visualize the flow of the work through a system.

Kanban board   Requirements are written on sticky notes or cards and are moved from the backlog to the different phases of the project to represent where the requirement currently is in the project life cycle.

Kano analysis   Kano analysis is an approach to sort customer requirements into five categories: must-be quality, one-dimensional quality, attractive quality, indifferent quality, and reverse quality.

Key performance indicators (KPIs)   KPIs are factors that show project performance. Agile uses four KPIs: rate of progress, remaining work, completion date, and costs remaining.

Knowledge-work projects   Agile projects are knowledge-work projects and are driven by creativity and brain power, rather than brawn and effort applied to defined processes and tasks. Software development is an example of a knowledge-work projects.

Lagging metrics   Lagging metrics are based on performance to this point of the project. Lagging metrics allow you to look for trends and then, based on what you find, predict the future with some degree of confidence. Lagging trends are proven.

Lead time   Lead time is how long a requirement takes to go through an entire process within the project.

Leading metrics   Leading metrics provide a view into the future. Leading metrics are trends that you predict will happen. Leading trends have uncertainty and are not yet proven.

Lean Product Development   Commonly called Lean, this agile approach uses a visualization of what needs to be done, creates requirements based on the customer's definition of value, and includes opportunity for learning and process improvement throughout the project.

Little's Law   A theorem that states "the average number of items in a queuing system equals the average rate at which items arrive multiplied by the average time that an item spends in the system." In other words, the more items that are in the WIP queue, the longer it will take the team to complete the items in the queue. When work is introduced into a system, such as your workflow, faster than the work is being completed, the queue time will increase for the work.

Low-tech/high-touch tools   Tools for agile project management that are not technology based are preferred because they are simple, clean, and direct like agile itself. Examples are Kanban boards and the WIP limit.

Manage stakeholder engagement   The third of the four processes in stakeholder management is to manage stakeholder engagement. This is an executing process. Managing stakeholder engagement is about communicating with, not just to, stakeholders. It's getting stakeholders involved, being transparent about all project news, sharing the project vision, and building energy and interest by delivering value in the project.

Maslow's Hierarchy of Needs   Maslow's Hierarchy of Needs describes the five levels of human needs: physiological, safety, social, esteem, and self-actualization. To be self-actualized means you have a sense of purpose in your work, which also means you're taking pride in your work and want to do it properly.

Medium   The medium, part of the communication model, is the intermediary device(s) that carries the message between the communication parties.

Metaphor   An XP practice is to create a metaphor for the project. A metaphor explains the goal and function in plain, understandable language for all stakeholders.

Minimal viable product (MVP)   The MVP is the smallest thing you can build that delivers value to the customer. You might also see the MVP referred to as the minimal marketable features (MMF).

Mitigation   Mitigation is anything that we do to reduce the probability or impact of a risk event.

Monitor stakeholder engagement   The fourth of the four processes in stakeholder management is to monitor stakeholder engagement. This is a monitoring and controlling process in which you monitor stakeholder engagement to identify stakeholders who may have fading interest or are drifting away from their responsibilities.

Monopoly money   Using Monopoly money is a requirements prioritization technique where participants "spend" pretend money on requirements. Participants spend their money on the requirements based on how valuable they perceive the items to be in the project. You then sum up the amount spent on each feature and rank them accordingly.

MoSCoW   MoSCoW is a prioritization schema for the product backlog. MoSCoW stands for Must have, Should have, Could have, and Would like to have but not at this time.

Net present value (NPV)   This calculation of the time value of money predicts a project's value more precisely than the present value formula. NPV evaluates the monies returned on a project for each period the project lasts and considers the investment into the project.

Noise Noise, part of the communication model, is anything that distracts from the message, such as static on a phone call.

Norming Norming is the third stage of Tuckman's Model of Team Development, when things have normalized in the project and people are going about the business of doing the project.

Osmotic communication Learning by overhearing others' conversations in a collaborative team space is osmotic communication.

Pair programming This is an XP approach where developers work in pairs; one person codes while the other checks the code. The pair switches roles periodically.

Parkinson's law Parkinson's law states that work expands to fill the time allotted to it. This law describes the danger of padding estimate sizes, as the work will expand to fill the size of the duration estimate.

Payback period The payback period is the duration it will take for the return on the investment to equal, or pay back, the project investment. This approach shows the management horizon, the breakeven point of the project.

PDCA (plan-do-check-act) cycle The PDCA (plan-do-check-act) cycle, based on Japanese quality initiatives, is also known as the Deming cycle. It's widely associated with quality assurance and quality control. PDCA prompts the project manager and the team to complete the actions of plan, do, check, and act to improve and control quality within the work.

Performing Performing is the fourth stage of Tuckman's Model of Team Development. As the team continues to work together, they begin to rely on one another, communicate more freely and transparently, and focus on creating value; they enjoy each other's company and are really firing on all cylinders.

Persona A persona represents a typical user of the system and addresses that individual's needs, expectations, and how they'll use what you're creating. It's a fictional character description of real people and it addresses their needs, wants, and concerns about the solution.

Plan stakeholder engagement The second of the four processes in stakeholder management is to plan stakeholder engagement. This is a planning process. While agile discourages lengthy planning documents, you still need a plan for how and when stakeholders will be engaged.

Planned value (PV) Planned value represents the percent of project completion the project should be at this time. Planned value is found by finding the percentage of planned completion times the budget at completion.

Planning poker Planning poker uses cards that have the Fibonacci sequence of 1, 2, 3, 5, and 8. The project manager and the team look at each user story and everyone privately chooses whichever poker card they think correctly sizes the story, and then everyone places their card face down on the table. Cards are revealed in unison and discussion follows each round of voting with the poker cards.

Predictive life cycle   The predictive life cycle works with fixed requirements for the project team to create a single delivery of the product, manage costs, and manage the project schedule.

Present value (PV)   Present value is what a future amount of funds is worth today. The formula for present value is $PV = FV / (1 + i)^n$, where i is the given interest rate and n is the number of time periods (years, quarters, etc.).

Prioritized backlog   A backlog of prioritized requirements based on the customer's opinion of what's the most important requirement, then the next, and the next, and so on. The team decides how much they can complete in the next iteration, plan the iteration work, and then deliver.

Process   A process is a set of actions that we follow to reach a predefined result.

Process analysis   Process analysis involves studying the processes of your project and how the project team gets work done. Process analysis takes the process flow, breaks it down, and identifies what items are needed for a process to work properly.

Process cycle efficiency   Process cycle efficiency is a metric in value stream analysis that is calculated by dividing the amount of value-added time by the total cycle time. The higher the process cycle efficiency value, the more successful the project is. Lower values indicate a high amount of non-value-added activity and waste in the project.

Product backlog   The product backlog is the long list of prioritized project requirements. The product owner is responsible for maintaining the product backlog.

Product boxes   A product box is a mockup of your project solution as if it were for sale and contained in a product box on a store shelf. The product box show the value of what the project is creating. It's a way of visualizing what the top features of the product are.

Product owner   This is a role in the Scrum agile methodology that describes the individual that manages the product backlog for the project.

Product roadmap   A product roadmap is a big picture of the functionality the team's deliverables and how that functionality satisfies the product vision. The product roadmap is a way of keeping our team and our stakeholders involved and keeping focus on the project result.

Product vision   The product vision is a summary to communicate the project's end goal. The product vision statement describes how the project's product will differ from competitors' products and support the overall strategy of the organization. It also sets the expectations of what the project will deliver and what it won't deliver.

Progressive elaboration   Progressive elaboration is an adaptive planning technique that starts with a broad idea of the project and then breaks it down into smaller and smaller items and components as the project progresses.

Project cycle time   Project cycle time is the duration of the entire project. However long the project lasts is the cycle time for the whole project.

Project leaders   Project leaders include the project manager, people on the project team, consultants, and subject matter experts who'll make key decisions on the project work.

Project pre-mortem   The project pre-mortem is an event that happens before any delivery occurs on your project. It's the earliest opportunity for your team to consider improvements to their software process. This event produces a detailed look from your team at all potential causes of failure on the project ahead, ranked by priority.

Project sponsor   The project sponsor is the champion for the project, with organizational authority to authorize the project and grant the project manager control over the project resources. The project sponsor signs the project charter.

Project tweet   Like a Twitter post, a project tweet defines the project in 280 characters or less.

Proxy customer   A proxy customer is a representative for a large group of project stakeholders.

Prune the Product Tree   Prune the Product Tree is a collaboration game that uses an illustration of a tree to demonstrate the priorities and requirements of the project. The trunk of the tree is what you already know or what you've already built. Then you draw branches off the tree, and you add sticky notes of ideas or new requirements on the branches. The closer the items are to the trunk, the higher the priority.

Qualitative analysis   Qualitative analysis is fast and subjective and isn't totally reliable. The goal of qualitative analysis is to decide which risks should go into quantitative analysis.

Quantitative analysis   Quantitative analysis quantifies the probability and impact of a risk event. Quantitative analysis takes more time to do, but it's much more reliable than qualitative analysis.

Quiet writing   Quite writing is a brainstorming technique where participants complete brainstorming as a solo activity before a meeting. Participants then come into the meeting already prepared with their ideas for group discussion.

Receiver   A receiver, part of the communication model, is the person who receives the message from the sender.

Red zone   In a red zone the focus is all about short-term and self-centered goals. The red zone encompasses all the negative aspects that may come with teams that aren't cohesive. People place blame and respond defensively. People feel threatened or wrong when others speak out against an idea. People hold grudges, shame mistakes, and accuse. People operating in a red zone experience binary thinking, which means it's all right or all wrong. A red zone is antithetical to the agile mindset.

Refactoring   Refactoring involves cleaning up the code to remove waste, redundancy, dependent connections, and shortcuts.

Regression testing   Regression testing confirms that what's been developed in the past still works once new code has been compiled into the software. Regression testing should happen on all functionality throughout the project. As the team compiles code, they do regression testing to ensure that what they've added to existing software doesn't break anything.

Relationship management   Emotional intelligence quadrant that requires people to work with others to communicate and keep the project moving along. This means that as a project manager you use your social skills to help develop others, promote teamwork, foster collaboration, and act as a servant leader.

Release plan   A release plan defines a set of requirements that when completed may be released. Release planning determines when we are going to have releases available. The project manager, the product owner, and the project team determine the next set of functionalities that can be released as part of an incremental approach.

Remember the Future   Remember the Future is a collaboration game involving the project team and key stakeholders in which the participants pretend to look back at the completed project. Participants take (for example) 20 minutes to write a report about how the project went. The participants imagine what went well, what threatened the project's success, and issues that weren't managed well. This game is a way of anticipating what's going to happen in a project.

Requirements prioritization model   In the requirements prioritization model, stakeholders vote on four factors of each proposed requirement on a scale of 1 to 9. The four factors voted on are benefit, penalty, cost, and risk.

Risk   Risk is anti-value in agile projects. In an agile project, risk is anything that threatens the success of the project and must be addressed sooner rather than later.

Risk burndown chart   A risk burndown chart is a stacked graph, similar to a user story burndown chart, that shows cumulative project risk severity. It charts the risk exposure from the beginning of the project through the end of the project.

Risk probability-impact matrix   A risk probability-impact matrix is a table of risk events that shows each risk's probability and impact, and a risk score or the expected monetary value of the risk event. The risk score is found by multiplying the risk probability times the risk impact.

Risk tolerance   Risk tolerance describes a person's or organization's willingness to take on risks in a project. High-priority projects generally have a lower risk tolerance than low-priority projects.

Risk-adjusted backlog   A risk-adjusted backlog adjusts the priority of user stories with a consideration of risks. This approach addresses risks earlier in the project, rather than later in the project. The risk-adjusted backlog takes on risks quickly to avoid significant damage or increased costs later in the project. Taking on risk project work earlier in the project helps determine if the project is feasible and if the project team can overcome the defined risks without investing too much time and costs into the project.

Risk-based spike   A risk-based spike is a brief investigation the team performs early in the project to identify and test risks within the project.

Risks   Risks are uncertain events or conditions that can have a negative effect on an agile project.

Rolling wave planning   Rolling wave planning uses waves of planning and then executing and is a characteristic of adaptive projects.

Root cause analysis (RCA)   Root cause analysis (RCA) is the analysis of the problem, the causal factors, and the determination of how the problem may be resolved. RCA defines the root problem, not symptoms that are causing those problems.

Round-robin   Round-robin is a brainstorming technique where the facilitator goes around the room and asks each person to give one idea. Each participant offers one idea until all ideas have been given and documented. There can be several rounds of this approach in the process.

Rule of seven   Whenever you have the results of seven consecutive measurements all on one side of the mean in a control chart, that represents a trend and is an assignable cause. That's called the rule of seven and it's a non-random event.

Schedule performance index (SPI)   SPI measures the project based on its schedule performance. The formula is earned value (EV) divided by planned value (PV). The closer to 1, the better the project is performing on schedule.

Schedule variance   The schedule variance is determined by calculating the earned value (EV) of the project minus the planned value (PV) of the project.

Screen design   A screen design is a mock-up of what the screen and interface will look like. It is a visualization of how the end result is going to look. The screen design can be created in PowerPoint or other software to show the product owner the interface the end user will see.

Scrum of Scrums Scrum   This is a meeting for larger Scrum projects where multiple teams are working together. Rather than having a huge Daily Scrum, the teams meet separately and then a representative from each team meets in a Scrum to report on each team's progress. The team representatives answer the same questions as in the Daily Scrum, but for the team rather than individuals. In addition, a fourth question is often posed: Will our team be putting something in another team's way?

ScrumMaster   The ScrumMaster ensures that everyone understands the rules of Scrum, removes impediments for the team, facilities Scrum meetings, helps the product owner groom the backlog, and communicates the vision of the project to everyone that's involved.

Secondary risk   Secondary risk occurs when one risk is solved but the risk solution inadvertently creates one or more new risks.

Self-awareness   Self-awareness is an emotional intelligence quadrant that means one has the confidence to ask why they are feeling an emotion, such as being upset or angry or not caring. Self-awareness causes a person to pause and use logic and reason to understand their own emotions.

Self-management   Self-management is an emotional intelligence quadrant that means one can manage their emotions. It requires being conscious of how you are acting and behaving and then making corrections when needed. Self-management means that a person can adapt their emotions based on the circumstances. Self-management affects drive and motivation and the ability to get things done.

Self-organized   A team that is self-organized decides who's going to do what in the current iteration and doesn't always rely on the project manager for instructions.

Sender   A sender, part of the communication model, is the person who is sending the message to the receiver.

Shore's Self-Assessment Chart   Shore's Self-Assessment Chart calls for the team to plot scores across the areas of planning, developing, thinking, collaborating, and releasing along a radar diagram.

Shu-Ha-Ri Model of Skill Mastery   The Shu-Ha-Ri Model of Skill Mastery describes three stages. In the first stage, Shu, you learn the skill by following the guidelines. In the Ha stage, you no longer rely on the guidelines and are able to work more intuitively. Ri is the stage at which you have fully mastered the skill and can innovate beyond the guidelines.

Sizing T-shirts   Sizing T-shirts is a way of determining and sorting the true sizes of user stories by comparing them. For example, comparing a user story previously labeled as medium to a small or large user story may reveal that the medium story is more likely a large or small. It's a type of affinity estimating.

Slicing   Slicing is the process of breaking down a large user story into smaller stories or tasks.

Smoothing   Smoothing in conflict resolution means you accommodate the conflict in order to move forward. A person exercising the smoothing technique does not consider the substance of the disagreement in any depth.

Social awareness   Social awareness is an emotional intelligence quadrant that means you have empathy for others, you understand where others are coming from, and you understand what's important in your organization. You understand the environment that you're operating in as a project manager.

Special causes of variance   Special causes of variance are unusual occurrences that influence project progress. For example, the power went out for two days, or three team members caught the flu, or there was an emergency in the business.

Speedboat game   The speedboat game (or sailboat game) is a collaboration game in which participants pretend that they're on a boat that represents their project. The facilitator asks, "What winds are pushing this project along? What anchors are holding our project back? What's the direction of the sailboat? And are there any rocks or other impediments in the way?" It's a game to explore the pros and cons of your project and forces for and against your project.

Sprint planning meeting   In this Scrum event, the development team determines how much work they can take on from the prioritized backlog for the next sprint. This determination is based on estimates of the items in the product backlog and past sprints. The selected items from the product backlog become the sprint backlog and the goal of the sprint.

Sprint retrospective   This Scrum event is held after the sprint review and before the next sprint planning meeting. It is just for the project team and the project manager, and they discusses what's worked well with people, product, and processes in the project, what needs improvement, and the feedback from the product owner from the sprint review meeting. Although this is typically used in Scrum projects, you can utilize a retrospective in an agile approach.

Sprint review   This Scrum meeting is held at the end of each sprint. The development team demonstrates for the product owner, the ScrumMaster, and other key stakeholders the work they've accomplished in the past sprint. This review is for the product owner to offer feedback on whether the work has reached the done stage, and, if it hasn't, describe what's missing and elaborate on corrections or modifications for the increment of work created. Although this is typically used in Scrum projects, you can utilize a retrospective in an agile approach.

Sprints   Scrum uses timeboxed iterations, called sprints, to create prioritized requirements for the customer. Sprints last from two to four weeks to complete the selected requirements for the current iteration.

Stakeholder register   The stakeholder register is a document that helps you know who's interested or concerned about what, their role and responsibility in the project, and to whom you'll communicate what information.

Storming   Storming is the second stage of Tuckman's Model of Team Development in which people jockey for positions, claim ownership of what they want to work on, or even voice strong opinions on project objectives. Storming can appear to be combative and full of conflict, but it's a natural part of team development.

Story points   Story points are points assigned to user stories for purposes of sizing them relative to each and estimating how long each will take to complete. Using story points provides a scale with which to size user stories relative to each other, such as a large story is worth five points, a medium story is worth three points, and a small story is worth one point.

Swarming   Swarming happens when multiple people, often the entire project team, attack a single problem, user story, or task.

Synergy   Synergy is the cooperation of two or more organizations or people to create something greater than the parties could do on their own. Synergy means we, the project team and the project customer, work together to create something unique, effective, and powerful to gain value.

Systems thinking   Systems thinking is a structured approach to do the work and includes analysis of the system's processes to reach the defined result.

Tabaka's Assessment Model   Tabaka's Assessment Model allows teams to score themselves on questions on self-organization, empowerment, and participatory decision making. With data in hand, teams can then focus on the areas with the lowest scores for improvement.

Tacit knowledge   Knowledge a person has gained through their experience and doing work is tacit knowledge. Teams have tacit knowledge about the project work and how things operate in their colocated environment.

Tangible business value   Tangible business value are derived from items like monetary assets, return on investment, stockholder equity, fixtures and tools your project creates or acquires, and the market share your project captures.

Task board   This board, like a Kanban board, represents the project tasks and their status. A task board is more closely associated with Scrum and it shows the status of the requirements in the sprint backlog rather than the requirements for the whole project.

Technical debt   Technical debt is the backlog of work that's caused if the team fails to do regular clean-up on the project code. It's the maintenance, standardization, and refactoring of the code. Technical debt can accumulate and cause the project code to become more complex.

Test-driven development   In test-driven development, an acceptance test is created before the code is written so the developers know what it takes to pass the acceptance test and can program accordingly.

The Declaration of Interdependence   This agile methodology document serves as a value system for agile project managers. The idea behind this document is that all participants in an agile project are interdependent on one another: the project manager, development team, customers, and other stakeholders.

Theory of constraints   The theory of constraints posits that there's always at least one constraint that is holding back the system, or project management approach, from reaching its maximum potential. A constraint is anything that limits your options: time, costs, scope requirements, people, software, hardware, and any number of other factors. You attack the constraint that is most restrictive until it's no longer the most restrictive constraint and then repeat the process with the next most restrictive constraint.

Three Cs of user stories   The three Cs of user stories are the card, conversation, and confirmation. A card is an index card or sticky note with just enough text to identify the story. A conversation is the details that are communicated between the customer and the development team. A confirmation is the customer confirmation that the story has been implemented correctly in the product.

Thumbs up/thumbs down   Thumbs up/thumbs down is a participatory decision-making technique in which participants show a thumbs up to indicate support for the decision or a thumbs down to indicate opposition to the decision. An additional option is to allow participants to display a sideways thumb to indicate they are neutral or undecided.

Timeboxing   A timebox is a predetermined, fixed duration for a project event.

Transference   Transference is anything that you do that transfers the risk to someone else, usually with a contractual relationship. You hire someone to manage that part of the risk.

Trend analysis   Trend analysis allows you to predict future performance based on what's happened already in the project.

Tuckman's Model of Team Development   Tuckman's Model of Team Development is a model that shows project team members moving from forming through storming, norming, and performing. Teams may shift back to earlier stages based on project conditions. Adjourning is a fifth stage that the team goes through when it disbands.

Usability testing   Usability testing is an approach that observes participants using the software. The participants try to complete certain tasks in the software while the project team or a few developers watch, listen, and take notes. The goal is to identify usability problems, collect data, and gauge how satisfied the users are with the software.

Use case diagram   A use case diagram models how a system works, including how people interact with the system. Use case diagrams include actors, which are the people and other entities, to show the activities that people involved with the system will do. Use cases represent the actions, the services, and the functions of the system.

User story   A user story is a small chunk of business functionality. User stories are written from the customer's perspective and describe a feature of the product you're creating.

User story backlog   The user story backlog, also known as the product backlog, contains all the requirements in a user story format.

User story formula   The user story formula includes role, functionality, and benefit and is seen as: As a <role> I want this <functionality> so that I'll receive this <benefit>.

Value management team   The value management team is composed of business people looking for return on investment for the project work. They look for opportunities to increase value, predict breakeven points, and forecast how the project will contribute to cutting costs in the organization and/or increasing revenue.

Value stream analysis   Value stream analysis is a Lean manufacturing technique that begins with identifying the product or service to analyze. Value stream analysis studies the current state of a process and then designs the future state for the process with a goal of efficiency and improvement. Value stream analysis gathers data across at least one iteration on what your process includes and determines overall efficiency for each iteration.

Value-based analysis   Value-based analysis examines the business value and assesses the worth of what the project will create. Value-based analysis is the business benefit minus the cost of the project.

Value-based decomposition   Value-based decomposition is a visual decomposition of the project scope, requirements, features, or risk. Value-based decomposition is a way to examine the requirements and determine the value of each requirement for prioritization and relationships among the components.

Velocity   Velocity is the capacity of work the team can complete per iteration. Velocity is defined by how many story points the team can complete in one iteration.

Vendor   A vendor is any entity that will provide resources to the project. Vendors are key stakeholders that need to be engaged and communicated with.

Voting with dots   Voting with dots, sometimes called multivoting, is a requirements prioritization approach where participants are given a list of requirements and vote on which ones they think deserve the highest priority by labeling them with dots, checkmarks, or even little sticky notes.

Wideband Delphi Technique   The Wideband Delphi Technique, sometimes called just the Delphi Technique, has rounds of anonymous surveys to create estimates, gather risks, or gather requirements. It helps to build consensus without everyone following one person's point of view.

WIP (work in progress)   The work in progress is what the team is working on right now.

WIP limit   WIP means work in progress. Kanban boards, task boards, and any hybrid approach to agile project management should set a limit on the number of requirements in the WIP.

Wireframe   A wireframe is a simple, straightforward diagram that shows your project solution. Wireframes often address the different elements in the user interface, screen and system organization, navigation paths, user interface look and feel, and user interaction with the solution.

Withdraw   One way to resolve a conflict, at least temporarily, is to withdraw from the situation and avoid further discussion. One party simply says, for example, "Let's discuss this later after we've cooled off" and leaves the room. This method requires a healthy level of emotional intelligence.

XP XP is short for eXtreme Programming and is an agile approach that is focused on software development. XP also uses iterations of development, but these iterations last for two weeks in a typical project.

Zero-sum reward A zero-sum reward means that only one person can win, such as employee of the month. That can create envy and make the non-winners feel poorly about their work and contributions.

INDEX